History, Cultural Traditions and Innovations in Southern Africa

Editors:
Michael Bollig and Wilhelm J.G. Möhlig

Volume 18

San and the State

Contesting Land, Development, Identity
and Representation

edited by
Thekla Hohmann

RÜDIGER KÖPPE VERLAG KÖLN

Bibliografische Information Der Deutschen Bibliothek

Die Deutsche Bibliothek verzeichnet diese Publikation in der Deutschen Nationalbibliografie; detaillierte bibliografische Daten sind im Internet über http://dnb.ddb.de abrufbar.

ISBN 3-89645-357-2

© 2003

RÜDIGER KÖPPE VERLAG
Postfach 45 06 43
D - 50881 Köln

www.koeppe.de

Text layout: Thekla Hohmann

Production: Richarz Publikations-Service GmbH, Sankt Augustin / Germany

Diese Arbeit ist im Sonderforschungsbereich 389 „Kultur- und Landschaftswandel im ariden Afrika, Entwicklungsprozesse unter ökologischen Grenzbedingungen", Köln, entstanden und wurde auf seine Veranlassung unter Verwendung der ihm von der Deutschen Forschungsgemeinschaft zur Verfügung gestellten Mittel gedruckt.

Preface

This volume deals with the multifarious relations between San communities and the state. In anthropological discourses San communities feature importantly: introductory books contain paragraphs which exemplify foraging mode of existence, band level organisation or shamanistic healing with ethnographic material on San communities. Interestingly it is mainly information on San communities in the Nyae Nyae/ Dobe area which got widely disseminated in anthropological circles disregarding the diversity of San cultures. In this volume none of the contributions adresses this very group of people; rather communities that have not been documented widely are portrayed: the Khwe of Western Caprivi (Namibia), the Haiḷḷom of the wider Etosha area (Namibia), the San communities of former Bushmanland West (Namibia) or South Africa's ǂKhomani and Botswana's !Ko are adressed. The Nama of South Africa's Richtersveld, of course, are not San but do speak a Khoisan language and interestingly many issues at stake for San communities (rising ethnicity, reinvigoration of cultural labels, increasing salience of ethnic boundaries) are at stake for them as well.

It is especially variation in the relation between local communities and the state (colonial and/or independent) which are discussed. Colonial regimes dealt quite differently with San communities: while some saw mobile and foraging San communities as an outright problem for an orderly land tenure system, others tried to differentiate San communities worth protecting and others not worth protecting. In many instances programmes were set up which were meant directly to help "Bushmen" communities. Colonial policies were ambigiuous and left varying spaces for local agency. While the Haiḷḷom were left no choice in 1954 and were summarily expulsed from the Etosha Park area, during the decades before Haiḷḷom eked out a living making use of the many resources of the area including employment for Park agencies and neighbouring white farmers.

The political moves in Namibia and South Africa in the 1990s have changed the field of options rather dramatically, the room for manoeuvre of local elites widened and many San leaders saw natural allies in other indigenous groups movements around the world. Tradition became a resource within the national and global context which is still being explored. The volume explores how local dynamics and globalisation work together and societies and cultures change rapidly. What will be the future of San communities? Will they be marginals dependent on governmental welfare and various donor agencies, will they be self-confident activists fighting for indigenous rights or both. The volume does not include the answers but fleshes out these questions in intriguing detail.

The volume was assembled within a year by Thekla Hohmann while she was associated to Cologne's ACACIA programme. Most contributions originate directly from the ACACIA programme which has facilitated research on man-environment interactions in arid Africa for eight years now. Two articles were contributed by South African and Botswanan associates of the ACACIA programme.

The editors would like to express their gratitude to the German Research Council for granting longterm research options in the region and WIMSA (Working Group for Indigenous Minorities, Windhoek) for facilitating part of the research. Rachel Lodder and Lee Clare have worked on the orthography, grammar and interpunctation of a volume in which native english speakers were a minority – a tedious task. Harald Sterly worked masterfully on the maps of the volume.

Cologne, March 2003   *The Editors*

Contents

San and the State:
An Introduction[1]

Thekla Hohmann

"San and the State" encompasses nine contributions resulting from recent anthropological work with various San communities in Southern Africa. The contributors shed light on the current situation of several San groups in the three Southern African states of Botswana, Namibia and South Africa. Small numbers of San are also residing in Angola, Zambia and Zimbabwe and a lot of what is said on the general situation of many San in this introduction as well as in the different contributions holds true also for them. However, they will not be mentioned in further detail here.[2]

The nine contributions assembled here highlight certain aspects of San contemporary history and their current situation. Contributions focus on relations between the San and the state and the consequences of these for local communities. Of special interest are the ways that recent developments in the broader regional, national, and international context influence San societies socially and politically. Whilst many contemporary contributions to San research stress that local socio-political structures result from external forces, local agency will be emphasised here. Authors discuss various aspects ranging from land tenure, natural resource management, language policy and political representation to the impacts of development initiatives and processes of identity formation.

This introduction is to set the scene for the contributions by first introducing "the San" as an ethnic label used to describe a certain part of the Southern African population. Furthermore 'the state' will be discussed briefly with its specific connotations in the Southern African context. Following this, anthropological research and non-scientific publications on San and the role that 'the state' has been playing in the analyses will be reviewed and contextualised historically.

---

[1] I would like to thank Gertrud Boden, Michael Bollig, Ute Dieckmann, and Thomas Widlok for comments on earlier versions of this introduction.

[2] For a discussion on San in Angola, Zambia and Zimbabwe see Robins et al. 2001.

Labelling 'the San'

The different population groups of Southern Africa nowadays summarised by the term 'San' have arguably not been existing until recently as the distinctive, cohesive group the title of this book suggests them to be. Different San groups developed varying economic strategies ranging from foraging to livestock herding, gardening, trading, iron forging and mining (cf. Barnard 1992). A variety of systems has also been shown for the social and political realm, including small-scale egalitarian hunting bands and chiefdom-like structures.[3] These different groups have however been subsumed under a common label in many of the publications that have appeared since the onset of anthropological research among them. A term consistently used has been 'Bushmen'[4]. More recently, for reasons of political correctness, the very same groups have been labelled 'San', a term however which implies equally pejorative connotations as 'Bushmen'.[5] 'San' nowadays is also most widely used by the Namibian and South African governments[6], development agencies and the press. The meanings, connotations and suitability of the two terms alone has led to lengthy discussions among anthropologists (cf. e.g. Guenther 1986; Barnard 1992:22-27; Gordon 1992:15-46; Widlok 1999:15-17). As Widlok points out, both 'San', a degrading term used for foraging peoples by their pastoral Khoekhoe neighbours, and the English term 'Bushman' or 'Boesman' in Afrikaans are not harmful due to their etymology, but because they are often used with negative attributes attached to them (cf. Widlok 1999:16-17). In this context one can understand the statement a San man in Tsumkwe District West once made when asked about the applicability of the two terms:

> To us it is not that important how someone is calling us. If you call me a bushman, yes, it is true, I come from the bush. My forefathers have come from the bush. And I am proud of that. If you want to call me a San, yes, you can do so, too. But what

---

[3] Cf. for a detailed comparison of different Khoi and San groups: Barnard 1992.

[4] See on questions of scientific terminology and classifications applied to San groups: Guenther 1986, Gordon 1992:15-46, Barnard 1992:7-28, Widlok 1999.

[5] Originally, 'san' is a Khoekhoe word for 'foragers' and can be translated as 'tramps', 'vagabonds', 'rascals', 'robbers', 'bandits', etc. (see Barnard 1992:8).

[6] In Botswana the term 'Bushman' has been replaced in government and public discourses by the term 'Mosarwa' (pl.: 'Basarwa'), a Setswana term expressing similar meanings like the original 'san' in Khoekhoe dialects (Barnard 1992:8).

> really matters is the way someone is treating us
> (fieldnotes Hohmann, February 1998).

In many instances, the labels that San groups would use to refer to themselves come from their own respective languages such as e.g. Jul'hoansi, !Xun, Hai‖om or ǂAkhoe, Khwe or Nharo. In recent years however the construction of a common San identity has been observed among various San groups. It has been in the context of an emergent elite of young educated school leavers, traditional authorities and of NGO- or state-run development initiatives emphasising a common identity that a self-labelling as 'San' and sometimes also as 'Bushmen' has become more salient among the people themselves (see Widlok 1999:17, and Hohmann this volume). The trend towards the usage of a common label by San communities themselves must be seen against the background of their rising self-awareness as a disadvantaged indigenous minority expressing unity in their struggle for development. Groups speaking different languages, having different cultural practices, residing hundreds of kilometres apart, and living in different political economies increasingly come to describe themselves by using the general label 'San' to express their unity with regard to certain aspects of their identity. The ethnic identity as San and common cultural ancestry is being constructed and re-shaped in the process, in some cases with direct reference to anthropological literature. Thus for instance rock-art has been constructed as evidence for the longevity of San culture.

Important characteristics ascribed to the entire group have been the economic strategy of foraging combined with spatial mobility (cf. Lee and DeVore 1976 and Barnard 1992:27), the prevalence of an egalitarian political structure (cf. Lee 1992:31, and Leacock and Lee 1982) and their usage of a language belonging to the Khoisan language family (cf. e.g. Köhler 1975 and for an overview of linguistic criteria used in classification Barnard 1992:20-27). In contrast, recent ethnographers tend to describe material poverty and marginalisation as alternative criteria for the identification of an individual as San by its neighbours or itself (cf. Taylor 2000:8 and this volume, Boden this volume, Gordon 1992 and Suzman 2000:107-108).

Since the late 1980s descriptions of San as indigenous people make use of these would-be common denominators defined by anthropologists. Global actors working for indigenous groups, NGOs and donor organisations on the one hand emphasise the San's marginalisation and discrimination, but on the other hand stress the survival of traditional values and structures among them. Just like the common ethnic label 'San' the label 'indigenous' is put to use in order to achieve cultural and political emancipation, greater security of land tenure and access to resources. Labelling local communities as 'indigenous' qualifies San to be continuous subjects of anthropo-tourism and of development projects geared to ethnic minorities.[7]

Contextualising 'the State'

The second component of this book's title, 'the state', just like the term 'the San', is a term describing a phenomenon with a variety of manifestations and connotations in the setting of Southern Africa. States have played changing roles for San over time and are having various meanings for the different San groups in Southern Africa today. According to Wilmsen states have influenced San socio-economic organisation since about A.D. 1000 (Wilmsen 1989:72, see also Segobye 1998:107). Pre-colonial states (e.g. Ondangwa, Tawana) had a definite influence on various San groups in the 18th and 19th centuries, but despite theoretical considerations on this issue there has been astonishingly little anthropological, historical and archaeological research on pre-colonial state-San relations. Pre-colonial states were superseded by colonial states imposing their discriminatory policy which culminated in South Africa and Namibia in the Apartheid political system. Features of the pre-colonial political system however have survived up until the period of the independent nation states one finds today. In the colonial period, pre-colonial structures of dominance and power were consolidated through indirect rule. Nowadays these very structures are re-formulated as traditional customary law and are re-confirmed by national law. In all South African states the San populations today are relatively marginalised, numerically small, politically and economically disadvantaged groups. The majority live in remote areas and are disadvantaged by laws of nature conservation. These laws prohibit foraging and poaching, a source of frequent confrontation between San communities and states (see Hitchcock and Masilo 1996). Globalisation and modernisation are affecting San and their expectations towards life with many of them hoping for change. At the same time however benefits from the modernising independent states such as school education, wage labour and new forms of political representation have remained little accessible to them. Le Roux (2000) for instance describes the ongoing disadvantages San pupils in the entire region are experiencing through national educational policy. Suzman (2001:23-25) shows that

---

[7]   Cf. Taylor 2000 for a case study of San in a development context, and Suzman 2001 for an assessment of various development initiatives among San in Southern Africa.

political representation of San in regional and national bodies of decision making is hardly existent. Although a number of strategies adopted by Southern African governments have been explicitly or indirectly aimed at improving the San's situation, by far not all have met this aim. This is partly due to the fact that government programmes have concentrated principally on welfare (see Hitchcock and Holm 1993 and Bollig this volume) and infrastructural development e.g. of roads and boreholes. Important components of the San's marginalisation such as disadvantaging local structures of domination, the lack of formal education, of representative political structures, secure land tenure and access to natural resources have been neglected (on state policies regarding San see Suzman 2001:20-23).

In Botswana, the Bushman Development Programme (BDP) had been introduced in 1974 to become the Remote Area Development Programme (RADP) later on.[8] The mere change of labels avoiding ethnic categorisation, whereby San (Bushmen) became rural area dwellers, demonstrates the integrationist strategy of the Botswanan Government. Anthropologists have repeatedly referred to the inefficiency of this policy in terms of positive development for San communities in Botswana (see for instance Hitchcock and Holm 1993, and Saugestad 1998). The programme also became increasingly criticised by development practitioners.

The situation in the two countries which have achieved democratic rule more recently – Namibia and South Africa – is different to that of Botswana. Some Namibian ministries have identified the San as a special target group and designed specific programmes to fit their needs. Ethnic pluralism is accommodated in Namibia's, as it is in South Africa's constitution. Nevertheless, generally speaking the Namibian Government has taken little significant and co-ordinated steps to alleviate the poverty and marginalisation of the Namibian San population.[9]

Generally a more supportive and promising basis for co-operation between San communities, NGOs and the government seems to exist in South Africa than in the other states of the region as Suzman (2001:23) explains: "South Africa's two major San communities [...] have proved able

---

[8] Cf. Wylie 1979 for an early description of the programme, Suzman 2001:21 for its major components, as well as Bollig, this volume.

[9] Suzman (2001:23) even describes the consequences by saying that "in the decade since independence the status of a significant proportion of San and other rural poor in Namibia has deteriorated and their dependency on state welfare has increased".

to exploit South Africa's relatively open political climate and have benefited from recent land redistribution initiatives." The South African context provides slightly more opportunities for San to achieve some of their goals if one takes into account e.g. successful claims for parts of their ancestral land (see Robins, Berzborn this volume), the granting of resettlement farms in the vicinity of Kimberley to !Xun and Khwe originating from Angola and Namibia and the establishment of a San cultural and training centre near Cape Town. Since the demise of the Apartheid political system in which they were subsumed under the ethnic category "coloured" the South African San have become eager to once again stress their San identity to achieve their position within the post-Apartheid society. The post-Apartheid Republic of South Africa even used a Khoisan expression from the extinct |Xam language in its coat of arms: "!Ke e: |xarra ||ke", literally meaning: "diverse people unite" (see Berzborn this volume). For historic reasons and political considerations however, "the response of the South African Government to the reclamations of Khoi and San during the 1990s has been mixed" (Robins et al. 2001:41). While in specific aspects e.g. land tenure and language policy the 'new South Africa' has been favourable for San interests, the government is careful in granting the San the exclusive status of 'indigenous' minority. Such prominent status would single them out among the group of South Africans who had all been discriminated against in the country's past and the present government wants to avoid further cases of aboriginal land claims.

Situating Anthropology

Social anthropology 'discovered' San as an attractive research subject early on. Given that San communities only constitute up to three % of the Southern African national populations (see Suzman 2001:5 for figures), they have found disproportionate interest amongst anthropologists. There is no textbook in anthropology in which San do not feature importantly. The following paragraph outlines some of the salient discourses of anthropological research.

Early Anthropological Research

Anthropological representations of San started to appear and to influence the pictures that others have of the group and their attitudes towards them at the beginning of European intrusion into South Africa with the first Dutch settlers at the Cape in the 17th century (cf. Kolb 1727, Dapper 1668; see also Szalay 1983 and Wilmsen 1989). In the early phase it was predominantly explorer-travellers or missionaries who began to describe what they perceived of San cultures and languages.[10] Different, sometimes contrary images of San emerged which could often be characterised along a continuum from 'exotic, noble, peaceful savages living in harmony with their environment by nature' to 'wild, dangerous, animal-like creatures' disturbing to members of the white colonial community, or, as Guenther termed it in the title of his article, "from 'brutal savages' to 'harmless people'" (Guenther 1980). The work of early San researchers especially from the second half of the 19th century onwards was heavily influenced by evolutionist and racist assumptions. Scientists belonging to the paradigm of anthropological evolutionism described San societies as among the most 'primitive' forms of human organisation. Cultural diffusionists such as Father Wilhelm Schmidt described the San as belonging to the "primitive culture circle of hunter-gatherers" (Schmidt 1939 [1937], see Barnard 2000:52). Such attitudes have come to the fore throughout anthropological publications. Up to the second half of the 20th century attention was often paid to the physiognomy of San with researchers in the tradition of racial categorisation and description spending a lot of their precious time in the field taking body measurements of San individuals. Their hair, skin colour and other physical features were described in often meticulous detail.[11] A driving force behind early San research was the assumption to find in them a 'window to the palaeolithic' providing information on the life and culture of stone age people.[12] These scientific discourses left their marks on public opinion as can be seen from a number of coffee table books and novels (e.g. Wannenburgh 1979, Marshall-Thomas 1959, van der Post 1961). This outdated evolutionist and mostly racist way of depicting the San has been harshly criticised and discarded by most researchers.

Early involvement of anthropologists in issues regarding colonial administration and politics concerning the San existed in the entire region and was intensified during Apartheid times in Namibia and South Africa. Anthropologists like Hoernlé, Schapera, Vedder, Schoeman and Coertze (cf. for details Gordon 1992:147-167, and Hammond-Tooke 1997) who during

---

[10] Cf. for instance the works of Hahn and Rath 1859, Anderson 1863, Galton 1889, and Schinz 1891.

[11] Cf. among others the publications of Schultze 1914; 1928, Seiner 1913, Gusinde 1953, and Tobias 1961. Physical anthropology though with different topics like genetics, sero-genetics and nutrition is still being undertaken by a number of researchers (cf. e.g. Jenkins 1986, de Almeida 1994, Soodyall 1998).

[12] See for a criticism and literature review of early San research in this regard: Wilmsen 1989:1-32.

that period worked directly for the South African administration or the South
African Defence Force (SADF) delivered anthropological data and analyses
to serve the Apartheid regime's intentions. The anthropologists working for
the SADF for instance contributed to the image of San men as individuals
suitable to become soldiers in a bush war 'by nature', especially because of
their tracking skills (Gordon 1992:185-192, and Sharp and Douglas 1996).
These considerations led to the formation of the two 'Bushman Battalions' in
the Caprivi and Bushmanland in 1974 and 78. In some cases the San
themselves make use of the images created by scientists in order to achieve
certain aims. Sharp and Douglas (1996) for instance describe the hope for
assistance from the state and potential international donors of a group of
!Xun ex-SADF-soldiers in Schmidtsdrift after 1994. They played on their
would-be 'primitiveness', their status as indigenous, 'real Bushmen' and
'harmless people' who the new government and SADF were claimed to be
indebted to. When given land to resettle in the vicinity of Kimberley, they
opted for a relatively remote tract in order to demonstrate their
connectedness to nature and bush life. Through emphasising foraging and
isolation in the bush as their prime mode of subsistence and way of life, they
hoped to receive state subsidies and attract tourists and donor money.

The Kalahari Debate[13]

The quest for hunter-gatherer communities untouched by food-producing
systems formed the basis for the anthropological approach to the San (see
Wilmsen 1989). Especially the Jul'hoansi of the Dobe area in Botswana
seemed to conform to the blueprint derived from neo-evolutionist paradigms.
From the mid 1960s onwards the members of the Harvard Kalahari Research
Group led by its most prominent member Richard Lee set out to the small
settlement of Dobe in the Kalahari to conduct fieldwork which resulted in an
immense number of articles and books on various aspects of the culture of
the resident !Kung[14]. Ideas on egalitarianism in foraging bands, the
importance of female gathering or the original affluent society later became
parts of introductory volumes to cultural anthropology. With the !Kung[15] –
and indeed the !Kung of a very limited geographical area – becoming a

---

[13] Cf. for previous descriptions and analyses of the Kalahari debate: Lee 1992,
Barnard 1992, and Barnard 1996:243-247.

[14] Cf, e.g. Lee (1979 and 1984), Tanaka (1980), Silberbauer (1981), Wiessner
(1982), Cashdan (1983), and Hawkes et al. (1991).

[15] Later on they were termed Jul'hoansi. Cf. second edition of Lee's monograph
(Lee 1993).

prime focus of anthropological work in Southern Africa, they also became the prototypical San group in academia and for the public.

From the late 1970s, the research of the Harvard Kalahari Research Group and others was criticised by a group of anthropologists and archaeologists. The so-called revisionist camp (see Wilmsen 1989, Schrire 1984, Myers 1988) claimed that Lee and others had depicted the San as isolated from the wider Kalahari environment, from global political and economic processes and from the influence of the state. Interestingly, Leacock and Lee themselves had previously argued that

> foraging societies can only be understood as the product of a triple dynamic: first, the internal dynamic of communal foraging relations of production; second, the dynamics of their historical interactions with farmers, herders, *and states*; and third, the dynamic of articulation and incorporation within the modern world system (Leacock and Lee 1982, emphasis added T.H.).

Largely however, the Harvard Kalahari Research Group had left out a detailed description and analysis of the !Kung's relations with outside stakeholders like state agencies. According to Lee they "had described relations with such outsiders, but [...] had de-emphasised them and placed them in a context of 'social change'" (Lee 1996:243). The so-called traditionalists did not consider change in San societies to be an important topic of their research. The revisionists saw much of what was deemed to be features of pure foraging as the product of an age-old dominance of food producers over foragers. These hunted because they were denied access to resources and even in this aspect they had to compete with outsiders who had better weapons (guns) and better means of transport (horses). They stressed the importance and historical depth of influences of the state and the world-system for the local context of the Kalahari. They emphasised class relations within a regional system in contrast to a would-be authentic culture of foragers.

In the years following Wilmsen's publication a number of scientists from various disciplines such as social anthropology, history and archaeology contributed their arguments to one view or the other. During the course of the debate Solway and Lee (1990) were the first to try to combine some of the arguments of the two sides in order to come to a more realistic and historically embedded picture of the !Kung.

Lee summarises the debate in 1996 when the most heated attacks and counter-attacks published in Current Anthropology had already been printed:

Thus none of these views of Bushman society is, in absolute terms, superior to any other. Each represents only part of the whole. They are like snapshots – each taken at a different time and in a different direction. Only by putting them all together do we get the larger 'picture' (Lee 1996:247).

Recent Developments and Challenges for Anthropological Research

In the 1990s profound political changes in Southern Africa brought new challenges for anthropological research. After Namibian Independence in 1990 and South Africa's first democratic elections in 1994 San groups in the two countries found themselves in the context of newly emerging independent democratic states. Greater incorporation into the regional and global political economy was following a period of segregation and relative isolation. Many San hoped for positive effects of the changed situation in the form of new opportunities to escape discrimination and marginalisation and gain access to economic and political resources.

The regional governments – including the one of Botswana since the launch of its Bushman Development-, or later, Remote Area Development Programme – have tried to foster development among the San mainly through settling them in remote areas serviced by the state and through subsidies in form of food aid, food-for-work programmes and pension schemes. Some educational and health support as well as infrastructure development have been granted to San communities. In the 1990s all Southern African states launched community based natural resource management (CBNRM) programmes which were meant to foster both nature conservation and rural development and were embraced by many San communities and development organisations working with and for them.[16] Besides this kind of state intervention development initiatives, San were being increasingly supported by the churches, the international donor community and development agencies. [17] As a consequence the first local

---

[16] On different aspects of CBNRM projects currently carried out among San populations in Namibia and Botswana see Bollig, Hohmann, and Taylor this volume.

[17] One has to mention that these efforts so far remain largely constrained to Botswana, Namibia and South Africa for a number of reasons: After the demise of Apartheid South Africa and Namibia became especially prominent targets for developmental support and Botswana has the largest San population regionally, while Angola, Zambia and Zimbabwe have small remaining San populations who are often hard to identify and difficult to reach in logistic terms. Cf. on the

San organisations, some of which I will briefly describe below were founded in Namibia, Botswana and South Africa in the 1980s and 1990s. These organisations became mediators between San communities and the state. In many instances NGOs and their development projects took over state functions such as the running of schools, health services and infrastructural development. Many of them received funding from USAID for CBNRM initiatives (see Hohmann this volume).

The development programme of San in the Nyae Nyae area in northeastern Namibia took its start in 1981. It was initiated originally as a 'cattle fund' to provide Jul'hoansi groups with livestock, tools, and seeds to enable them to successfully keep their own cattle and move out of Tsumkwe town back into their original n!oresi[18]. Over the years the project grew into a multi-faceted development programme that is characterised by close co-operation between an NGO, the Nyae Nyae Development Foundation (NNDFN), and a community based organisation (CBO), the Nyae Nyae Farmers Cooperative (NNFC). NNFC was registered as the the first of the Namibian communal area conservancies, the Nyae Nyae Conservancy (NNC) in 1998. This development effort aims at the empowerment of Jul'hoansi communities through participatory planning and implementation of political, economic and cultural projects. NNFC has received assistance from various sides, including donors in Southern Africa, Europe, and America. Emphasis is placed on social and economic development as well as human resource development involving formal and non-formal education and training.[19] The Nyae Nyae area has since grown into a regional centre of state services and activities with various ministerial offices, a police station and hospital and the only junior secondary school in the area. Infrastructural maintenance and development as well as food programmes are being administered from Tsumkwe, the centre of the Nyae Nyae area. The Jul'hoansi's attitudes to the state however are ambivalent. The state is seen both as a provider and as an enemy when state services seems not that readily accessible as they are to the inhabitants of other regions.

---

history and current situation of San in Angola, Zambia and Zimbabwe; Robins et al. 2001.

[18] N!ore (pl.: n!oresi): According to Wiessner (1982:62) "areas of landrights [..] the right to exploit the resources of the land along with others who inherit similar rights," according to Dickens' dictionary "territory, country, land (especially that belonging to a village)" (Dickens 1994).

[19] Cf. for more details on the development initiative among the Jul'hoansi of Nyae Nyae: Hitchcock and Biesele 2000, and Hitchcock and Biesele 2002.

Anthropologists have been active in the Nyae Nyae area since the high time of the Harvard Kalahari Research Group both scientifically and often in an applied way working as consultants within the development context.

An early and fast growing development initiative among San in Botswana has been the Kuru Development Trust (KDT) officially registered in 1989 and since 2001 transformed into the KURU Family of Organisations carrying out projects in various fields among San in several regions of Botswana (see Bollig this volume for a description and analysis of its work).

The NGO First People of the Kalahari (FPK) was established in 1993 on the initiative of a group of San from the central Kalahari in Botswana who has been focusing mainly on the plight of the residents of the Central Kalahari Game Reserve (CKGR) whose residence inside the reserve has been threatened by removal through the Government of Botswana and finally ended with the cutting back of state services in January 2002.[20] A constitutive and continuous field of FPK's activity – the fight against removals of San from CKGR – has thus been characterised by conflict with state agencies resulting from the San's perception that their very existence is being threatened by government.

For South Africa, the South African San Institute (SASI) established in 1996 is the largest NGO working towards the development of San on a national and regional level. Its prime tasks are described on the SASI homepage:

> Presently SASI is mandated to work on a national and regional level through the creation of multi-disciplinary development projects in areas such as education, leadership training, cultural resources management, land rights, intellectual property rights, oral history collection and new approaches to community mobilisation.[21]

With the beginning of the 1990s, delegates of various San groups and local San organisations in Southern Africa began to work towards the creation of a regional network of Southern African San communities. This intention as well as two big Southern African conferences on San development issues held in Namibia in 1992 and in Botswana in 1993 led to a needs assessment carried out by two local consultants among San groups in

---

[20] For more detailed accounts of the history of the CKGR see Cassidy et al. 2001:26-28, Hitchcock 1999, Ditshwanelo 1996, and WIMSA 2002.

[21] http://www.san.org.za/sasi/home.htm.

Botswana, Namibia, South Africa, Zimbabwe and Zambia in 1994. As a consequence, the regional Working Group of Indigenous Minorities in Southern Africa (WIMSA) and a WIMSA/Botswana branch were established in 1996. WIMSA has committed itself to supporting San communities on the local, national and regional level. According to WIMSA's website and reports the NGO's general tasks are to provide a platform to advocate and lobby for San rights, to ease information exchange on San issues and ensure ongoing training and advice to San communities on administrative procedures, developmental issues, land tenure and tourism.

WIMSA consists of San member organisations throughout Southern Africa – currently 24 of them which are indigenous CBOs or VOs (village organisations). Additionally WIMSA presently has 11 registered support organisations, defined as "organisations which work with indigenous minorities nationally, regionally or internationally, and which share the aims of WIMSA" (paragraph 5.5.i of WIMSA's constitution)[22].

Table 1: WIMSA Membership Organisations[23]

Country	Organisation
Botswana	Maiteko Tshwaragano Development Trust
	D'kar Village Organisation
	Kuru Development Trust
	First People of the Kalahari
	Groot Laagte Village Organisation
	West Hanahai Village Organisation
	Dobe Village Organisation
	Tshobokwane Village Organisation
	Qoshe Village Organisation
Namibia	West Caprivi Development Trust
	Nyae Nyae Farmers' Co-operative
	Omatako Valley Rest Camp Committee
	Sonneblom/Dokerbos Committee
South Africa	!Xun & Khwe Trust
	Southern Kalahari San Association

According to the WIMSA mission statement of 1997, the main areas in which the San shall receive assistance from WIMSA are their striving for political recognition, for secure access to natural and financial resources, for

---

[22] Ibid.
[23] Source: WIMSA Annual Report 1998.

increased human rights awareness among their communities, for self-sustainability through development projects and for a common identity and pride in their culture which would improve their self-esteem. The ultimate goal is "to form a Regional San Council that will be fully representative of the San in Southern Africa" (cf. Brörmann 2002:46). With the foundation of WIMSA, the San are further escalating their effort in entering a dialogue with international organisations. From 1996 onward several San delegates were able to take part in conferences of the United Nations Working Group on Indigenous Populations (UNWGIP) in Geneva and at other international exchanges of views and experiences.

Looking at the aims defined by the various young San or San support organisations introduced above, there can be no doubt that a lot of their activity is likely to cause conflict with state policy or with what they perceive as the state. Many of their initiatives are aimed at changing existing legislation e.g. pertaining to land rights. State services like health and educational services are criticised for existing shortcomings and government decisions such as the ones to remove the San inhabitants from CKGR in Botswana or from Khwe land in West Caprivi (see Orth and Boden, this volume) are condemned and fought against. The development programmes implemented by Southern African governments do not always meet the San's demands and sometimes even appear to have negative effects on them (see e.g. Hitchcock and Ebert 1989, Hitchcock and Holm 1993).

The San and the image(s) that exist of them remain popular in public discourse, in the media, film and tourism industry and of course among social anthropologists working on Southern Africa. Today, probably more than previously, the influence that these discourses have on San identity and politics is one of the central issues in anthropological studies. As Lee interestingly asks: "On this new and expanded political terrain an interesting question concerns how hunters and gatherers themselves regard hunter-gatherer studies" (1992:42). The character and implications of research on San is not only discussed by academics themselves, but increasingly also by NGOs supporting indigenous peoples' movements like WIMSA, SASI, KURU etc. One problem connected to research and also the work of journalists for the San are the sometimes unwanted and potentially harmful presentations and images of them generated and spread in publications. Another problematic field currently widely discussed are the San's intellectual property rights when it comes to the scientific and commercial usage of their knowledge. It is not a new phenomenon that it can potentially be put to unwanted or detrimental uses – e.g. for political objectives or commercially without compensating the San. Take for example the

Traditional Authorities issue in Namibia where data on the political organisation, the land tenure system and the history of several San groups (recent migration or 'owners of the land') can have very practical effects on their chances to achieve official recognition and equal rights for their leaders. One example of a recent case of commercial use of research results is the one of the *Hoodia gordonia* succulent. Its active ingredients forming the basis of its hunger and thirst suppressing qualities known for generations by Southern African San groups have been patented without informing the San by American Pharma-Companies in 1997 and 1999. This has become the subject of ongoing negotiations and a memorandum of understanding between the Council for Scientific and Industrial Research (CSIR) and the South African San Council in 2002 (cf. for details: WIMSA 2002:59-60). To prevent such cases is one of the aims which WIMSA is actively supporting by having drawn up a contract that San groups or WIMSA can sign with researchers or journalists. Anthropology – including the research which resulted in this publication – has never been and will never be conducted in a political vacuum. The wider settings in which it has taken place – previously the Apartheid political system and currently the emerging arena of politicised San fighting for their rights and aims often in conjunction with a powerful group of globally interconnected NGOs and donor organisations – always has its implications for research and researchers. Research and its results can have unwanted side effects or be misused in unexpected ways. Anthropologists whether they want it or not are a part of the political discourse involving San presentation, development and politics rather than neutral bystanders. These are considerations that they must be aware of and that they are increasingly reflecting upon.

Current Answers to the Challenges

In the context of these developments new currents in anthropological research are emerging. The younger generation of anthropologists currently active in conducting research among San including the contributors to this volume have tried to find a way beyond the Kalahari Debate and distance themselves from both the traditionalists' and the revisionists' paradigms. Revisionists had depicted the San as victims of the political and economic processes around them while traditionalists had seen San society as conditioned by an arid environment and the unpredictability of resources. Both had left little space for agency. In a number of recent studies, anthropologists emphasise new aspects of culture and life of different San groups that they found to be of relevance during their fieldwork. Emic perspectives of San, neglected by traditionalists and revisionists, generally receive more attention in the published results of fieldwork than they did previously.

Where Lee and Wilmsen were primarily conducting analyses of their findings on a relatively abstract theoretical level, recent anthropological research on San has changed both in terms of its content and in terms of the way that it is presented. Widlok (1999), Taylor (2000) and Suzman (2000) for instance underline much of what they have to say on the background of their analytical methods and theorising through using a polyphony of different quotes from local actors. The subjects of the research thus become personally visible. The stress is clearly on the empirical basis of the analyses whereas theoretical orientation is pushed more into the background. What can be realised from the above work as well as a number of other publications (cf. Kent 1996, Sylvain 1999, Klocke-Daffa 2001) is a concentration on San groups that little had been published on before.

Development and the effect of regional and global processes are among the new topics of social anthropological research. Ethnic identity and the way it is currently used as a means by various stakeholders in the development process to gain access to political and economic resources is also among the new topics of research. The post-Apartheid state becomes a counterpart in more or less conflicting negotiations for development and is seen as an agency that is responsible for offering opportunities to achieve it. Thus, in recent anthropological research the state is thus more or less directly taken into account as an important stakeholder in San social and political affairs. The interaction of San in different areas of Southern Africa with the states in which they are situated has become the subject of a few anthropological studies during the recent decade.[24] Lee interprets the work of Clastres (1989) by saying that for relatively egalitarian, non-centralised societies like the San

> the main problem was resisting becoming a state; [...] resisting not only the imposition of a state from outside but also resisting the pressures building up within, pressures leading toward accumulation and concentration of wealth and power (Lee 1992:40).

This shows that specific problems and dynamics must be connected for San groups to their growing incorporation into the nation states' fabric. At the same time San are becoming integrated into even larger networks on a global

---

[24] Cf. Gordon 1992, Hitchcock and Holm 1993, Douglas 1997, Hitchcock and Biesele 2000, Taylor 2000, Anderson and Ikeya 2001, and Tshireletso 2001.

level especially through the involvement of NGOs. The San's connection to the growing international movement for indigenous rights and self-determination has been playing a major role in recent processes in San societies, taken note of in anthropological work e.g. in all of the contributions to this volume. In the context of the recent tendencies in San development anthropologists also engage in applied research carried out for donor organisations, NGOs and sometimes governments themselves.[25]

The San and the State: Historical Perspectives

San are seen and progressively identify themselves as the descendants of Southern Africa's indigenous inhabitants who have been the sole population group in the entire sub-continent, before the immigration of Bantu settlers started in the first millenium AD. After the in-migration of Bantu cattle herder-farmers, state-like political systems started to evolve in the region. Some San communities were contained in their spatial movement by these states and partly incorporated into their dynamics, but a lot of them were merely in contact with them through trade and working relationships (cf. Iliffe 1995:35-36; 97-103). Enslavement of San was a phenomenon occurring at a later stage of their integration with Bantu pre-colonial state systems as is especially documented for the Tswana kingdoms in the Kalahari in the 19th century (see Morton 1994, Iliffe 1995:175). However, generally speaking, little data are available on how exactly their integration was structured.

San history, as it can be reconstructed from archival records, oral history and scientific publications, becomes more detailed at the onset of the second major transition of the sub-continent after the Bantu expansion. The first direct contact between Europeans and San – called *Sonqua* by the Khoekhoe and the early Dutch settlers (Barnard 1992:157) – started at the Cape of Good Hope in 1652. It has to be stressed though that no clear distinction was made at the time, nor can be made today, between Khoekhoe and San, as "Khoe-speaking herders who lost their livestock could easily have become 'Bushmen' and vice versa" (Barnard 1992:159). Generally the area of the Cape was marked by regular friendly and unfriendly contacts between various population groups of a San, Khoekhoe or Bantu background up to the late 19th century (cf. Barnard 1992:158). Few sources are available on the

---

[25] See publications that resulted from such applied work of anthropologists, e.g.: Hitchcock 1993 and 1996, Bollig et al. 2000, Bollig and Hohmann 2001, Suzman 2001.

earliest encounters of Europeans with the local peoples of this area[26]. Some San were pushed beyond the colonial frontier while others became involved in the Dutch trading network. San were also incorporated into the colonial economy as translators, workers and slaves. This process implied frequent liaisons and offspring of white settlers or administrators and San women. Especially during the last quarter of the 18th century San groups organised strong resistance against the colonial encroachment (Szalay 1983:194-196). The settlers' response to this were organised 'kommandos' to fight back the San resistance in an often brutal manner (Szalay 1983:196-202; Wright 1971). While men were often killed, many women and children were captured to become workers on the European farms (Guenther 1980:131ff.). Kommandos thus served at the same time the colonial expansion and the integration of captured San, and continued under British rule into the second half of the 19th century (Eldredge 1994:114). During the further expansion of the Dutch colony South African San lost access to their ancestral land entirely and became subsumed under the label Coloureds until the end of Apartheid rule in 1994. As a result, San identity in South Africa has become largely denied by descendants in South Africa and disappeared from its ethnic landscape until very recently.

The geographical expansion of the Cape colony implied restrictions of the territories available to the African population, a trend continued also in colonial Namibia, Botswana and the other Southern African states not dealt with in this volume. During the initial period the San's major coping strategy was obviously to withdraw from colonial influences into more remote areas beyond the internal frontier. At the same time their growing incorporation into the colonial regional and global economy offered new opportunities and some San found ways to profit considerably from their interactions with traders, hunters and missionaries (see Gordon 1992:33-40; Wilmsen 1989). At later stages however the San's key economic strategy of hunting and gathering and their mobility were curtailed by land loss. The territorial order in the region was altered dramatically. Free access to land and natural resources was denied to local populations and their traditional property arrangements widely disregarded in the process. Land was taken over as farmland by white settlers and the resident population dispossessed and often incorporated into the farming system as cheap workers. The establishment of native reserves in 1913 in South Africa and 1923 in Namibia left local populations in marginal areas on less productive land. However, in some

---

[26] See Szalay 1983, Elphick 1979 and on the history of Khoisan populations Maingard 1931.

areas like Ghanzi District in Botswana (see Bollig et al. 2000:13) and Grootfontein area in Namibia an integration of farmwork and foraging evolved. Access to land was not denied to San completely, as farm labourers they were still allowed to move freely and had permission to use farm water points. "The relationships between San and the freehold farmers were essentially symbiotic ones in the beginning" (Bollig et al. 2000:13). However, with the fencing of freehold farms in Ghanzi from the 1960s onwards and in Grootfontein farming area in these San were also largely dispossessed and became landless labourers.

Restrictive colonial nature conservation legislation was one further factor having negative effects on San mobility and economic sustainability (see Dieckmann this volume). Nature conservation areas were created as spaces reserved for wildlife and free from local people so that many were removed from their ancestral land (see table 2).

Table 2: National parks, game reserves, and conservation areas in Southern
Africa that resulted in the resettlement of San populations

Park or Reserve Area	Date of Establishment	Size (km²)	Country	Comments
Central Kalahari Game Reserve	1961	52,730	Botswana	1,100 Gǀwi, Gǁana and Boolongwe Bakgalagadi were resettled outside the reserve in 1997 in nearby areas
Etosha National Park	1907	22,175	Namibia	Haiǁom were resettled outside the park or sent as workers to freehold farms
Gemsbok National Park, became Kgalagadi Transfrontier Park in April 1999	1931	37,991	South Africa, Botswana	ǂKhomani and Nǀamani San were resettled out of the park in the 1930s

Kruger National Park and its predecessors	1926	~19,000	South Africa	Around 2-3,000 people were moved from Sabi Game Reserve in 1903; Makuleke were relocated to the Ntlaveni area in 1969
Hwange (Wankie) National Park (declared a National Park on 29.01.1950)	1927	14,620	Zimbabwe	Batwa (Tuya, Amasili) were rounded up and resettled south of Hwange Game Reserve in the late 1920s
Moremi Game Reserve	1964	3,880	Botswana	Bugakhwe (‖Ani-khwe) were relocated out of Moremi in the 1960s
Nata Sanctuary	1989	230	Botswana	Shua lost access to the sanctuary and its resources
West Caprivi Game Park, since 2000 Bwabwata National Park	1963	5,715	Namibia	Khwe and Mbukushu were resettled in the early 1960s and Khwe and !Xun San went to South Africa in the 1980s

(Source: Hitchcock 2001:140 and Carruthers 1995:xi; 43; 99)[27]

New national boundaries were drawn sometimes dividing the residential areas of local communities as in the case of the Jul'hoansi in the border area between what is now Namibia and Botswana[28]. Homelands were created as territories reserved for the settlement of local populations, separated according to Apartheid ideology along what administrators perceived to be existing ethnic lines. For the group defined as 'Bushmen' of South Africa and Namibia the Homeland 'Bushmanland' was created in Northeastern

---

[27] I thank Ute Dieckmann for compiling this table and making it available for this introduction. Information on some additional nature conservation areas like e.g. Khaudom National Park in Namibia is not included because little researched.

[28] See for a description of the history and current situation of "The Jul'hoansi under two states" Hitchcock and Biesele 2000.

Namibia. Social anthropologists and an international lobby were of vital importance for enforcing the necessity of such a reserve and for defining the criteria that 'real' Bushmen suitable for staying in the reserve should have.[29]

In Bushmanland as well as in the Caprivi strip the colonial state established a number of SADF camps and recruited several thousands of San men in the 1970s. Through this the state induced a directed militarisation of San men and the absorption of their family members into a military political economy (see Lee and Hurlich 1982, Gordon 1992:185-192, and Sharp and Douglas 1996).

The San and the State: Mutual Influences

The following paragraph will briefly characterise today's interaction of San with the states they are living in and with state representatives. The most relevant aspects of this interaction will be summarised. The topics introduced are treated in detail by the contributors to this book in their case studies.[30]

Land

Land in the history of Southern Africa's colonies has been a most contested resource. The European settlers' quest for farmland and the states' political measures to ensure their economic and hegemonial interests conflicted with the local population since the early stages of European settlement. In the early phase of European settlement of the colonies, San together with other population groups were either forced to leave newly established farm areas or integrated into the commercial farming system as cheap labourers seasonally or permanently. Some remained on the farms with their families and lived off the meagre payments they received, often in kind, sometimes in cash. During a second phase of territorial organisation of the colonies reserves and homelands were established and the rest of the San population was restricted to live in the small part of the territory reserved for them under mostly unfavourable environmental conditions. As already mentioned above, the states' nature conservation policies since the beginning of the 20th century have been an additional obstacle to the San's access to

---

[29] See Gordon (1992:147-167) and Dieckmann (2002) on the interaction of anthropologists and the South African administration in Namibia.

[30] See for a detailed assessment of today's general situation of the various San populations dealing among others with the topics summarised here: Suzman 2001.

land and resources. Parts of their territories were set aside for conservation purposes and from the 1950s onwards they were cleared of the local population.

As a result, the San have lost secure access to most of their natural resource base. San currently have access to their ancestral land in only very few places in Botswana, Namibia and South Africa. In several places state interventions kept threatening their position on the land throughout the past years (see e.g. Barnard 1992:240-241, Boden and Orth this volume). Many San are still today living on farmland as labourers often under very precarious conditions (cf. Sylvain 2001, Suzman 2000 and 2001). San staying in towns are often suffering from a lack of formal education and from ethnic prejudice which severs their chances for paid employment. The status of San on state land like in West Caprivi and the Central Kalahari Game Reserve to take but two examples is often complicated by their lack of political power and representation and of effective property regulations to secure their access to the land and the resources on it. The state-initiated and strongly subsidised settlement programme in Botswana does not offer the San self-administered access to land either and has created new problems because of the remoteness of most of the settlements and their dependency on state welfare (see Bollig, this volume). Recently some success can be noted in South Africa where the San of the Kalahari and Schmidtsdrift have managed to receive land to resettle. In Namibia San have so far hardly been able to profit from resettlement schemes. Although agricultural land has been granted to San in Omaheke and Tsumkwe Districts and in West Caprivi these have not been functioning well and reaping hardly any economic benefits. Altogether the land problem remains one of the most pressing ones that San are currently experiencing and a lot of their recent attempts at improving their standing in Southern African states have involved questions of land and resource security.

Education and Employment

Equal access to formal education had been denied to the African population by the colonial regimes in Southern Africa. Access to qualified employment and effective political representation on a national level were impossible without the skills that could only be acquired within the formal education system. For San the situation has proven especially difficult because of their high geographical flexibility, the remoteness of the areas where they live and their frequent employment in the farm sector where their employers and sometimes they themselves did not regard school education as necessary to conduct their work.

With the end of the colonial era education has become a basic right for all and the countries' constitutions and policies in writing provide their citizens with equal chances to receive education. Illiteracy however is rife among San, school attendance rates are far lower than those of other population groups and drop-out rates are higher. Recent studies have shown that perceived discrimination on the basis of their ethnic background is a problem for San students (Le Roux 2000, Felton 1999). Furthermore, schools are often far from children's homes in the remote areas where most San are living. This increases the childrens' difficulties in adapting to the new and sometimes hard situation in school. Another problem is the difficulty for many San parents to finance their children's school and hostel fees. Where they can get exemption from this because of poverty, they are often not aware of it or allegedly told otherwise by school staff (see Felton 1999 and Le Roux 2000). Mother-tongue education currently is not offered to the majority of San children because of a lack of San teachers and of teaching material in the San languages.[31] Although national educational policies has begun to attend to the specific problems of San learners[32], educationalists and the affected themselves still expect a lot of improvements from the side of the respective governments.

Indigenous Peoples Movement and Political Representation

Power relations between San and the states are undergoing a process of redefinition with the San's recent involvement in the global movement of indigenous peoples. Many San groups have gained political strength and negotiation power especially since their quest is being strongly supported by NGOs and international donor agencies. The movement is concentrating on diverse topics like the recognition of basic human rights, the fight against discrimination, poverty reduction, struggles for land and natural resources, better access to education, the labour market and healthcare, political representation, cultural self-determination and the recognition of intellectual property. Open and increasingly confident struggles for the recognition of the San's plight in various fields have recently led to direct conflicts with governments' views and policies. A major part of this process is the San's fight for a recognised political leadership, most clearly demonstrated by their effort in Namibia to gain the government's approval of their elected

---

[31] See for the described problems in the case of Tsumkwe Constituency: The Namibian, 08.10.2002. *Education a Major Challenge at Mangetti.*

[32] E.g. in the Namibian case with the ministry's intersectoral task force for educationally marginalised children.

traditional authorities (see Felton 2000, Boden and Orth this volume). San are also beginning to actively involve themselves in national politics, make use of their right to vote and run as party candidates (see Hitchcock and Holm 1993:328-331 for the Botswanan situation). In the struggle for political representation and equal rights with outside stakeholders, political organisation within San societies is in a process of transformation. Newly emerging leaders are often young men with basic school education co-operating closely with NGOs. They are trying to find their position in the political economy in relation to governments, other state representatives, NGOs and donor agencies and have rapidly adapted to their new roles. At the same time they are trying to define and secure their position among their communities. As a result, new types of political organisation and power struggles are evolving.[33]

State Services: Domination and Dependency

Government policies towards the San in Botswana, Namibia and South Africa have contributed to dependency (see for example Hitchcock and Elbert 1989, Hitchcock and Holm 1993, Bollig and Hohmann 2001, Suzman 2001, and Bollig this volume). Government policy regularly favours high subsidisation in terms of infrastructure, food and employment instead of systematically increasing the San's opportunities to make their own independent achievements and decisions. As a consequence, San in many areas have become increasingly dependent on state bureaucracy and services. In some respect the effect of NGO input in 'San development' can be regarded in the same vein (see Bollig and Berzborn 2002). State decisions and NGO programmes which are sometimes planned without sufficient participation of San themselves can lead to new forms of external domination as

> various governmental and non-governmental organizations (NGOs) settle, train and otherwise organize the new lives of former forager populations [...] Economic domination – by farmers, employers or traders – is eclipsed by bureaucratic domination in this new social context (Hitchcock and Holm 1993:306).

Domination and dependency are perceived as problematic not only by the authors of this volume quoted above and other researchers or NGO staff, but

---

[33] See also Hitchcock and Holm 1993:321-324, and McCall 2002.

also by many San who seek their own path to what they understand as development.

Cultural Self-determination and Identity

A core activity of NGOs working among San and of recently established San CBOs is the quest for cultural self-determination. Recently the powerful global discourse emphasising minority rights, anti-racism and anti-discrimination has had its impact on Southern African San communities. International organisations trying to implement related values have created a platform for San to move towards the (re)construction and representation of their history and identity in internal discourses as well as in contacts with outsiders. Attempts to stress San indigenous identity with the ultimate aim to change their precarious situation are on the one hand contrary to the states' attempts at nation building. On the other hand there have recently been government decisions and legislation for instance pertaining to land rights, access to natural resources and political representation which support a stronger emphasis on ethnic identity (see Orth and Hohmann this volume). Ethnic identity inevitably becomes the basis of the 'community', a criterion used by governments and NGOs alike in identifying a given group as being eligible for e.g. land titles, a recognised traditional authority or a conservancy. San, and especially an evolving young San elite, have become aware of the advantages that an image as a cohesive ethnic group can have and increasingly stress ethnic markers like land use practices, plant and medicinal knowledge, initiation rites, dances and music, dress and language[34]. A similar trend to emphasise a cohesive and distinct identity can be caused in a context of conflict and competition with neighbouring groups as shown in this volume for the cases of the Khwe in West Caprivi (Orth and Boden) and the !Xun in Tsumkwe West (Hohmann).

The overall relationship between the San and the states they are living in must be characterised by the mutual influences that both sides have on each other. It would be a simplification to depict the San as merely being at the states' and NGOs' mercy or their passive victims. Their situation and coping strategies must be analysed more deeply which is what the contributors to this volume do. They demonstrate in many instances how the San's reactions to their wider social and political environment exert their own influence on it and how they make use of the conditions and the opportunities they have in order to live according to their own terms.

---

[34] On the role of language in this regard see especially Berzborn, this volume.

References

Anderson, Charles John
1863   *Der Okavango Strom. Entdeckungsreisen und Jagdabenteuer in Südwest-Afrika.* Leipzig: Wolfgang Gerhard.

Anderson, D. G. and K. Ikeya
2001   Managing Hunting Practice and Identity within State Policy Regimes. *Senri Ethnological Studies 59.* Osaka: Museum of Ethnology.

Barnard, Alan
1988 a Structure and Fluidity in Khoisan Religious Ideas. *Journal of Religion in Africa* 18:216-236.

1988 b Cultural Identity, Ethnicity and Marginalization among the Bushmen of Southern Africa. In: Rainer Vossen (ed.). *New Perspectives on the Study of Khoisan.* (Quellen zur Khoisan-Forschung 7.) Hamburg: Buske:9-27.

1992   *Hunters and Herders of Southern Africa: A Comprehensive Ethnography of Khoisan Peoples.* Cambridge: Cambridge University Press.

1992   *The Kalahari Debate: a Bibliographic Essay.* Occasional Paper No 35, Centre of African Studies, University of Edinburgh.

Bollig, Michael, R. Hitchcock, C. Nduku and J. Reynders
2000   *At the Crossroads: The Future of a Development Initiative. Evaluation of KDT Kuru Development Trust. Ghanzi and Ngamiland Districts of Botswana.* Bonn: EED.

Bollig, M. and Th. Hohmann
2001   *An Evaluation of Maiteko Tshwaragano Development Trust, Zutshwa, Botswana.* Bonn: EED.

Brörmann, Magdalena
2002   WIMSA. *Cultural Survival Quarterly.* Spring 2002, Vol. 26, Issue 1:45-48.

Cashdan, Elizabeth
1983   Territoriality among Human Foragers: Ecological Models and an Application to Four Bushman Groups *Current Anthropology* 24:47-66.

Cassidy, Lin, Kenn Good, Isaac Mazonde and Roberta Rivers
2001   An Assessment of the Status of the San in Botswana. *Regional Assessment of the Status of the San in Southern Africa*. Report 3 of 5. Windhoek: Legal Assistance Centre.

Clastres, Pierre
1989   *Society against the State: Essays in Political Anthropology*. New York: Zone Books.

Dapper, Olaf
1668   *Naukeurige Beschrijvinge der Afrikanisher Gewesten*. Amsterdam: J. van Meurs.

De Almeida, Antonio
1994   *Os Bosquimanos de Angola*. Ministério do planeamento e da Administracao do Território Secretaria de Estado da Ciencia e Tecnologia. Instituto de Envestigacao Cientifica Tropical.

Dieckmann, Ute
2001   'The Vast White Place': A History of the Etosha National Park in Namibia and the Hai‖om. *Nomadic Peoples* (2001), Volume 5, Issue 2:125-153.

Ditshwanelo
1996   *When Will this Moving Stop? Report on a Fact-Finding Mission of the Central Kgalagadi Game Reserve*. Gaborone: Ditshwanelo – The Botswana Center for Human Rights.

Douglas, S.
1996   Prisoners of their Reputation? The Veterans of the 'Bushman' Battalions in South Africa. In: Skotnes et al. (eds.) *Miscast: Negotiating the Presence of Bushmen*. Cape Town: University of Cape Town Press:323-329.

1997   Reflections on State Intervention and the Schmidtsdrift Bushmen. *Journal of Contemporary African Studies* 15 (1):45-66.

Eldredge, Elizabeth A. and Fred Morton (eds.)
1994   *Slavery in South Africa. Captive Labor on the Dutch Frontier*. Pietermaritzburg: University of Natal Press.

Elphick, R.
1979   The Khoisan to c. 1770. In: Elphick, R. and H. Giliomee (eds.). *The Shaping of South African Society, 1652-1820*. Cape Town and London: Longman:3-40.

Felton, Silke
2000   "We want our own chief" – San Communities Battle Against Their
        Image. In: Le Beau, Debie and Robert J.Gordon (eds.). *Challenges
        for Anthropology in the 'African Renaissance': A Southern African
        Contribution*. Windhoek: University of Namibia Press, Publication
        No. 1.

Felton, Steve
1999   *Listen to Us. Challenges Facing San Children in Education*.
        WIMSA: Windhoek.

Galton, Francis
1889   *Narrative of an Explorer in Tropical South Africa*. London, New
        York and Melbourne: Ward, Lock and Co.

Gordon, Robert J.
1992   *The Bushman Myth: The Making of a Namibian Underclass*.
        Boulder: Westview Press.

Guenther, Mathias
1980   From "Brutal Savages" to "Harmless People". Notes on the
        Changing Western Image of the Bushmen. *Paideuma* 26, 1980:123-
        139.

1986   'San' or 'Bushmen'? In: Biesele, M., Robert Gordon and Richard
        Lee (eds.). *The Past and Future of !Kung Ethnography: Critical
        Reflections and Symbolic Perspectives. Essays in Honour of Lorna
        Marshall*. (Quellen zu Khoisan-Forschung 4.) Hamburg: Buske:27-
        51.

1990   Convergent and Divergent Themes in Bushman Myth and Art. In:
        Karl-Heinz Kohl et al. (eds.). *Die Vielfalt der Kultur*. Berlin:
        Reimer:237-254.

1999   *Tricksters and Trancers: Bushman Religion and Society*.
        Bloomington, Indianapolis: Indiana University Press.

Gusinde, Martin
1953   Anthropological Investigations of the Bushmen of South Africa.
        Anthropological Quarterly 26:20-28.

Hahn, H. and J. Rath
1859   Reisen der Herren Hahn und Rath im südwestlichen Afrika. Mai bis
        September 1857. *Mittheilungen aus Justus Perthes' geographischer
        Anstalt über wichtige neue Erforschungen auf dem Gesammtgebiete
        der Geographie von Dr. A. Petermann*:295-303.

Hammond-Tooke, W. D.
1997   *Imperfect Interpreters: South Africa's Anthropologists 1920-1990.*
        Johannesburg: Witwatersrand University Press.

Hawkes, Kirsten, Nicholas Blurton Jones and Patricia Draper
1994   Foraging Returns of !Kung Adults and Children: Why Didn't !Kung
        Children Forage? *Journal of Anthropological Research*, 50:217-248.

Hitchcock, Robert
1993   Indigenous Peoples, the State, and Resource Rights in Southern
        Africa. In: Veber, H., J. Dahl, N. Wilson, and E. Wähle (eds.).
        *"Never Drink from the Same Cup." Proceedings of the Conference
        on Indigenous Peoples in Africa.* Tune: IWGIA:119-132.

1996   *Bushmen and the Politics of the Environment in Southern Africa.*
        Tune: IWGIA document No. 79.

1999   A Chronology of Major Events Relating to the Central Kalahari
        Game Reserve. *Botswana Notes and Records* 31:105-117.

Hitchcock, Robert, J.I. Ebert, and R.G. Morgan
1989   Drought, Drought Relief and Dependency Among the Sarwa of
        Botswana. In: R. Huss-Ashmore and S.H. Katz (eds.). *African Food
        Systems in Crisis. Part One: Microperspectives.* New York: Gordon
        and Breach:303-336.

Hitchcock, Robert and J. Holm
1993   Bureaucratic Domination of Hunter-Gatherer Societies: A Study of
        the San in Botswana. *Development and Change*, Vol. 24:305-338.

Hitchcock, Robert and Rosinah Rose B. Masilo
1996   Subsistence Hunting and Resource Rights in Botswana: An
        Assessment of Special Game Licences and Their Impacts on Remote
        Area Dwellers and Wildlife Populations. *Botswana Notes and
        Records* 28:55-64.

Hitchcock, Robert and Megan Biesele
2000   The Jul'hoansi San under Two States: Impacts of the South West
        African Administration and the Government of the Republic of
        Namibia. In: Peter Schweitzer, Megan Biesele and Robert Hitchcock
        (eds.). *Hunters and Gatherers in the Modern World. Conflict,
        Resistance, and Self-Determination.* New York: Berghahn
        Books:305-326.

2002   Controlling their Destiny: The Jul'hoansi San of Nyae Nyae.
        Cultural Survival Quarterly. Spring 2002, Vol. 26, Issue 1:13-15.

Iliffe, John
1995   *Africans. The History of a Continent.* Cambridge: Cambridge
        University Press.

Jenkins, T.
1986   The Prehistory of the San and the Khoikhoi as Recorded in Their
        Blood. In: R. Vossen and K. Keuthmann (eds.). *Contemporary
        Studies on Khoisan. Quellen zur Khoisan-Forschung* 5.2. Hamburg:
        Buske:51-78.

Kent, Susan (ed.)
1996   *Cultural Diversity Among Twentieth Century Foragers: An African
        Perspective.* Cambridge: Cambridge University Press.

Klocke-Daffa, Sabine
2001   *„Wenn du hast, mußt du geben" – Soziale Sicherung im Ritus und
        im Alltag bei den Nama von Berseba/Namibia.* Studien zur sozialen
        und rituellen Morphologie, Bd. 3. Münster: LIT.

Köhler, O.
1975   Der Khoisan Sprachbereich. In: H. Baumann (ed.). *Die Völker
        Afrikas und ihre traditionellen Kulturen.* Wiesbaden: Steiner:305-37.

Kolb, Peter
1727   *Naauwkeurig en Uitvoerig Beschryving van de Kaap de Goede
        Hoop; Nevens een Beschryving van den Hottentotten.* 2 Vols.
        Amsterdam: Balthazar Lakeman.

Leacock, Eleanor and Richard Lee
1982   Introduction. In: Leacock, Eleanor and Richard Lee (eds.). *Politics
        and History in Band Societies.* Cambridge: Cambridge University
        Press:1-20.

Lebzelter, Viktor
1934   *Die Eingeborenenkulturen in Südwest- und Südafrika.*
        Wissenschaftliche Ergebnisse einer Forschungsreise nach Süd- und
        Südwestafrika in den Jahren 1926-1928. Leipzig: Verlag Karl W.
        Hiersemann.

Lee, Richard B.
1979   *The !Kung San: Men, Women, and Work in a Foraging Society.*
        Cambridge: Cambridge University Press.

1982   Politics, Sexual and Non-sexual, in an Egalitarian Society. In:
        Leacock, Eleanor and Richard Lee (eds.) *Politics and History in
        Band Societies.* Cambridge: Cambridge University Press:37-59.

1984   *The Dobe !Kung*. New York: Holt, Rinehart and Winston.

1992   Art, Science, or Politics? The Crisis in Hunter-Gatherer Studies. *American Anthropologist* 94, 1992:31-54.

1993   *The Dobe Ju/'hoansi*. New York: Hartcourt Brace.

1996   Laurens van der Post and the Kalahari Debate. In: Skotnes et al. (eds.) *Miscast: Negotiating the Presence of Bushmen*. Cape Town: University of Cape Town Press:239-249.

Lee, Richard and Irven DeVore
1976   *Kalahari Hunter-Gatherers*. Cambridge: Harvard University Press.

Lee, Richard and Susan Hurlich
1982   From Foragers to Fighters: South Africa's Militarization of the Namibian San. In: Eleanor Leacock und Richard Lee (eds.). *Politics and History in Band Societies*. Cambridge: Cambridge University Press:327-345.

Le Roux, W
2000   *Torn Apart: San Children as Change Agents in a Process of Acculturation*. Windhoek: Kuru Development Trust / Working Group of Indigenous Minorities in Southern Africa.

Maingard, L.F.
1931   The Lost Tribes of the Cape. *South African Journal of Science* 28:487-504.

Marshall-Thomas, Elisabeth
1959   *The Harmless People*. London: Secker & Warburg.

McCall, Grant S.
2002   *Egalitarian Tensions of Ju/'hoansi in a Capitalist Economy: Foraging Ideology and Adaptations to Cash Income*. Paper presented at the Ninth International Conference on Hunting and Gathering Societies, 9th to 13th September 2002, Edinburgh.

Morton, Barry
1994   Servitude, Slave Trading, and Slavery in the Kalahari In: Eldredge, Elizabeth A. and Fred Morton (eds.). *Slavery in South Africa. Captive Labor on the Dutch Frontier*. Pietermaritzburg: University of Natal Press:215-250.

Myers, Fred
1988   Critical Trends in the Study of Hunter-Gatherers. *Annual Review of Anthropology* 17:261-282.

Robins, Steven, Elias Madzudzo and Matthias Brenzinger
2001   An Assessment of the Status of the San in South Africa, Angola, Zambia and Zimbabwe. *Regional Assessment of the Status of the San in Southern Africa*. Report 2 of 5. Windhock: Legal Assistance Centre.

Saugestad, Sidsel
1998   *The Inconvenient Indigenous: Remote Area Development in Botswana Donor Assistance and the First People of the Kalahari.* Tromsø: Faculty of Social Science, University of Tromsø.

Schinz, Heinz
1891   *Deutsch-Südwest-Afrika.* Leipzig: Schulze'sche Verlagsbuch-handlung.

Schmidt, Sigrid
1989   Catalogue of the Khoisan Folktales in Southern Africa. Part II: The Tales. In: Vossen, R. (ed.) *Quellen zur Khoisan-Forschung 6.2.* Hamburg: Buske.

1995   Representatives of Evil in Khoisan Folktales. In: Traill, A., R. Vossen and M. Biesele (eds.). *The Complete Linguist. Papers in Memory of Patrick Dickens.* Cologne: Köppe:115-134.

Schrire, Carmel
1984   *Past and Present in Hunter-Gatherer Studies.* Orlando: Academic Press.

Schultze, Leonard
1914   Südwestafrika. In: Hans Meyer (ed.). *Das Deutsche Kolonialreich*, vol. 2, pt. 2. Leipzig: Verlag des Bibliographischen Instituts.

1928   Zur *Kenntnis des Körpers der Hottentotten und Buschmänner. Zoologische und anthropologische Ergebnisse einer Forschungsreise im westlichen und zentralen Südafrika.* Vol. 5, Part 3. Jena: Gustav Fischer:147-227.

Segobye, A. K.
1998   Early Farming Communities. In: Lane, P., Reid, A., and Segobye, A. K. (eds.). *Ditswa mmung: the Archaeology of Botswana.* Gaborone: The Botswana Society:101-114.

Seiner, Franz
1913   Beobachtungen an den Bastard-Buschleuten der Nord-Kalahari. *Mitteilungen der Anthropologischen Gesellschaft in Wien* 43:311-324.

Sharp, J. and S. Douglas.
1996.   Prisoners of their Reputation? The Veterans of the 'Bushman'
        Battalions in South Africa. In: Skotnes et al. (eds.) *Miscast:*
        Negotiating the Presence of Bushmen. Cape Town: University of
        Cape Town Press:323-329.

Silberbauer, George
1981   *Hunter and Habitat in the Central Kalahari Desert.* Cambridge:
        Cambridge University Press.

Solway, Jacqueline and Richard Lee
1990   Foragers Genuine or Spurious: Situating the Kalahari San in History.
        Current Anthropology. Vol. 31, No. 2:109-146.

Soodyall, H. and T. Jenkins
1998   Khoisan Prehistory: The Evidence of the Genes. In: A. Bank (ed.).
        Proceedings of the Khoisan Identities and Cultural Heritage
        Conference Held at the South African Museum, Cape Town, 12-16
        July 1997. Cape Town: The Institute for Historical Research at the
        University of Western Cape and Infosource CC:374-382.

Suzman, James
2000   *'Things from the Bush'. A Contemporary History of the Omaheke*
        Bushmen. (Basel Namibia Studies Series 5.) Basel: P. Schlettwein
        Publishing.

2001   An Introduction to the Regional Assessment of the Status of the San
        in Southern Africa. *Regional Assessment of the Status of the San in*
        Southern Africa. Report 1 of 5. Windhoek: Legal Assistance Centre.

Sylvain, R.
1999   *'We work to have life': Ju/'hoan Women, Work and Survival in the*
        Omaheke Region, Namibia. PhD thesis. Toronto: Graduate
        Department of Anthropology.

2001   Bushmen, Boers, and Baasskap: Patriarchy and Paternalism on
        Afrikaner farms in the Omaheke Region, Namibia. *Journal of*
        Southern African Studies, 27:4, 2001:717-738.

Szalay, M
1983   *Ethnologie und Geschichte: Zur Grundlegung einer ethnologischen*
        Geschichtsschreibung. Mit Beispielen aus der Geschichte der Khoi-
        San in Südafrika. Berlin: Reimer.

Tanaka, Jiro
1980   *The San: Hunter-Gatherers of the Kalahari. A Study in Ecological Anthropology.* Tokyo: University of Tokyo Press.

Taylor, Michael,
2000   *Life, Land and Power. Contesting Development in Northern Botswana.* Unpublished PhD Thesis, University of Edinburgh.

Tobias, P.V.
1961   Physique of a Desert Folk. *Natural History* 7 (4):16-25.

Tshireletso, L.
2001   Issues, Dilemmas and Prospects on the State Provision of Education to Traditional Hunter-Gatherer Societies in Botswana. In: Tanaka, J., M. Ichikawa and D. Kimura (eds.) *African Hunter-Gatherers: Persisting Cultures and Contemporary Problems.* African Study Monographs. Suppl. 26. Kyoto: The Center for African Area Studies:169-184.

van der Post, Laurens
1961   *The Heart of the Hunter.* London: Penguin.

Wannenburgh, Alf
1979   *The Bushmen.* Johannesburg: Struik.

Widlok, Thomas
1999   *Living on Mangetti. Bushman Autonomy and Namibian Independence.* Oxford: Oxford University Press.

Widlok, Thomas and Kazuyoshi Sugawara (eds.)
2001   *Symbolic Categories and Ritual Practice in Hunter-Gatherer Experiences.* African Study Monographs. Suppl. 27. Kyoto: The Center for African Area Studies.

Wiessner, Polly
1982   Risk, Reciprocity and Social Influence on !Kung San Economics. In: Leacock, Eleanor and Richard Lee (eds.) *Politics and History in Band Societies.* Cambridge: Cambridge University Press:61-84.

Wilmsen, Edwin
1989   *Land Filled with Flies: A Political Economy of the Kalahari.* Chicago: University of Chicago Press.

WIMSA
2002   *Working Group of Indigenous Minorities in Southern Africa; Report on Activities April 2001 to March 2002.* Windhoek: WIMSA.

Wright, John B.
1971   *Bushman Raiders of the Drakensberg, 1840-1870.* Pietermaritzburg:
        University of Natal Press.

Wylie, L.
1979   Official Policy Towards San Hunter-Gatherers in Modern
        Botswana – 1966-1978. *NIR Working Paper No. 23.* Gaborone:
        National Institute of Development Research and Documentation.

Yellen, John E.
1977   *Archaeological Approaches to the Present: Models for
        Reconstructing the Past.* New York: Academic Press.

The Impact of Nature Conservation on the San:
A Case Study of Etosha National Park

Ute Dieckmann

> "In conflict between good and evil the solution is simple – seek the triumph of good over evil. But in the conflict between good and good the balancing of conflicting moral imperatives is painful and trying, and without clear implications for a correct course of action. The resident peoples issue is clearly in this latter category." (West 1991:xix).

Introduction

In Southern Africa, sizeable portions of land have been declared national parks or game reserves during the last century (Table 1, see Introduction, this volume). The national park concept includes the idea that people do not live within the protected area, nor consume its resources (Brechin et al. 1991:7-10). Under the illusion of being natural systems apart from, and not at all influenced by the political, social or cultural developments around them, national parks have become important tourist attractions. But appearances are deceptive: those areas have become off-limits to local people who have been living on that land for centuries.

In Southern Africa, areas of far more than 100,000 km² are now restricted for use by local people. During the colonial era, national parks were often established in arid areas not suitable for farming. For a long time, those areas served as refuges or niches for (former) hunter and gatherer groups before nature reserves were established and people were resettled. Thus, San belong to the people most affected in Southern Africa by the establishment of those parks or by nature conservation legislation in general (Taylor 2000, Hitchcock 2001, Ikeya 2001).

In Namibia, about 13.6% of the total land area is designated as national parks and game reserves (Blackie and Tarr 1999:13). One can only estimate how many people have been affected by the establishment of these parks, either by relocation or by grave restrictions on the use of natural resources within the reserves. The fact that exact data about the consequences for the resident people are missing for most of the reserve areas can be viewed as a sign of the lack of relevance taken for the local people in the planning and realisation of these parks. Compensation for lost land or lost resources has never been paid to the people who were forced to abandon their areas for the sake of national parks or game reserves.

This article outlines the development of Etosha National Park as one example of the impact nature conservation has had on local people. Whereas other articles in this volume deal with more recent approaches of nature conservation (Hohmann, and Taylor, this volume), which are thought to combine the protection of natural resources with community development, and therefore begin to include local people in the planning and realisation of conservancy areas, this chapter will – with its focus on Etosha – explore the more 'traditional' approach. It has pretended that nature conservation is a goal in itself (which it in fact never was) and mostly disregarded the people affected by the establishment of national parks, game reserves and conservation areas.

I compare the 'history'[1] that can be reconstructed from archival material with perspectives from within, from the people themselves who were affected. It will become clear that the combined analysis of different source material – oral history and archival documents – offers another understanding of the past than the examination of just one of these.

This article is based on archival work done in the Namibian National Archives[2] in 1999 and on interviews conducted during my adjacent fieldwork in Outjo and Etosha between 1999 and 2001. The knowledge that I gained in the archives influenced my approach in the field, but the 'history' presented by the local people held a different interpretation than I had expected.

---

[1] The quotation marks for 'history' are meant to emphasise that history always includes interpretation. Therefore, there is no single 'history', but many different 'histories' about the past. However, we can only approach the past through the different histories about it.

[2] The 'history' constructed from archival material may be found in Dieckmann 2001.

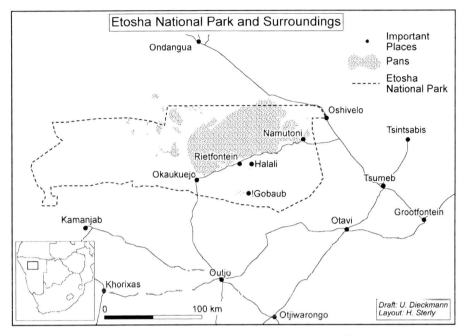

Map 1: Etosha National Park and surrounding

The Area and People

Etosha National Park (22,270 km²) is one of the world's largest national parks and the premier tourist attraction in Namibia (Mendelsohn et al. 2000:34). The popularity of this park is based on the abundance of wildlife: most of Namibia's lions, elephants, rhinos and other large animals live within the boundaries of the park. In 1997, about 98,100 tourists visited Etosha; two-thirds of all foreign tourists to Namibia include Etosha in their itinerary. Etosha is obviously the best opportunity in Namibia to see African wildlife, a major motivation for western tourists to visit Africa (Mendelsohn et al. 2000:30, 34). Today, when tourists travel on the comfortable roads of the park they think of themselves as travelling in a virgin natural environment. But the area south of Etosha Pan, where most of the tourist roads run, has long been the home of a hunter-gatherer community. It belonged to people who were generally categorised as one of the "Bushman" or San groups of Namibia,[3] and who came to be known as the Hai‖om during the 19th century. During that time and into the beginning of the 20th century, the Hai‖om lived in the region stretching from Ovamboland, Etosha, Grootfontein, Tsumeb, Otavi and Outjo to Otjiwarongo in the south (some authors claim that the southern limits extended to Rehoboth, e.g., Bleek 1927, Schapera 1930), and were enmeshed in trade networks and sociopolitical relations with surrounding groups. The park was created in the early 20th century, but initially and for a long time afterward, the Hai‖om were accepted as residents within the game reserve,[4] while the surrounding area was increasingly occupied by white settlers. Today, the Hai‖om are left without legal title to any land in Namibia (Widlok 1999:32).

The Beginning: Precolonial Times and the German Period (1850-1915)

In the 19th century, the region around Etosha Pan was visited by travellers (e.g., Anderson 1863, Galton 1889, Schinz 1891) and missionaries (e.g., Hahn and Rath 1859), who mentioned Bushmen living there. These travellers often employed Bushmen for odd jobs during their journeys (e.g., Schinz 1891:339) and reported about their contacts with Oshivambo-speaking people in the north and their copper mines near Otavi (Hahn 1867:286, Schinz 1891:340, see also Widlok, this volume). Galton (1889) observed that the Bushmen regarded the 'Ghou Damup' (now known as Damara) as inferior and had taught them their language (Galton 1889:154)[5].

Germany took control of the territory in 1884, but only some fourteen years later, the colonial administration was in a position to prepare plans to exert control over the Hai‖om. In 1898, a treaty was signed with Aribib, one

---

[3] The label "Bushman" is no longer popular in the official discourse in Namibia, and the term "San" is used instead. But in informal conversations, people, especially farmers, still talk of "Bushmen." I use the term "Bushmen" in the context of historical sources, since the attitudes and actions of the Administration and of white society at large was motivated by their ideas about 'Bushman.' Even academics disagree about the politically and/or scientifically correct term; for a discussion see Gordon (1992:4f., 17ff.) and Widlok (1999:6f.).

[4] Most of the earlier writers did not distinguish between the different San groups. Thus, even when specific cases are mentioned, it is not easy to determine which group a given author means. But since the area of Etosha was always 'Hai‖om-country,' one may assume that references to Bushmen living there indicate the Hai‖om.

[5] The ideology about the Bushmen, which, grounded in evolutionary assumptions, was to become popular later, was not expressed as openly in 19th century travel accounts as it was in 20th century accounts.

of the Hai‖om 'leaders,' in order to incorporate the Hai‖om into the colonial system. Aribib ceded to the Germans a large piece of land between Outjo and Grootfontein for the annual payment of 500 Marks, protection and the permanent right to forage in the area (Gordon 1992:50). Köhler comments: "The purpose of the treaty was to get the Hei-‖um Bushmen of the Etosha Pan under German control and create some order between the Bushmen and the colonists" (Köhler 1959:19).

The idea of creating a game reserve in northern Namibia came into discussion at the very beginning of the 20th century. In 1902, the district administrator (*Bezirksamtmann*) of Outjo – a town situated approximately 100 km south of Etosha – suggested declaring the Etosha area a game reserve, mainly to close the area to traffic in order to keep hunters out (SWAA Nature Conservation and Tourism:iv)[6]. Control posts south of Etosha Pan at Namutoni, Rietfontein and Okaukeujo had already been erected in 1896-1897 in order to prevent stock movement as a consequence of the outbreak of rinderpest during those years (de la Bat 1982:12).

In 1907, Governor von Lindequist proclaimed the Etosha region one of three game reserves[7]. According to this ordinance (Ordinance 88 of 1907), the hunting of kudu cows, eland, zebra, buffalo and giraffe was prohibited in game reserves, and vehicular traffic required written permission of the government (SWAA Nature Conservation and Tourism:iv). Lieutenant Adolff Fischer, commander of Fort Namutoni at that time, became the first warden of the game reserve. Fischer was transferred in 1910, and two years later Fort Namutoni was abandoned by the Germans. Private farm ownership was still allowed within the boundaries of the game reserve, but this lapsed in 1935 (Berry 1980:53).

---

[6] Hunting had become an economic enterprise in the northern parts of Namibia, including the Etosha area, during the second half of the 19th century. Game, especially lions, rhinos and elephants, had become scarce. The last herd of elephants was killed at Klein Namutoni in 1881. By 1886, no white rhino were left, and black rhinos had found refuge only in the most inaccessible spots. By the turn of the century, lions had been completely exterminated in the Namutoni area (Germishuys and Staal 1979:110-111).

[7] "[...] Als Wildreservate werden bestimmt: [...] 2.) Das Gebiet südlich, westlich und nordwestlich der Etoscha-Pfanne in den Bezirken Grootfontein und Outjo, welches durch folgende Linien begrenzt wird: Im Osten und Süden die Westgrenze des Ovambolandes vom Kunene bis Osohama. Von dort nach Koantsab und über Ondowa, Chudop, Obado [?], Aigab, Vib, Chorub nach Gub. Von Gub über Otjokaware (Kowares) bis Oachab. Von Oachab das Hoarusib-Rivier bis zum Meere. Im Westen vom Meere. Im Norden vom Kunene bis zur Grenze des Ovambolandes [...]" (Ordinance 88 of 1907, ZBU MII E.1).

The explicit reason for the establishment of game reserves was to protect game in specific areas, since game had become scarce in the territory over the preceding century[8]. However, economic motivations are clearly articulated in the explanatory paper for establishing the game reserves:

> [...] The high economic value of game in the country is known to everybody. In some kitchens you can find game as fresh meat. The practical value of the skin as straps and whips, etc., is known. No statistics are available, but if you calculate its value by taking the average price of meat as a basis, you would get a sum of more than 200,000 M. If you took this sum as annual pension, the capital that we have in the game population in the country would exceed several million. We all get this pension for free [...] Thus, each inhabitant should try to protect game because it is in the interest of every individual [...] The use of game reserves for the country might be the following: Centres could be established where game could multiply without disturbance. This increase may mean that game would have to spread out to other grazing areas and eventually reach the farms, where it could be shot and processed [...] I must add the following remarks to the different paragraphs of the proclamation. To §1: The defined reserves comprise areas that, because of their nature, are not fit for farms either now or in the near future [...]"[9]

Therefore, the conservation of nature served specific purposes, and the settlers and colonial administration were to benefit in a direct and material way: Game meat was pinpointed as a crucial resource for the colony. For this reason, it was essential that the game reserve was not fenced. No hints could be found that any need of administrative control over the Hai‖om living in that area was taken into consideration in the decision to declare the Etosha area a game reserve.

The proclaimed Game Reserve No. 2 included today's Etosha National Park, as well as Kaokoland from the Kunene River to the Hoarusib River, an area of 93,240 km² (de la Bat 1982:12). Since its proclamation, Game Reserve No. 2 has undergone many minor and several major boundary

---

[8] The Germans had proclaimed the first game laws in South West Africa some years before the establishment of game reserves (Germishuis and Staal 1979:110f.).

[9] ZBU MII E.1, translation U.D.

alterations under the South African Administration (Berry 1980:53, de la Bat 1982: 14, 19f.)[10].

During the German period, the Hai‖om were permitted to stay in the reserve. The goals of nature conservation and the policy towards 'natives' were contradictory and not strongly related to each other. The prohibition of hunting in this area applied only to hunting with guns, but not to bow and arrow. Archival documents do not give detailed insight into the policy in regard to people within the park. In 1908, it was suggested that more Bushmen from the area outside the game reserve should be settled near Namutoni[11]; this idea cropped up again during the South African period (see below). In 1910, the District Chief (*Distriktchef*) Zawada asked for more police patrols to round up Hai‖om at the different waterholes and bring them to Namutoni, where they should work and be fed with maize, in order to protect the game living in the reserve[12]. But the administration did not follow up on this plan. Lieutenant Fischer summarised the attitude of the German colonial government towards the Hai‖om in a comment in his report on an expedition to the Omuramba, Ovambo and Okavango in 1908: "With the advancement of settlement, the Heigum will soon face the choice of becoming farm labourers or moving to areas where they will eventually disappear under more unfavourable living conditions. The tribe of the Heigum is not essential for the development of the colony."[13] Whereas game was worth protecting for the sake of the colonial economy, the extinction of Bushmen was not considered to be a loss for colonial development.

Although there was various discourse during the German and South African colonial periods (e.g., by farmers, missionaries and the administration) concerning the treatment of Bushmen that were by no means consistent, they all shared some underlying assumptions grounded in the racist and pseudo-Darwinist ideology of the time, which viewed Bushmen on the lowest rung of human evolution, in an order just above that of animals. It was supposed to be merely a matter of time before Bushmen disappeared

---

[10] The reasons for and discussions about those changes would themselves be worth a detailed analysis.

[11] ZBU W II B.2, Kaiserlicher Bezirksamtmann Grootfontein an das Kaiserliche Gouvernement, 15-8-1908.

[12] ZBU WII O.4, Distriktamt Namutoni, Bericht, 10-3-1910. If the the above quotation is taken to its logical extreme, one could conclude that the Hai‖om should be fed with maize in order to keep the meat for the white settlers.

[13] ZBU F XIII B.4, 15-1-1909, translation U.D.

completely from the face of the earth[14]. The Hai‖om, or Bushmen in general, were rarely regarded as subjects, but rather objects that had to be subjugated as much as possible in order to serve the colonial powers, a fact clearly reflected in the language used. The control over and necessary assimilation of the people would eventually lead to their inevitable extinction.

Views from Within

The majority of people still alive today did not personally experience the German colonial period. Therefore, it is difficult to draw a picture based on the few statements concerning those times,[15] nevertheless, some aspects may be noted.

The Hai‖om lived in family groups near the various waterholes inside the park. According to informants, every group occupied a specific area that often included a number of waterholes, specific bushfood areas or hunting grounds, comparable to the social organisation of some other San groups (Barnard 1986). Headmen (very rarely headwomen) were responsible for peace and order; they were called to settle disputes and to mediate between individuals. They had to be asked permission by people from other areas for hunting or gathering rights. Usually people moved within their area according to season, and extended family networks guaranteed access to natural resources in other areas. But their detailed knowledge was often limited to their specific area, and they didn't know specifics about the headmen of other areas, seasonal mobility within that area, etc.

Contact with other groups also existed: The Hai‖om exchanged meat, salt or ostrich eggs for *mahangu* or tobacco with Ovambo. This contact intensified when Oshivambo-speaking men were recruited as contract labourers for the farms further south. On their way back home they crossed the area inside the game reserve. These contacts were not always peaceful: attacks and robberies from the Hai‖om occurred occasionally. The elder people in Etosha whom I talked to could not remember Damara staying there during their lifetime, but they were told by their grandparents that Damara were used by the Hai‖om to carry meat for them.

---

[14] The idea of the "vanishing race," or the extinction of indigenous people, was not only restricted to the San in southern Africa. The same idea was long held the paradigm of research among the indigenous people of North America (see Heinz 1993:44).

[15] In addition, most, if not all, of the elder people are illiterate and not really concerned about dates. It is often difficult to reconstruct any kind of chronological order.

In the memory of the Hai‖om, Aribib is not such a unique man. Some did not know him at all, others claim that it was not Aribib, but in fact ǂArixab, who signed the treaty with the Germans. Later on he ran into difficulties with the German colonial administration and fled to Ovamboland. A photograph of Aribib/ǂArixab (stored in the National Archives in Namibia) circulated in the 1990s among some of the Hai‖om communities, perhaps influencing their knowledge about him and his significance as well.

I came across an interesting point of view that was mentioned by an elder man, a proud Xomkhoeb (a Hai‖om from Etosha Pan[16]), concerning the Hai‖om's relationship with the Germans and the settlement of white farmers south of Etosha:

> K: [...] Some people did not have leaders. They just moved around.
>
> Q: But were there problems when they came into the area of another leader?
>
> K: Yes, there were problems. They were coming to steal also, they went away again. Not all the people were good people.
>
> Q: Did they not know the law?
>
> K: They were certainly wild people [laughing]. There were also wild bushmen [laughing]. They were wild people, it is true! Yeah. I have seen it myself. Also at the farm, when I was young ... That side ... [south of Etosha], they had those habits. [In] the German time, they made the Germans angry. My grandfather has told me that. The Germans had come with the cattle. Now, they [the 'wild' Hai‖om] did not want to struggle hunting, the cattle are tame.... So they started to slaughter the cattle. Germans became angry because of that! [...] When they started to shoot, it was not the mistake of the Germans. All the old people, they know that actually the wild bushmen, the wild Hai‖om, it was they, who made the people angry. So the Germans decided, all right, we have to fight back now.
>
> (K.K., 21.04.01, translation U.D.[17])

---

[16] Several geographic subgroups of the Hai‖om (e.g., Xomkhoen, ‖Khomakhoen, Kokarakhoen, Sêkhoen) existed, obviously with a high identificational value.

[17] I worked with a translator (Hai‖om–English) at the beginning of my field research. Later on, I conducted most of the interviews in Afrikaans and these translations are my own (the translator is indicated below each quotation).

For this man, the Germans were not guilty of taking the land south of Etosha that had already been settled by Hai‖om people. He considered the Hai‖om in that area to be the ones causing conflict with the Germans. It is important for the interpretation of this perspective to remember that this man lived in Etosha nearly all of his life and that Etosha was a kind of protected area during that time, and nobody had considered settling there to farm[18]. The Hai‖om themselves were not a united group, and relationships to the colonial administration varied significantly, certainly dependent upon which way the people were affected by the colonial state geographically (either by staying in the game reserve, by being exposed to the advancing settlement south and east of it, or to the Oshivambo-speaking people in the north) or individually.

> They [the people south of the game reserve] made problems. When they made them [the settlers] angry on that side, they ran away up to Etosha, here to Xoms [Etosha Pan]. Oh!! That time, my grandfather, he was a policeman of the Germans, they just caught them [the escaping people], they tied them/fastened them. Called the police, the police came... they did not want to have trouble here, they heard, the men had stolen, they had run away to here. So they just looked for them slowly, and they caught them and tied them. Later, somebody called the police.

(K.K. 21.04.01, translation U.D.)

Working for the police could ensure a good and secure relationship with the Germans, which they didn't want to threaten by hiding other people's offences. Is it necessary to stress that the Hai‖om who lived in the area initially settled certainly had another perspective?

Change: South African Period (1915-1940s)

During World War I, South African troops invaded the Etosha area and occupied Fort Namutoni. Prohibitions concerning the hunting of specific game were lifted for the duration of the war since the military required food and Game Reserve No. 2 offered a vast supply of fresh meat[19] (Germishuis

---

[18] Ruins from German houses can be found at some waterholes. But according to informants, the houses were abandoned after the battle between the Ovambo and Germans at Namutoni in 1904.

[19] Again, it becomes clear that nature conservation or game protection is neither a goal in itself nor a moral issue, but serves specific purposes that can change over time and depend on the various interest groups involved.

and Staal 1979:112f.). Later on, the German Proclamation was repealed by Ordinance No. 1 of 1916 and amended to suit the new situation. Among other things, the ordinance made provision for hunting licenses and introduced penalties for offences. Specific game (e.g., elephant, rhino, buffalo, giraffe, zebra) were declared 'royal' and could be hunted only for scientific reasons.

The South African Military Administration reconfirmed the borders of Game Reserve No. 2 (SWAA Nature Conservation and Tourism:iv). Permanently manned police posts were established at Namutoni and Okaukuejo. The sergeants of these stations were also responsible for tourism, which was slowly starting to develop (de la Bat 1982:12). They had to write regular reports about their areas concerning the game, stock in the game reserve, Bushmen living within their areas, native employment, visitors, etc.[20] In the beginning, Captain Nelson assumed the post of game ranger for Game Reserve No. 2. In 1928, the post was abolished and the native commissioner of Ovamboland, Major Hahn,[21] took over and acted as part-time game warden.[22] It involved a remarkable combination of duties: He was responsible for both game and 'natives.' The abolition of the post of game ranger may document the lack of significance of nature conservation (for whatever purpose) for the South West African Administration during that period.

It is impossible to find exact figures on the number of Hai‖om living in the game reserve during those days. The monthly and annual reports were written by people responsible for different areas (e.g., Namutoni or Okaukuejo), which also included land outside the game reserve. Additionally, the accounts given are based only on estimates, since the officers did not have any detailed knowledge about the Hai‖om living in their areas, a fact which they often mentioned in their reports:

> In Ovamboland proper there are few real Bushmen [...] It is impossible to give accurate figures [...] of the Bushmen inhabiting the country which falls under the control of this office – including the game reserves – [...] It must be remarked [...] that Bushmen come and go according to season. This is particularly the case with the wild Bushmen inhabiting Eastern

---

[20] E.g., NAO 33/1. These reports resulted in a huge number of archival documents that help to reconstruct the development of the park and the relationship between the Hai‖om and the representatives of the South African Administration.

[21] Up until the 1940s, Major Hahn occupied this post (Gordon 1992:248).

[22] SWAA A511/1, Administrator to the Commandant, S.W.A. Police, 24-8-28.

Ovamboland who roam from place to place in that vast area
following the water and game [...][23]

Analogous to typologies of animals, the administration distinguished
between 'wild' and 'tame' or 'domesticated' Bushmen, sometimes adding to
these the category of 'semi-wild.' Originally, this typology was meant to be
spatial and economic: the 'wild' Bushmen were those not permanently
incorporated into the administrative system, and generally living beyond the
Police Zone, while 'semi-wild' Bushmen came from beyond the Police Zone
to work temporarily on farms. Finally, the 'tame' Bushmen were those who
were permanently employed on settler farms (Gordon 1992:90). However,
the officials used this categorisation quite arbitrarily. Some officers used
'blood' as a criterion for the distinction, implying crude racial concepts.
Others were of the opinion that stock thieves were automatically 'wild,' and
sometimes the border of the Police Zone was simply used as the marker
between 'wild' and 'tame.' Thus, it is difficult to grasp whom the officials
exactly meant when talking about 'wild', 'semi-wild' or 'tame' Bushmen.

But regardless of these problems, it can be concluded that a few hundred
to one thousand Hai‖om lived in the park, mainly inhabiting the southern
part of Etosha Pan. Lebzelter (1934:83) even estimated that 1500 Hai‖om
lived around Etosha Pan in the 1920s. The number varied with economic and
environmental circumstances, such as the need for labour on surrounding
farms or the seasonal availability of wild foods, but no clear trends can be
identified, and had there been one, the officials, anxious to document
everything, would most probably have described them.

Within the reserve, the Hai‖om lived mostly off hunting and gathering. In
the 1920s,[24] the game ranger received instructions from the government
regarding various subjects, one of which fell under the heading Bushmen:

> The Ranger should take every opportunity on his patrols, of
> getting in touch with Bushmen and of endeavouring to persuade
> them either to hire themselves out to employment with farmers
> or others to take up their residence away from the vicinity of
> occupied farms, in the [Game] Reserve. It should be noted that
> wild Bushmen should not be prosecuted for offences committed
> beyond the Police Zone, except if of a most serious nature.

---

[23] NAO 11/1, Annual Report 1937.
[24] Without exact date.

> Breaches of the Game Law, for example, should pass unnoticed
> unless firearms are used.[25]

In regard to Bushmen in the area, the policy offered two possibilities: either employment on farms, which meant a direct integration into the colonial system, or living within the boundaries of the park. It was the lesser evil to have Hai‖om staying there than to have them on the farms 'roaming around' and disturbing farmers and the development of the colony. It becomes evident that the park was seen as kind of refuge for Bushmen in the colonial system.

Some Hai‖om kept dogs within the boundaries of the game reserve. Hunting with dogs was not allowed and could only be controlled by a complete ban on dogs, which was introduced in 1930[26]. But generally, hunting by the Hai‖om was not seen as a problem in the 1920s and 1930s, as the following comments indicate: "The amount of game shot by Bushmen is by no means decreasing the game" (1926)[27] or, ten years later, "The game of the pan was on the increase, even after making liberal allowance to the Bushmen there."[28] There were undoubtedly certain limitations (no firearms, no dogs, no shooting of giraffe, kudu, eland, impala and loeffelhund),[29] but even the violation of these prohibitions was not generally punished. On one hand, some officials were of the opinion that it was better to have Bushmen live within the game reserve and kill game for their own consumption than to have them move out and commit stock thefts at the occupied farms. In 1926, the game warden wrote to the native commissioner "I encourage the Bushmen to leave the vicinity of occupied farms and to reside in the Game Reserve, where their activities can be controlled to a certain extent, this does not apply to 'tame Bushmen.'"[30] On the other hand, station commanders at Namutoni or Okaukuejo were sometimes concerned about strange Bushmen moving in and killing game: "I have the honour to report that it would appear from investigations that quite a lot of Bushmen have made their appearance in the Reserve within the last two months [...] The continuance

---

[25] NAO 33/1: Instructions for the Guidance of Game Ranger. The border of the Police Zone passed through Etosha (see Hartmann et al. 1998: map viii).

[26] NAO 33/1, Secretary for S.W.A. to the N.C., Ovamboland, 24-10-1930.

[27] SWAA A50/26, Game Warden to the N.C., Ovamboland, 20-8-1926.

[28] NAO 33/1, Magistrate Grootfontein to the Secretary, 24-8-1936.

[29] NAO 33/1, Officer in Charge, N.A., Ovamboland to the Post Commander, S.W.A. Police, Namutoni 17-9-1928.

[30] E.g., SWAA A50/26, 20-8-1926.

of Game being destroyed is a daily routine [...]"[31] The Secretary for SWA pointed out in October 1930 that the Bushmen's 'privilege' of being able to shoot game for their own consumption did not extend to Bushmen not resident in the reserve "who merely come in following game [...]"[32] The possibility of using the park as a refuge for Bushmen was obviously limited. But at that time, the problem did solve itself for a while: Only one month later it was reported that Bushmen were gradually leaving for farms to the south of Etosha.[33]

In addition to hunting and gathering, a lot of families had livestock: especially goats, but also a few cattle and donkeys. In the 1920s, there was uncertainty among the officials about the number of stock that should be allowed[34]. It was decided then that the Bushmen should not keep more than ten head of large and fifty head of small stock per person within the borders of the reserve[35]. But the issue of livestock was to be raised again later. During the 1930s, there were fair numbers of livestock at some waterholes; for example, at Okevi in 1939 there were twenty-eight cattle, two donkeys and sixty-nine goats belonging to different owners[36]. The station commander at Namutoni again suggested a reduction in numbers, and the Monthly Report two months later states that all Bushmen stockowners had reduced their herds considerably[37].

Besides foraging and raising stock, there were several opportunities for seasonal or regular employment, either inside or outside the game reserve. In the 1920s, a number of Hai||om were employed in the Bobas mine near Tsumeb[38]. They could also seek work on farms around the park, a possibility that several men chose temporarily and seasonally throughout the first half

---

[31] NAO 33/1, Post Commander, Namutoni to the N.C., Ovamboland, 17-10-1930.

[32] NAO 33/1, Secretary to the N.C., Ovamboland 24-10-1930.

[33] NAO 33/1 Monthly Return, November 1930.

[34] E.g., NAO 33/1 correspondence of N.C., Ovamboland and Post Commander, S.W.A. Police, Namutoni, July-August 1929.

[35] NAO 33/1, Officer in Charge, N.A., Ovamboland to the Post Commander, Namutoni, 17-10-1929.

[36] SWAA A511/1, Station Commander, S.W.A. Police, Namutoni to the N.C., Ovamboland, 11-10-1939.

[37] SWAA A511/1, Station Commander, S.A. Police, Namutoni to the N.C. Ovamboland, 1-12-1939.

[38] ADM 5503/1, Game Warden Namutoni to the Secretary for S.W.A, 5-10-1922, 1-6-1924, SWAA A50/26, Game Warden to the N.C., Ovamboland, 20-8-1926.

of the 20th century[39]. Furthermore, there was a lot of employment available within the game reserve. Hai‖om were employed in road construction gangs, constructing and repairing roads in order to ensure more comfortable trips for administrative officers, hunters and tourists[40]. Between 1938 and 1940, for instance, approximately fifty Hai‖om were permanently engaged in repairing or constructing roads[41].

Some of the men[42] were employed to keep waterholes clean[43] or by the police at Namutoni and Okaukuejo[44]. Their names appear again and again in the Monthly or Annual Reports[45]. Payment for work varied substantially. Sometimes the only payment was the permission to stay in the park, sometimes they were given rations such as *maize meal*, sugar and tobacco, and sometimes they received additional wages. At least within the game reserve, a trend could be observed over the years ranging from simply being allowed to remain in the reserve (albeit under the threat of being expelled), to being paid with rations of *maize meal*, sugar, tobacco, to 'proper' wages and supplements of meat to the food rations, a development that certain did not pertain to the farms outside the reserve. Nevertheless, the wages earned by the Hai‖om were always considerably lower than those paid to Ovambo labourers[46].

Views from Within

The past remembered by the Hai‖om is a time when they were no longer living exclusively from hunting and gathering. There were new opportunities

---

[39] E.g., ADM 5530/1, Game Warden Namutoni to the Secretary for S.W.A, 30-1-1924.

[40] E.g., SWAA A511/1 Monthly Return April 1929, NAO 33/1, N.C., Ovamboland to the Secretary, 22-10-1932, Station Commander, S.W.A. Police Namutoni to the N.C., Ovamboland, 8-8-1938.

[41] SWAA A50/26, N.C. Ovamboland to the Chief Native Commissioner Windhoek, 5-9-1940.

[42] Hai‖om women are rarely mentioned in these reports.

[43] E.g., NAO 33/1, Note for the Post Commander, S.W.A. Police Namutoni, 25-5-1932.

[44] SWAA A511/10 Station Commander, Okaukuejo to the N.C., Ovamboland 15-7-1948.

[45] Of course their European names (e.g., Fritz, Izak, Joshua) were mostly meant, and not their Hai‖om names or surnames, which were too difficult to pronounce and nearly impossible to write.

[46] LGR 2/20/2 Annual Report Native Affairs 1937.

besides the accustomed strategies to make a living. Some men temporarily went to farms to work, and besides foraging they kept some livestock.

> D: [...] they could keep the animals at their waterholes: goats, donkeys, and dogs, which they had bought from the Oshivambo-speaking people. So if they [the Oshivambo-speaking people] had come, they bought these donkeys and everything from these people, and they had all these kinds of animals on their own.
>
> (D.K. 26.01.00, translation V.G.)

The police stations were already established, and when in need of a labour force, the police came to specific waterholes, such as Rietfontein (more or less half-way between Namutoni-Okaukuejo, see map 1) in order to find men for temporary jobs such as road construction or work at the police stations. I suppose the different sergeants knew people at the waterholes near the former road between Namutoni and Okaukuejo quite well, and they knew which men were available to work.

> K: Rietfontein [a waterhole and permanent settlement] was previously a station where the police could meet together and the Hai‖om people have signed contracts there. That was the time while they were still staying here in the Game Park that they have been free as they were moving. But they have signed contracts with the employers to work in the road construction. And then about the cattle, I heard that the Hai‖om people previously were having the cows, but after I have been born there were only goats, but [...] the families were far from each other, that is why I could maybe not see a cow of another family, but I heard about it, that the people were having the cows.
>
> Q: And did every family have goats as well?
>
> K: Each and every family had a kraal for the goats, and as a child has been born, then I have been given a small goat so as I grew up I knew this one is mine. It was happening like that when I got a gentleman, when I had my own family, I had my own goats.
>
> Q: And what did you do with the goats?
>
> K: In times that it was very hard, that they have suffered from hunger, then they were getting meat from the goats. If they have

maybe hunted and have not got something, then they have to take one of the goats. And they were also milking the goats [...] the first milk, after the goat has given birth, now, that was also milked. And when the baby is born it could also drink from the goat's milk.

(K.K. 6.03.00, translated by V.G.)

From the informant's point of view, the relationship with the police was usually good, and the work was done voluntarily.

Q: Why did they do the work?

K: They were getting this information from the Police because at Okaukuejo and Namutoni, there were already Police Stations, so it was a must.

Q: Were they been forced to work in the road construction?

K: They were not forced, but if you want then you have to work. And the lazy people, they stayed behind. But there was some remuneration to get from the employers.

Q: What do you mean with remuneration?

K: You are getting salary.

Q: What did you get?

K: They got 10 cents and 5 cents.

Q: And did they get some meat during that time?

K: The meat was shot, like zebras for them.

(K.K. 6.03.00, translation V.G.)

Life in Etosha was not isolated 'from the outside': new opportunities and limitations arose from the creation and administration of the game reserve. From the perspective of the Hai‖om, the changes were not seen as a threat to their way of life, rather, they represented the broadening of options. The (changing) way of life in the 1920s, 1930s and the beginning of 1940s was integrated in the wider sociopolitical and economical system, and involved various economic strategies that could be employed simultaneously. The money earned was used to buy blankets and other commercial goods at specific farms that kept small shops. Stock keeping was a strategy to cope with risk (besides symbolising the owner's wealth). In using these different strategies, the Hai‖om of Etosha were no different from other Hai‖om or other San groups (e.g., Guenther 1986, Suzman 2000, Widlok 1999).

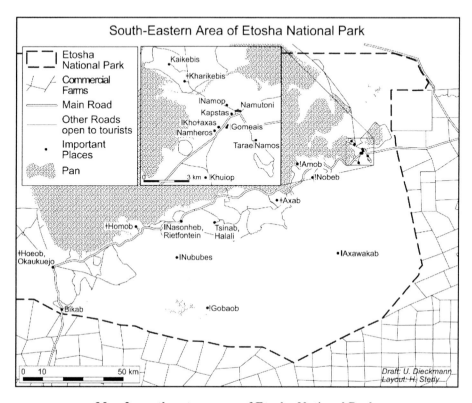

Map 2: southeastern area of Etosha National Park

The Development Leading to Eviction: 1940s – 1954

Life within the park changed over the years, new laws were made, and new opportunities arose. Legislation was tightened, particularly in the 1940s. In 1948, after a period of twenty years without amendments to the laws concerning hunting by Bushmen, a limitation was imposed regarding the species that were allowed to be killed. The Hai‖om were only allowed to hunt wildebeest and zebra, and it was specified that "[...] action, under the Game Law, will be taken against them if they continue to shoot other species of Game [...]"[47] This new limitation was probably connected to the

---

[47] SWAA A511/1, correspondence of the Secretary and the N.C., Ovamboland, 23-2-1948, 24-3-1948.

appointment of the first full-time game warden, A. A. Pienaar, in 1947[48].
The question of enforcing these laws remained, especially in remote areas
within the reserve. Additionally, instructions were issued in 1948 that
stockowners were no longer allowed to possess more than five head of large
stock and ten head of small stock each[49] in order to control foot-and-mouth
disease[50].

However, these developments cannot be attributed to a single cause;
several factors were involved. The necessity of controlling foot-and-mouth
disease was one such factor; but the increasing interest in tourism[51] – and the
potential of nature conservation in this context – was undoubtedly another
major factor that influenced, for instance, the appointment of a full-time
game warden. Kruger National Park in South Africa, established in 1926
(Carruthers 1995:64), was held out as the shining example to be followed,
and as late as 1954, Schoeman wrote: "Concerning the tourist facilities,
Etosha Game Reserve is still in its infancy compared to Kruger Game
Reserve."[52]

The people living inside the game reserve never played an important role
in the perceptions of visitors. In the earlier accounts, one rarely finds more
than stray references to the people in the park. Obviously, at that time
concepts of nature and the enthusiasm for wilderness excluded people[53].

---

[48] SWAA A511/1: Jaarsverslag 1953/54 van die Afdeling wildbewaring van SWA
van P.J. Schoemann. In the same year, the Kaokoland portion of Game Reserve
No. 2 was set aside "for the sole use and occupation by natives." During the
same year, 3406 km² were cut off from Etosha and partitioned into farms (de la
Bat 1982:14).

[49] Based on the numbers of stock reported by the Station Commanders over the
years, one cannot notice a tendency towards stock accumulation between 1929
and 1945, and even in 1947, the Station Commander of Okaukuejo reported that
there was enough grazing for game and livestock in his area (SWAA A511/1,
1947).

[50] SWAA A511/1, correspondence of the N.C., Ovamboland and the Secretary for
S.W.A., 5-2-1948, 13-4-1948.

[51] SWAA A511/10.

[52] SWAA A511/1, Jaarsverslag van die Afdeling Wildbewaring van S.W.A, April
1953-Maart 1954.

[53] "Footprints of Bushmen" (Heck 1956:85) are referred to, or a mention is made of
"another exciting experience [that] was a hunt and 'kill' by a party of Bushmen
who then had their werft at Rietfontien" (Davis 1977:142, writing about 1936).
The idea of wilderness or 'pure nature' does not inevitably exclude native
people. For the concept of wilderness including the Indians in North America in
the first half of the 19th century see Spence (1999:11ff.).

Bushmen Policy in General and the Hai‖om Discussion

To understand the developments that finally led to the expulsion of the Hai‖om from Etosha, we have to turn to the overall policy of the South African Administration of Namibia regarding Bushmen over the years. In the very beginning of the South African Mandate period, official attitudes towards Bushmen were remarkably tolerant. As Gordon notes, "Initially, the South African Occupation Forces were concerned to show the world how much better they were then their German predecessors and consequently were more tolerant toward Bushmen." But he also adds, "Below the level of magisterial rhetoric aimed at superiors, a different world existed" (Gordon 1992:89). In 1921, the Native Reserves Commission (the body responsible for the development of segregation as policy) was of the opinion "that 'the Bushmen problem [...] must be left to solve itself' (supposedly with the extinction of the group), and that 'any Bushmen found within the area occupied by Europeans should be amenable to all the laws'" (South West Africa 1922, quoted in Gordon 1992:91). But the 'problem' did not solve itself. In the early 1920s, the magistrate Van Rynefeld was murdered by Bushmen (Gordon 1992: 92f.). Ovambo labourers were occasionally attacked and robbed on their way back to Ovamboland, and this obviously endangered the system of migrant labour that was indispensable for the economy of South West Africa. In addition, farmers complained regularly about the Bushmen, whom they held responsible for stock thefts, grass fires and attacks[54]. They pressured the administration to solve the problem. For instance, E. Schwarz, a farmer, wrote to the magistrate of Grootfontein in 1926, painting the Bushmen in the darkest colours:

> [...] The above said proves that the Bushmen put themselves outside the law, they are a danger for life and property of all human beings. Therefore, the State has not only the right but the duty, in the interest of its citizens, to make very severe and drastic laws for and against the Bushmen.[55]

The administration took action, and laws were amended: the Vagrancy Proclamation was passed in 1927,[56] the Arms and Ammunition Proclamation passed in 1928, and Bushmen bows and arrows were included under the

---

[54] SWAA A50/26.

[55] SWAA A50/67, 2-7-1926.

[56] SWAA A50/27, 1927, Proclamation No. 32.

definition of 'firearms' (Gordon 1992:130). Thereafter, a slight improvement was reported in the situation[57].

Another discussion about the 'Bushmen problem' occurred simultaneously to these developments; namely, the suggestion to create a Bushmen reserve, a suggestion that had already made during the German Colonial Period (e.g., von Zastrow 1914, ZBU 1911[58]), but put aside at the time as impracticable. In 1936, the issue was raised once again, shortly after the Empire Exhibition in Johannesburg, where a number of Bushmen families were exhibited for public curiosity. The question now arose whether Bushmen, with their "fascinating" habits and customs, were not worthy "of being preserved for all time in South Africa."[59] This question was also addressed to the administration of South West Africa in regard to the Bushmen there[60]. The administration itself was sceptical about the idea of a Bushmen Reserve,[61] but demonstrating good will, it agreed to undertake an ethnological enquiry funded by the Carnegie Corporation[62]. Isaac Schapera, a social anthropologist, was entrusted with ethnological investigations. He drew up a questionnaire that the district administrative officers were supposed to complete. The officers' replies were by no means enthusiastic,

---

[57] E.g., LGR 17/15/6, Annual Report 1930.

[58] Kaiserliches Bezirksamt Outjo an das Kaiserliche Gouvernement: Betr.: Erhaltung der Buschleute: „[...] Meines Erachtens muß es das Bestreben der Verwaltung sein, aus dem vagabundierenden Buschmann einen seßhaften und nützlichen Arbeiter zu machen. Sollten diese Versuche mißlingen, so bleibt nichts übrig als den Buschleuten den Aufenthalt im besiedelten Lande derartig zu verleiden, daß sie sich in Gebiete zurückziehen, wo sie dem Weißen nicht gefährlich werden können (etwa in der Namib oder im Betschuanaland). Reservate für sie zu schaffen wäre mit der Schaffung eines Sammelplatzes für Viehdiebe und Straßenräuber gleichbedeutend. Das wissenschaftliche Interesse muß gegen das Interesse der Sicherheit der weißen Ansiedler und der farbigen Arbeiter insbesondere der arbeitsuchenden Ovambos zurücktreten." (ZBU W II O.2, Kaiserliches Bezirksamt Outjo an das Kaiserliche Gouvernement, 12-11-1911), see also Gordon 1992:60ff. for the discussions during that time.

[59] SWAA A50/67, 24-9-1936, article in The Star.

[60] The scientific community, especially anthropologists, with their own specific interests, took an active part in these discussions about Bushmen reserves (Gordon 1992:147f.).

[61] SWAA A198/26, Smit, Secretary for Native Affairs, to Courtney Clarke, Secretary for S.W.A., 26-8-1937.

[62] SWAA A198/26, Courtney Clarke to Smit, 2-9-1937.

and the information collected was not very useful[63]. With the outbreak of World War II, the matter was dropped once again[64].

The Hai‖om played only a minor part in this discussion, since their status as 'pure Bushmen' was questioned by both academics and administrative officers[65]. But the need to deal with them existed, especially with those living outside the game reserve. Opinions about how to go about this were by no means consistent. In 1921, the deputy commissioner of police in Outjo reported that the "district is infested with Bushmen who undoubtedly do a great deal of harm to the stock of farmers [...] and who are more like jackals than human beings."[66] In 1936, an inquiry was made concerning the possibility of prosecution even inside the game reserve. The police considered the game reserve as a possible haven for "Bushmen criminals" and wanted to send patrols into the reserve, but they were denied permission[67]. In 1938, there was a contradictory suggestion: Move all the Hai‖om of the region into the game reserve[68]. In 1940, the native commissioner of Ovamboland suggested that Bushmen families should either be moved inside the game reserve or to Ovamboland. In reference to a former letter to the Secretary of SWA he wrote:

> [...] I do not consider the Bushmen population of the Game Reserve excessive; in fact I thought that room could be found for more wild families and that these could be settled at places other than the main springs and game watering places, where

---

[63] SWAA A198/26, e.g., Assistant Native Commissioner Runtu, 14-8-1939.

[64] SWAA A198/26, Courtney Clarke to the Chief Native Commissioner, Windhoek, 23-5-1946.

[65] According to common typologies for which racial, geographic, as well as linguistic parameters, were used by academics, the Hai‖om could not be identified as 'prototypical Bushmen.' Their language is more closely related to Nama/Damara than to other Bushmen languages, they lived for a long time in an multi-ethnic environment, and their appearance was not really 'Bushman-like.' It was often supposed that they were a 'racial mixture' or 'hybrids' (e.g., von Zastrow 1914:2-3, Fourie 1959 [1931]:211f., Bruwer 1965:58, Gusinde 1954:56).

[66] ADM 3360, Deputy Commissioner, S.W.A. Police to the Secretary for S.W.A., 6-9-1921.

[67] SWAA A50/67, Station Commander, S.W.A. Police, Outjo to the District Commandant Omaruru 30-9-1939, Commissioner S.W.A. Police Windhoek to the Secretary for S.W.A. 14-10-1936, N.C., Ovamboland to the Secretary for S.W.A. 14-11-1936.

[68] SWAA A50/67, District Commandant, Omaruru to the Commissioner, S.W.A. Police, Windhoek 15-10-1938.

big concentrations of various species of game even proved so attractive to visitors. I pointed out too that the Bushmen in the Reserve form part and parcel of it and that they have always been a great attraction to tourists.[69]

His comments are exceptional, insofar as in the same letter he suggested involving both Hai‖om and Ovambo in the discussions.

After World War II, the issue of how to deal with the Bushmen regained prominence, partly due to a strong white farmers' lobby, which continued to approach the officers to solve the Bushmen problem. The first step taken was the formulation of a general policy in regard to the future treatment and control of "wild Bushmen": "befriend" them rather than "scare them off." This included food donation schemes, as well as a peaceful and confidence-seeking attitude by the police towards the Bushmen. The police were issued small supplies of tobacco, salt and maize meal to hand out when necessary in making contact with Bushmen. Supplies of the same items were also available for old and sick Bushmen, or in cases of severe drought. The main purpose was to prevent further stock thefts[70]. In subsequent years, the station commanders from Okaukuejo and Namutoni, amongst others, submitted regular requisitions for supplies of maize meal, salt and tobacco[71].

Under this new policy, the Commission for the Preservation of Bushmen[72] was appointed in 1949, and P.A. Schoeman and Dr. L. Fourie were among its members. Schoeman was known as a famous writer and anthropologist actively involved in developing a cohesive doctrine of Grand Apartheid. Fourie was a 'Bushmen expert' and the medical officer of the Mandate granted by the League of Nations to the Union of South Africa to administer South West Africa (Gordon 1992:144, 160f.). The commission undertook official tours to investigate the 'Bushmen question' and wrote several reports with different suggestions. Although, in its preliminary report, the commission suggested a Hai‖om reserve be created near the game reserve, this suggestion was dropped in the final report, without giving any convincing explanation for the change[73]. All Hai‖om (except twelve families

---

[69] SWAA A50/26, 5-9-1940.
[70] SWAA A50/67, Deputy Commissioner, Windhoek to the District Commandants, S.W.A. Police, 3-4-1947.
[71] SWAA A50/67.
[72] Note the terminology: 'Bushmen' should be 'preserved' as nature should, but at separate places.
[73] The explanation given was: "The Commission for the Preservation of Bushmen has found that, since presenting its preliminary report, developments have taken

still employed within the park) were to leave the game reserve and move either to Ovamboland or to farms south of Windhoek, where they were expected to look for work[74]. The reasons for the decision to expel the Hai‖om without any compensation were not clearly expressed anywhere. This harsh recommendation might seem surprising, because until then there had been no consistent complaints about game being targeted by the Hai‖om living there. Indeed, the Hai‖om in the game reserve were sometimes considered 'part and parcel' of it, or, at least, as not disturbing the game population. An article about Etosha Pan Game Reserve, prepared by an officer of the South West African Administration for a publisher in Johannesburg in 1949, stated: "Perhaps one should also mention the Bushmen, although nowadays they are no longer classed as 'game'! They certainly fit into the picture and help to give to the Etosha Pan something of the atmosphere of the old wild Africa that is fast disappearing everywhere [...]"[75]

The proposals were undoubtedly influenced by the fact that one of its members, the anthropologist P. A. Schoeman, had been responsible for Etosha as full-time game warden since 1951. He recognised Etosha's tourist potential and had already started to develop tourist infrastructure in the game reserve by constructing bungalows for tourists, improving roads, and drilling new bore-holes (de la Bat 1982:15). The general opinion that the Hai‖om were not 'real Bushmen' was certainly yet another factor, for the final report of the commission mentioned that

> Nowhere did your [the Administrator's] commissioners receive the impression that it would be worthwhile to preserve either the Heikum or the Barrakwengwe [Kxoe, another group labelled "Bushmen"] as Bushmen. In both cases the process of assimilation has proceeded too far and these Bushmen are already abandoning their nomadic habits and are settling down amongst the neighbouring tribes to agriculture and stock breeding [...][76]

---

place in the Etosha Pan Game Reserve which make its previous recommendation – that a Reserve for the Bushmen should be established along the border of the Game Reserve – impracticable [...]" (SWAA A627/11/1, n.d.).

[74] SWAA A50/67, Secretary to the Administrator-in-Executive Committee, 20-8-1953.

[75] SWAA A511/1, 9-5-1949.

[76] SWAA A627/11/1, 1956.

We are faced here with a monumental ignorance of historical facts: The necessity to integrate the Hai‖om into the economic system, which did not stop at the borders of Etosha, almost inevitably led to their assimilation. This implied, without doubt, the alienation from an exclusively foraging way of life, and this in turn finally produced the opinion that the Hai‖om were not worth 'preserving.'[77]

The attitudes of white farmers also played a role in the recommendations, even if the protection of game was the officially expressed reason for the decision. The farmers needed labour, and perhaps this explains why the Hai‖om were ultimately not forced to shift to an area south of Windhoek. Instead, it was accepted that they be moved to farms neighbouring the game reserve. The game warden Schoeman himself was afraid of informing the Hai‖om in the reserve about the government decision, and the Native Commissioner of Ovamboland was appointed for this task: "[...] because he considers that their removal from the Game Reserve is bound to [lead to] antagonism amongst these Bushmen, Dr. Schoeman feels that he should not present the matter personally as such antagonism may hamper his work in the Game Reserve. There is, therefore, no alternative but to ask [the Native Commissioner of Ovamboland] to take the necessary steps for their removal [...]"[78] And he did so; later he reported to the Chief Native Commissioner that:

> I addressed 24 men, 33 women and 35 children [...] on the 30th January 1954 at Namutoni and 14 men, 15 women and 21 children [...] on the 31st January at Okaukueyo, in the following terms:

> 'I have come here to tell you that it is the order of the Administration that you move out of Game Reserve No. 2. The reason for this order is that you are destroying the game. You may go into the Police Zone and seek work on farms South of Windhoek, or elsewhere. You must take your women and children with you, also your stock. There are many farmers who will take you into their employ and I am sure allow you to have your stock with you. Those of you who do not wish to go and work on farms must move into Ovamboland, but without your stock of any description, i.e., cattle, horses, goats, donkeys,

---

[77] Preservation of 'pure' peoples had now become desirable. The disastrous consequences of this racist ideology are well known.

[78] SWAA A50/67, Chief Native Commissioner to the N.C., Ovamboland, 28-12-1953.

fowls, dogs etc. You will have to be out of the Game Reserve the 1ˢᵗ May, 1954. If you are still in the Game Reserve on that day you will be arrested and will be put into gaol. You will be regarded as trespassers [...] None of you will be allowed to return to Game Reserve No. 2 from Ovamboland. Those of you who go to farms will not be allowed to return to the Game Reserve unless you are in possession of a permit issued by a Magistrate [...] I hope you understand this message. If you have something to say I will listen but I wish to tell you that there is no appeal against this order. The only Bushmen who will be allowed to continue to live in the Game Reserve are those in the employ of the Game Wardens. Convey what you have heard today to your absent friends and relatives.'

Replies made by some of the Bushmen at Namutoni do not deserve any comment. Those of Okaukueyo made no representations [...] I should have held these meetings with the Bushmen in November but was asked to postpone them by your telegram [...] In the meantime 80% of the Bushmen have already left the Game Reserve and have taken up employment in farms in the Outjo, Tsumeb and Grootfontein districts. Although I told those remaining at Namutoni and Okaukueyo that they should seek work on farms South of Windhoek, I added, or elsewhere, as the whole object is to get them to leave the Game Reserve. It would be impracticable and certainly undesirable to try and compel them to take up employment on farms in a particular portion of South West Africa. I understand that since November, 1953, certain farmers were given permits by Magistrates to enter the Game Reserve for the purpose of recruiting Bushmen labour. [...][79]

Through analysis of the archival documents, one comes to realise that the problem of taking control over the Bushmen, followed by the idea of creating a Bushmen reserve, existed from the beginning of the colonial period, sometimes higher on the agenda than in other years. The Hai‖om, by being Bushmen, had also to be taken into consideration in the general Bushmen discussion, but they were surely not regarded as the most difficult part of it. The game reserve had been a protected area both for animals as well as for Bushmen for more than 40 years, but things changed. With Schoeman's appointment to the Commission for the Preservation of

---

[79] SWAA A50/67b, 1-2-1954.

Bushmen as well as to full-time game warden for Etosha, ideas about nature conservation and tourism became part of the general discussion about Bushmen[80]. The preservation of nature and the 'preservation' of people now had to take place as separate issues in separate places. A solution had to be found for the Hai‖om still living in Etosha, as well as for other Bushmen groups. The criterion of 'pureness' in the discussion about Bushmen reserves led to the belief that the Hai‖om were not worth 'preservation' because they were already 'too assimilated.' Thus, they had to leave Etosha for the exclusive sake of nature conservation and were subsequently left without any land.

The search for other documents (e.g., articles, books about Etosha) that mention the eviction met no success. The former Chief Game Warden of South West Africa, Bernabé de la Bat (1982), who was appointed biologist in the park and stationed there until 1963, did not mention these events in his article about the history of Etosha. He only writes that "In 1955 the Administration decided to establish a permanent section to deal with game and game reserves [...]. Our total staff establishment in Etosha consisted of three whites, 12 Wambo and 16 Heikum Bushmen [...]" (1982:15). Reminiscing about "those days" he writes, "The small number of Heikum Bushmen still living in the park were induced by the Bantu Commissioner, Harold Eedes, to settle at the rest camps where proper housing, medical care and work opportunities were available. They became our trackers, builders, camp workers and later our road grader and bulldozer operators." (1982:16). Dieter Aschenborn, the famous Namibian painter, who was game warden in Okaukuejo between 1952 and 1954, did not mention the Hai‖om in his highly readable and amusing memoirs about those two years in Etosha (Aschenborn 1957).

Views from Within

I will summarise what I got to know in the various interviews concerning the eviction. Some events cannot be traced exactly according to chronological order.

In the beginning, there were just police stations at Namutoni and Okaukuejo. Tourists visited the park from time to time, but the park was closed for the rainy season every year. Police went out with the tourists to go

---

[80] This combination of duties reminds us of the combination of the tasks which Major Hahn (as native commissioner and part-time game warden) had to fulfil in the 1920s.

to waterholes where Hai‖om still lived. At these occasions, the people often gathered at specific places such as trees to wait for the tourists, who gave them sweets or fruits and took some pictures. The Hai‖om appreciated the remuneration they got from the tourists for being 'looked at'. No informant remembered anything annoying about the tourists.

Later on, representatives of nature conservation appeared, and they made the decision to remove the Hai‖om. The Administration started to hand out rations (meat or tobacco) to the people. This rationing is always mentioned in the context of the removal, apparently the people interpret the rations as one step in the bigger plan of expulsion.

Schoeman and de la Bat are well known by many people.

> It is a long story, but I will try it. When it was the free life, I was still young. But I was very awake, I always listened [to the words of the older people]. This place was first [...] only a police station [...] But the tourists were coming all the time [...] And later in time, slowly, the Nature Conservation came in [...] Schoeman came first, then Aschenborn, those men came. They just worked. They went out, when the tourists went out, they went with the people [...] There is now another story. Now the people got a ration, food and meat, that time [...]

(K.K. 7.11.00, translation U.D.)

Whereas the police sergeants are often described in a positive way, Schoeman in particular was obviously not very popular. He is thought to be responsible for the decision for removal. As it seems, his attempts to avoid antagonism amongst the Bushmen by not informing them of the removal himself failed.

Due to the vast area and the lack of roads to each and every settlement, people could not just be rounded up and brought out. Several informants mentioned that they were firstly 'tamed' (an obvious adoption of the colonial discourse about the Bushmen) before they could be removed. They got used to the rations, they were not allowed to hunt anymore, and they were gathered at a couple of waterholes that were easily accessible from the police stations.

> J: [...] And later, they said, nee, all the people have to move away from the waterholes to Namutoni, that you will stay there at Namutoni, the people will give you food, you will get tobacco there, so all the people moved from the waterholes to ‖Khoe ‡Axas [a waterhole near Namutoni] to stay there... so we

stayed there, we thought that we would stay, stay, stay, and then we saw that the people were moved out from there.

Q: So first the whites told you to move to ||Khoe ‡Axas...

J: Yea, to move to Namutoni, so that the people stayed near the closest water there and then perhaps meat would be shot there, and you would get some porridge, the people said so, I have just heard from the old people, the old people told me that, so the people said, ok. The people all moved away from the waterholes, there from !Gobaub [far in the south] to ||Nasoneb [Rietfontein], some people, and some people [Namutoni, ||Khoen‡Axas]. And the people from Tsinab [near Halali, which did not yet exist], they moved to ||Nasoneb. And we who have been close to here, we moved to Namutoni. From there, we just have seen the cars which have come and they took the people and they brought the people to Outjo, some went to the side of Tsumeb. I was together with grandmother, so we went to the farm Onguma where we stayed until I became big.

(J.T., 22.04.01, translation U.D.; see map 2 for the places mentioned)

Some waterholes were more than 50 kilometres away from the police stations or the main road, thus, it took a while to contact the Hai||om and convince them to move. In the Hai||om's perception today, the development leading to the eviction was a slow process, and it took some years for the representatives advocating nature conservation to perform the requirements necessary for eviction.

I cannot remember the year, when the Game Park has been taken over, but what I can remember was that when the tourists were visiting, the people, the people of the Nature Conservation said that dogs are making noise, now, they must be prohibited from being in the Game Park, and so, little, little, they decided, no, these cattle must also be out and then, this bow and arrow must also be stopped, and no one has to hunt. And people were in a big number around Rietfontein. And they decided, the Nature Conservators, that they will shoot for them every month, and then give them meat each and every time, and so, things have been stopped.

(D.K. 26.01.00, translation V.G.)

But eventually, the necessary requirements were fulfilled, and all that was needed was a meeting to inform the people about the decision. I came across one elder man who remembered the meeting at Namutoni when the people were told to move out quite well:

> H: [...] 1951, February month, they just have called all the Boers and there was one ... [?], he stayed there at Vamboland, he was an Englishman. He called them there, and they then had a meeting there, and we came also.

> Q: Where was it?

> H: It was at Namutoni.

> Q: So the Englishman of Ovamboland was also there?

> H: Yes. His name was Eedes, that was a white man. He was Englishman.

> Q: What was his name?

> H: Ietz/Eedes, but I don´t know his surname.

> Q: And it was 1951?

> H: 1951. 2nd or 5th of February. And that year, it rained, it rained a lot, the pan was full with water.

> Q: The Englishman came to Namutoni?

> H: Yes, he came.

> Q: And all the Hai‖om...

> H: ... had to come together. And they have held a meeting. So they said, ok, this is now our place. That is not your place anymore. You now have to go, there are now donkeycarts and horsescarts and motorcars, everything is there. And the Boers said, thank you, thank you, that we can get people. And they had listened [?], some people, who did not..., with the wives and the children, they were loaded [onto the transport], for the farms, to the farms. There were just a few old men, who..., Ou Isaak...

> Q: And you said, it was 1951, I thought it was 1954.

> H: Yes, no, no, 1951, I was a big man, I know very well. But now, one old man, Ou Isaak...

Q: But I thought that during that time you have been working at Vergenoeg [farm]?

H: Yes, yes. They wrote a letter, the Police brought the letter with the bicycle there, that there would be the meeting. So the wife of the Baas, she loaded some men, the Sergeant had said, bring H., because H. has a keen mind, so that H. can translate, that is why those Boers brought me there so that I could translate.

Q: Then the Boers loaded the people onto the cars...

H: Onto the cars and they brought them to the farms. And the few people who stayed behind, were Ou August and Ou Isaak, Ou Isaak had cattle, now he asked there, what shall I do with the cattle? So they said, you just have to take your cattle and go. Any Baas who will rule you, you just can stay there with your cattle. Ok, from there he also moved with his cattle to Vergenoeg.

Q: Isaak?

H: Yes.

Q: With his cattle. And August?

H: August, he did not have cattle, but he just went there. And Ou Karl. Ou Karl went to Onguma [farm].

Q: And August went to Vergenoeg?

H: Yes. Yes. August went to Vergenoeg. My Oom, the oldest brother of my mother, Ou Fritz, he stayed at Okevis [waterhole near Namutoni], he stayed there with his wife and children, he also went to Vergenoeg. So now, there are just the people who worked there who could stay there.

Q: You did go back to Vergenoeg?

H: Yes. I have just translated and I went back again. And later on, I worked for road construction...

(H.H. 27.3.01, translation U.D.)

Can we assume that this man is talking about the same meeting that the Native Commissioner of Ovamboland described in detail (see above)? On one hand, there are many facts that let us believe it is the same meeting: The name of the native commissioner of Ovamboland *was* Eedes. The meeting took place at Namutoni. The farmers' need for labourers was mentioned as well.

On the other hand, I have no explanation for the discrepancy between the dates: 1951 (his version) and 1954 (official version). The informant quoted above is one of the few people who remembers dates quite well: he knows the dates of birth of his children, he knows the years when he moved form one farm to another, etc. Both versions at least agree on the fact that it was a very rainy year (this can be read in the monthly reports of 1954). It becomes obvious how difficult, or impossible, it is sometimes to form a consistent story from different source material.

Another issue is touched on again in this man's description: The integration of the Hai‖om in the colonial system was not en-groupe. Individuals were integrated differently. This man was called a translator, others also had active roles in connection with the removal, for example, as drivers. People at waterholes close to the police stations were well known by the sergeants and were called for specific jobs. However, families who stayed at distant waterholes did not have as much contact with the police or tourists, and were not called for jobs, but moved easily to farms in the vicinity to take up employment. Thus, even the removal of the Hai‖om affected individuals quite differently.

Let us return to the quotation by the Native Commissioner of Ovamboland about the meeting and removal. He mentioned that 80% of the Hai‖om had already left the park. This is a fact that some informants mentioned as well. Most of the people went voluntarily during that period; the final consequences had not yet been anticipated (see following section).

One woman complements the official report of the speech given by Mr. Eedes' (assuming that both were describing the same event), who merely mentioned that "replies made by some of the Bushmen at Namutoni do not deserve any comment":

> Q: Can she remember the time when the whites came, this Englishman of Ovamboland who told the people that now is the time you have to move out?
>
> K/F: She is not sure about the year, but she remembers that man.
>
> Q: What does she still know, what did that man tell the people?
>
> K/F: The man has come, he said, here this land, you have to move out now. So he came and he said, the people they have to

go out.... But the old man, Isaak, he worked for the police, he talked, he said, the animals, we people, we don't kill the animals, we don't chase the animals away, but the rifle, that chases the animals away. Our bow and arrow, it cannot chase the animals away. He came out and talked like that. But when they explained, he was alone, he talked alone to the Englishman, now, he has lost. The other men did not support him, they stayed silent, he had just talked alone...

(F.A. 30.03.01, translation to Afrikaans: K.K., to English: U.D.)

Isaak's objections were not taken seriously and did not have any consequences. The people had to move. Most went by foot, and some were brought with lorries to Namutoni and Okaukuejo, where lorries were already waiting to transport people to different farms in the vicinity of the game reserve. The Hai‖om had to give up their bows and arrows to the police, and people were divided and brought to different farms. Some farmers came to the game reserve in search of suitable labourers.

[ ] Later in time, the Government decided, they said, Schoemann and Aschenborn, and the police worked also together with [...] the Nature Conservation to bring the people out, to bring them away from the waterholes. But they were not transported, they were just told, "go to Okaukuejo." Some went by foot, others were brought with the cars. So we came here, and here they divided the people. Those people who should go out to the farms and those who should stay here to work for the Government. We were also from the people who had to go out. There at Namutoni, that other area, from Halali the other side, they did the same. Those who should stay with the Government stayed behind, other people: out. The people were called, and the farm owners came and they have chosen by themselves, how many and whom they wanted to take. They asked which people are from one house, so the people from one house [family] were taken by one man, one man took those people. So we were brought out. There was no gate, there was no border, there was nothing. We went there to the farms, we stayed there [...].

(K.K., 7.11.2000, translation U.D.)

These various voices about the eviction are personal reminiscences. They have not been transformed into oral tradition about the removal in the form of a unanimous account of exodus. Instead, we are left to puzzle over the different perspectives and interpretations of the events.

And after? The South African Period (1954-1990)

Let us shift back to the official version. In the same year as the eviction meeting, 1954, the SWA Parks Board was accorded responsibility for the maintenance and expansion of game reserves (Gaerdes 1957:43). More funds were made available for the expansion of tourism, resulting in more specific planning and development. At least some Hai‖om could stay in the park, although no longer at the various waterholes, but under tight control at the rest camps at Okaukuejo and Namutoni and near the two gates, Lindequist and Ombika.[81] In the 1950s, regular patrols were undertaken to apprehend Bushmen at the different waterholes. Those who were caught were charged for being there without a pass. But, due to a lack of time, the patrols were often restricted to waterholes near the police stations and/or rest camps, or the main road between Namutoni and Okaukuejo, a fact regretted by the officers.[82]

After 1958, Game Reserve No. 2 became Etosha National Park (Berry 1980:53). Due to the shift in objective from game reserve to national park, fencing became both an important and difficult task. The first fences at Etosha were erected by European farmers on the southern boundary during the period between 1955 and 1960, but the fences were discontinuous and easily broken. In 1961, an epidemic of foot-and-mouth disease in the northern regions of Namibia resulted in the erection of a 'game-proof' fence along the eastern and southern boundaries. The complete fencing of Etosha was finished in 1973 (Berry 1980:54). Since governmental interest in tourism had increased significantly, especially in the 1960s under the Administrator of SWA Daan Viljoen (Viljoen 1961:3-9), and a greater awareness of conservation had also became evident (de la Bat 1982:20), there was no lack of labour in the following years for the few remaining Hai‖om. Tourist facilities were expanded or constructed, and a new location for 'black' employees was built.[83] Women were employed to clean rest camps, and as domestic workers for the sergeants and game wardens. Men were employed in road construction, as cleaners, mechanics, and assistants

---

[81] Since 1967, some have also stayed at Halali, an additional rest camp opened during that year (Berry et al. 1996:38).
[82] NTB N 13/3/2: Monthly Reports Namutoni, e.g., July, December 1957, May 1958.
[83] NTB N 13/3/2, 1958.

of the *veldwagters*. Until the 1960s, they were also still engaged as tourist attractions, dancing 'traditional' dances in 'traditional' clothes for visitors twice a week in the Okaukuejo rest camp[84]. No explanation could be found in the documents consulted for the abolition of this custom.

Those who were born in the park were given permission to stay there for the rest of their lives[85]. In 1984, 244 Hai‖om lived in the park at Okaukuejo, Halali, Namutoni and the two gates (Marais 1984:37f.).

Views from Within

As mentioned above, the complete consequences of the removal were not anticipated by many people. Before the 1950s, the Hai‖om lived in Etosha, but went to farms to work for a couple of months or they visited family members who were already staying and working regularly on a farm. Thus, in the beginning, it was nothing really new for them. And since there were no fences, they thought that it would be easy to return to those waterholes not under regular inspection from park officials. But after a while they realised that things had indeed changed:

> K: [...] But the old people, they said, come, we are going back [to the park]. They decided, come, we are going, back, what are we doing here [on the farms]? We cannot stay here for a long time! We want to go back home! [...] We are going back home! We are going to ‖Nasoneb [Rietfontein].

But they met the police sergeant on their way back home, and he asked them what they were doing there.

> K: We said, we are coming back! He said, where are your papers, passes, where are your passes? We said, what kind of a pass? We just come back!!! No, not again, it is finished, you won't come again! You, as you look for work, look to other places for work! Not here! You don't have to come here! We went back to Oberland.
>
> J: [...] So they thought perhaps we shall come back. They said, we are just going there to work [to the farms], we will always come. So like K. said, when you come back, you need a pass

---

[84] SWAA A511/1, n.d.

[85] I did not get the exact information about the date, but both the Chief Game Warden and Hai‖om informants assured me that they could stay there if they had been born there.

You have to come with a pass, you must not come like that. Go
back. They were hunted away and they stayed, stayed, stayed,
but you don't forget! Your place, you are coming back, this side
... [?] What is this man looking for? Tell him that he comes!
When you pass here, there were a few people ... [?], he was a
police man, at the police man. He is going there [?]. What are
you looking for? I just visit these people. No, you have to bring
your pass! Where is your pass? He [the "trespasser"] is locked
up. He is going to jail [laughing]. Until we nearly forget this
place! The old people, the old people were very afraid for the
whites that time! [...talking Hai‖om...] you will be beaten. We
are going back! We went back to the farms, we stayed, stayed,
stayed. But I never forgot this place, I came always, then I
worked here [...]

(K.K. and J.T. 22.04.01, translation U.D.)

Shortly after the expulsion, the Hai‖om encountered problems whenever
they met the police or tried entering through the gate when returning to the
park. It was not advisable to visit waterholes situated near the main road, the
stations or rest camps, but otherwise, their movements could not be
completely controlled. People remember two Hai‖om who stayed
continuously at !Gobaub near the southern boundary of Etosha until at least
the end of the 1960s. Others went back 'home' for some time (weeks or
months), but returned to the farms or the rest camps later on. What is said for
the animals applied for people as well: "Initially the definition of Etosha's
boundaries made virtually no impact on the movement of wild animals [...]
Physically the boundaries consisted of surveyed points and later firebreaks
were cleared along some of them" (Berry 1980:54).

An interview with a white woman who owns a farm along the border of
Etosha supports this assumption. The Hai‖om who worked on the farm
sometimes went back 'home' to hunt meat, which she would find later on
near the houses of the workers. Discussions about it would have meant the
discovery of an offence, thus, she kept silent and did not inquire[86].

---

[86] Q: Zurückgegangen?
T: Doch, vielleicht, um mal nen Gemsbok oder was zu holen, so n bisschen
gegangen, Fleisch war bei ihnen also das, wirklich das, was, worum ihr ganzes
Leben...Und manchmal, wenn ich dann an dem Pontoks (?) ankam, wo die
wohnten, dann siehste da Fleisch und du siehst da so'n, so'n Spieß, so, und du
siehst noch, da, das Fleisch, das hangt da in den Bäumen, und du weißt, das ist
nicht deins, [...], du hast es nicht gegeben, aber du sagst nichts, du machst, als ob

Some Hai‖om first went to farms, but legally returned to the park after a couple of years to take up employment. A labour force was needed within the park due to the development of tourism.

> The fence is now put up. The gate is there now. We came there, they said, no, you are not coming in anymore. Who is on that side, stay on that side. Who is inside, stay inside. We were lucky. We came in before the fence was put up. That time we were already here. And the people who stayed behind, they came there, the gate was there, it was said, no, you should not come, you will stay outside, you are not coming in anymore. The people they tried, no, we are coming back... but that was still a little bit better, the men they came to look for work, and they came in at the gate. Later they said, no you have to have a permit to enter. But as long as you are a Hai‖om you could come in if you are looking for work. So they got a job.

(K.K. 7.11.00, translation U.D.)

The informants emphasise that Hai‖om could always get regular employment within the park. It was accepted – even by advocates of nature conservation – that the Hai‖om had been the former residents of the area. People vividly describe their relationship to certain officers, game rangers and sergeants who were employed within the park. They obviously appreciated the dances for the tourists on Wednesday and Saturday evenings and some can exactly explain the events:

> Yes, 5 o'clock, about 5 o'clock, the *voorman* had to make the fire. A big fire. Then one Ford, a car, the car of the Administration, would load the women [at the location of Okaukuejo] and bring again and load again, and bring and load and bring, and load all around and bring. They [the women] wore skins now. And my father, those had skins as well. Then we danced there, there were busses and busses and busses, which had come. Uh! And they played!

(T.G., 13.09.01, translation U.D.)

---

du's nicht siehst. Denn se ham sich nen bischen von ihrem Zuhause was geholt. Wir warn ja ungefähr nur drei, dreitausend Meter von, von...[Unterbrechung] Dann weißt du genau, sie sind mal n bischen nach zuhause gewandert, ham sie irgendwo nen Wildebeest geholt oder was, du sagst nix, eisern, du machst, als ob du das überhaupt nicht siehst. Denn wenn du da, das nun zur Kenntnis nimmst, dann mußt du sie fragen, und das war ja strafbar. (E.T., 3.3.00)

On the same evenings at Okaukuejo, another tourist attraction was presented before the Hai‖om dances: game rangers and tourists visited a specific waterhole for so-called 'lion parties.' A zebra was slaughtered and the tourists could watch a lion devouring the meat. Another zebra would be slaughtered for the Hai‖om. Both attractions were stopped in the early 1960s. It was difficult to find an explanation for this cessation. One informant mentioned that the lion parties stopped because the old lion, Castor, who was 'tame' and lazy (he was used to the visits to that waterhole and the offered meat), was killed by another lion who moved away with the two lionesses that had been with Castor. It was not possible to lure new lions willing to regularly visit that waterhole. But he has another explanation for the cessation of the Hai‖om dances:

> The Hai‖om did change as well. They did not want to dance any more. The young people, they did not want to dance anymore. They did not want to dance. But that time, that man, de la Bat, he said: The people have to continue with their tradition! But they said: no, we are not any more wild, we won't continue! They stopped by themselves. It is true! They are talking about traditions today, but the Hai‖om did stop by themselves! De la Bat, he said, the Hai‖om, who were brought out, all have to come back. But they did not come back, those who came back, they just made trouble and were brought out again. They did stop by themselves with those traditional things. But he talked nicely [de la Bat?], he said: come back and do your traditional work/things.

(K.K. 29.10.01, translation U.D.)

This is an interesting perspective. Instead of accusing the policies of nature conservation, he places the responsibility on the younger Hai‖om, who were no longer interested in "tradition." It is noteworthy that this particular informant was employed in Etosha most of his life until his retirement and had a good relationship with his employers.

During the time of the liberation struggle in the 1970s and the 1980s, men were recruited for the South African Defence Force (SADF) as trackers. Every year, they were called upon for a couple of weeks, and the payment was good. It was impossible to refuse. Otherwise, the men would have been accused of supporting the South West African People's Organisation (SWAPO). Some were also employed as soldiers on a regular basis for some years. Etosha National Park was not protected against the influences of the war. The location at Okaukuejo was sometimes combed by security forces.

People don't talk a lot about that time, and in this they are not exceptional in Namibia.

The people who stayed in Etosha after the expulsion were better off than those who had left the park. Wages were considerably higher than those paid on farms, and the men, often working on road construction or with rangers, had the opportunity to visit their old places. Some rangers were also particularly interested in the knowledge the Hai‖om[87]. This sharing of knowledge reinforced the feeling that Etosha is actually their place.

Life on the farms was often tough. The wages and rations that were paid, as well as treatment and workload, depended entirely on the farmers' discretion. Some farmers were well known for their cruelty, others treated their employees acceptably. Only a few Hai‖om stayed at any one farm for the rest of their lives; the majority moved from one farm to another, and some of them worked on more than twenty farms in the region around Outjo and Otavi.

Independence

With Namibia's independence in 1990, the political environment changed. The following assessment of Kruger National Park is valid for Namibia, too: "In the African version of wildlife conservation history, the experience has been that game reserves are White inventions, which elevate wildlife above humanity and which have served as instruments of dispossession and subjugation" (Carruthers 1995:101). Thus, with independence, new concepts of nature conservation and tourism needed to be developed. Now, the impact on, and the eventual benefits to, the local population had to be taken into consideration. Hitherto, no general method had been found to reconcile the interests of local people with those of conservation. Several initiatives were taken, especially by the Ministry of Wildlife, Conservation and Tourism (now the Ministry of Environment and Tourism [MET]) to approach this issue. Community Based Natural Resource Management (CBNRM) is one important approach towards reconciling such apparent contradictions of interest. It aims at providing "communal area residents with appropriate incentives to use their resources sustainably and combines reform of policy and legislation with implementation at

---

[87] One ranger in Okaukeujo told me, for example, that he owed much of his knowledge about the park to one Hai‖om man, still employed at Namutoni. The Hai‖om themselves talk about specific wardens or rangers who were particularly interested in their knowledge.

community level" (Jones 1999:2). Community-based tourism is another relevant concept being developed in communal areas as well (see e.g., Research Discussion Papers of the MET 1994-1999).

Since the majority of the Hai‖om do not live in communal areas, they have not benefited from these initiatives.

Views from Within

Today, people often glorify the 'good old days' when they were still allowed to stay in Etosha, interestingly more in terms of life today, than to after the eviction.[88] There was no hunger, no diseases like today, and there was no war. Landlessness is seen as one of the most important problems by the majority of the Hai‖om (which fits very well in the actual discourse about land in Namibia; see Widlok, this volume). In the interpretations of this, some people focus on the eviction from Etosha, others focus on the withholding of a 'homeland' for the Hai‖om during the Apartheid Era.

Many Hai‖om all across the region regard Etosha as their 'homeland,' even if their direct ancestors never stayed in the area that later became Etosha National Park. This is not surprising, since Etosha was the last area where the Hai‖om could at least partly continue to lead a relatively autonomous life. Oshivambo-speaking groups had already occupied areas north of Etosha for centuries, and white farmers increasingly occupied the areas adjoining the park to the south and east, especially since the early 1900s once the railway line to Tsumeb, Otavi and Grootfontein was completed in 1908 (Gordon 1992:54). Today, most of the Hai‖om live on farms owned by others or in the towns of the Kunene and Otjozondjupa Regions.

Many elder Hai‖om claim that life worsened after independence. We can only speculate about the reasons for this. Maybe promises of the prospective government played a role, maybe living conditions became more difficult in some respects, maybe it is part of the human character to glorify the past. People who were formally employed in the game reserve and are still there today, complain that their children do not get jobs within the national park anymore. According to their perspective, the former government respected the fact that the Etosha area was formerly occupied by Hai‖om, which led to the employment of Hai‖om within the park. We could conclude that land rights as subsistence rights on this land, and not only ownership (see Widlok,

---

[88] This is true not only for the people who could stay in Etosha after 1954 due to their employment, but also for the residents of Outjo and farmworkers.

this volume, for discussion about the concept of land rights) were an acceptable form of 'land rights.' Today, young people living in Etosha are confronted with difficulties in getting employment, and the Hai‖om have no better chances than people from other language groups.

I assume that they do not feel like citizens of the new nation, especially the elder Hai‖om. They do not feel able to actively take part in shaping policy in independent Namibia. This can be partly explained through their powerlessness over the past century. The Hai‖om, like other San groups, were often treated as objects rather than subjects by most others, a fact that may have influenced their self-perception in regard to the 'outside,' or the wider political system in which they are involved. Another important aspect may be their involvement in the SADF. They did not actively fight for the liberation of the country, nor do they feel that they benefit from this liberation. This may partly explain the revitalisation of a Hai‖om identity that can be observed today.

There have been some attempts made to improve the Hai‖om's situation. They are struggling to unite their communities into a stronger political organisation. The NGO Working Group of Indigenous Minorities in Southern Africa (WIMSA), a San organisation whose activities are focused particularly on land tenure, institutional capacity building, education, training and networking of the various San communities in Southern Africa supports the Hai‖om in their aspirations (Brörmann 1999:22, 2000:3). In 1996, the Hai‖om elected a chief to represent them on the Council of Traditional Leaders,[89] but he was never recognised by the government, and over the years he lost the support of most Hai‖om[90].

In 1997, a demonstration at the gates of Etosha National Park was organised by the Hai‖om to re-claim their ancestral land. Thus, Etosha has become a reference point for identification. Seventy-three people who were

---

[89] Traditional leaders in Namibia now play vital roles at the national and local levels, as defined by the Traditional Authorities Act of 1995. At the national level, their task consists of advising the President, through the Council of Traditional Leaders, on "the control and utilisation of communal land." The council also provides a means for information to be communicated from the government to the people, and traditional leaders have to be recognised by the Ministry of Regional and Local Government and Housing (Blackie and Tarr 1999:17).

[90] Hai‖om are no exception; several San communities still struggle for political representation and recognition by traditional authorities. They are often confronted with statements like: "You people never had leaders. Why do you need leaders today?" (‖Useb 2000).

demonstrating at the gates and blocking roads were jailed, some were granted bail and later the charges were dropped[91]. It was the first time that the fate of these people achieved national and international recognition,[92] but due to internal struggles for representation within the Hai∥om community, these steps were not followed up on. The potential for a group experience from this event was lost. New elections for a traditional authority are always in discussion, but have not yet taken place. Because the establishment of a recognised Hai∥om Traditional Council has continued to fail, another strategy to unite the different Hai∥om communities under one umbrella organisation was taken. In 2001 the ∥Naisa !Nanis San Development Trust was established with the support of WIMSA and Centre of Applied Social Studies (CASS), but hitherto the initiative of the trust is still in its infancy (see Widlok 2002, also this volume).

Conclusion

Several issues must be stressed. The first needs to be mentioned, even if it is not surprising and also is part of the methodological aspect. It concerns the different source material, either archival material or oral history, and the different 'histories' we discover in these perspectives: from the local people on one hand, and on the other, from the representatives of the colonial state. To merely interprete one source independently from the other one would create quite a different picture.

Furthermore, it can be misleading to draw conclusions from the analysis of the material from one side about the other side. When reading archival material about the Bushmen and the development of Etosha National Park, one would expect a far more antagonistic attitude from side of the Hai∥om. Two points, the event and the discourse, will serve as illustration:

a) The eviction could make us think that the Hai∥om would have developed a far more critical attitude towards nature conservation or the whole colonial power than they apparently do. But by analysing their perspectives, we can

---

[91] Allgemeine Zeitung, 24. June 1997. *Buschleute frei.*
[92] The Namibian, 16. January 1997. *Copaction slammed: 21 Hai∥om remain in jail.*
The Namibian, 23. January 1997. *San vow to fight to bitter end for land.*
The Namibian, 31. January 1997. *Government giving urgent attention to Hai∥om case.*
Allgemeine Zeitung, 21. January 1997. *Premier verteidigt Polizeieinsatz.*
Allgemeine Zeitung, 21. January 1997. *DTA fordert Freilassung der Hai∥om-Demonstranten.*
Republikein, 13. January 1997. *Boesmans beleër Etosha.*

infer that the eviction is just one point in a long story of subjugation, dispossession and disempowerment that was not reversed with the independence of Namibia in 1990. Their heritage not only consists of landlessness and conflicts within the Hai‖om 'community' scattered about large areas of northern Namibia, but it also implies a critical attitude towards the new government, which has not yet managed to solve the problems and continues to create a problematic self-perception in regard to their own power or co-determination in the new nation.

b) The language often used by the officers does not pretend to imply a very human attitude. However, we have to take into consideration that theory and practice, in this case language and behaviour, are two sides of a coin. It is quite possible that the official reports we got to know are not completely consistent with the actual behaviour of those officers. They adapted to the official discourse about the Bushmen, but also got to know some of them quite well and treated them in a way that was acceptable to the people[93].

However, we must differentiate further: the material from both sides does not present a consistent perspective. Due to the individuals involved in the whole process, people developed varying viewpoints. The opinions of representatives of the colonial administration were not by no means unanimous. The same is true for Hai‖om voices. They are not uniform in their interpretations, and there is no single oral tradition about the events.

I will now leave the standpoint regarding the different perspectives and interpretations and shift back to a bird's-eye-view of the impact of nature conservation on the local people. Regardless of interpretations, we can note that some one hundred Hai‖om were evicted from Etosha National Park during the 1950s. In contrast to many other ethnic groups, the Hai‖om were not granted any 'homeland' under the South African Apartheid Regime. Today, the Hai‖om are scattered over a huge area, with the majority living in townships in commercial areas, on farms or in some areas of the four O-Regions (see Widlok, this volume). Thus, in addition to other sectors of the South African policy during their mandate period, nature conservation legislation was one important aspect that resulted in their landlessness. Along with other San groups, the Hai‖om are one of the most marginalized people in Namibia (UNDP Report 1998,1999), which is partly a result of their landlessness.

---

[93] Needless to say, this interpretation should not be understood as any kind of justification.

Since 1990, new approaches in Namibia have been taken. They aim to combine the interests of local people and protect natural resources in the planning and realisation of conserved areas. These attempts are mostly limited to communal areas and therefore do not affect the Hai‖om. Political pressure on the government from the people who have lost their land for the sake of nature conservation interests is not (yet?) strong enough to create serious official attempts of compensation. Regarding the need and struggle for a general land reform, which is actually taking place in Namibia, this is not surprising at all.

The old approaches towards resettling local people have not (yet?) been completely thrown on the scrap-heap. In 1997-1998, G|wi and G‖ana were resettled to the Central Kalahari Game Reserve in Botswana (Ikeya 2001). But today, in general, the tendency to integrate local people into the plans of conservation projects can be observed. The question about the loss of land by the people who were resettled during the colonial era remains. There are some sparks of hope. In South Africa the ǂKhomani San have managed to regain rights to parts of their ancestral land in the Kgalagadi Transfrontier Park (formerly the Kalahari Gemsbok National Park) from the South African Government (Hitchcock 2001:140), hitherto the only case in Southern Africa. Certainly, the regaining of land rights to ancestral land is not the only solution for local people who were affected by nature conservation legislation during the colonial period, but political discussion about possible ways to deal with it are still necessary.

References

Books and Articles

Anderson, Charles John
1863   *Der Okavango-Strom. Entdeckungsreisen und Jagdabenteuer in Südwest-Afrika.* Leipzig.

Aschenborn, Dieter
1957   Zwei Jahre Wildschutzwart. *S.W.A. Annual* 1957:99-105.

Barnard, Alan
1986   Rethinking Bushman Settlement Patterns and Territoriality. In: *Sprache und Geschichte in Afrika* 7.1 (1986):41-60.

Berry, Hu
1980   *Final Report: Ecology, Behaviour and Population Dynamics of Blue Wildebeest at the Etosha National Park.* Afdeling Natturbewaaring en Tourisme Suid-wes-Afrika Administrasie (Okaukuejo).

Berry, Hu et al.
1996   *Bedeutung und Ursprung der Ortsnamen im Etoscha Nationalpark, Namibia.* Windhoek.

Blackie, Rob, and Peter Tarr
1999   *Government Policies on Sustainable Development in Namibia.* Research Discussion Paper 28, January 1999. Directorate of Environmental Affairs. Ministry of Environment and Tourism: Windhoek, Namibia.

Bleek, Dorothea F.
1927   The Distribution of Bushman Languages in South Africa. In: *Festschrift Meinhof: Sprachwissenschaftliche und andere Studien.* Hamburg: Kommissionsverlag von L. Friedrichsen und Co:55-64.

Bollig, Michael
1998   The Colonial Encapsulation of the North-Western Namibian Pastoral Economy. *Africa* 68 (4) 1998:506-536.

Brechin, Steven R., Patrick C. West, David Harmon, and Kurt Kutay
1991   *Resident Peoples and Protected Areas: A Framework for Inquiry.* In: West and Brechin (eds.). Resident Peoples and National Parks: Social Dilemmas and Strategies in International Conservation. Tucson:5-28.

Brörmann, Magdalena
1999   *Working Group of Indigenous Minorities in Southern Africa: Report on Activities April 1998 to March 1999.* Windhoek: WIMSA.

2000   *Working Group of Indigenous Minorities in Southern Africa: Report on Activities April 1999 to March 2000.* Windhoek: WIMSA.

Bruwer, Johannnes P.
1965   Die Khoisan- en Bantoebevolking van Suidwes-Afrika. In: *Die ethnischen Gruppen in Südwestafrika.* Windhoek:45-73.

Carruthers, Jane
1995   *The Kruger National Park: A Social and Political History.* Pietermaritzburg: University of Natal Press.

Davis, Sey, and S. Davis
1977   Etosha Revisited. *S.W.A. Annual* 1977:142-144.

De la Bat, Bernabé .J.G.
1982   Etosha, 75 Years. *S.W.A. Annual* 1982:11-26.

Dieckmann, Ute
2001   'The Vast White Place': A History of the Etosha National Park in
        Namibia and the Hai‖om. *Nomadic Peoples* Vol. 5, Issue 2:125-153.

Dierks, Klaus
1999   *Chronology of Namibian History.* Windhoek: Namibia Scientific
        Society.

Fourie, L.
1959 [1931]   Subsistence and Society among the Heikum Bushmen. In:
        A.L. Kroeber and T.T. Waterman (eds.). *Source Book in
        Anthropology.* New York: Harcourt, Brace and World, Inc:211-221.

Gaerdes, F.
1957   Nature Preservation and the Works of the Monuments Commission
        in S.W.A.. *S.W.A. Annual* 1957:41-47.

Galton, Francis
1889   *Narrative of an Explorer in Tropical South Africa.* London, New
        York and Melbourne: Ward, Lock & Co.

Germishuys, Hugo, and Hermann Staal
1979   *The Vast White Place: An Introduction to the Etosha National Park
        of South West Africa.* Manuscript. National Archives Namibia.

Gordon, Robert
1992   *The Bushman Myth: The Making of a Namibian Underclass.*
        Boulder, etc.: Westview Press.

1997   *Picturing Bushmen: The Denver African Expedition of 1925.* Ohio:
        University Press.

Guenther, Mathias
1986   From Foragers to Miners and Bands to Bandits: On the Flexibility
        and Adaptability of Bushmen Band Societies. *Sprache und
        Geschichte in Afrika* 7.1 (1986):133-159.

Gusinde Martin
1954   Ergänzende Beobachtungen an den Buschmännern. *Journal of the
        South West African Scientific Society* 10:55-60.

Hahn, Hugo, and Rath
1859   Reisen der Herren Hahn und Rath im südwestlichen Afrika. Mai bis
        September 1857. *Petermanns Geographische Mitteilungen*
        1859:295-303.

Hahn, Hugo
1867   Hugo Hahn's Reise von Otjimbingwe zum Kunene, 1866.
        Petermanns Geographische Mitteilungen. 1867:284-297.

Heck, Lutz
1956   Etoshaland. *S.W.A. Annual*:75-85.

Heinz, Marco
1993   *Ethnizität und ethnische Identität: eine Begriffsgeschichte.* Bonn.

Hitchcock, Robert K.
2001   'Hunting is Our Heritage': The Struggle for Hunting and Gathering
        Rights among the San of Southern Africa. In: Anderson and Ikeya
        (eds.). *Parks, Property, and Power: Managing Hunting Practice and
        Identity within State Policy Regimes.* Osaka.

Hohmann, Thekla
2000   *Transformationen kommunalen Ressourcenmanagements im
        Tsumkwe Distrikt (Nordost-Namibia).* Unpublished MA Thesis.
        University of Cologne.

Ikeya, Kazunobu
2001   Some Changes among the San under the Influence of Relocation
        Plan in Botswana. In: Anderson and Ikeya (eds.). *Parks, Property,
        and Power: Managing Hunting Practice and Identity within State
        Policy Regimes.* Osaka.

Jones, Brian T.B.
1999   *Community Management of Natural Resources in Namibia.
        International Institute for Environment and Development,* Issue
        Paper no. 90. London.

Köhler, Oswin
1959   *A Study of the Grootfontein District.* Pretoria: The Government
        Printer.

Lebzelter, Viktor
1934   *Eingeborenenkulturen in Südwest- und Südafrika.* Leipzig: Verlag
        Karl W. Hiersemann.

Marais, François and Partner
1984   *Ondersoek na die Boesmanbevolkingsgroep in Suidwes-Afrika.*
        Windhoek: Direktoraat, ontwikkelingskoördinering.

Mendelsohn, J., S. el Obeid, and C. Roberts
2000   *A Profile of North-Central Namibia.* Windhoek: Gamsberg
        Macmillan Publishers.

Neumann, Roderick P.
1998   *Imposing Wilderness: Struggles over Livelihood and Nature
        Preservation in Africa.* Berkeley: University of California Press.

Taylor, Michael
2000   *Life, Land and Power. Contesting Development in Northern
        Botswana.* Unpublished PhD Thesis, University of Edinburgh.

Schapera, Isaak
1930   *The Khoisan Peoples of South Africa.* London: Routledge and Kegan
        Paul LTD.

Schinz, Hans
1891   *Deutsch-Südwest-Afrika: Forschungsreisen durch die deutschen
        Schutzgebiete Gross-Nama- und Hereroland nach dem Kunene, dem
        Ngami-See und der Kalahari 1884-1887.* Oldenburg und Leipzig:
        Schulze'sche Hofbuchhandlung und Hof-Buchdruckerei.

Spence, Mark D.
1999   *Dispossessing the Wilderness: Indian Removal and the Making of
        the National Parks.* New York/Oxford: Oxford University Press.

Suzman, James
2000   *"Things from the Bush": A Contemporary History of the Omaheke
        Bushmen.* Basel: P. Schlettwein Publishers.

United Nations Development Programme
1998   *Namibia. Human Development Report 1998.* Windhoek.

United Nations Development Programme
1999   *Namibia. Human Development Report 1999.* Windhoek.

|Useb, Joram
2000   *'One Chief is Enough?' Understanding San Traditional Authorities
        Within the Namibian Context.* Paper read at the Annual International
        Conference "Africa's Indigenous Peoples: 'First Peoples' or
        'Marginalised Minorities?'" May 24-25, 2000. Edinburgh: Centre of
        African Studies. University of Edinburgh.

West, Patrick C.
1991   Introduction. In: West and Brechin (eds.). *Resident Peoples and National Parks: Social Dilemmas and Strategies in International Conservation*. Tucson:xv-xxiv.

Widlok, Thomas
1999   *Living on Mangetti: 'Bushman' Autonomy and Namibian Independence*. Oxford: Oxford University Press.

Widlok, Thomas
2002   Hai‖om Trust in the Hai‖om Trust. *Cultural Survival Special Issue*.

Viljoen, Daan
1961   *Plans to Make S.W.A. a Tourist Paradise. S.W.A. Annual* 1961:3-9.

Von Zastrow, B.
1914   Über die Buschleute. In: *Zeitschrift für Ethnologie* 46:1-7.

Files, National Archive Namibia

German Era, ZBU
M II E.1: Wildreservate – Generalia
W II O.2: Buschleute – Spezialia, Bd. 2
W II O.4: Buschleute unter Jan Aribib
W II B.2: Berichte über Eingeborenen-Verhältnisse, 15-8-1908
F   XIII   B.4:   Geographische   und   ethnographische   Forschungen: Caprivizipfel und Okavangogebiet

ADM (Military Administration)

3360: Bushmen – General, Treatment of Vagrants: General
5503/1: Game Reserve Namutoni Reports – General

SWAA (South West African Administration)

Nature Conservation and Tourism, 1959-1981: List of Files. Introduction.
A511/1: Game Reserves General
A511/9: Game Reserves: Protection of Fauna and Flora
A511/10: Etosha Pan Game Reserve: Tourist Facilities, 1938-1951
A50/26: Bushmen Depredations Grootfontein (Part I)
A50/27: Native Affairs: Native Vagrants
A50/67: Native Affairs: Bushmen (1)
A50/67: Strandloopers and Bushmen
A198/26: Ethnological Enquiry into the Bushmen: Control of Bushmen

A627/11/1: Native Affairs: Bushmen Reserve

NAO (Native Affairs Ovamboland)

33/1: Namutoni Game Reserve
11/1: Native Affairs: Monthly and Annual Reports

LGR (Magistrate Grootfontein)

LGR 2/20/2: Annual Reports, Native Affairs
LGR 17/15/6 Annual Report 1930

NTB (Natuurbewaring)

NTB N 13/3/2: Natuurbewaring Maandverslae Namutoni 1957-1963

The Needy, the Greedy and the State:
Dividing Hai‖om Land in the Oshikoto Region

Thomas Widlok

Introduction

The point of departure for this chapter is evidence from recent political events surrounding land reform in Namibia which suggests that the land question is not only a matter of great concern to landowners and to landless people like the Hai‖om and other San[1] but also to the nation state itself. State claims to sovereignty and of being the legitimate trustee of the national territory depend critically on a successful land policy. In Namibia the land policy to date has been focused on land redistribution and this chapter investigates the background of this policy, which is based on notions and practices of land division rather than of land sharing.

The case material presented here relates to the development of state land politics with respect to San living in what used to be known as eastern Owamboland and is now become known as the eastern portion of the "4 'O' Regions", Omusati, Oshana, Ohangwena and Oshikoto (see map 1). I argue that in areas that were marginal to main centres of political power various modes of sharing the land, that is, of parallel use of land by multiple users, have gradually been replaced by attempts to divide and distribute the land. I suggest that this background sheds more light on the necessity that San people in the region experience today to form community-based organisations and trust funds in order to become negotiation partners that are accepted by state agencies in negotiations about land.

---

[1] In this chapter I use the term "San" instead of the locally more widely used "Bushman" because it has become the official term in Namibia for Khoisan-speaking people with a background in hunting and gathering and it is commonly used in matters relating to land ownership and land use, the subject matter of my contribution. For more details on the issue of ethnic labels see Widlok (1999).

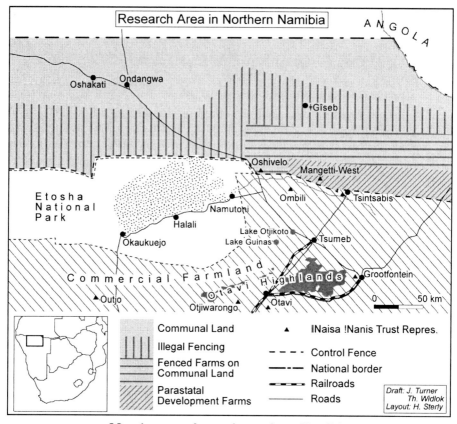

Map 1: research area in northern Namibia

The Namibian State (of) Affairs

When Zimbabwean president Robert Mugabe visited Namibia on Africa Day in May 2000, at the height of farm occupations by war veterans in his country, Namibian papers reported his speech with headlines like "Grab the land if you have to"[2] Addressing Namibian President Sam Nujoma and a large audience in Ondangwa Mugabe said that "if the other neighbouring countries have problems similar to the ones we have encountered why not apply the same solution as Zimbabwe. It is a simple solution."[3] At this point the land debate in Namibia had already been fuelled by events in Zimbabwe

---

[2]   The Namibian, 26.5.2000.
[3]   The Namibian, 26.5.2000.

which some feared to be a "dress rehearsal for Namibia"[4]. The Namibian National Farmer's Union and the Namibia Non-governmental Organisations' Forum talked of the crisis in Zimbabwe as 'a wake-up call' for commercial farmers in Namibia who "failed to seek solutions in the national interest"[5]. Subsequently, Namibian politicians including P. Ithana, Minister for Land, Resettlement and Rehabilitation, tried to diffuse fears that Namibia would take the same path as Zimbabwe[6] while at the same time promising to landless people, specifically the San, that "the government will continue to give land to landless Namibians" and "to intensify its efforts to redistribute the land"[7]. Clearly, Namibian politicians were, like Mugabe, "using land as [a] trump card"[8] in their political strategies. They announced that the government would "take land" for redistribution[9], give "land to the landless"[10] and that "the international community must not lose sight of the fact that the hunger of the Namibian people for land cannot go on unanswered indefinitely"[11], even though for the time being the Namibian government maintained its policy of "willing-seller, willing-buyer". Land redistribution in Zimbabwe, too, had operated on a willing-seller, willing buyer principle for the first ten years after its independence in 1980. The principle was later replaced by a Land Acquisition Act which empowered the government to buy land for redistribution compulsorily, at first with compensation, later without it[12]. In his speech commemorating twenty years of Zimbabwe's independence, Mugabe called the land question "the last colonial question heavily qualifying our sovereignty."[13] This is in tune with voices from the Namibian ruling party who maintain that the "central question of the war of liberation was land"[14].

The political events surrounding the violent seizure of farms in Zimbabwe show two things. First, the question of land is not simply a domestic issue for landless people like various San groups in Namibia but it

---

4   Windhoek Observer, 6.5.2000.
5   The Namibian, 29.5.2000.
6   Republikein, 29.5.2000.
7   New Era, 3.7.2000.
8   New Era, 12.5.2000.
9   The Namibian, 16.5.2000.
10 New Era, 3.7.2000.
11 The Namibian, 15.6.2000.
12 New African, June 2000.
13 New African, June 2000.
14 The Namibian, 16.5.2000.

is also driven by developments on national and international levels. Second, land is not only crucial for economically and politically marginalised people like the Hai‖om and other San people in Namibia. It is also crucial for the state, its claims to legitimacy and sovereignty. The Namibian government has always emphasised that the San communities are an integral part of the Namibian nation. However, democratic states do not own their members. Citizens have an exit option and occasionally they use it.[15] States need not be land owners themselves but their claim for legitimacy is based on their keeping a territory in trust across generations and beyond individual movements. "The land question", as it is commonly called in southern Africa, is therefore more than just one policy field among others. For the state as a landed entity, it is crucial that it can prove itself successful at looking after the territory with which it is entrusted because otherwise it would lose its legitimacy. The extent to which the state becomes a land-owning and land-distributing agent is not pre-determined by its being a territorially-based entity in principle. In practice, however, social relations are critically effected by the ways in which land as an economic good can be converted into land as a moral good (i. e. as a basic good that constitutes legitimacy, group membership and social order) and vice versa. Large privately owned farms are an issue for the Namibian state, not only because they form more than half of the agriculturally usable land but because they are sometimes seen as 'states within the state'. This challenges the claim for sovereignty maintained by the national government, which, according to its constitution, may expropriate property in the public interest (subject to just compensation). This vested interest in land held by the state, I argue, is often downplayed by state agents who present their role as one of determining "how much the land greedy are greedy and how much the land hungry are hungry, and how to reconcile the two" (H. Geingob, Namibian Prime Minister, quoted in New African, June 2000). In this chapter I approach the land question not only in terms of the needy, nor simply in terms of a conflict between the needy and the greedy, but also in terms of a crucial moral resource for the state to establish its position with regard to its citizens and for land owners to establish their position in the social system.

---

[15] The best known examples from Namibia are that of San people, some of whom chose to live at Schmidtsdrift in the Republic of South Africa (see Gordon and Sholto Douglas 2000:199), and others who fled to Botswana from the Caprivi.

Land for Share

In the heated and morally loaded debate about land reform in southern Africa the land question to many seems unresolvable because the need for land by far exceeds the land available and because the current land owners simply "won't share" the land[16]. It needs to be pointed out that, historically, both conditions are probably more recent developments than we may think. Goody argues that "traditionally", not land but manpower was the scarce resource in Africa (Goody 1973:23). Arguably the violent conflicts at the beginning of German colonisation in Namibia were the first conflicts about the control of land rather than about the control of people. However, it seems that land occupation, at least in the central north of Namibia, has, well into the colonial period been characterised by the habitus of the "internal African frontier", that is to say, by the specific developmental dynamics of the pastoral and agropastoral social systems in the area that involved the splitting-up and subsequent movement of social segments in what was conceived to be either "empty" or at least readily accessible space (see Kopytoff 1989, Widlok 2000). San people occupied the space that served Owambo from the north and Herero from the south and east (and also Nama from the deep south) as a marginal area for their transhumant migrations but also as a *hinterland* (or more precisely a *"vorderland"*) for pursuing their political strategy of reproducing social entities and maintaining their social organisation as a whole through processes of expansive segmentation. The historical record suggests that the Khoisan-speaking foragers did share their land and its resources with these neighbouring groups, not out of some superior altruism but because for a long time it was beneficial for them as well (see Widlok 1999, 2000). This is not to downplay or deny any of the violent clashes that took place in this period but simply to underline that sharing the land was a viable option for a long period, moreover, an option that did not immediately disappear with the onset of colonisation, even though it became more difficult to realise. Similarly, it should be pointed out that despite wide-spread ignorance about the political dynamics of the internal African frontier, at least some of the colonisers seem to have seriously considered the option of sharing the land, that is, of parallel use-rights of different groups with different interests who share a piece of land. H. Vedder, a German missionary who worked with Hai‖om at the beginning of the 20th century, presented the following account of settler-San relations, which he also recommended for the future:

---

[16] See New African, June 2000.

> The path taken over the last 50 years is the following: A farmer
> settles where, since time immemorial, an extended family of
> Bushmen have found their water, have hunted their game and
> collected wild fruits. The farmer positions himself as friendly to
> these people and promises them neither to chase them away nor
> to take away their water, game and wild food. He can do that
> without any disadvantage because the farmer wants pasture for
> his livestock and a piece of land for vegetable and maize
> farming. The farmer cannot do much profitably with what the
> Bushman wants [from the land]. And the Bushman does not
> know what to do with what the white man needs, namely
> pasture and grass. Both interests, excluding the hunt, are not in
> conflict with one another. (Vedder 1953:80-1, my translation).

Vedder continues to suggest that the farmer should not try to turn the old
people into farm labourers but to arrange with them that the younger
generation should stay in work. He also warns farmers to prohibit neither the
use of water nor the hunt in order to avoid violent conflict. Given the
evidence on violent settler-San relations (see Gordon 1992) we cannot take
this at face value as a reliable account of the situation. The "promise not to
chase them away" was often not kept – if it was given at all. However, it
does prove that among the settlers, too, exclusive land ownership was not
considered the only option, that access to manpower did matter to the
farmers and that some shared use of land and its resources was considered a
viable option. This raises the question as to how and why this option was not
pursued further and why it seems to have lost out to what I call the
distributive approach to land.

Nationalising the Land, Dividing the Land

Looking back in history, we see that there has been considerable sharing
of land and overlapping uses of it by different parties, not only before
colonisation but long into the colonial period. The tendency to divide the
land, rather than to share it, did not come 'naturally'. In fact, there seems to
be no compelling reason why it would have to come that way at all. A
crucial factor seems to be the state ideology of apartheid, which was always
predicated on the division of land. After independence the new government
made it quite clear that it considered the apartheid land policy to be grossly
unfair and that the new resettlement programme was also meant to address
some of the injustices created through apartheid. The new policy was clearly
one of nationalising and of redistributing the land, instead of carving it up
into semi- or pseudo-autonomous units and instead of reconstituting

ancestral rights to land. However, both processes, nationalising and redistribution, again implicate the division of land, rather than the sharing of it. In order to nationalise the land, the government had to divide what was previously (at least in theory) shared communal land into "unutilised land for resettlement" versus "land not available for resettlement" (TCCF 1992:29). The commercial farms, too, were divided into a number of categories. Farms owned by non-Namibians and farms owned by multiple farm owners were put into categories of land likely to be nationalised (NCLR 1991:32). Once the government had purchased or otherwise nationalised land for resettlement the first measure that was taken was to divide the land into small plots, which were given to landless people like the San as a long term loan. The government took a very critical stance towards the illegal fencing off of communal land into farms (see Widlok 1999). However, it seems that this was primarily a reaction not to fencing as such but to the fact that some headmen in some parts of the communal areas claimed the right to partition the land as they see fit while the state government claimed this as an exclusive national right (see below).

I therefore suggest to understand the increasing division and decreasing sharing of land not in terms of historical origins but rather in terms of state objectives that are being pursued. The objective of the apartheid policy was the protection of settler land by pre-empting indigenous claims. The strategic measure was the division of land, as well as the division of whatever else may have been subject to rivalling claims (public space, political power etc.). The objective of the independent government was the nationalisation of the people and the land. The strategic measure was the redistribution of land, as well as resources in other domains that were identified as needing "affirmative action" (the job market, public institutions etc.). Redistribution implicated prior pooling of resources, unification in a sense, but also increasing division, even though along quite different lines than before independence. The Namibian government, through its Ministry of Lands, Resettlement and Rehabilitation (MLRR) was reported in the media to be in need of 486 million hectares of land to resettle 243,000 people for agricultural purposes[17]. The estimate is based on an average need of 2,000 hectares "for each person earmarked for resettlement", including Namibians who returned from exile since independence in 1990, disabled people, the marginalised San, former farm labourers and retiring workers who want to farm[18]. The problem is that Namibia's landmass only amounts to 82.5

[17] The Namibian, 23.5.2000.
[18] The Namibian, 23.5.2000.

million hectares, which means that an area nearly six times as large as
Namibia would be needed for this kind of resettlement. The figure, as
ridiculous as it is, indicates that the logic of dividing the land – by first
pooling and then redistributing it – is so pervasive in the policy of the state
government and, it seems, of development agencies, donors and the
Namibian public that it overrides what would otherwise seem to be the
obvious alternative, namely to diversify the rights held in a particular piece
of land, i. e. to increase the number of people sharing land instead of trying
to increase the amount of land that can be redistributed. At the same time,
calculations and figures like those quoted above serve another function in
Namibia's heated land debate. While some land-owning farmers may take it
as an argument against the reasonability of any land claims made by landless
people, it also serves as an excuse for the government's inability to cater for
all land needs, and consequently not to be able to go ahead with a land
reform that goes beyond land redistribution. Furthermore, one ridiculous
figure gives rise to other ridiculous figures, or at least supports them. Instead
of trying to increase the number of people who either share land or who can
receive gain from resources without actually owning the land, the size of
individual plots has been reduced below the limit of what seems useful for
any of the traditional land use practices such as pastoralism, farming,
hunting or gathering. For instance, the state land distributed after
independence to resettle San in the Caprivi and Western Bushmanland was
given out in 5-7 ha plots, clearly insufficient for any serious farming (or
foraging) purposes (see photo 1).[19] Moreover, land is handed out for a
limited set of land-use forms, namely farming and livestock holding. Those
who have been resettled are not given freehold title over the land but they
are under constant threat of losing their land again if they fail to make
"productive use of their land" in the above sense. Those who try to lease out
the land they received from the state because they cannot work it themselves,
do this illegally and are likely to lose their land if they are found out[20].

---

[19] It seems that the Ministry has more recently moved away from its initial policy
of handing out plots of equal size all over the country despite the fact that the
quality of the land and the climatic conditions limiting its use vary greatly
(Werner pers. com.). Nevertheless, there is a tendency among state agencies to
treat land as a standardised entity and to divide it into interchangeable plots.

[20] The Namibian, 17.5.2000.

Photo 1: Three Namibian Ministers distribute the first demarcated plot of land to a San family at M'kata, Western Bushmanland, November 1990 (M. Hausiku, Minister of Land, Resettlement and Rehabilitation; P. Mueshihange, Minister of Defence; P. Ithana, Deputy Minister of Wildlife, Conservation and Tourism)

The statistics leave little doubt that demand is exceeding supply and that the pressure on the government to provide rights in land is very real. However, the only alternatives to receiving land from the government envisaged in the public debate, it seems, are either for people to buy their own land or not to have any access to land at all if they could not, or would not, do any farming. The whole land debate in Namibia is characterised by what may be called 'the pie image' of land reform, namely that there is a limited amount of land available in Namibia that is to be (re-)distributed as individual or household-owned plots for farming. There are very few, if any, suggestions for ways in which the land could be *shared*, based on the variety of land use rights, rather than *divided*. Insistance on finding the right way of dividing the land has led to an impossible situation for land distributors and land receivers alike. This development was not inevitable but could have taken a different direction at least at two transition points, first at the onset of colonialism at the end of the 19th century and again at the end of the colonial period with the arrival of Namibian independence. Things could have developed differently and given the protracted difficulties in formulating a land reform, there are strong reasons to suggest that things should develop differently. How did dividing up the land into plots with exclusive use rights became the dominant mode of land allocation?

Dividing the Colonial Land

In Namibia, as in other African countries including South Africa, Europeans began dividing the land even before the colonial state was formally in place. In Namibia the land 'purchases' by the tradesman A. Lüderitz are renowned. He gained large stretches of land by drawing up contracts with some indigenous leaders. The leaders were often left in the dark about the implications of the transaction and often did not have the legitimate right to alienate the land in the first place. The colonial administration later followed the same pattern in its dealings with Hai‖om leaders (see Gordon 1992:50, Dieckmann this volume). But even after the German state stepped in (upon Lüderitz' request), trade corporations continued to be very active in southwestern Africa. In 1892 German and English traders asked the German government to sell a concession for the exploration of central-northern Namibia (around Otavi and Tsumeb) to them (Drechsler 1996:84). For that purpose they founded the "South West African Railway and Mining Co. Ltd", abbreviated as SWAC or SWACo) as a shareholding company for landholding and mining purposes. The concession included 13 000 square kilometres of land ("Grund und Boden") which was declared to have been *terra nullius* ("Niemandsland") and it meant that the colonial government transferred exclusive rights of exploitation to the corporation (Drechsler 1996:84). The company became dominated by the interests of Cecil Rhodes, who was a major shareholder. Several exploration companies turned out to be economic failures but SWAC and other successful exploration companies produced considerable profits for their shareholders and – to a much more limited degree – for the colonial state, which had put high hopes into the companies (Drechsler 1996:328). It was part of the ideology of land holding corporations that enlarging the number of shareholders, i. e. increasing the number of people who owned land in the colonies, would strengthen colonial politics (Drechsler 1996:324). The colonial state, by contrast, was ambivalent towards the land holding companies. While it relied on them to be able to make political claims as a colonial power, it was also suspicious towards them, especially if there were large amounts of foreign capital involved, as in the SWAC case. In a sense it may therefore be said that the land corporations and the colonial state formed an alliance by dividing the land and its profits between them.

As I have shown elsewhere (Widlok 2000), it is very instructive to study the archival records that document early land disputes involving SWAC. In the so-called Leinhos case the South West Africa Company and a descendant of the game hunter and trader Frederick Green fought about a piece of land just to the northwest of Grootfontein. The proceedings of that court case, which are kept in the Namibian National Archives, include the testimonies of some well-known authorities on the early colonial period (among them C. von François, G. Hartmann, M. Rautanen, and H. Vedder) but also of local people of all ethnic groups involved (labelled as "Bastard", "Hai‖om", "Herero", "Hottentot", "Owambo"). The disputed land, called "Berg Aukas" by the Germans, "Okauua" by the Herero, and "!Uin Aokos" by the Hai‖om "Bushmen", was claimed by Ida Leinhos, Green's daughter. She argued that this land rightly belonged to her family because it was given to them by the Herero chief Maharero Tjamuaha, supported by his son Samuel Maharero, in 1884. Moreover, the plaintiff claimed that she was a descendant of Maharero on her mother's side so that the court case was also one of Herero versus colonial claims over land. Leinhos had the support of prominent Herero chiefs whose testimonies exhibit Herero practices and aspirations beyond this individual case. SWAC, undoubtedly interested in the mining potential of the area, argued that the land never belonged to the Herero in the first place, who, consequently, could not make a gift of it. The case went on for decades, probably not to the satisfaction of any party involved. The witnesses could not agree whether the land was that of the Herero or, more precisely, whether the "Bushmen" whose land it was were dependent subjects of the Herero, of the Owambo or of no-one at all. Partly because of this unclear situation, the Leinhos case provides rich insights into the interrelation between the Herero and Owambo expanding their pastoralist economies, and into the position of the Hai‖om "Bushmen" in this region.

From a present day perspective it is striking that the court could not reach a decision because all witnesses basically agreed that the land in question was in fact the land of the "Bushmen". One of the written sources of evidence, formulated in 1893, years before the case hearings began, by Major von François, certainly not a "Bushman" activist, concluded: "If we consider the question as to whose land the Grootfontein and Otavi area rightfully is, then it should be granted to the Haiumgo [sic] Bushmen, as the oldest population group in this area [...]" (I/42).[21] In his witness record von François reiterated this judgement by saying that at the time the "Bushmen" "were completely independent" and that he "never heard that they ever were in a dependency relationship to anyone" (I/180). While the latter point was

---

[21] All documents of the Leinhos vs. SWAC case are quoted according to the files found in the National Archives, Windhoek, under GWI 361 056/04 Vol. I/II.

disputed, none of the witnesses doubted that the "Bushmen" occupied the land in question – and none of them seriously considered the possibility that this should result in the land being given to the "Bushmen". Today the Leinhos judgement ought to be considered a miscarriage of justice because the land was distributed without any benefit to those who were the legitimate owners, the "Bushmen". However, even in the current situation in Namibia, hunting and gathering are usually not considered sufficiently "productive" forms of land use that would result in rights to land (see Widlok 1994).

But the indecisiveness of the witnesses and of the court are also noteworthy in and of themselves. It shows that the social institutions of hunter-gatherers, their engagement with the environment, was not deemed sufficient to grant land rights. Furthermore, not only the status of the farm itself was uncertain but also the institutionalising processes that would make it an integral part of Herero or Owambo society. It was only for the purposes of clarifying the institutional rights of Owambo and Herero that the question of "Bushman" involvement in these polities was seriously considered at all. The revised judgement in the Leinhos case, reached in 1914 was to *divide* the farm in question into two equal halves, one for the Leinhos family and one for SWAC. It is probably fair to say that this judgement did not influence the overall course of Namibian history. In fact, the court case continued even further and dragged on into the period of the South African administration. However, the case illustrates that in the transition period at the beginning of colonisation, the state decided to ignore evidence of shared land use. The court, the conflicting parties and most of the expert witnesses not only worked with the expectation that land would need to be divided in portions of exclusive use-rights but that dividing the land was also considered to be the most appropriate strategy of dealing with conflicting claims to land.

The problem remains that in historical sources like the Leinhos case files, the statements on record are coloured by the largely unknown motivations of the witnesses who in this particular case may have wanted to either support Leinhos or SWAC or who followed their own agenda. While all parties and witnesses involved recognised the occupation of the land by the Hai‖om, all of them, except for the Hai‖om themselves, conclude that it was "free" land nevertheless. They considered it to be land which was up for grabs for either Owambo nor Herero or any other recognised authority who claimed it. By contrast, the acknowledgement of "Bushman" land rights would have gone against the vested interests of both parties involved in the case, against that of most witnesses who, after all, benefited from colonial rule, and, ultimately, against the legitimation of the court itself as a supreme colonial office with its claim of a sovereign right to distribute land. Given the limitations of the evidence, we can only reconstruct that there seem to have been two distinct but related strategies for defending the legitimacy of the rights of agropastoralists vis à vis the "Bushmen". The Europeans were seeking to establish whether the recognised institutional foundations for "tribal" land ownership were applicable for the area in question – with the important qualification that only certain institutions, namely tribute collection, establishment of cattle-posts, treaties and chiefly authority were considered legitimate institutions at all. The Herero, by contrast, were seeking to show that the area was indeed an institutional vacuum which would justify their appropriation (and subsequent alienation) of it. The Europeans largely thought of the situation in terms of the colonial frontier while the Herero interpreted it on the basis of their experiences on the internal African frontier (see Widlok 2000). The San witnesses protested that "the place [of the farm in question] is situated in the land of the Hai‖om Bushmen. The Herero chief had no right to give away a place in our area [...]" (II/92-3). Their account makes clear that although the Hai‖om shared the land and its resources (not only pasture for cattle but also copper) with their neighbours, this did not in and of itself compromise their own view that the right to decide as to who would have access to the land was vested locally, in the hands of families and communities: "Bushmen do not have private ownership in places but each larger family or sib has its own place where it lives and where the members of other sibs are not allowed to hunt or to gather *veld* fruits" (II/95). San voices were heard and put on the record by the colonial court, but this did not help their cause. As I will show in the remainder of this paper many San voices have been heard and documented since Namibian independence but the question remains as to whether it has helped to improve their situation with respect to their neighbours and with respect to the state.

Contemporary History

For the remainder of this paper I will focus on the contemporary history, that is to say, events that I have witnessed over the last 12 years of my work in Namibia. With independence in 1990 came the formal end of colonisation, a period of transformation comparable to the point when SWAC and other colonial agencies were appropriating land a hundred years earlier. This is not to say that there were no relevant changes between the two points in time. Dieckmann (2001 and this volume) has documented considerable changes in the policy concerning Hai‖om residency in the Etosha National Park during the South African administration of Namibia. The change from initial co-existence of nature conservation, tourism and Hai‖om occupancy towards greater segregation and finally expulsion seems to have primarily followed the opportunism of native commissioners and nature conservationists like P. Schoeman (see Widlok 1999:25, Gall 2001:137). It followed the same logic of dividing the land that already emerged from the Leinhos case. Somewhat surprisingly, suggestions for a Hai‖om reserve never materialised (see Widlok 1999:23). In hindsight former government ethnologists and German-speaking farmers in the area consider this to be one of the greatest mistakes of the pre-independence government. The administration did not object to the plan on principle grounds but simply followed more influential interest groups, namely the nature conservation lobby and the representatives of ethnic groups in the country that were (and still are) more powerful than the Hai‖om.

Independence, by contrast, had the potential to bring about a veritable transformation of conditions, at least this was a wide-spread expectation. But the expectations of the Hai‖om community were not met; they were not compensated for the loss of land that they had suffered. In 1997, as a reaction to "empty promises", about a hundred Hai‖om decided to block the gates to the Etosha Park (see WIMSA 1997:29), which led to the first post-independence court case dealing – indirectly – with Hai‖om land claims. In contrast to the Leinhos case, the Etosha case received considerable media attention. Not only is Etosha one of the main tourist attractions in Namibia (see Dieckmann 2001) but the harsh treatment that protesters received from the Namibian police seemed rather reminiscent of police actions before independence and consequently caught the attention not only of the press but also of human rights NGOs in the country. 73 men and women were arrested, later bailed out with money collected by the community, with the help of money provided by the Working Group of Indigenous Minorities in Southern Africa (WIMSA). The case was eventually dropped (see Dieckmann this volume). As a consequence of these events, the Ministry of Lands, Resettlement and Rehabilitation later offered the group under the leadership of Willem |Aib to receive resettlement plots on farms south of Etosha that the government had taken over from a rich farmer. However, |Aib underlined that they wanted a share in the profits accrued in the Etosha Park and that they were not prepared to settle for a portion of a farm administered by the government (|Aib interview 2000). The Ministry in turn emphasised that it would not give exclusive land rights on ethnic grounds, since this would be segregation. At the same time it continued a policy of maintaining the strict division between established nature reserves, freehold commercial farms and government-owned resettlement farms, which excluded the possibility of regaining access to Etosha or of gaining communal land for the Hai‖om. Since it had offered the protesters some land, the ministry felt that it had responded adequately to Hai‖om demands. Again the strategy had been one of dividing land rather than sharing it, even though a division along ethnic lines was explicitly rejected.[22] Since the charges against the protesters were dropped, the Hai‖om land issue was not elaborated on in court but only – to some extent – in the press. I will now report on other land cases involving Hai‖om which made it neither to the courts nor to the press but which provide insights into the relations between the San and the state during the transition period in which colonial rule in Namibia came to an end.

The Offence

Fencing-off is an offence. President Nujoma, in his address to the national land conference in 1991, declared the fencing-off of communal areas by rich Namibians to be "illegal, inhuman and unpatriotic behaviour towards fellow Namibians [which] must come to an end forthwith" (NCLR 1991:6). In fact, substantial parts of the communal land area in Owambo and Kavango had already been fenced with the permission of the traditional authorities and the South African administration (and therefore arguably legal) before independence. There seems to have been no objection at the time against this de-facto privatisation of communal land, most probably because the land concerned was then permanently occupied 'only' by Bushmen. Also there were no attempts after independence to undo this privatisation. But when the vested interests of other livestock owners began to be infringed, fencing came to be considered a problem.[23] During the first years of independence there were more and more reports of fencing going on

---

[22] There is another spin-off of the events of this case: it provided Willem |Aib and his followers in Outjo with considerable publicity, which in turn later provided a problem for large sections of the Hai‖om community who became dissatisfied with |Aib and who have struggled to have other representatives recognised by the government. |Aib himself has fallen out with WIMSA, the largest San NGO in Namibia following disagreements about the bail money.

[23] This is also true for the pre-independence era. In 1987 I witnessed a major conflict in "Hereroland" about fences, which had been bought from German development funds to introduce rotational grazing patterns. The fences had been left unused because of disagreement within the community of herders. There was resistance against fencing amongst some and attempts to appropriate the fences by others.

in large parts of "Hereroland" and "Owamboland", accelerating considerably the enclosure of communal rangelands that had started before independence (Tapscott and Hangula 1994). The Ministry of Lands, Resettlement and Rehabilitation had no control over the situation and moreover, felt powerless, since many of the 'illegal' fences were erected with the knowledge and permission – but without the full control – of traditional authorities in the communal areas. Above all, fencing was carried out by influential businessmen or retired public servants and politicians. Tapscott and Hangula conclude:

> Those enclosing land comprise a powerful alliance of senior traditional leaders, the local business elite and senior political figures, including some members of the Cabinet. Without the support of this group, calls for land reform from the north are largely muted. (1994:14)

In 1991 there were four large farms being fenced off in my research area. Since the places were not easily reached by car, these fencing operations were costly enterprises. It usually involved bringing in a drilling machine (see photo 2) to open a borehole. The drilling crew I met in the field said that the cost for a borehole at the time would amount to at least 28 000 Namibian Dollars (and this was the third drill they had done for the same individual). Once the borehole was there, a team of workers with equipment needed to be paid and provisioned for weeks as they were putting up the fence. All four fences were financed by absentee cattle owners, one of whom turned out to be a police commissioner and one was said to be the brother of a government minister. Arguably, therefore, the offence committed was not only one of illegal fencing but also of abusing a position of power (not unlike the situation that gave rise to the Leinhos conflict). Given that this was a shady field, it was not possible to establish to what extent the headmen knew and approved of what happened. The assumption was that the cattle owners had paid the headmen considerable sums of money.

Collecting the Evidence

When visiting the area around Botos, Sanab and ǂGiseb on the district boundary between Oshikoto and Ohangwena in March 1991, the local San reported that an Owambo man with a police escort had visited the place, claiming that he was in charge of all water pumps in Namibia. He had told the locals that the pump at Sanab, which had been blocked by the army during the war to prevent SWAPO insurgents using the water, would be repaired. He demanded that they had to clear the road from encroaching bushes so that a truck would be able to get through. When I asked what kind of truck he was talking about, one of the local San replied that it would not only be a truck with machinery to repair the pump but also a truck filled with food. I pointed out that this was most likely to be food for his workers. But the rumour stuck that food would be given to the locals as well. Other rumours flourished as various people reported bits and pieces of what the Owambo said and what he was going to do. Some insisted that the policemen said that not only the San but also local Owambo should help cut the bushes that had started to grow all over the place due to overgrazing. The local San welcomed the idea of a good source of water and they certainly welcomed the prospect of a truck of food to which they might get access if they were wanted as workers. But there were also critical comments on the things to come. Some feared that the whole thing would be a trick. Shortib, a local San who had worked on commercial farms and as a kitchen boy with the army, said: "We are not paid for clearing the road. When the pump is being repaired Owambo will sit on top of it. Many Owambo will come with their cattle and we will be chased away, as it has happened before." ‖Ubcb, another local, feared that the Owambo would not repair their pump at Sanab at all but that they would drill their own borehole, fence it in, lock the gates and sit there to control who was using the water. Since the policeman had announced his return to Sanab a few days later, I decided to wait and speak with the man himself. However, a few days passed and nothing happened. Two Hai‖om men decided to cut a few bushes. When I asked why they did it, since it seemed that the man was not to return after all, they replied: "What shall we do? After all they are the one's with the red shoulder flaps [i. e. policemen]."

photo 2: A borehole drilling team (hired by a wealthy Owambo businessman) at work in the northern part of the Oshikoto region

The policemen did not return for many weeks but eventually a few contract labourers appeared with wire and tools to start fencing the area. As the workers were supposed to cut their own '*droppers*' (fence poles) from local wood, work proceeded rather slowly and was repeatedly interrupted. Dagmar Widlok and I took photos of the work camp (see photo 3), which was deserted at the time, and of the existing fences, which indicated that the owner of the fence was planning to fence in a large piece of land on both sides of the road and with the old pump of Sanab in the middle of it. The San would soon find themselves fenced in.[24] We sent a note of urgency to the Lutheran World Federation Office (LWF, a development NGO for whom D. Widlok worked as a consultant) and to the Bishop of the Evangelical Lutheran Church in Namibia since the two organisations were planning a project in the area that was supposed to assist local San.[25]

photo 3: Illegal fencing in the Northern Oshikoto region
        (locality: Oshanashatemba)

---

[24] Other cases from the "4 O" regions have been reported where whole villages had been fenced in (Namibian, 23.5.00).

[25] The project in the end never got off the ground, as the Lutheran World Federation closed its office in Namibia after a quarrel between the two largest protestant churches (ELCIN, the former Finnish mission in the north, and ELCRN, the former Rhenish mission in the south). ELCIN then decided to focus on missionary work and no longer engage itself as a development NGO. Local staff changed either to the Ministry of Land, Resettlement and Rehabilitation or worked for projects funded by organisations from abroad.

LWF sent one of its staff members, J. Nujoma, to investigate. We took him to Sanab where the worker's camp was once again deserted. More work had been carried out on the fence. We went to Botos and ǂGiseb, the neighbouring sites where Owambo herders were living. They too were concerned about the fencing as it would inhibit the movement of their herds, and possibly their own movements too. Some were clearly not keen to see any townspeople interfering in their local affairs and they appeared to include myself and Nujoma in this group. When Nujoma approached some Owambo men at ǂGiseb, he was told by a spokesmen that he had dreamt of a hyena that would come to eat all their cattle. The situation was tense and Nujoma left without any results but with the promise to get in touch with the headmen responsible for this area who were staying at considerable distance from Sanab. In April 1991 M. Hausiku, then Minister for Land, Resettlement and Rehabilitation, came to visit the area and to meet with Haiǁom whom I had assisted in sending letters to the Ministry in which they expressed their concern about losing access to land and in which they made specific land claims. The Minister expressed his sympathy with the needs of the San in the area and promised that his Ministry would pursue the matter further.

The Bush Meeting

Months passed without any official visiting Sanab and the remote area around it. Instead, members of all groups with an interest in land were asked to come to Windhoek in June to air their views at the National Land Conference (see NCLR 1991, Widlok 2001). At the conference illegal fencing was once again condemned and the San were identified as receiving priority in the distribution of land. A technical committee was set up to deal with the issues that emerged from the conference (see Widlok and Widlok [1992a, 1992b] for submissions dealing with illegal fencing and the situation of Haiǁom). Finally, at the end of November 1991 ELCIN and LWF staff brought together the relevant headmen, the Ndonga tribal secretary, the owners of fences that had been put up, and – once again – the Minister of Lands, Resettlement and Rehabilitation and some of his staff. We were told to ask San from various places to come along to Sanab, where they were supposed to meet with the convoy of the minister, the headmen and others who started their journey in Ondangwa. With considerable delay, due to a number of car breakdowns, the meeting took place at Sanab. It turned out that none of the headmen who had some authority over distributing this land had been in this area before. Staff of the MLRR had also not seen the area. Only one of the government drivers recalled having been here not long ago with a government minister who was soon retiring and who had been looking for a suitable place to establish a farm!

photo 4: Bush meeting at Sanab between Hai‖om, local headmen, owners of fences in the area, representatives of the Ministry of Land, Resettlement and Rehabilitation, of ELCIN (the local church) and of the Lutheran World Federation (a development NGO) held in November 1991.

Since all office holders involved were Owambo, except for the Minister himself who was originally from the Kavango, discussions took place in Oshiwambo. The Hai‖om men present were bilingual and therefore theoretically able to participate in the discussion but for most of the time they were not really included in the debate. They were sitting separately while the Owambo men were discussing the fate of Sanab (see photo 4). Initially, however, the headman addressed the San men, confirming that the land around Sanab was that of the San, and he asked one of them to specifically name the places that they had always stayed at. Abakub, a local Hai‖om man, then listed a whole number of places but this remained the only active participation of the San. The headmen then continued and argued that there are Ndonga, Kwanyama and San all "mixed" (he used the English word) living in this area and that the San should select someone who would allocate land (to other San) around Sanab. The church representatives said that Sanab would become a place with a school and clinic for the settlements nearby. There seemed to be agreement among headmen, Minister and church representatives that this was an area of open access. People may be prohibited from putting up fences but not to moving into the area from other parts of Owamboland, nor to using their own money to drill boreholes, to install pumps and to move their cattle here. When I was asked to comment I brought up issues that concerned the San in the debates that I had witnessed earlier. I pointed out that problems may arise when San are chased away from water sources, that there is overgrazing, that to say that this is their land would have to include that they have a say in the decision as to who is settling at a specific place and who has use-rights to water and land. J. Nujoma, who had translated parts of what I had said, commented that to prohibit people from moving in with their cattle and from settling here would be segregation and therefore not acceptable. He later told us that the headmen and business men were already complaining that too much provisions were made for the San. It is quite clear that those debating agreed that the communal land distribution system of the Owambo was able to cope with any San needs so that no special requirements would have to be made. Only when the discussion turned to the specific fences that had already been put up, some disagreements surfaced and the debate got more heated. Finally, the headmen, the minister, and church representatives concluded that the fence as it stood was extending too far south and that it should stop north of the Omboto-Sanab road which extends east to west. It was agreed with the businessmen that no more fences should be erected between Sanab and Onashie in the south and Botos in the east. Beyond these points no commitment was made. When being asked whether any signs or boundary markers would be put up to the effect, J. Nujoma responded that there is no need for signs since land allocation would continue to go through the headmen and if any problems and disagreements would arise people should contact the headman at Ohumbula (not far from Ondangwa).

The Result

It is striking that the Bush meeting in a sense came to the same decision based on land distribution as the colonial courts dealing with the Leinhos case. The farm Berg Aukas was divided into two equal parts, similarly the proposed fenced farm around Sanab was also divided into two roughly equal parts. Fencing was allowed north of the road from Sanab to Botos but prohibited south of it. This result is the more suprising since the overall ideology and rhetoric was one of "shared land", namely that no "segregated" land was to be permitted. De facto, a segregation did of course take place, not along ethnic lines but along lines of wealth and political influence. Those who had capital and would invest in paying the headmen, in putting up fences and drilling waterholes could reserve a piece of land for their exclusive use. The others, San and Owambo herders who were not well-to-do, were relegated to a shrinking communal land that would be overgrazed even more and effectively be treated as an open access resource since the headmen who could control access or mediate in conflicting demands were located so far away that complaints by San and sanctions against misuse were practically impossible.

It is probably fair to say that the solution did not satisfy either the Owambo business man in question, nor the San. The Owambo had already invested time and money into fencing an area that was now declared off limits. Moreover, he felt that he was "developing" the area and therefore should be welcomed for this effort and not be bothered with "interference" from the San, the church or the state. The San men remained sceptical as to what would happen in the future. Over the following two years Sanab was developed for cattle but not for the people living there. Fencing was stopped and the pump was repaired, which, not unexpectedly, led to a dramatic influx of livestock and accelerated land degradation. No facilities like a school or a clinic were established in Sanab; in fact, with the church's withdrawal from development work no such services reached Sanab at all. Moreover, the pump, operating with a diesel engine, failed as a reliable source of water for the people living in the area. Whenever it broke down, it took a long time for it to be repaired. Occasionally, it also ran out of diesel, which was bought by Owambo cattle-owners since the San were not able to afford it. To save money, the cattle-owners at times used their control over the pump to shut it down, for instance when the cattle would find water in open pools. Several years later very few San were still resident near Sanab. A group that had split from the Ombili Foundation, which is "re-educating" San on a farm south of the "red line" (the veterinary control fence separating the "communal" north from the commercial south [see map 1]), to return to what they considered their land. They found no supporting services whatsoever, a rather harsh treatment by local Owambo and a *veld* that had less wild fruit than it used to have. After several members of the group had died the others returned grudgingly to Ombili, where some were re-admitted after working several weeks without pay – according to the farm management "to even out the work input that the others had provided in the meantime" (B. Mais-Rische pers. com.). Five individuals from that group did not return to Ombili and went to a newly established resettlement farm near Tsintsabis.

None of the San men who were present at the bush meeting were able to keep Sanab as a main residence. They all visited Sanab regularly over the next few years but saw no prospect in living there and returned to Mangetti-West or other farms where most of them still live on a mixed economy based on gathered food, shared labour income/pensions and government or church handouts. Also, none of the men present, nor any other San person who planned to live at Sanab and who tried living in the area since independence, has acquired any legal ownership rights for any piece of land. It seems that those who had the most demonstrable and vivid links to land that at the time of independence was not yet appropriated by herders, had lost out most. They not only lost their land but they are now even further away from any prospect of regaining control over land and resources than former farm workers among the Hai‖om who have settled at places like Tsintsabis. This is largely due to the fact that Hai‖om at Tsintsabis and other places that were thoroughly under colonial control and more clearly dependent on state support are also the ones who find it easier to organise themselves as the kind of corporate entity that states (but also non-governmental organisations) require before they extend their services and before they are ready to negotiate about rights in land and other crucial matters (see Widlok 2001). None of the board members at the recently established ‖Naisa !Nanis San Development Trust (see below) has ties to Sanab and the other places in the area. The extension services of NGOs like WIMSA do not include Hai‖om living north of the red line. They are not excluded categorically but simply pragmatically since the area is too remote and the negotiations with Owambo farm owners and headmen would introduce more problems than a dispersed and fragile network such as the ‖Naisa !Nanis Trust could handle.

The Trust

In October 2000, nine years after the "bush meeting" at Sanab and the Land conference in Windhoek, and three years after blocking the gates of the Etosha Park, Hai‖om people established the ‖Naisa !Nanis San Development Trust. The name ‖Naisa !Nanis refers to particular topographical feature of the Etosha pan, namely a belt of vegetation on the open plain which was selected to represent "the fact that the trust is open to all people" and that "it holds and embraces everybody" like a belt (Gebhardt 2000:1, see Hohmann, this volume, for a parallel case). The name therefore is an expression of the fact that at the beginning of colonisation Hai‖om people were occupying a large area in northern central Namibia, covering Etosha pan and its surrounding areas, where they now live as dispersed communities. It is probably this central position more than any other "cultural feature" that may distinguish the people concerned from any other group of San that had, and still has, important implications for the relations between local Hai‖om on the one hand and their neighbours and the state on the other (see Widlok 1995, 2002). Initially Hai‖om benefited from this position.[26]

However, under the firm establishment of colonial structures, the Hai‖om began to suffer greatly from being in such a central position. Their land was divided up among mining corporations, settler farmers and the Owambo groups. While they were initially allowed to continue living in the Etosha reserve, they were expelled from there in the 1950s on the grounds that due to their extensive contact with other groups they could not be considered "real Bushmen" anymore (see Widlok 1999, Dieckmann 2001). Given their contacts as well as some intermarriage with neighbouring groups, Gusinde and others who had a racial definition of ethnic identity denied that the Hai‖om could claim a San identity at all. The newly established trust is a "San" Trust rather than only a "Hai‖om" trust because there are also !Xun-speaking people participating. This illustrates that the Hai‖om today have no doubt about their San identity nor about their "ethnic allegiance" with neighbouring !Xun. After the loss of all land, of political power and the continuing denial of self-determination in matters of identity, being Hai‖om became very difficult. At the 1991 national census only 7,506 people claimed to speak Hai‖om at home, much less than previous estimates had suggested. However, with the emergence of Hai‖om community organisations as San organisations, it is likely that this number will increase in the future and that Hai‖om will become more visible in the regions as well as nation-wide. This, at least, is one of the hopes of those supporting the new trust. ‖Naisa !Nanis is explicitly labelled a "development trust" because its main purpose is "to act as a conduit in supporting the developmental projects of the community" (Kamanja 2000:1).

Since Namibia's independence, a number of funding bodies, government and non-government agencies have shown an interest in supporting Hai‖om, who had previously been in the shadow of the better known Jul'hoansi of the Nyae Nyae area or the ex-servicemen in the Caprivi and elsewhere. A major problem with incoming money is that it has to be held and managed by somebody. Development agencies and private donors require that a group constitutes itself as a fiscally responsible corporate community and that it

---

[26] Hai‖om in this area had access to copper that was valued by the Owambo, they had access to rich hunting grounds and later on they had some control over movements between the densely populated north and the labour-demanding settlers in the south. Owambo kings were keen to incorporate Hai‖om into their society, German colonial officers signed treaties with them, and the first ethnographers wrote extensively about them.

fulfills other formal requirements before it can hold funds and receive support more generally.

In Tsintsabis a community trust fund was initially established in the form of a bank account into which a private donor has contributed money for the people of Tsintsabis. However, that fund remains unused to date, given that four signatories have to be consulted and that it is contested as to who should be a signatory representing the 'community'. After the first trustees were named, other residents of Tsintsabis came forward asking that these representatives be replaced because they were not trustworthy. In a situation of rapid change and of unequal access to the institutions of the new state and the new non-governmental sector, Hai‖om find it difficult to know whom they can trust sufficiently for running a trust fund. But there is an institutional problem to it too, in that there are genuine logistical difficulties in establishing and running a trust fund which caters for a fairly large, fairly diverse and fairly dispersed group of people who value neither hierarchy nor internal differentiation.

These difficulties became apparent to representatives of WIMSA (the Working Group of Indigenous Minorities in Namibia) and of CASS (the Centre for Applied Social Sciences) who carried out meetings in various Hai‖om settlements between Outjo and Tsintsabis in May 2000 (in which I participated as an observer). The goal set by WIMSA and CASS was to have two representatives elected in each of these 'communities' who would travel to further meetings in which the idea of a Hai‖om Development Trust (later called the ‖Naisa !Nanis San Development Trust) would be discussed and established. Establishing such an organisation seemed the prerequisite for channelling development funds to the Hai‖om settlements that, so far, had been much more politically marginalised than the spatially more remote 'communities' in the Nyae Nyae area or in the Caprivi. Hai‖om all over northern Namibia hope that with the help of a development trust fund they could facilitate communication and transportation between Hai‖om settlements, increase their political presence on regional and national levels and create a network of mutual assistance for a variety of needs that are currently not sufficiently met. But paradoxically, it is precisely this lack of communication and transportation facilities and the costs involved in forming an effective network, which are major obstacles in founding and maintaining an organisation such as a Hai‖om Trust Fund.

The dilemma is further aggravated by the fact that not all organisational forms that have been developed by (or for) other "San" groups in the region can serve as a model for the Hai‖om. Given the spatial dispersion and the diversity of backgrounds, Hai‖om at various settlements made it clear that they would want a Hai‖om-owned organisation which would have a strong 'federal' structure, that is, it should provide the local trust funds with a maximum of autonomy. The situation is further complicated by the fact that in many places between Oshivelo in the northwest, Tsintsabis in the northeast and Outjo in the south Hai‖om live in close neighbourhood with !Xun (or !Kung) speaking people so that some of the local branches will have Hai‖om as well as !Xun members. A more serious problem is that representation has to be vested in individuals who are expected to speak for a 'constituency'. The meetings held during WIMSA's fact finding mission showed that many Hai‖om, especially women, do not like to speak at meetings, nor do they like being elected as representatives, which would put them in the position to speak about and for others in important matters. At the same time some individuals have realised the potential benefits of being in a position to make decisions. The case of the first acclaimed Hai‖om chief after Namibian independence who has fallen out with WIMSA and many of the Hai‖om is a constant reminder of this fact. There is a demand for new forms of representation and possibly a chance of using modern technology innovatively to allow for more participation where at this stage the focus is primarily on representation as the mode of organising associations like community trusts (see Widlok 2001).

The first hurdle in this process was taken when members of various Hai‖om settlements met in 2000 for a workshop and drew up a draft resolution for the ‖Naisa !Nanis San Development Trust (see WIMSA 2000:10-11). This draft constitution specifies ten specific aims and purposes for the Trust:

1   To "build one San identity within and abroad the region" (networking with WIMSA)
2   To "strive towards San self-reliance and self-sufficiency" (political representation)
3   To "ensure social security for San" (access to health)
4   To "ensure that San benefit on social welfare" (access to pensions etc.)
5   To ensure that "San children [...] have access to education" (includes promoting San languages)
6   To promote "San culture and tradition" (setting up cultural centres)
7   To facilitate San participation "in tourism and agriculture" (running a camp in Etosha)
8   To educate San "on their rights and ensure that their rights are upheld" (advocacy)

9   To "generate income" (craft production etc.)
10   To "regain land"[27]

In the reports of the workshop at which this constitution was drafted with the help of CASS personnel (Gebhardt 2000; Kamanja 2000), there is only one specific reference to land. This concerns the possibility to put up a conservancy and a lodge which would involve the acquisition of land (Kamanja 2000:3) possibly in the southern area of Etosha (Gebhardt 2000:1).

The organisational structure of the trust follows a standard arrangement with three main organs, namely branch committees (elected informally in each local community), the Annual General Meeting (AGM, with representatives from all branches plus the board) and the board of trustees (elected by the AGM) (see WIMSA 2000). The overall format is therefore that of a trustee corporation with representative membership (see Widlok 2001:21). That is to say, membership is representative, not participatory, since only two members of each branch committee attend the AGM. It is a trustee and not an agent corporation since trustees act for the benefit of the group as a whole but are not directly under the direction of the group as an agent would be. It seems that this organisational form was pre-selected by the CASS advisors probably on the grounds that most San are not familiar with the different legal organisational forms of trusts. With this trust the Hai‖om in these dispersed settlements possess a new tool for their dealings with the state. How effective this tool will be with respect to the land issue remains to be seen.

Conclusion

There is a lot of political play with the colonial past in Namibia. Those who were politically powerful before independence emphasise the infrastructure, architecture and 'western' institutions that were put into place in the country during colonisation – and which they now see threatened by the SWAPO government since independence. The ruling party in turn emphasises the negative legacy, structures of injustice and marginalisation that it inherited from the colonial past. In this paper I have given one answer to the question as to how distribution and division rather than sharing have

---

[27] It is interesting to note that point 10 was added in pencil on the copy of the draft constitution that is held on file by WIMSA. This explains why the draft contains specific objectives for each of these aims except for item number 10, the land issue.

become the dominant modes of dealing with land issues. I have emphasised that the nation state is not the neutral or disinterested mediator between conflicting parties as its representatives sometimes suggest. Since independence the Namibian government is constitutionally obliged to treat all citizens in an equal way. However, as the recent history of San land issues shows, state ministries and the NGOs involved have their own interpretation of what constitutes equal treatment. This interpretation tends to consider not only claimants but also the land to be equal in the sense of being interchangeable. Plot sizes were harmonised and any existing ties to particular pieces of land were disregarded, at least in the case of the Hai‖om who were denied the particular places they had asked for and were offered substitutes instead. At the same time government policy not only considers land to be an economic good, but also a moral good. It is considered a moral good insofar as the moral entitlement to land ownership is underlined. However, land title is not given to any individual citizen but only to parties that are recognised as moral persons. This excludes people who – for whatever reason – do not work the land that they are given but decide to rent it out. It also excludes people who do not pursue the recognised land uses, namely agriculture and pastoralism. Finally, a moral person, eligible for receiving land, not only needs to engage in a limited set of pre-defined land uses, the person also needs to be held responsible. In order to constitute this responsibility, individual San need to form a corporate person, e. g. a trust, which can then interact with government and non-governmental agencies. In other words there are a number of largely implicit premises held by those driving the land reform which have fostered the distribution or division mode of land allocation in favour of a sharing approach to land. These implicit premises leading to land division are particularly difficult to challenge because they are couched in a rhetoric of "sharing the land" but here understood as open access to land – eventually dominated by individuals with sufficient wealth and influence.

The first ten years of independence have not been used for an innovation of the premises on which the Namibian land use system has been based since colonisation began. From the perspective of the Hai‖om living in the Oshikoto region I have underlined the fact that the two dominant parties involved in shaping the transition, namely the colonial administration and the independent government, despite the different dominant groups behind them, had rather similar ideas and practices about what constitutes the role of the state. The old regime propagated the division of land, the new state was concerned about the re-distribution of land. Both were trying to preclude claims based on indigenousness or first comer status – even though with very different measures, the former by spatialising ethnic identity and by codifying it from above, the latter by largely disregarding ethnic group membership. In other words, independence did not bring a reversal to pre-colonial forms of land distribution but it was a continuation of state orchestrated land division now with a strong rhetoric of "sharing" as a means of pre-empting land claims based on indigenousness. I suggest that both ways of dealing with the land gave the state a crucial role in dealings with the land and that both did not seriously consider alternative options of sharing the land.

Acknowledgements

Field research in Namibia was carried out in seven periods between 1987 and 2000 (a total of 32 months) with financial support from a number of sources. I gratefully acknowledge the funding provided by the following institutions: University of London, J. Swan Fund (Oxford), Max Planck Institute for Psycholinguistics (Nijmegen), Deutsche Forschungsgemeinschaft, Max Planck Institute for Social Anthropology (Halle/Saale). Thanks to Ute Dieckmann, Thekla Hohmann, and Michael Bollig for helpful comments on earlier drafts of this paper.

This paper is dedicated to Tomab ||Gam||gaeb who died near Sanab in a desperate attempt to occupy and cling to his land despite extreme hardships and lack of external support.

References

Dieckmann, Ute
2001   'The Vast White Place': A History of the Etosha National Park in Namibia and the Hai||om. *Nomadic Peoples* Vol. 5, Issue 2:125-153.

Drechsler, Horst
1996   *Südwestafrika unter deutscher Kolonialherrschaft. Die großen Land- und Minengesellschaften.* Stuttgart: Franz Steiner.

Gall, Sandy
2001   *The Bushmen of Southern Africa. Slaughter of the Innocent.* London: Chatto and Windus.

Gebhardt, M.
2000   *Report on the Training Workshop Held in Grootfontein to Set up the ||Naisa !Anisa San Trust (9-12 Oct. 2000).* No place.

Goody, Jack
1973   Bridewealth and Dowry in Africa and Eurasia. In: Jack Goody and
        Stanley Tambiah (eds.). *Bridewealth and Dowry.* Cambridge:
        Cambridge University Press:1-58.

Gordon, Robert
1992   *The Bushman Myth. The Making of a Namibian Underclass.* Boulder
        etc.: Westview Press.

Gordon, Robert and Sholto Douglas
2000   *The Bushman Myth. The Making of a Namibian Underclass.* Oxford:
        Westview Press.

Kamanja, A
2000   *Report on the Training Workshop Held in Grootfontein to Set up the
        ‖Naisa !Anisa San Trust (9-12 Oct. 2000).* No place.

Kopytoff, Igor
1989   The Internal African Frontier: The Making of African Political
        Culture. In: Igor Kopytoff (ed.). *The African Frontier. The
        Reproduction of Traditional African Societies.* Bloomington: Indiana
        University Press:3-84.

NCLR, National Conference on Land Reform
1991   *National Conference on Land Reform and the Land Question,
        Windhoek, 25 June - 1 July 1991.* Volume 1: Research Papers,
        Addresses and Consensus Document. Windhoek, Office of the Prime
        Minister: National Conference on Land Reform.

Tapscott, Chris and L. Hangula
1994   *Fencing of Communal Range Land in Northern Namibia: Social and
        Ecological Implications.* Windhoek: Multi-Disciplinary Research
        Centre, University of Namibia.

TCCF, Technical Committee on Commercial Farmland
1992   *Report of the Technical Committee on Commercial Farmland.*
        Windhoek, Office of the Prime Minister: Technical Committee on
        Commercial Farmland:188.

Vedder, Heinrich
1953   *Buschmänner in Südwestafrika.* Afrikanischer Heimatkalender:67-
        81.

Widlok, Thomas and Dagmar Widlok
1992a   *Legal and Economical Control of Mangetti-West as Commercial Farmland. Submission to the Technical Committee on Commercial Farmland.* Windhoek.

1992b   *Increasing Commercial Holding of Communal Land in the Eastern Ovambo Region. Submission to the Technical Committee on Commercial Farmland.* Windhoek.

Widlok, Thomas
1994   *Problems of Land Rights and Land Use in Namibia: A Case Study from the Mangetti Area.* Social Science Division Discussion Paper 5.

1995   Enteignet für den Etosha-Nationalpark. Die Hai‖om-Buschleute finden in Namibia zu wenig Gehör. *Pogrom* 185:12-14.

1999   *Living on Mangetti. 'Bushman' Autonomy and Namibian Independence.* Oxford: Oxford University Press.

2000   On the Other Side of the Frontier. Relations between Herero and 'Bushmen'. In: Michael Bollig and Jan-Baart Gewald (eds.). *Herero on Bushman Land. People, Cattle and Land.* Cologne: Köppe:497-522.

2001   *Equality, Group Rights and Corporate Ownership of Land.* Max Planck Institute for Social Anthropology Working Paper No. 21. Halle: Max Planck Institute for Social Anthropology.

2002   Hai‖om Trust in the Hai‖om Trust. *Cultural Survival Special Issue.*

WIMSA
1997   *Report on Activities.* April 1996 to March 1997. Windhoek.

2000   *Draft constitution. ‖Naisa !Anisa San Development Trust.* No place.

Files

National Archives of Namibia, Windhoek, *GWI 361 056/04 Vol. I/II*

Newspapers and Journals

Republikein, 29.5.00

Namibian, 16.5.00, 17.5.00, 23.5.00, 26.5.00, 29.5.00, 15.6.00

Windhoek Observer, 6.5.00

New Era, 12.5.00, 3.7.00

New African, June 2000

Identity as Dissociation:
The Khwe's Struggle for Land in West Caprivi

Ina Orth

> "What have we to say to a person who *knows* that
> God gave the land to his ancestors at the beginning
> of time, to be inhabited by their descendants in
> perpetuity? That their notions do not fit with
> theories of ethnicity of the 1990s? That indigenous
> ideas of heritage, and indigenous identities, are just
> a product of colonialism?"
> (Barnard 1997:3)

Introduction

Since Namibia's independence in 1990, the issues of land rights and access to land in the communal areas have been a regular source of conflict between neighbouring ethnic groups, as well as between ethnic groups and the state. Access to land and the right of access regulation have manifold implications ranging from political and economic power to the very existence and survival of a community. Especially the latter is true for the San communities in Namibia, which – with regard to their political self-determination and economic resources – range among the most underprivileged communities in the country (see Suzman 2001).

The situation of the Khwe[1] in West Caprivi reflects the above-mentioned problems in many ways. Located in a region severely lacking in infrastructure, with few to no prospects for cash income, only very limited options for agricultural or pastoral land-use, and harshly restricted use of natural resources such as wildlife and plants, West Caprivi is nevertheless

---

[1] The spelling of "Khwe" (as well as of other San groups) in this article follows the guidelines drawn up in the *Penduka Declaration on the Standardisation of Ju and Khoe Languages* (2001). This, of course, does not apply to quotations from earlier publications, where spellings such as Kxoe (e.g., Brenzinger 1998) or Kxoé (Köhler) are used.

intensely utilised economically by various ethnic groups (see map 1). This setting has, in the past and the present day, led to conflicts concerning access to the limited resources in the area. Those conflicts have been, and still are, closely related to the question of political power in the region. Indigenous identity, with all its political, economic and social implications, has become a major issue in the Khwe's struggle for obtaining political and land rights. Crucial in this process is their application for recognition of the Khwe Traditional Authority as official representatives of their community, as this is regarded – in the context of the current legal situation – as the only means to guarantee that land claims are considered by regional (state) authorities.

In early 1998, when I conducted short-term field research on land rights in West Caprivi,[2] the Khwe's endeavours to obtain formal land rights and political self-determination stood at a crossroads. As early as 1992, at the request of the Ministry of Wildlife, Conservation and Tourism (now the Ministry of Environment and Tourism), a community-based natural resource management (CBNRM) programme had been initiated with the intention of integrating the local population (mainly Khwe, and, to a lesser extent, Vasekele, San immigrants from Angola, and also a few Mbukushu residing in West Caprivi) into nature conservation and establish a system of community game guards (CGGs) engaged in wildlife protection. The Khwe community strongly approved of these projects, and a great number of community members were involved in the process (see Weaver, Affidavit 1997). In the following year, the Khwe, with considerable help from international donors,[3] had started a highly ambitious tourism project, the N‖goavaca campsite, situated on the banks of the Okavango River close to a local tourist attraction, the Popa Falls. The project was aimed at initiating a

---

[2] The research was carried out in cooperation with the Working Group of Indigenous Minorities in Southern Africa (WIMSA) and the Legal Assistance Centre (LAC), both located in Windhoek, and its results, as well as historical evidence from Namibia's National Archives, formed the basis for my MA Thesis "Landrechte und Identität bei südafrikanischen Wildbeutern: Eine Fallstudie zu den Kxoe in West Caprivi (Namibia)" ("Land Rights and Identity of South African Foragers: A Case Study on the Kxoe in West Caprivi (Namibia)") in 1998.

[3] In particular, the United States Agency for International Development (USAID) and the World Wildlife Fund (WWF), but also local non-government organisations (NGOs) such as Integrated Rural Development and Nature Conservation (IRDNC) were involved in the CBNRM project, of which the campsite formed an integral part (see Owen-Smith, Affidavit 1997:§10–20 and Weaver, Affidavit 1997:§2 10).

(in the long run) self-sustaining community-based campsite with income- and know-how-generating potential for the Khwe community. The campsite was officially opened in May 1997 and seemed to prosper right from the start, raising high hopes for economic improvement among the Khwe community.[4]

At the same time, however, these hopes were massively threatened by a decision made by the Namibian government in 1996 to lay claim to the very plot the Khwe had chosen for the establishment of their campsite four years earlier, in order to expand the grounds of a prison camp, the Divundu Rehabilitation Centre, located exactly at the turn-off from the Trans-Caprivi Highway to N‖goavaca campsite. The Khwe Traditional Authority, fearing the community's eviction from the campsite, sought assistance from the Working Group of Indigenous Minorities in Southern Africa (WIMSA) and the Legal Assistance Centre (LAC), and submitted their case to the Namibian High Court. The issues raised in their Notice of Motion (Legal Assistance Centre 1997) of December 23, 1997, perfectly reflect the complex situation concerning land-use, as well as social and political structure in West Caprivi. The document shows how features such as settlement history, colonial influences, neighbourly relationships (and ethnic conflicts, respectively), ethnic identity, recognition of traditional leaders, and, not least, economic survival are mutually interdependent and in many ways interwoven with the question of land rights and access to land in West Caprivi. In this article, I will try to show how the Khwe, by using a multi-layered strategy, try to obtain legal certainty concerning political and economic autonomy, and, at the same time, create a wider lobby in this struggle. First, I will outline briefly the history of settlement of the Caprivi Strip in pre-colonial and colonial times and its effects on the present-day situation. Then I will show how the flexibility in, and the ability to shift between, various economic strategies and land-use patterns have effectively been used for risk-minimisation and how this practice is presently under threat by the current[5] situation of legal uncertainty. Finally, it will be shown how the Khwe have started to follow new paths in pursuing their goals since Namibia's independence. By presenting themselves as a cohesive ethnic

---

[4] These hopes did not seem to be unfounded, as shortly after opening the campsite, the Co-director of the local NGO IRDNC, Garth Owen-Smith, described the project as "a sustainable and economically viable business enterprise" (see Owen-Smith, Affidavit 1997:§28).

[5] As Boden (this volume) shows, this uncertainty has not been resolved within the past four years, but, quite to the contrary, has rather been very aggravated.

entity, and searching for new allies, the Khwe community has started to play an active role on Namibia's political stage. This strategy, however, does not seem to be aim for association with the state's political structure and hierarchies, but rather for dissociation from national integration policies. Ethnicity and the issue of shared history and cultural heritage are pivotal in this process. In addition, engagement in CBNRM and new land-use patterns form a strategy of taking possession of inhabited land. At the same time, it opens up ways to cooperate with international (donor) organisations, and thus participate in the regional as well as the global discourse with and about indigenous minorities.

A Brief History of the Caprivi Strip

Owing to favourable natural conditions, marked by the rivers Okavango in the west, Luyana in the north, Mashi/Kwando crossing the area from north to south, Zambezi in the northeast and Chobe in the south, the area around the Caprivi Strip was densely populated by various ethnic groups in pre-colonial times (see Holub 1879). This situation has prevailed until present time and is still representative especially of the eastern part of the Caprivi Strip (see map 1). East Caprivi, between the Kwando and Zambezi Rivers, was politically under the domination of the Lozi since the end of the 17th century (Fisch 1996:53). In the region west of the Kwando River, stretching down to the banks of the Okavango, hardly any surface water can be found, except for the areas close to the rivers. Thus, this part of the Caprivi Strip was "only sparsely settled by hunter-gathering Khoé (Kxoé, Kwengo)"[6] (Fisch 1996:68). According to Fisch, the Mbukushu, who at the time settled east and west of the banks of the Okavango River, regarded the Khwe as their subjects, but nevertheless did not control them directly (ibid.).

The relationship between Khwe and Mbukushu is described – especially in the older literature – as one of dependence and subjugation on the side of the Khwe. J. H. Wilhelm, who travelled the region of southeast Angola in 1917 reports: "According to statements by the bushmen, the Mbukushu rape women and drag them, as well as men and children, into slavery. Having no rights whatsoever, they have got used to recognising the Mbukushu as their master"[7] (Wilhelm 1955:20).

---

[6] "[...] nur dünn von wildbeuterischen Khoé (Kxoé, Kwengo) besiedelt" (Fisch 1996:68).

[7] "Nach den eigenen Aussagen der Buschleute werden von den Mbukushu Frauen vergewaltigt und ebenso wie Männer und Kinder in die Sklaverei geschleppt. Sie

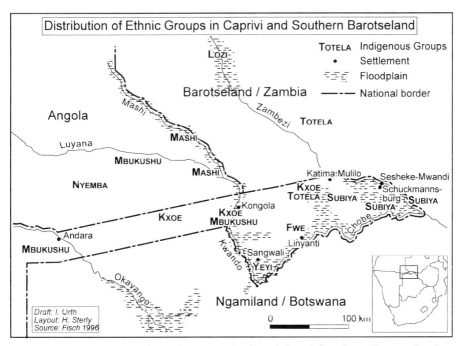

Map 1: distribution of ethnic groups in Caprivi and Southern Barotseland

Khwe-Mbukushu interactions, however, have not exclusively been marked by hostility. Köhler (1989:203-204) gives examples of trade and inter-marriage, as well as, during the 20th century, of Khwe wage labour for Mbukushu agriculturalists. According to Köhler, the Khwe not always perceived immigrants in their settlement area as a threat to their survival, but, on the contrary, were quite willing to allow access to strangers, as long as the "master of the settlement" ("Herr des Wohnplatzes", Köhler 1989:203) was asked permission to make use of the settlement's water resources. Some of my informants in West Caprivi also reported of this habit of asking one another for permission to use land, but were clearly referring to some former time. At the same time, they regretted that, in the present open-access situation in Namibia's communal areas, this custom is no longer in use.

Access to land and natural resources has been, and still is, the main issue marking Khwe-Mbukushu relations. Owing to the mobile lifestyle of both

stehen vollkommen rechtlos und haben sich auch daran gewöhnt, den Mbukushu als ihren Herrn anzuerkennen" (Wilhelm 1955:20).

groups, migration was no solution for the Khwe, when at the end of the 19th century more and more Mbukushu started claiming access to Khwe settlement areas after being forced to migrate out of their own settlements by invading Tawana groups from the south (see Brenzinger 1998:347).

> But even by moving away, a strategy which might have worked with other intruders, this did not work that well with the Mbukushu, who were quite mobile themselves. They are described to have shared a semi-sedentary lifestyle and after 1800 were spread over an area similar to that of the Kxoe, concentrating along rivers" (ibid.).

Seiner, a German geographer who travelled the region at the beginning of the 20th century, describes how several Khwe communities were driven away from their villages by incoming Mbukushu and forced to settle further north, extending their hunting grounds up into today's Angolan territory (Seiner 1913:299). With the beginning of Namibia's colonisation and the drawing of national boundaries in the region around West Caprivi, however, this strategy of spatial mobility in order to avoid conflicts has – especially under South African rule – become increasingly restricted.

German Rule

When the region of today's Namibia became the German colony Deutsch Südwest-Afrika in 1884, the area east of the Okavango River was not originally concerned; it belonged to the British protectorate Bechuanaland. Only in 1890, with the Helgoland-Zanzibar Contract between Germany and Great Britain, was a narrow stretch of land 450 km in length added to the German colony on its northeastern border. In exchange, the British government received the islands of Zanzibar, then under German colonial rule, and Helgoland in the North Sea (see Fisch 1996:12-13). Germany's intention in this contract was to find a navigable way from South West Africa via the Zambezi River to its other colony, German East Africa, today Tanzania. Due to the many cataracts of the Zambezi, this plan proved impossible, so that South West Africa was now in possession of a narrow stretch of land lying in one of the least accessible regions of the colony, sharing borders only with British and Portuguese colonies. The German administration was largely ignorant of any economic or strategic use of this area. Named after Georg Leo Earl of Caprivi, then German Imperial Chancellor, the region was called "Caprivizipfel" (Caprivi Strip) (ibid.).

In order to gain some clarity at least about its economic potential, the geographer and journalist Franz Seiner was sent to the Caprivi Strip in 1905 and 1906 by the German government. Seiner was one of the first Europeans to travel the region and drew up an extensive survey on geography, geology, climate and quality of soil (Seiner 1909 a and b; 1910). He came to the conclusion that only the eastern part of the Caprivi Strip, east of the Kwando River, was to some extent economically interesting. In spite of the rich wildlife, he was sceptical about the region's value concerning hunting and fishing. Only with regard to agriculture and, to a lesser extent, livestock breeding, did he consider the Strip to be useful (Seiner 1909a:9). Seiner regarded the area west of the Kwando as "culturally inferior" ("kulturell minderwertigere Niederungswaldsteppe") (ibid.:13), marked by a substantial lack of water.

Therefore, it was not surprising that in 1908, the German government installed their first administration for the Caprivi Strip in eastern Caprivi. A second reason for this selection of an administrative site was the fact that the royal seat of the Lozi kings during this time was in Sesheke in East Caprivi. Following the principles of British *indirect rule*, the first German Administrator[8], Streitwolf, had his residence built close to the village of Sesheke-Mwandi, then also the seat of the British administration of the Protectorate Bechuanaland. Streitwolf travelled the eastern part of the Caprivi Strip extensively, negotiating with the local authorities about the future administration of the region. He was only interested in West Caprivi insofar as it would have proved useful in finding a direct road from East Caprivi to the Okavango River, thus avoiding having to travel across land owned by the British crown to reach his residence (Fisch 1996:97). While travelling in the western part of Caprivi in mid-1909, Streitwolf hardly seemed to have come into contact with Khwe (whom, like Seiner, he called Hukwe). According to his travel report, he was "[...] astonished at how low a level the Hukwe are. They live like animals in the forest, without permanent settlements"[9] (Streitwolf 1911:175). Considering this impression and the fact that Streitwolf estimated the number of Khwe residing in West Caprivi to be 300 at most, it is clear that the German administration at the time had no interest in the San population of the Caprivi Strip whatsoever. As far as the administration was concerned, they were not part of the political structures and hierarchies of the region, and in the reports of early travellers they only were rarely mentioned as being enslaved by Mbukushu

---

8   Or "Kaiserlicher Resident", as was his position within the German administrative hierarchy.

9   "[...] erstaunt, auf wie niedriger Stufe die Hukwe standen. Sie leben wie die Tiere im Walde ohne bleibende Wohnstätte" (Streitwolf 1911:175).

or Barotse (Holub 1981 II:51; Seiner 1910:360; 1913:208 as cited in Fisch 1996:57; also see Köhler 1989:459, 463).

Thus, there was no administration in the western part of the Caprivi Strip during German colonial times. If at all, German administration applied to the area east of the Kwando River. West Caprivi remained, until the official end of German colonialism, widely unknown and 'untouched' territory. European settlements had not yet been founded in West Caprivi (see George, Affidavit 1997b:§12).[10]

However, with the arbitrary distribution of land as drawn up in the Helgoland-Zanzibar Contract, neither the political nor the economic structures already existent in the region were taken into consideration. Concerning the relations between the different ethnic groups in the region, whose settlement structures had certainly not followed national borders, the demarcation of boundaries had long-lasting negative effects, with substantial potential for conflict until the present day.

South African Administration

With the end of World War I and the Peace Treaty of Versailles, German South West Africa, and thus also the Caprivi Strip, was put under South African administration. During the first years of its mandate, the new administration didn't seem to put too much effort into controlling one of the most remote parts of the country, which is evident in a statement in one of the first Annual Reports of the South West African administration:

> The natives concerned live along the northern border of this territory and in the Caprivi Zipfel and are separated from European influence by a large stretch of intervening country which for the most part of the year is waterless. Intercourse with them has in the past been difficult [...] they have been left to rule themselves according to their customs without interference

---

[10] This affidavit contains statements about Khwe settlements and land rights in West Caprivi and was drawn up in 1997 to support the case of the Khwe concerning their land claim for the N‖goavaca campsite before the Namibian High Court. It was kindly put at my disposal by the Legal Assistance Centre in Windhoek.

on the part of this Administration. (SWA Annual Report 1923:18).[11]

Compared to the enormous effort put into the administration of other regions in South West Africa, which has left behind a flood of files and records in today's Namibian National Archives, the amount of files concerning the Caprivi Strip reflects this attitude of 'laissez faire'. The region well beyond the Police Zone seemingly offered little to encourage investments or administrative control through the government. While East Caprivi was declared a native reserve in 1940, West Caprivi remained largely unnoticed. A letter of the Magistrate and Native Commissioner in Katima Mulilo in East Caprivi to the Secretary for Indigenous Affairs in Pretoria, dated November 30, 1943, states that "The portion bordering the Okavango River is in fact administered and controlled but the portion between that River and our boundary near the Kwando River is not in fact controlled" (SWAA / A503/1). Like their German predecessors, the South African administration didn't seem to find any value in the western part of the Caprivi Strip, as the then Native Commissioner in Rundu put in clear words. "The Western Caprivi Zipfel, east of the Okavango River, is a useless strip of country, approximately 126 miles long by 20 miles wide. It is unsuitable for agriculture away from the rivers, and has only a meagre supply of water for the greater part of the year, and is, in consequence, unsuitable for stock" (SWAA / A503/1, letter dated 15/01/1944). Neither this letter to the Chief Native Commissioner in Windhoek of the year 1944, nor most of the other files on the Caprivi Strip of that time mention the Khwe as inhabitants of West Caprivi at all. Living beyond the Police Zone, they belonged to the category of *wild bushmen*, the "least civilised" of the three bushmen categories used by administrators and scientists at the time to classify the country's San population[12].

---

[11] Unlike the inhabitants of the neighbouring Bechuanaland, the residents of the Caprivi Strip were not even forced to pay so called "hut taxes" (SWA Annual Report 1928:107).

[12] "The typology of 'wild', 'semi-tame or wild' and 'tame' Bushmen became well established by the early 1920s in the settler discourse on understanding Bushmen behaviour. The basis of this typology was both spatial and economic. 'Wild' Bushmen were those who were not permanently incorporated into the settler economy and generally lived beyond the Police Zone. Then there were the 'semi-tame or wild' Bushmen, who came from beyond the Police Zone to work on settler farms on a temporary or seasonal basis. Finally there were the 'tame'

It was not until the 1950s that the South West African administration drew their attention to the Khwe, whom they called "Barrakwengwe" or "Black Bushmen". In the administration files of 1950, one can find the *Temporary Report of the Commission for the Preservation of the Bushmen Population in South West Africa*[13] (SWAA 433 A50/67, vol. 3). The aim of this commission was to draw up a detailed survey of the different San groups in South West Africa, their numbers and their regional distribution. Chairperson was P. J. Schoeman, professor of anthropology, who, while working at the University of Stellenbosch, was one of the architects of South Africa's "Great Apartheid" (Gordon 1992:160, 163), the doctrine of classifying the country's population along ethnic and racial lines[14]. In the report, the Khwe were described as being "tremendously different" from the other ethnic groups in South West Africa, so that the commission at that stage was unable to recommend where this group should best be settled in the future[15] (SWAA 433 A50/67, vol. 3). The commission estimated the number of Khwe (or "Swart Boesmans" as they were labelled in this report) at 700 to 800 individuals, only referring, however, to the region around Bagani and Andara, close to the Okavango River (ibid.). Their being "tremendously different" and their classification as "hybridised" (meaning somewhat of a "mixture" between San and Bantu), "who can pass for natives in so far as stature is concerned" (SWAA 433, A50/67, vol. 4:1[16]), seemed to be the reason for the Bushman Commission to suggest in 1953 officially granting the Khwe permission to work as migrant labourers in the mines at Witwatersrand and within the borders of the Police Zone. Thus, the Khwe became a new target group for the South West African Native Labour Association (SWANLA) in their efforts to satisfy an ever-growing need for cheap labour for the South African economy.

Bushmen, who were permanently 'habituated' to employment on settler farms" (Gordon 1992:90).

[13] *Voorlopige Verslag van die Kommissie vir die behoud van die Boesmansbevolking in Suidwes-Afrika.*

[14] This policy, in later years, built the 'legal' foundation for mass resettlements of the black population in the so-called homelands.

[15] "Aangesien hul taal en stamgebruike hemelsbreed verskil van dié van die ander stamme in Suidwes-Afrika kan u Kommissie in hierdie stadium van sy ondersoek nog nie aanbeveel waar hulle uiteindelik gevestig moet word nie" (SWAA 433 A50/67, vol. 3).

[16] Letter by the Bushman Commission to the Chief Native Commissioner, dated December 19, 1953.

Until the end of the 1940s, only a few Khwe had migrated to work as farm labourers due to the poor working conditions on the farms, especially for San, who were seldom paid in cash but rather in kind, and quite often had to endure harsh treatment, including corporal punishment, by the farmers (Gordon 1992:101, 138, 170-171).

After the end of World War II, labour migration became more attractive to many Khwe men, when two offices of the SWANLA and the Witwatersrand Native Labour Association (WNLA) were opened in Katima Mulilo in East Caprivi and Shakawe in Bechuanaland (Köhler 1966:135). During the 1950s and 1960s, many Khwe signed 16-18-month contracts and migrated to the Witwatersrand to work in the gold mines. Due to the above-mentioned limitations of their rather traditional economic strategies, the Khwe were strongly dependent on those contracts (Brenzinger 1998:345); however, they were for the first time able to accumulate some sort of prosperity.[17]

The report by the Bushman Commission for the first time recognised the Khwe as residents of the Caprivi Strip and, concerning ethnic terms, framed them as a cohesive group, separate from neighbouring Bantu-speaking peoples. On the other hand, the topos of hybridisation expounded earlier by Streitwolf and Seiner was thereby taken up once again.

> The Barrakwengwe or Black Bushmen appear to be a mixture between the Kung and the Bantu and reside as a separate entity in the Western Caprivi Zipfel. There would appear to be no object in shifting them. They are at home in the area they now occupy and get on well with the surrounding native tribes. Your Honour's Commissioners recommend, therefore, that they be allowed to remain where they are and that water be opened up for them (SWAA 433, A50/67, vol. 4:1).

The same politics of non-intervention were applied in the following years and confirmed in the final report of the Commission of Inquiry into South West Africa Affairs (the Odendaal Commission[18]). The commission considered the Khwe to be one of the three main San groups in South West

---

[17] Köhler (1997:9; 365-387) gives several reports of ex-migrant labourers, telling of goods they could buy with their wages, such as coats, trousers, underwear, and the like.

[18] The aim of the Odendaal Commission was to work out the foundation for enlarging the *native reserves* and transforming them into *homelands* following the guidelines of Apartheid politics.

Africa and stated that "The Barakwengo [Khwe, I. O.] live along the lower part of the Okavango area [...] and in the Western Caprivi almost up to the Kwando River" (Republic of South Africa 1964:30). Therefore, the commission recommended "that homelands be created for the Bushmen, these areas to be known as (i) the portion of the Western Caprivi east of the Okavango River, and 587,671 hectares in extent for the Barakwengo Bushmen; and (ii) Bushmanland, 1,805,000 hectares in extent [...] for the other Bushmen [...]" (ibid.:99).

Whereas the commission's recommendations concerning the homeland "Bushmanland" were followed, this was not the case for Western Caprivi. On request of the Department of Nature Conservation, the South West African administration declared the entire area between the Okavango and Kwando Rivers a nature reservation with the name "Caprivi Game Park" on March 20, 1968 (Republic of South Africa, Government Notice 19 of 1968). Unlike the Hai||om of Etosha, the Khwe were still given permission to reside within the borders of the new game reserve; however, the options to further follow their economic strategies, be it hunting and gathering or agriculture, were substantially limited (Adams and Werner 1990:121, also see below)[19].

During the time of my field research, many of the Khwe expressed their suspicion that nature conservation was neither the only, nor the main, reason for West Caprivi's proclamation as a game reserve. Rather, they suggested that this was quite an effective means for the administration to control population movements in this frontier area so close to the Angolan border, and thus prevent any possible turmoil in connection with the Angolan civil war (also see George, Affidavit 1997b:§35). This suspicion is not unfounded considering the activities of the South African Defence Forces (SADF) in the region that started in the early 1970s. In 1973, the SADF built their first army camp in West Caprivi, Alpha, which was re-named Omega in 1976, (Uys 1993:59, see map 2). Since the proclamation of the Caprivi Game Park in 1968, as well as the closing of the Botswana border in the mid-1970s, had triggered off a major setback in Khwe economy, the arrival of the SADF in the Caprivi Strip must have come as an economic salvation to the poverty-stricken community of the Khwe. Massive recruitment campaigns started in 1973 after the Alpha camp had been built, and Khwe men were employed as

---

[19] In the course of the CBNRM programme at work in West Caprivi since 1992, there have been attempts by the Khwe to have the reserve de-proclaimed. At present, a cabinet decision for the de-proclamation of, at least, parts of the area exists, but up to now has not been put into action, so that the status of the area remains unchanged (see Boden, this volume).

trackers in the battle against SWAPO guerrilla in the bush. In the following year, the camp was enlarged to take up San refugees from Angola, whose number totalled 3,000 individuals by 1978 (Gordon 1992:185). Male refugees were recruited either by SADF or the South West Africa Territorial Force (SWATF), and their dependents were provided for by the military forces. Gordon (ibid.) objects to the assumption that recruitment was mainly on a voluntary basis: "The relatively high salaries and services received for signing up easily created the delusion that it was an act of 'free choice'. ...[T]he army acknowledged that bushmen refugees had very little choice in the matter. They had either to sign up or leave the region entirely" (Star, November 24, 1982, as cited in Gordon 1992:186).

Map 2: army camps in West Caprivi

In 1974/75, the Bushman Battalion 31, consisting of Khwe and Vasekele, was established, and by 1980 the additional military bases Bwabwata, Bagani, Buffalo, Guiga and Omega III were built (ELCIN/NORAD 1994, 4-5; see map 2). From these northern bases, the SADF supported the struggle of the Angolan guerrilla movement União Nacional para a Independência Total de Angola (UNITA) against the ruling Movimento Popular da Libertação de Angola (MPLA). The military presence in West Caprivi was expanded tremendously in the following years, which had a massive impact on Khwe social and economic life. Almost all Khwe families were involved directly as soldiers, or indirectly as family members with the SADF. In

1989/90, the total number of San army servicemen in Western Caprivi (including dependents) was estimated at 6,000 souls (ibid.).

The comparatively high wages paid to the bushmen soldiers enabled them not only to support their extended families (Gordon 1995:1), but even to buy luxury articles such as clothing and high-heel shoes available in the camp shops (Köhler 1997:11). Besides changes in living standards, Köhler observed a major impact on Khwe social structure as a result of the younger generation moving to the army bases, while most of the elder people remained in their former settlements. Thereby, Köhler (ibid.) suggests that oral tradition as a socially important means of passing on knowledge, as well as cultural norms and values, was widely interrupted, and thus evoked a generational, as well as a social gap in Khwe society.[20]

The Khwe's major economic dependence on the army and the risks involved in case it withdrew from the region was publicly recognised long beforehand: "Virtually the entire Bushmen population of the Western Caprivi is supported by the military. If they go, the entire socio-economic structure will collapse" (Eastern Province Herald, February 2, 1980, as cited in Gordon 1992:186). This prediction closely matched reality when the SADF withdrew from the region shortly before independence, and left those Khwe who decided to remain in West Caprivi virtually facing starvation (Gordon 1995:1). As San had been employed as "auxiliaries" in the military forces, they had no pension rights or any other privileges resulting from their services (ibid.:2).

Changing Economic Strategies

Flexibility, regarded as a salient marker of San societies in anthropological literature (see, for example, Vierich 1982 and Günther 1996), has always been the Khwe's most effective survival strategy. Shifting between a variety of economic activities, the Khwe have at all times practised hunting and gathering as but one of their means to make a living. Even in pre-colonial times, agriculture has played a major role in Khwe economic life. Moreover, Köhler (1986:254, 1991:7) has shown that Khwe were part of far-reaching trade networks with neighbouring ethnic groups during these times. After the arrival of the Portuguese in Angola, Khwe

---

[20] This indeed seems to have been one of the aims of the SADF in West Caprivi. The camp Omega, for example, was perceived and described as a "model of 'upliftment', of guided acculturation [   ]" by one army anthropologist (Gordon 1995:1).

hunters were involved in fur and ivory trade with Portuguese salesmen (Köhler 1991:5). The process of continuing land dispossession in West Caprivi as described above culminated in the cordoning off of the entire area by the South African Defence Forces in the 1970s. For a period lasting 20 years, it almost entirely obstructed any hunting and gathering, as well as agricultural activities by the Khwe. At the same time, mobility, as the key risk-minimisation strategy used by the Khwe when under political, economic or environmental constraints, has become increasingly illegalised[21]. As a result, a massive change in economic strategies and, concurrently, relations to the land, by the Khwe population in West Caprivi have taken place. During the period of the South African administration, an increasing number of Khwe men made use of the opportunity for earning cash income through wage labour, at first mainly through labour migration to farms and mines, later as soldiers for the SADF. A closer look at economic change and Khwe land-use patterns is thus necessary to fully understand current Khwe strategies of claiming West Caprivi as their "ancestral"[22] land.

Khwe System of Land Allocation

In literature on West Caprivi, there are hardly any descriptions of Khwe structures of land allocation to be found. However, in some of Köhler's oral texts on Khwe life, one can find hints that it was always possible for Khwe villagers to deny outsiders – be they Khwe or non-Khwe – access to the land they lived on, as well as the natural resources surrounding a settlement (e.g., Köhler 1997:710). In February 1998, I gathered more detailed information on Khwe land allocation during group interviews in the communities of Mutc'iku, Chetto, Omega and Omega III. With the limitation of the Khwe migration area by national borders with today's Angola, Botswana and Zambia, rights of access to and use of land and resources have changed. Although all the land[23] is *de jure* state property, it is regarded and used as

---

[21] Though this practice is still widely used until the present, as the migration movements of many Khwe to Botswana in recent years have illustrated (see Boden, this volume).

[22] The term "ancestral" was frequently used during interviews as well as in personal communication with chief George and was obviously referring to West Caprivi as the remainder of the once much larger migration area of the Khwe.

[23] When the community members spoke of "the land" or "Khwe country" in interviews, they always referred to the whole of West Caprivi between the Okavango and Kwando Rivers.

common property by all the communities[24]. Khwe communities divide the land into privately used and communally used parts. Privately used land refers to land that is inhabited by a family, i.e., where they have built a house and made a garden. The rights for using this piece of land are usually passed on from a user to his/her children after death. Individuals also have the option to apply for use rights of a plot from communally used land. The principles of land allocation differ slightly between the communities. In Mutc'iku, for example, the chief was considered the person in charge of land allocation, whereas the headmen seemed to be responsible for this task in Omega III and Chetto[25]. The situation in Omega was described as more complex due to the presence of an office of the Ministry of Land, Resettlement and Rehabilitation (MLRR), which has been engaged in the implementation of a resettlement scheme since 1991, and thus takes part in land allocation (ELCIN/NORAD 1994:7-8)[26]. But here the headmen of the community are also involved in the process.

Consensus in all the communities is that, associated with the rights to use a plot, comes a set of rights and responsibilities that the user or "owner" has to accept. Supreme is the rule that privately allocated land must not lay bare. Users are obliged to care for their plot, fence it, clear the land from weeds, build a house on it and grow a garden. Although this tends to describe the 'ideal case', which, particularly with the unrest in the area since 1998, cannot always be maintained, informants were very concerned about this point. Furthermore, users are responsible for the natural resources on the land, i.e., the felling of big trees or the destruction of edible plants is prohibited. Some of the informants considered obedience towards the local traditional authority as a precondition for land-use rights. Social sanctions and even the rescinding of use rights were listed as consequences in the case of severe failure to obey to the rules, although the latter seemed, according to the informants, to be extremely rare incidents. It is important to note that it was made absolutely clear during interviews that there was no reason to deny a member of the Khwe community access to a plot of land for

---

[24] As far as relations to land and attitudes towards ownership of land are concerned, the following statements are based on the information gathered during community interviews.

[25] This might be due to the fact that during the time of my research, Chief George resided in Mutc'iku and was thus consulted by the community headmen in all land matters.

[26] For details concerning the resettlement scheme and its impacts on the Khwe population in West Caprivi see Boden, this volume.

individual use if nobody else could claim ownership (or use rights) for that particular plot.

A similar set of rights and responsibilities as mentioned above applies to the communal land. Within the borders of West Caprivi – with the exception of the private plots – all the land and natural resources are regarded as the common property of the Khwe. The issues of resource protection and nature conservation were also considered of paramount importance on communal land, which might in part be due to the presence of conservation activists in the area in recent years. This applies also (and especially) to the in-migration of non-Khwe, mainly Mbukushu, into West Caprivi, who, according to the Khwe, do not treat the land and natural resources properly (see below).

Thus, the Khwe community today is no longer willing to grant access to their land to non-Khwe. Community members regard the contemporary 'open access' situation, which allows every Namibian the right of free movement within the country, as a major problem, viewing this freedom on the case of others as a limitation to their own freedom, and thereby perceive their rights of land allocation neglected by the national government. Recognition of the Khwe Traditional Authority as the land-allocating body in West Caprivi is therefore seen as a key issue in the Khwe's struggle for political and economic self-determination.

Foraging

Hunting and gathering has at all times been one of the Khwe's major economic activities. Even today, *veldkos* (bush crops) such as honey, wild nuts, edible roots and leaves, berries and wild onions make up a substantial part of their diet. According to a study of nature conservationists in 1992, the Khwe of West Caprivi gather 25-50% of their food from the bush (Brown and Jones 1994:174, as cited in Brenzinger 1998:344). But, whereas in former times gardening was used more as a supplementary strategy to foraging, the situation today is vice versa. Especially in times of meagre harvests, or when garden crops have to be sold for cash income, the gathering of *veldkos* comprises the major alternative for survival in a marginal region like West Caprivi, where the options for wage labour are close to nonexistent.

Hunting, on the other hand, has become almost impossible since the proclamation of West Caprivi as a game reserve in 1968. Since then, the hunting of game has been regulated by the Ministry of Wildlife, Conservation and Tourism (today the Ministry of Environment and Tourism, MET) (ELCIN/NORAD 1994:12). These regulations prohibit hunting within the borders of West Caprivi[27], especially in the "core conservation areas" (see map 3). In the so-called multiple-use areas, small groups of Khwe occasionally hunt rabbits and other small animals (Brenzinger 1998:344). Today, a more pressing problem for Khwe hunters is the enormous decrease of game through poachers, who often use automatic weapons and even "attempt to kill witnesses, such as Kxoe hunters, who run into them in the bush" (ibid.).

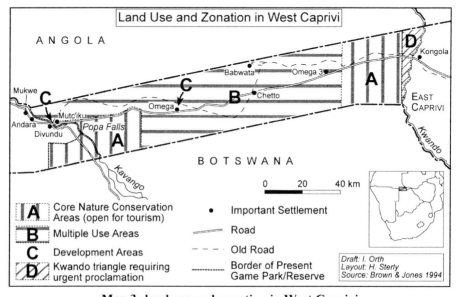

Map 3: land use and zonation in West Caprivi

Poaching, as well as the increasing destruction of plants on their land are of great concern to the Khwe community. Particularly the 'export' of natural resources such as grass and wooden poles, which many Mbukushu cut in West Caprivi and transport over the Okavango River to use for building houses, is regarded as a threat to the Khwe's environment – and thus to their very survival – and as theft of their property.

Protection of the environment and natural resources has recently become a trajectory for excluding outsiders from using resources in West Caprivi.

---

[27] This, at least, is true for the local population. However, two trophy-hunting concessions are still held by tour operators, one in Buffalo and on the banks of the Okavango River, and the other in the Kwando Triangle (Gertrud Boden, pers. com.).

Khwe employment in nature conservation as a novel strategy to legitimise access to and use rights to the land will be described below.

Agriculture

Agriculture is currently the main means for survival by the Khwe. In pre-colonial times to the 1940s, gardening was practised as shifting cultivation, integrated both into the yearly cycle and the cycle of hunting and gathering. Historical evidence of fenced gardens in West Caprivi is given by early travellers (Gibbons 1904:208, as cited in Köhler 1966:124; Wilhelm 1955:23). During these times, Khwe mainly employed agriculture as a supplement to hunting and gathering.

The first major change came in the 1940s with the opportunity of wage labour on farms in South West Africa, and later in the mines at Witwatersrand in South Africa. The cash income enabled many Khwe families to buy livestock and ploughs, and thus intensify their agricultural activities. Viewed in light of political events, particularly the beginning of the Angolan war of independence in 1961, which led to a massive in-migration of San refugees into West Caprivi and thereby caused increasing population pressure in the region, this change was the only possible alternative to hunting and gathering. In addition, as mentioned before, the proclamation of West Caprivi as a game reserve heightened the pressure on the Khwe to engage in different economic strategies.

During the 20 years of military presence in West Caprivi in the 1970s and 1980s, most Khwe families were concentrated in army camps, which resulted in a severe loss of male work power in local agriculture. In this period, the Khwe were mainly dependent on the incomes of those men employed with the SADF or the SWATF and on the goods available in the army shops.[28] Those Khwe who were not employed by the military forces were entirely dependent on food rations given to them by the South African administration (cf. Köhler 1989:515-516). Today, especially the old people nostalgically refer to these times as being well-cared for by the government. Thereby, of course, they clearly express a change in their relationship to the Namibian government since independence, which seems to be marked by the Khwe feeling neglected by the government.

---

[28] According to Köhler (1989:517), this period was called "times when we ate tins" ("Zeit, da man Dosen ißt") by the Khwe, as the food rations were distributed in cans to the bushmen soldiers and comprised a substantial part of the Khwe's diet.

After the SADF withdrawal, some 1600 Khwe accepted an offer by the South African government and moved to Schmidtsdrift, a military camp north of Kimberley, South Africa (Brenzinger 1998:341). The main reason for this move, besides the lack of economic perspectives, was a substantial fear of possible acts of revenge by the SWAPO-led government of independent Namibia, as many of the San soldiers had worked as trackers for the SADF in their battle against SWAPO. For those Khwe who remained in the region, agriculture again was the only means to ensure economic survival. "Those Bushmen who wanted to stay [in Namibia, I. O.] were confronted with a bleak future without salaries, food, housing, and social services after the withdrawal of the SADF" (ELCIN/NORAD 1994:5). To reduce poverty in the region, the Bushmen Ex-Servicemen and Dependants Rehabilitation and Settlement Programme was carried out by the Evangelical Lutheran Church in Namibia (ELCIN) between 1991 and 1996. Their major aim was "[...] to create homes for landless Namibians by allocating arable land to them to settle on, use and develop in order to make a living as individuals, families or groups (Republic of Namibia/MLRR, n.d. as cited in ELCIN/NORAD 1994:6). Participating families in West Caprivi were resettled in the four villages of Bagani/Mutc'iku, Omega, Chetto and Omega III, each receiving four hectares of arable land. It was problematic, however, that the plots were neither chosen nor distributed according to Khwe ideas of land allocation. Instead, the resettlement scheme distributed plots according to issues such as economic effectiveness (ELCIN/NORAD 1994:7-8) – not always, however, taking into consideration what the Khwe thought to be effective and profitable. Problems like these lead back to the cornerstone of Khwe economic and political self-determination in West Caprivi today: the uncertain status of land and political authority, the latter of which definitely has a say in the former. At the time of my research in early 1998, it was unclear whether the Khwe participating in the rehabilitation programme were *de jure* owners of that particular piece of land or whether they only held use rights (ibid:8; Hitchcock and Murphree n.d.:5)[29] that could easily be withdrawn. The indeterminate status of land in West Caprivi was viewed as a major obstacle for development in the region by analysts:

> The land act of 1936 which is still applicable in the communal
> areas stipulates that Government is the state land allocating
> body but in practice chiefs and headmen perform these duties.
> Till this legal impasse has been resolved and individual land

---

[29] In the meantime, the plots in West Caprivi are registered in the names of the owners (Gertrud Boden, pers. com.).

grant certificates or PTOs (Permission To Occupy) have been issued to the Bushmen plot occupants, the situation of insecurity of tenure and ambiguous land rights will remain. Given the particular background of the settler families this may indeed provide a serious disincentive for future development" (ELCIN/NORAD 1994:8).

During my interviews, the Rehabilitation and Settlement Programme or its effects on the community were hardly ever mentioned.[30] I suggest that this might be due to the fact that, in the perception of most Khwe, the headmen remained the responsible persons in questions of land allocation rather than some unfamiliar government officials. However, it has to be mentioned that the programme did have an impact on infrastructure in the region. In several food-for-work projects, bore holes and water pumps were installed, streets were built between the villages and fields, and a demonstration plot for teaching in agricultural methods was founded in Bagani.

Two significant aspects attached to agriculture by Khwe people are of particular interest in the context of this article. Economically, agriculture was seen as the major risk minimisation strategy in the light of ever-decreasing options of other economic activities, be they 'modern' or 'traditional'. Statements like "[the garden yields] keep people from starvation"[31] show the gardens' important role as food- and income-generating means. Furthermore, those families who are able to yield sufficient crops from their fields are responsible for members of their extended families, thus providing some kind of insurance. In addition, in the case of an especially good harvest, even a little cash income can be obtained through the sale of crops; this was mentioned by many informants as one means to pay school fees for the children or, sometimes, clothes. Of course, these are usually only meagre incomes, especially due to the lack of cattle, which could make ploughing much more effective. In 1998, only a few Khwe families were in the possession of cattle. After the outbreak of Contagious Bovine Pleuropneumonia (CBPP) in northern Botswana in 1996, many families in West Caprivi were also forced to have their cattle slaughtered without any compensation by the government (The Namibian,

---

[30] With the exception of the village of Omega, where the regional head office of the Ministry of Resettlement and Rehabilitation is located and some sort of co-existence of the two systems of land allocation seemed to be in practice.

[31] Field notes 02.02.1998.

08.02.1999). According to Chief George[32], only Khwe families were affected by the slaughtering; others, like Mbukushu and Mafwe, had a stronger 'lobby' and were able to save their cattle. It is neither possible nor important to judge whether this impression holds true or not, more interesting is the fact that it illustrates the deep mistrust of the Khwe towards neighbouring ethnic groups and particularly the national government.

The second aspect is more symbolic. Working on the land was described as a sort of "cultural heritage", especially by elder community members. Many times the fact was stressed that the Khwe learned agricultural practices from their parents and grandparents, *not* from neighbouring Bantu groups, and certainly *not* from the Mbukushu. Working on the land with one's own hands and making it produce food gave a "deep meaning" to the land, and at the same time was perceived as something that made the land belong to the person who worked on it[33]. By laying such emphasis on agriculture as something inherent to Khwe culture and tradition, the community simultaneously expressed some sort of historical and economic independence from their worst rival on the local political scene, the Mbukushu.

During the interviews, the most violently discussed topic was the indeterminate status of the land[34]. Working on, and thus investing a lot of energy, in the land without knowing when the government, one of its ministries or the Mbukushu chief might next come to lay claims on it, was perceived as extremely dissatisfying.

Need for Transition

On the previous pages, I outlined those economic strategies practised by the Khwe that are closely related to the use of land and natural resources. Although, as mentioned above, these were never the only means of survival for the Khwe, a strong involvement in – and thus, dependence on – the monetary system only occurred when the South African administration 'discovered' the Khwe as a potential labour force for work on farms and in the South African gold mines.

---

[32] Field notes 03.02.1998; Kipi George, pers. com.
[33] Field notes 31.01.1998.
[34] Strangely, again, this discussion was not connected with the implementation of the Rehabilitation and Settlement Programme.

It has been shown that, through political changes, the Khwe's main options for cash income, be it labour migration or military employment, had definitely come to an end with the withdrawal of South Africa's military forces in 1990. As, with Independence, the new Namibian government recognised the tragic economic and social conditions of most San communities, they became one of the main targets of resettlement schemes, aimed at opening up access to land to the many landless groups in Namibia. These measures, however, where not without constraints, as they often disregarded the socio-economic realities of San communities (cf. Gordon 1995:7). In the case of West Caprivi, the resettlement scheme did not take the difficult ecological conditions such as the extreme unpredictability of rainfall into consideration (Mendelsohn and Roberts 1998), nor the variability of Khwe economic strategies. Agriculture, though an important strategy in Khwe economy during the last decades, was never the only one. Any programme for resettlement and "sedentarisation" in the area should therefore be designed as flexible, leaving options for the participants to employ supplementary strategies. The intricacy of the West Caprivi situation is acknowledged in the final evaluation report of the Bushmen Ex-Servicemen and Dependents Rehabilitation and Settlement Programme. Admitting that the project has partly neglected the *communal* aspects of natural resource management such as gathering bush crops and utilisation of grazing areas and forests (ELCIN/NORAD 1994:31), the authors strongly recommend that: "[...] in future, Bushmen residential and resource utilisation practices be more seriously taken into consideration when planning for and designing resettlement schemes, agricultural lot demarcations and physical layouts [...]" (ibid.).

Considering the severe lack in infrastructure and, consequently, in job opportunities, in West Caprivi, it becomes quite clear that many Khwe are eager to participate in recently established projects aimed at improving the region. Many of these projects follow a participatory approach in nature conservation and thereby try to combine environmental issues with the Khwe's struggle for the recognition of land rights and new ways of creating jobs in the impoverished region of West Caprivi.

Visions of Land Rights: New Strategies of Land Tenure in West Caprivi

The picture portrayed above of Khwe economic history shows how spatial and economic flexibility has been the Khwe's main strategy to survive in an ever-changing ecological, political and social environment. However, this flexibility has been increasingly limited through massive intervention of external forces, both colonial and post-colonial governments, as well as neighbouring ethnic groups competing for access to land and resources. It is obvious that the security of land rights and the stability of internal authority structures are and will increasingly be decisive for the socio-economic development of the region of West Caprivi. To obtain this security and stability, the Khwe have employed alternative strategies since the 1990s, including the new political, economic and legal frameworks of independent Namibia. At the root of these strategies lies identity: the Khwe's ambition to represent themselves as a cohesive and thus distinct ethnic group, to strengthen Khwe self-esteem and to claim legitimacy as an indigenous people in the national, regional and global discourse.

Dissociation

> "Did the Mbukushu give birth to us like they gave to themselves?"

This exclamation made by an elder woman of the Mutc'iku community[35] as an answer to my question why the Khwe feel so vehemently threatened by Mbukushu in their struggle for land rights and oppose any in-migration of Mbukushu on their land, provoked a lively discussion on the membership in the Khwe community. In the course of this discussion, it became clear that certain rights, and especially the rights of access to land and natural resources, were inseparably connected with membership in the Khwe group. The primary marker of this group membership was the usage of Khwedam as mother tongue. The question "what makes a person a Khwe?" was unanimously answered with "he or she must be born as a Khwe and speak Khwedam as his/her mother language" or the like[36]. "Born as a Khwe" included that at least one parent had to be Khwe, and, above all, that the person had to be raised in Khwe traditions. Tradition is quite an abstract category and was as such used by the community members in connection with various aspects of their culture and history. I will deal with the different facets of Khwe tradition further below. By means of examples, the informants tried to give this category meaning. Besides the use of Khwedam, certain aspects of economy, i.e., hunting with bow and arrow, gathering of bush crops and typical preparations of food and medicine, as well as participating in particular rituals and feasts were mentioned as markers of Khwe tradition. None of those examples was further specified during the interviews. It became obvious that, to members of the Khwe community, the

---

[35] Field notes 31.01.1998.
[36] Field notes 31.01.1998, 02. and 03.02.1998.

importance of tradition was not to be found in their *content*, but rather in the *difference* between the Khwe ways of doing things and those of other peoples, especially and most often mentioned, the Mbukushu.

These perceived differences deserve closer attention. De facto, the Mbukushu way of life is not so much different from that of the Khwe. Khwe-Mbukushu relationships have a long history and are marked by mutual dependence. Both societies share a semi-sedentary lifestyle, many Mbukushu gather bush crops to supplement their earnings in agriculture, and even cross-cultural marriages are quite frequent (Köhler 1989:395). I suggest that stressing the difference in tradition and lifestyle on the part of the Khwe serves as a manifestation of their own identity in contrast to the group they perceive as the most threatening to their survival and well being. As a matter of fact, it is the Mbukushu who strongly deny something such as a distinct Khwe identity, but rather present the Khwe as a Mbukushu "sub-group", subordinate to the Mbukushu Traditional Authority.

Revitalisation of Traditions

In the introduction to the second volume of "Die Welt der Kxoé-Buschleute im südlichen Afrika"[37], Köhler acknowledges that his field research among the Khwe was funded by various institutions "[...] which were open-minded towards the task of the documentation of a dying people and its traditional ancient culture"[38] (Köhler 1991:XXV, also see Brenzinger 1998:321). However, the above-mentioned developments within the Khwe community show quite a different situation. The meaning of language in this context has been described above. Brenzinger (1998:321), in his socio-linguistic study of the use of Khwedam in West Caprivi, comes to the conclusion that "Kxoedam, however, is not a dying language [...] there is even some evidence to the very contrary." Similar to my own findings, he further stresses the meaning of the mother tongue as an important issue of group membership: "'He/she is a Kxoe' means therefore that the person's mother tongue is Kxoedam" (ibid.:323). According to many elder Khwe, language is historically important, and points towards a common Khwe tradition. The fact was stressed that many places in West Caprivi have Khwedam place names that are still used today and thus prove that the area

---

[37] *The World of the Kxoé-Bushpeople in Southern Africa* (Köhler 1991:XXV).

[38] "[...] die der Aufgabe der Dokumentation eines aussterbenden Volkes und seiner traditionellen alten Kultur aufgeschlossen gegenüberstanden" (Köhler 1991:XXV).

is Khwe "ancestral land"[39]. Brenzinger states that "members of the Kxoe community in West Caprivi constantly stress the use of their own language and their own terms in contexts of daily life. They complain, for example, about the use of non-Kxoedam names for places in West Caprivi, such as Buffalo, Chetto, Omega III, Mashambo etc. and claim that their own names should be used instead [...]" (Brenzinger 1998:330). Whereas Köhler, during his thirty years of research in West Caprivi, found that many Khwe learned and used Thimbukushu[40], a development quite to the contrary can be said to exist today. "Kxoedam is the language dominantly used in West Caprivi and it is employed as a lingua franca. [...] Kxoedam, according to these findings is definitely not a receding language" (Brenzinger 1998:335).

A brief look at game hunting offers a second example of how Khwe use a feature of everyday life as a common cultural marker. I have mentioned before that, currently, hunting has almost entirely lost its economic importance, given the diminishing presence of game in West Caprivi and the region's status as a game reserve, which makes every hunting activity illegal. Although many Kxoe still 'poach' smaller animals such as rabbits or tortoises[41] (traditionally more a gathering activity of Khwe women), hunting as economic strategy has diminished considerably. This is not the case, however, with regard to its significance as a common tradition. Unanimously, members of all communities emphasised hunting with bow and arrow as one of the prime markers of Khwe culture that reveals a common Khwe history[42]. Thus, game hunting today is an important example of the fact that "the cultural life of the Khwe is still very much based on the cultural traditions of the past generations"[43]. In a similar context involving Botswana Basarwa (San), Taylor (2001:157-158) suggests "that hunting and gathering is important in understanding Basarwa identities, not because Basarwa represent leftovers of a prehistoric way of life, but because contemporary contexts make 'hunting and gathering' an important label of self-designation by Basarwa in certain contexts. In other words, the salience of hunting and gathering today is more as a *symbol* that carries meaning to both Basarwa and their neighbours [...] especially considering experiences of dispossession and alienation from land and wildlife."

---

[39] Field notes 31.01.1998; 02. and 03.02.1998.

[40] This was true especially during the times when men of both groups worked as migrant labourers at Witwatersrand (Köhler 1997:12).

[41] Axel Thoma and Magdalena Brörmann, pers. com.

[42] Field notes 31.01.1998; 02. and 03.02.1998.

[43] Field notes 02.02.1998.

'New' Traditional Authorities

> Our problems regarding land issues are manifold. On the one
> hand we might be forced by the Namibian government to leave
> part of our ancestral land and on the other hand an attempt to
> undermine my position as chief of the Kxoe might lead to the
> complete loss of the Kxoe's ancestral land (George 1997a:2).[44]

When asked about Khwe political organisation, informants stated that
there was a long tradition of Khwe political leadership in West Caprivi. This
structure was, however (with one exception), not specified in regards to
which persons held which political positions in the past. The exception was
Martin Ndumba, uncle of the late Chief Kipi George, who became chief in
1953 and held the position until his death in 1989 (George, Affidavit
1997b:§63). According to Köhler (1989:515), Ndumba was *foreman* of the
Mutc'iku community, appointed by the Mbukushu chief. The Khwe would
have vehemently opposed this, as during the interviews they constantly
referred to Ndumba as chief, and furthermore, as their most important and
best remembered political leader of the past.[45] In one of the oral texts Köhler
recorded between 1977 and 1980, Ndumba was referred to as "T//axa"
(ibid.:514), which more closely matches the English *chief*. This example
clearly shows that the question of indigenous political authority is a rather
sensitive one, and dependent on one's viewpoint. Nevertheless, community
members stressed the fact that Khwe political leaders were at no time
appointed by non-Khwe such as Mbukushu chiefs or by the South African
administration before Namibia's independence. In 1998, Kipi George was
regarded chief of the Khwe by the community,[46] and, when asked,
community members were able to name the acting members of the Khwe
Traditional Authority of their village (i.e., headmen and councillors) at the
time, as well as their duties within the community. Whereas the headmen's
duties lay in dealing with minor crimes such as theft, etc., and the
distribution of land, the main duty held by the chief was representing the

---

[44] Quotation from a speech given by Chief George in front of the United Nations
Working Group on Indigenous Populations (UNWIP) in Geneva, 1997, where he
participated as WIMSA chairperson in the 15th UNWGIP session on "Land and
environment in relation to indigenous people" (WIMSA 1998:14).

[45] Field notes 02.02.1998.

[46] This could be concluded from the statements made during interviews and
became even more obvious during informal meetings and encounters, when
Chief George was treated with great respect both by community members and by
San visitors from Tsumkwe District West.

community. Supported by his councillors, the chief functioned as a mediator between the national government and the local community, conveying information, claims made by the Khwe community and the respective reactions of ministries and the like back and forth between both parties. In 1998, the Khwe had put high hopes in their chief – with special regard to their land claims – as Kipi George not only represented their community, but had already acted as representative of all Southern African San on the international stage.

The Khwe's struggle for the recognition of their political authority clearly shows the significance of the whole issue of indigenous political leadership in Namibia today. Namibia's rural population, ethnically and economically heterogeneous as it may be, is increasingly dependent on access to communal land. This access is based – in contrast to the official rejection of former Apartheid structures – on ethnic group membership, as local traditional authorities are in the position to grant or deny land (use) rights. This makes the situation particularly troublesome for the San communities in Namibia. In contrast to most Bantu communities in the country, they have been (historically) and still are denied autonomy as ethnic groups and thus an autonomous political structure. Whereas Herero or Ovambo receive recognition as ethnic entities, San are still artificially homogenised and today fight vehemently for recognition as Hai‖om, Jul'hoansi, !Xun or Khwe. In the case of the Khwe, this situation was resolved in the subordination of the Khwe under Chief Erwin Munika Mbambo, recognised political leader of the Mbukushu, who successfully claimed his superiority over the Khwe, whom he considered his subjects.[47]

It comes evident that the struggle for the recognition of traditional authority is closely connected with the struggle for land rights (see also Hitchcock and Murphree n.d.:4). As long as traditional authorities in Namibia hold the monopoly for the distribution of communal lands, this situation will remain unchanged.

---

[47] The national position in this question is revealed in the fact that Kipi George, who formerly received payment as chief by the Namibian government, had his payment reduced to that of a "headman" after Chief Mbambo announced that he himself was chief of all inhabitants of West Caprivi (George, Affidavit 1997b:§71). An appeal to the Namibian High Court to receive official recognition of the Khwe Traditional Authority is currently being prepared by the LAC. For more information on the issue of traditional authority in West Caprivi and the consequences for the Khwe community see Boden (this volume).

When, in 1998, the Namibian government officially recognised the leaders of 31 "traditional communities"[48] and put them into quite influential political positions by making them members of the Council of Traditional Leaders, none of the six San chief designates were recognised, while the Mbukushu Traditional Authority received recognition (WIMSA 1999:13; Republic of Namibia, Government Gazette No. 1828 of March 31, 1998). For the Khwe, this means that to the present day, the Namibian government negotiates most questions of land distribution with the Mbukushu and is still able to leave Khwe land claims aside. This has undoubtedly contributed considerably to the Khwe's deepening mistrust towards both the national government and the neighbouring Mbukushu in political matters.[49]

I suggest that the Khwe's struggle for the recognition of their political authority be looked at from two perspectives: First, it serves as an internally stabilising factor for the Khwe community, ultimately enhancing the communal spirit of all Khwe, especially those residing in West Caprivi. On this level, traditional authority functions – as does the use of Khwedam in daily life and the stressing of common traditions within the community – as another element of Khwe 'cultural identity', and is used in the same way to dissociate from other ethnic groups. Secondly, viewed on the national level, the constitution of an autonomous political structure is the crucial element to secure the Khwe a say in the matter of communal politics, and thus in accomplishing land claims in West Caprivi.

Environment, Tourism and Identity

Taylor (2001:157) shows the salience of contemporary natural resource management carried out by Basarwa in northern Botswana in their attempt to

---

48 "Traditional community", as defined in the Traditional Authorities Act 17 of 1995, is "an indigenous, homogenous, endogamous social grouping of persons comprising families deriving from exogamous clans which share a common ancestry, language, cultural heritage, customs and traditions, recognises a common traditional authority and inhabits a common communal area; and includes the members of that community residing outside the common communal area" (as cited in WIMSA 1999:13).

49 As a result of an initiative of the San traditional leaders and WIMSA, later that same year an improvement of the situation could be reached when the !Kung and Jul'hoan traditional authorities of Tsumkwe Districts West and East received official recognition as members of the Council of Traditional Leaders (WIMSA 1999:14; Government Gazette No. 307 of 1998). For the Khwe Traditional Authority, however, conditions have remained unchanged.

achieve land rights and access to natural resources. He argues that, by participating in a programme of Community-Based Natural Resource Management (CBNRM), Botswana Basarwa try to "reverse the trend of alienation from land, wildlife and natural resources" and thereby places "expressions of identity by Basarwa within the wider context of debates over CBNRM [...]" (ibid.). The argument applies to the situation of Khwe in Western Caprivi as well. I have mentioned above that, by utilising the habit of hunting and gathering not merely as an economic strategy, but, recently, more as an expression of Khwe culture and tradition, the Khwe community reinforces a salient marker of ethnic identity. By doing so, the Khwe stress their attachment to the land and natural resources in West Caprivi, and therefore express a *moral* claim on this land and the resources thereon[50].

Since 1992, the Khwe have begun to engage in a number of CBNRM projects, including an eco-tourism project. From the start, this engagement was appreciated and promoted by the Ministry of Wildlife, Conservation and Tourism, which arranged for sponsorship of a CBNRM programme in West Caprivi through the WWF-US. Aiming at integrating the Khwe into nature conservation, the goals of the programme were: "(1) to build up the region's natural resource base, (2) to strengthen the capacity of local communities to manage and conserve natural resources, and (3) to facilitate the return of social and economic benefits from natural resources to local communities" (Hitchcock and Murphree n.d.:2)[51]. At the same time, a programme for community game guards (CGGs) and community resource monitors (CRMs) was established, which functions both as a measure for nature conservation and a source of cash income for the participating individuals.[52] These jobs as CCGs and CRMs were oriented towards the 'traditional' gender-based division of labour: men were employed as game guards, involved in matters concerning the region's wildlife, and women worked as resource monitors, surveying the availability of bush crops, teaching the plant classifications to community members and offering alternatives to certain plants in case of shortages. The CRMs especially functioned as mediators between the Khwe community and foreign eco-activists working in the region (Hitchcock and

---

[50]   Taylor (2001:165) finds a similar situation in northern Botswana: "[...] the moral economy that Basarwa vocalise is more than an appeal to customary rights of tenure, but a very identity that is based largely on the use of these resources."

[51]   For the more general aims of CBNRM also see Hohmann, this volume.

[52]   In 1997, 24 CGGs were employed on a full-time basis and 18 CRMs worked part-time within the programme. Except for three Vasekele men working as CGGs, all employees were Khwe (Hitchcock and Murphree, n.d.:2-3).

Murphree, n.d.:2-3). In addition to integrating the local population into environmental issues, the CBNRM programme intended to mitigate the many conflicts between the interests of the local population on the one hand and those of nature conservation on the other; conflicts that in the past have mostly been at the cost of the community living in a nature conservation area. As but one example, the severe damage to bush crops, gardens and even human lives that elephants have caused in West Caprivi shall be mentioned here. In the past, the Khwe have had no legal rights to prevent these damages due to the region's status as a game park and the total prohibition of hunting within its borders.

From the Khwe's point of view, the crucial significance of the CBNRM programme lies in its potential for the social and economic development of their environment. The programme offers opportunities for active participation in developing land-use concepts and thus for literally taking the land and the natural resources in West Caprivi into possession[53]. Furthermore, in the Khwe's perception, the income-generating capacity of CBNRM contributes considerably to the economic upgrading of the poverty-stricken region. This latter aspect is true particularly for the tourism project, which aimed at founding a community-based campsite on the banks of the Okavango River. The N‖goavaca campsite is[54] situated near the local tourist attraction of Popa Falls, a tiny waterfall in the Okavango, close to the Bagani Bridge and not far from the Trans-Caprivi Highway, a route highly frequented by tourists travelling from Namibia to Botswana, Zimbabwe or Zambia. Whereas finances for the building of the campsite, training of future employees in tourism, management, bookkeeping, etc., were supplied by international donors, the major aim of the project was for it ultimately to be self-sustainable. Even shortly after the opening of the campsite in 1997, IRDNC Co-director Garth Owen-Smith estimated this goal as quite realistic in the near future (Owen-Smith, Affidavit 1997:§9-28) – thus reinforcing the Khwe's hopes concerning the project – and stated that

---

[53] In the course of the CBNRM programme, with the assistance from IRDNC, the Khwe community tried to establish a conservancy in parts of West Caprivi. Due to the region's status as a game reserve, this plan proved impossible. For details on the subject of conservancies within San communities, see Hohmann (this volume).

[54] The description of the campsite is given here in present tense, for the site itself is still existent. Unfortunately, due to the political and military events since late 1998 (see Boden, this volume), the site is currently deserted and out of use.

It is a highly significant step forward in social empowerment for
a marginalised community. This small enterprise is a key factor
in bridging an underdeveloped community into the modern
commercial world of developing Africa (ibid.:§10)[55].

The massive conflict over land rights in West Caprivi that was fought
with vehemence between the Khwe, the Mbukushu and the Namibian
government in 1997/98, had been triggered by a government decision in late
1996 to force the Khwe community to vacate the N‖goavaca campsite. This
was justified by government plans to expand a rehabilitation camp for
prisoners that had been built close to the campsite in 1995, without ever
asking permission or even the acceptance of the Khwe Traditional Authority
(see Hitchcock and Murphree n.d.:4). To worsen the situation, consultations
had taken place, but between government officials and Erwin Mbambo, the
Mbukushu chief, who had given his permission for the extension of the
prison camp; this disregard of the Khwe's land claims and their traditional
authority considerably sharpened the Khwe's mistrust of their national
government. They perceived their very survival to be at stake, including
"employment opportunities; natural resources; access to the Okavango
River; income from tourism; [and] part of their land" and feared that they
would "thus lose the essential base for any further development" (George
1997a:2). To prevent this worst-case scenario, the Khwe Traditional
Authority, assisted by the Legal Assistance Centre (LAC) and WIMSA,
made an application to the Namibian High Court in 1997 to claim Khwe
supremacy over the land in West Caprivi and at the same time official
recognition of the Khwe Traditional Authority (Legal Assistance Centre
1997). Although the case was never heard in front of the court, an out-of-
court agreement was reached and the government withdrew the order to
vacate the campsite in 1999, no doubt responding to the considerable
pressure exerted by the NGOs assisting the Khwe community.

However, conflicts like the above-mentioned one show the importance of
guaranteed land rights for development in marginalised regions. Insecurity is
de-motivating for individuals and the community, and thus hinders any
effective cooperation between development organisations with the local
population. If the land on which a promising project has been started might
have to be vacated at any time, why start at all? Furthermore, and more

---

[55] All above-mentioned information on N‖goavaca campsite is drawn from the
affidavits of IRDNC Co-director Garth Owen-Smith and the LIFE (Living in a
Finite Environment) Programme Chief of Party Larrye Chris Weaver. Both
papers were given to me by the Legal Assistance Centre (LAC).

critically, such government actions probably deepen the gap between the state and local populations, as Kipi George lucidly illustrated in his speech before the Working Group on Indigenous Populations in Geneva:

> If both the Mbukush [sic!] chief and the Namibian government succeed with their plans [to subordinate the Khwe under Mbukushu rule and have N‖goavaca campsite vacated] the already poor Kxoe community will be even further marginalized and deprived of development opportunities. We have lost trust in the Namibian government, as it seems that it only pays lip service when it comes to rights for minorities. It will be my responsibility to prevent this from happening to the Kxoe community. The solidarity of other indigenous people and the international community at large is imperative" (George 1997a:2).

Conclusion: New Strategies against a bleak future?

This article has shown that security of land rights is of crucial importance for the survival of the Khwe community in West Caprivi. The entire region suffers from a massive lack in infrastructure, and thus offers extremely meagre employment opportunities for its inhabitants. At the same time, due to a great extent to the political and military intervention by colonial administrations as well as the current government, neither agriculture nor foraging activities can supply the Khwe with enough earnings to secure their own subsistence without being dependent on food aid from the national government or international donors.

In this situation of uncertainty, efforts by the Namibian government as well as the Mbukushu Traditional Authority to claim parts of West Caprivi in order to accomplish their own ends, represent a hazard for the Khwe's economic and social survival. Recent efforts by the Khwe community to achieve an economic upgrading of their land by actively participating in new concepts and projects in nature conservation are also put to threat. Security of land rights is the major precondition to make these endeavours, as well as the conservation projects themselves, successful and sustainable over the long term.

Since the beginning of the 1990s, the Khwe have started applying alternative strategies to strengthen their position on the national and international stage. The formation of ethnic identity is salient in this process. Besides an emphasis on ethnic identity as *Khwe*, which serves for strengthening the community's internal stability, Chief George's statement cited above, spoken in front of an international body concerned with the matters of indigenous peoples in a global setting, demonstrates that the Khwe have begun to search for new allies in their struggle. On the national level, this process of increasing ethnic identity seems contradictory at first: on the one hand, enforced emphasis on membership in the Khwe community serves as a means for dissociation from other ethnic groups in Namibia. This strategy can, on the other hand, also be regarded as a way of associating with a society that, after one decade of independence, is still structured along ethnic lines. Acceptance of certain aspects and rules of the Namibian society, such as, e.g., the conditions of the Traditional Authorities Act, require the dissociation from other parts of it in the local setting. At the same time, this opens up the way for the Khwe to participate in the wider community of *all San* in Southern Africa[56], and thus get involved in the global discourse on indigenous peoples.

During the time of my field research in February 1998, the Khwe were active participants in this process of 'indigenous globalisation'. Chief George, as representative of the community, not only spoke excellent English, but was also well trained in conversation with national and international organisations, cognisant of the 'vocabulary' used both by anthropologists and donor agencies and how to use it in his endeavours for the community's well-being. Besides reinforcing ethnic identity as *Khwe* on the community level, as shown above, the Khwe were engaged in the formation of a regional ethnic identity as *San* and, furthermore, on the global level as *indigenous people*. I suggest that this active self-labelling, oscillating according to changing contexts, is employed as a strategy of dissociation from a long history of external classification. Whereas in the past, anthropologists, ethno-linguists and, not least, governments have employed labels such as "San" or "Bushmen" as etic concepts, the objects of these labels, by filling these concepts with their own (emic) meanings, use this very discourse today to accomplish their aims.

When I wrote my MA thesis in 1998, the Khwe's prospects for the future weren't that bleak at all. Community members were enthusiastic about their campsite, conservancy plans and participation in natural resource management. Chief George was a well-respected political leader within the community, and hopes were high that he would in due course be recognised

---

[56] For details on the process of local, regional and international networking and lobbying of Southern African San communities, see Hohmann, introduction to this volume.

as an official member of the Council of Traditional Leaders. Brenzinger (1998:351) presents a remarkably positive outlook for the Khwe community:

> Given the increasingly stable regional environment, it appears [...] that the Kxoe community may now be entering a phase of consolidation. In this process, there are big opportunities for the Kxoe to strengthen their cultural identity. [...] West Caprivi, with its recently established traditional authority structure, could develop into a vital centre for all the Kxoe-speaking communities.

But, once again, from late 1998 until the present, the Khwe community has found itself caught in the middle of political and military upheavals (see Boden, this volume). Many of the projects in nature conservation, as well as the N‖goavaca campsite project, have virtually come to an end. With them, the Khwe's hopes for improvements in infrastructure, employment opportunities and regional upgrading have largely been crushed. Again, officially guaranteed land rights and the acceptance of the Khwe Traditional Authority through the Namibian State could form the basis for more stability in West Caprivi. And again, flexibility seems to be the most promising strategy for the Khwe to cope with this uncertainty.

References

Barnard, Alan
1997   *Problems in the Construction of Khoisan Ethnicities.* Paper presented at the Conference on Khoisan Identities and Cultural Heritage at the University of the Western Cape. Cape Town, 12-16 July 1997.

Brenzinger, Matthias
1998   Moving to Survive: Kxoe Communities in Arid Lands. In: Schladt, Mathias (ed.). *Language, Identity, and Conceptualization Among the Khoisan.* Research in Khoisan Studies 15. Cologne: Köppe:321-357.

Brown, C.J. and B.T.D. Jones (eds.)
1994   *Results of a Socio-Ecological Survey of the West Caprivi Strip, Namibia. A Strategic Community-Based Environment and Development Plan.* Directorate of Environmental Affairs, Ministry of Wildlife, Conservation and Tourism. Namibia. Windhoek.

Fisch, Maria
1996   *Der Caprivizipfel während der deutschen Zeit 1890 – 1914.* History,
       Cultural Traditions and Innovations in Southern Africa 2. Cologne:
       Köppe.

George, Kipi
1997a *Namibian Government Deprives Kxoe Community of Rights to
       Ancestral Land.* Brief report presented to the 15th Session of the
       Working Group on Indigenous Populations. Geneva, 28 July-1
       August. Unpublished manuscript.

1997b *Affidavit.* Unpublished manuscript.

Gibbons, A.S.H.
1904   *Africa from South to North through Marotseland.* Vol. 1. London
       and New York: Routledge.

Gordon, Robert J.
1992   *The Bushman Myth. The Making of a Namibian Underclass.*
       Boulder, San Francisco, Oxford: Westview.

1995   *The Demilitarization of the Bushmen in Namibia.* Unpublished
       manuscript.

Guenther, Mathias
1996   Diversity and Flexibility: The Case of the Bushmen in Southern
       Africa. In: Kent, Susan (ed.). *Cultural Diversity Among Twentieth-
       Century Foragers. An African Perspective.* Cambridge: Cambridge
       University Press:65-86.

Hitchcock, Robert K. and Marshall W. Murphree
n.d.   *The West Caprivi Region of Namibia: Human Rights, Conservation,
       and Development.* Unpublished manuscript.

Holub, E.
1879   *Eine Culturskizze des Marutse-Mambunda-Reiches in Süd-Central-
       Afrika.* Wien: L.C.

1881   *Sieben Jahre in Süd-Afrika: Erlebnisse, Forschungen und Jagden
       1872–1879.* Bd. II. Wien.

Jansen, Ruud, Neville Pradhan and John Spencer
1994   *Bushmen Ex-Servicemen and Dependants Rehabilitation and
       Settlement Programme. West Bushmanland and Western Caprivi,
       Republic of Namibia. Evaluation, Final Report.* Windhoek:

Evangelical Lutheran Church in Namibia (ELCIN) and Royal Norwegian Embassy / NORAD.

Kent, Susan (ed.)
1996   *Cultural Diversity Among Twentieth-Century Foragers. An African Perspective.* Cambridge: Cambridge University Press.

Köhler, Oswin
1966   Tradition und Wandel bei den Kxoe-Buschmännern von Mutsiku. In: *Sociologus* 16 (2):122-140.

1986   Allgemeine und sprachliche Bemerkungen zum Feldbau nach Oraltexten der Kxoe-Buschleute. In: Rottland, Franz and Rainer Vossen (eds.). *Sprache und Geschichte in Afrika* 7 (1). Hamburg: Buske:205-265.

1989   *Die Welt der Kxoé-Buschleute im südlichen Afrika Eine Selbstdarstellung in ihrer eigenen Sprache. Vol. 1: Die Kxoé-Buschleute und ihre ethnische Umgebung.* Berlin: Reimer.

1991   *Die Welt der Kxoé-Buschleute im südlichen Afrika. Eine Selbstdarstellung in ihrer eigenen Sprache. Vol. 2: Grundlagen des Lebens.* Berlin: Reimer.

1997   *Die Welt der Kxoé-Buschleute im südlichen Afrika. Eine Selbstdarstellung in ihrer eigenen Sprache. Vol. 3: Materielle Ausrüstung: Werden und Wandel.* Berlin: Reimer.

Legal Assistance Centre
1997   *Notice of Motion submitted to the High Court of Namibia, Windhoek.* Unpublished manuscript.

Mendelsohn, John and Carole Roberts
1997   *An Environmental Profile and Atlas of Caprivi.* Windhoek: Gamsberg Macmillan.

Nyae Nyae Development Foundation
1993   *Report on the Aboriginal Saami and San Meeting in Namibia 14-28 November 1993.* Windhoek.

Owen-Smith, Garth
1997   *Affidavit* Unpublished manuscript.

Republic of Namibia / Ministry of Lands, Resettlement and Rehabilitation
n.d.   *Draft National Resettlement Policy.* Windhoek.

Republic of Namibia
1998   *Government Gazette* No. 1828 of March 31st 1998. Windhoek.

1998   *Government Gazette* No. 307 1998. Windhoek.

Republic of South Africa
1964   *Report of the Commission of Enquiry into South West African Affairs 1962-1963*. Pretoria: Government Printer.

1968   *Government Notice 19 of 1968*. Pretoria: Government Printer.

Seiner, Franz
1909a   *Die wirtschaftsgeographischen und politischen Verhältnisse des Caprivizipfels*. Berlin: Wilhelm Süsserott.

1909b   Ergebnisse einer Bereisung des Gebietes zwischen Okawango und Sambesi (Caprivi-Zipfel) in den Jahren 1905 und 1906. In: *Mitteilungen aus den deutschen Schutzgebieten* 22 (1):2-106.

1910   Die Buschmänner des Okawango- und Sambesi Gebietes der Nord-Kalahari. In: *Globus* 97 (22, 23):341-345, 358-360.

1913   Ergebnisse einer Bereisung der Omaheke 1910–1912. In: *Mitteilungen aus den deutschen Schutzgebieten* 26 (3):296-304.

Streitwolf, K.
1911   *Der Caprivizipfel*. Berlin: Wilhelm Süsserott.

Suzman, James
2001   *Regional Assessment of the Status of the San in Southern Africa. An Assessment of the San in Namibia*. Report No. 4 of 5. Windhoek: Legal Assistance Centre

Taylor, Michael
2001   Narratives of Identity and Assertions of Legitimacy: Basarwa in Northern Botswana. In: Anderson, David G. and Kazunobu Ikeya (eds.): Parks, Property and Power: Managing Hunting Practice and Identity Within State Policy Regimes. *Senri Ethnological Studies* 59. Osaka: Museum of Ethnology:157-182.

Thoma, Axel
1997   *Eine Lobby für die San. afrika süd* 1/1997:33-34.

Uys, Ian
1993   *Bushman Soldiers. Their Alpha and Omega*. Germiston: Fortress Publishers.

Vierich, Helga
1982   Adaptive Flexibility in a Multi-Ethnic Setting: The Basarwa of the Southern Kalahari. In: Leacock, Eleanor and Richard Lee (eds.). *Politics and History in Band Societies*. Cambridge et al: Cambridge University Press:213-222.

Weaver, L.C.
1997   *Affidavit*. Unpublished manuscript.

Wilhelm, J. H.
1955   *Die Hukwe*. Jahrbuch des Museums für Völkerkunde zu Leipzig XIII/1954. Leipzig.

WIMSA
1996   *Report on the San Conference Held at Gross Barmen, Namibia on 8–12 September 1996*. Windhoek: WIMSA.

1998   *Report on Activities – April 1997 to March 1998*. Windhoek: WIMSA.

2001   *The Penduka Declaration on the Standardisation of Ju and Khoe Languages*. Windhoek. Unpublished manuscript.

National Archives

A 50/67 vol. 3. Native Affairs, Strandloopers and Bushmen. July 1950 – June 1952.

A 50/67 vol. 4. Native Affairs, Strandloopers and Bushmen. July 1952 – June 1953.

A 503/1. Control: Western Caprivi Zipfel. 30.11.1943.

A 503/1. Control: Western Caprivi Zipfel: Control Of. 15.01.1944.

SWA Annual Report, 1923.

SWA Annual Report 1928.

Newspaper Articles

The Namibian 08/02/1999: *Hunger Haunts the San people*.

Star, 24/11/1982.

Eastern Province Herald, 02/02/1980.

'Caught in the Middle'
Impacts of State Decisions and Armed Conflicts on Khwe Economy and Ethnicity in West Caprivi between 1998 and 2002[1]

Gertrud Boden

Introduction

Since October 1998, the lives and prospects of the Khwe[2] people in West Caprivi have experienced some major changes. In chronological order these changes are the uncovering of the separatist movement in East Caprivi and consequent security sweeps throughout both East and West Caprivi, the cabinet decision to re-proclaim Caprivi Game Park as Bwabwata National Park, the overspill of the Angolan civil war into northeastern Namibia, and the rejection of the Khwe application for government recognition of their leadership in August 2001. These developments have made the past years a period of continued frustration for the Khwe people, who felt increasingly neglected, disregarded and misunderstood by the Namibian government and its security forces.[3]

---

[1] Thanks are due to the Deutsche Forschungsgemeinschaft (DFG), which has sponsored research within the special research unit *Arid Climate Adaptation and Cultural Innovation in Africa*. I also wish to express my gratitude to the Khwe people, who have supported my research, and to Susanne Berzborn, Michael Bollig, Matthias Brenzinger, Ute Dieckmann, Thekla Hohmann, Karine Rousset and Axel Thoma for comments on earlier versions of this article.

[2] The orthography used here is in accordance with "The Penduka Declaration on the Standardisation of Ju and Khoe Languages" by San representatives (April 2001). The name for the same group of people used by linguists before is 'Kxoé' (Köhler, e.g., 1989) or 'Kxoe' (Brenzinger, Heine, Kilian-Hatz and Schladt, in e.g., Schladt 1998).

[3] It goes without saying that the security situation has also affected the conditions for my fieldwork, which lasted from November 1998 till February 1999, July till December 1999, and October 2000 till February 2001. I first arrived in West Caprivi only after many Khwe had left because of security sweeps in October/November 1998. Due to the political tensions in the area, I decided to start my fieldwork at Mutc'iku (see map 1), the Khwe settlement furthest away

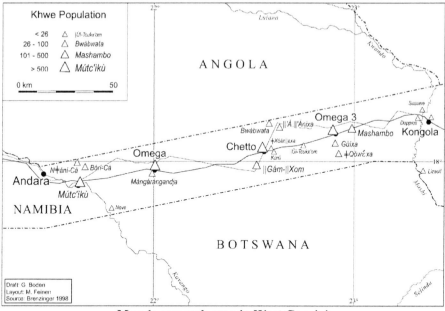

Map 1: research area in West Caprivi

The denial of government recognition of Khwe leadership implies that the Khwe people in West Caprivi, together with the land they live on, fall

from the secessionist upheaval in East Caprivi. During my first stay I only paid day-visits to Khwe villages further east, including Bwabwata, close to the Angolan border, where I planned to later extend my fieldwork. However, when I returned to West Caprivi in July 1999, I changed my mind and chose Mashambo as a second location after a number of encounters with intelligence and security forces during the course of which I was warned to stay away from the border. Mashambo emerged as a good option. Whereas the villagers of Bwabwata, with those of Omega III and many others, had left their homes in January 2000 after the overspill of the Angolan civil war, Mashambo turned out to be the most stable Khwe community in the eastern part of West Caprivi. During my last stay, I nevertheless decided not to overnight there, but went in and out from Kongola, relying on the military escort for transport. In Mutc'iku, even daytime work turned out to be impossible, as army officers advised me not to stay in the area. Thus, I had to pick up people and work with them at my home base across the Okavango River, from which I could still hear almost daily shootings and occasional mine blasts. I am thus ready to admit that assessments made here are influenced by my own feelings of insecurity as well as the lack of assurance concerning my relationship to people who themselves feel so highly embattled.

under the sovereignty of the already state-recognised Traditional Authority of their Mbukushu neighbours. This, obviously, brings the Mbukushu leadership into a much better position politically and economically than that of the Khwe.

The struggle for land rights and political recognition in independent Namibia has been on the Khwe agenda well before 1998. Orth (this volume) convincingly argues that the formation of ethnic identity[4] as 'Khwe' on the local level, 'San' on the wider regional level, and 'First People' on an international level, backed by regional and international non-governmental organisations (NGOs), is a promising political strategy in this respect. The two recent armed conflicts in the region, however, have shown the other side of the coin of Khwe ethnic distinctiveness. To be Khwe now meant to be suspicious and accused of subversive attitudes and actions against the Namibian state, and to be treated respectively by security forces. That is to say that 'visibility' as a distinct ethnic group can bring both advantages and disadvantages, depending on whether one is seeking protection and aid, or avoiding attack and victimisation (cf. James 1994).

In order to explain their current relationships, Khwe reasoning most prominently referred to their former enslavement by Mbukushu people and their employment by the South African Defence Forces (SADF) in colonial times. At the time, for the Khwe the latter meant liberation from Mbukushu oppression, protection from infringement and a 'social uplifting' (Erasmus 1997).[5] In the long run, however, it brought them under the rule of their

---

[4]   Today, it is generally agreed that the 'ethnic group' is a social construct and, therefore, subject to change. Ethnic or tribal identities have to be understood as essentially political products of specific situations, socially defined and historically determined (Fukui and Markakis 1994b). To discuss Khwe notions of their ethnic distinctiveness would open another subject matter. Yet, it can be said that such notions refer primarily to language (cf. Berzborn, this volume), subsistence and a process of discrimination or victimisation. 'The Khwe' in this article are to be understood as an interest group formed along ethnic lines in a political context that is structured in a way to promote ethnicity. The task of the article will mainly be to highlight and contextualise the notions and perceptions of this Khwe interest group, and not to give an objective account of all parties involved. It is understood that there are different interest groups also within the Khwe, e.g., concerning the candidates for the currently vacant post of the chief. Such differentiation must, however, remain the subject of another paper.

[5]   Erasmus discusses two possible reasons why the Khwe and other San let themselves become involved in the war: 'hate' and 'upliftment.' There were, however, also important economic reasons: i.e., the prohibition to hunt in a

former enemies of war, the South West Africa People's Organization (Swapo), which constitutes the ruling party in Namibia since its independence. History has caught the Khwe in the middle.[6] They are themselves victims of rebel intimidation and attacks, and, at the same time, accused of collaborating with the rebel movements. Khwe ethnic distinctiveness embodies the chance of gaining political recognition by the state, but, on the other hand, it means being the target of harassment, rights abuses and the threat of death by the same state's security forces. Khwe economic options are constrained by national and international interests in nature conservation and the competition for resources by members of other ethnic groups in the area. Development aspirations are blocked by the current conditions of insecurity[7] and, above all, by the lack of a safe legal base concerning land rights and political representation in a state that controls the allocation of resources and is felt to be less than fair by Khwe people.

After sketching the West Caprivi setting and the events therein since October 1998, the article is going to describe their impacts on Khwe economy, in terms of food security as well as of development aspirations. The catalysing effects of recent state decisions and armed conflicts to endow ethnicity will be analysed. The focus is on how Khwe people have

---

nature conservation area, the stop to migrant mine work in South Africa as borders were closed due to the militarisation of the area and an increased pressure on resources due to the in-migration of people from Angola fleeing the war there. In addition, allegations have been made that the SADF used force to persuade the San to join (Gordon 1992:186, Sharp 1994, Erasmus 1997).

[6] 'Caught in the middle' is a section title in a reader on "Ethnicity and Conflict in the Horn of Africa" edited by Fukui and Markakis (1994a), which presents case studies on ethnic groups that, like the Khwe, are worn down between the interests of more powerful allies and enemies. Two similar titles "Caught in the Crossfire" (Biesele and Hitchcock 2002) and 'Caprivians Caught Between two Fronts' (New Era, 15-18.1.2001) have been found for the Khwe situation by other authors.

[7] Up until now, the state of insecurity has blocked the implementation of the plans by the Ministry of Environment and Tourism (MET) for Bwabwata National Park. This can, however, change in the near future, as the recent death of Unita leader Jonas Savimbi on the 22nd of February 2002 and the cease-fire agreed upon on the 4th of April, contain a chance for peace in Angola, and thus also in northeastern Namibia. Information in this article only includes the period up to the end of April 2002.

experienced their relationships during the past few years and how they explain the developments by referring to history and past relations.

The West Caprivi Setting

West Caprivi is the narrow strip of land between the Okavango and Kwando Rivers that connects the heartland of Namibia and East Caprivi. The whole of Caprivi owes its affiliation with Namibian national territory to German colonial interests, which wanted a territorial connection to the German colonies in East Africa via the Zambezi River, what, however, turned out to be a hope frustrated due to the river's cataracts. Under South African administration, West Caprivi became a nature conservation area in 1963 and a military deployment zone of the SADF during the 1970s and 1980s. The SADF employed many Khwe as soldiers and trackers, and used them against the PLAN fighters of the Swapo as well as supporting the União Nacional para a Independência Total de Angola (Unita) in Angola (Uys 1993).[8]

Caprivi has experienced frequent changes in administrative responsibilities during colonial times, and even after independence, administrative boundaries have changed twice. In 1992, the border between the Okavango and Caprivi Regions was marked as 21° East, and West Caprivi considered part of the Caprivi Region. In 1998, the Okavango Region was renamed Kavango and West Caprivi was divided so that, currently, the western part falls within the Mukwe constituency of Kavango Region and the eastern part within the Kongola constituency of Caprivi Region. The border between the two administrative regions is at 22°30' East, just west of Chetto (see map 1). The latest revision of regional boundaries has been interpreted by the Khwe as a government action to split their community. It has caused frequent confusion about administrative responsibilities, and people have been sent back and forth between offices in

---

[8]   The role of the Caprivi strip during the liberation war is dealt with in Kangumu (2000). He demonstrates that, while regarded as a 'dream frustrated' by the German administration and useless by the early South African administration, its very remoteness and international borders made it a 'useful corridor' and gave it utmost strategic importance to the SADF from the 1970s and after. Zeller (2000) also points to the strategic value of Caprivi.

the regional capitals of Rundu and Katima Mulilo in order to get their business settled.[9]

West Caprivi is also at the centre of the much larger Khwe settlement area, which formerly extended north into southeastern Angola to the Luyana River and even beyond, and extends across the Botswana border into northern Ngamiland and south to the Selinda spillway (Brenzinger 1998: map on page 329). Pursuant to a sociolinguistic census carried out in 1996, the number of Khwe in West Caprivi was nearly 4,000 (Brenzinger 1998). Apart from the Khwe, several hundred !Xun and Mbukushu lived in the area, as well as small numbers of individuals of other ethnic affiliations.

During the past thirty years, the international borders on both sides of the 32 km wide strip have marked zones of refuge for politically motivated moves by Khwe people. The 1970s saw large numbers of Khwe flee the war in Angola[10] and cross the border into Namibia (Brenzinger 2000: map on page 17). Since October 1998, Namibian Khwe have sought refuge in neighbouring Botswana in order to escape from armed conflicts in which their home country was engaged. These conflicts are the East Caprivi secessionist rebellion and Namibia's commitment in Angola's civil war. In both conflicts, the Khwe were suspected of collaborating with enemies of the Namibian state: the Caprivi Liberation Army (CLA) and Unita.

But even without armed conflicts, the Khwe's stand is more difficult than that of other San in Namibia.[11] Not only is West Caprivi a nature

---

[9]   Field notes 3.12.1998; letter by the Swapo Coordinator in Mutc'iku, West Caprivi and the Treasurer of the West Caprivi Committee to the Permanent Secretary of the National Planning Commission, 3.5.2001.

[10]   !Xun people were also among the San people who fled southeastern Angola and were employed by the SADF. Angolan Khwe and !Xun had also previously been engaged as soldiers and trackers by the Portuguese colonial army (Uys 1993). Many of the Angolan !Xun and Khwe have been resettled to South Africa when Namibia became independent. Some !Xun later moved to Tsumkwe district (Brenzinger 2000). The !Xun do not make a claim for land rights in West Caprivi and are, simply due to their small number, much less visible as an ethnic group than the Khwe in the local context, although also suspected of Unita collaboration.

[11]   The view that the Khwe are even worse off than other San groups in the country is also held in the recent 'Regional Assessment of the Status of the San in Namibia' (Suzman 2001: 61) and in the public media. Labels such as 'most neglected,' 'most marginalized,' 'disadvantaged,' 'poverty stricken,' 'politically

conservation area, but the Mbukushu chief also lays claim of Mbukushu sovereignty[12] over the Khwe and the area they live in. Relations between the Khwe and Mbukushu have been manifold since the in-migration of the latter's ancestors into the Khwe settlement area during the 19th century. These relationships have ranged from the oppression and enslavement of Khwe by Mbukushu people, from the economic dependency of Khwe families on Mbukushu, to family relations, friendship, and mutual help. Within the current political arena, however, in which representation and power are crucial for gaining land rights and other state-regulated resources, Khwe ethnic distinctiveness has become a matter of contest in itself. Interest groups form along ethnic lines and the shared history is referred to by both sides to substantiate arguments. The Khwe have brought forward their identity as first people and regard their subordination under the Mbukushu Traditional Authority as an unlawful continuation of enslavement by the members of this ethnic group in the past. From the former subordination of the Khwe the Mbukushu chief draws his own right to rule Khwe people and land.

Political self-determination and land rights have come to be regarded as the most important cornerstones for emancipation and development of indigenous minorities worldwide (e.g., Hitchcock 1996). Namibian legislation of prime importance concerning these issues comes along as the Traditional Authority Act 17 of 1995, and the Nature Conservation Amendment Act 5 of 1996, respectively. According to the first, recognised Traditional Authorities will become members of the Council of Traditional Leaders, advise the President on land matters and are the legal bodies to be addressed by ministries and entrepreneurs for planned activities in the area under control of a Traditional Authority. The latter act enables communities in communal areas to establish so-called conservancies, within the boundaries of which they are entitled to use and decide upon natural resources, especially wildlife. Revenues of wildlife tourism and trophy hunting are the only chance for substantial economic development in an area that is underdeveloped in economic terms like West Caprivi. A conservancy

---

vulnerable' or 'embattled' are regularly added to characterise Khwe people in newspaper reports (The Namibian, 1998–2001).

[12] Actually, the Mafwe chief also claims sovereignty over West Caprivi and has appointed a Khwe headman (Field notes 4.8.1999; Brenzinger 1998: 343). The Mafwe, commonly known as supporters of the opposition party DTA, however, do not have as powerful allies in the Namibian government as does the Mbukushu chief.

application for West Caprivi was prepared as early as 1996. The community could, however, not go further ahead "[...] as the legislation making provision for communal area conservancies expressly excludes proclaimed game parks or nature reserves from being included in or being part of a conservancy".[13] Thus the inhabitants of West Caprivi had to wait for a government decision on the status of the land.

In applying for a conservancy and for their leadership to be granted official recognition by the state, the Khwe were in the company with a number of other San groups in Namibia,[14] and hoping for a better future based on these legal devices. They are assisted in their efforts mainly by two non-governmental organisations: Integrated Rural Development and Nature Conservation (IRDNC) and Working Group of Indigenous Minorities in Southern Africa (WIMSA). IRDNC has dedicated itself to the implementation of Community Based Natural Resource Management (CBNRM), and one of its main objectives is to assist communities in setting up conservancies (MET 2001). WIMSA is mainly engaged in political matters of self-government, legal and human rights, and networking.[15] WIMSA has supported the Khwe in applying for their Traditional Authority to gain official government recognition.[16] Both NGOs' programmes are in accordance with the increasingly convergent world agenda on indigenous people's rights (Biesele and Hitchcock 2000) and nature conservation.

As far as land rights and representative bodies are concerned, Namibian legislation is, however, not consistent with respect to the underlying concept of how a community is defined (cf. Piek 1998). Whereas the conservancy regulations refer to local communities independent of their ethnic affiliation, literally "a group of persons, resident on a demarcated piece of communal land," the Traditional Authority Act refers to ethnic groups and their leadership organisation. According to the act, traditional authorities are

---

[13] Letter by MET Permanent Secretary U. Hiveluah to Chief Kipi George, 2.12.1996.

[14] Only two San Traditional Authorities have been recognised so far: the Jul'hoan Traditional Authority in Tsumkwe East and the !Kung Traditional Authority in Tsumkwe West (Government Gazette No. 307 of 1998). The Nyae Nyae Conservancy in Tsumkwe East is the only conservancy established by San people. It was registered in February 1998 with 752 members (MET 2001).

[15] www.san.org.za/wimsa/wimsabody.htm.

[16] Support also came from the Centre of Applied Social Sciences (CASS), and for litigation procedures the Khwe have been represented by the Legal Assistance Centre (LAC), a Namibian human rights organisation.

regarded as the leaders of a 'traditional community,' defined as "[...] an indigenous homogenous, endogamous social grouping [...] [that share] a common ancestry, language, cultural heritage, customs and traditions, recognise a common traditional authority, inhabit a common communal area [...] [and include] the members of that community residing outside the communal area." Both acts, thus, require different strategies. Whereas the Khwe in West Caprivi were advised to work together with local Mbukushu by IRDNC in order to launch a conservancy application, they were advised by WIMSA to stress their exclusive rights to reside in West Caprivi, as well as their distinctiveness as a cultural group. Both strategies, though inconsistent to a certain degree, are, however, in accordance with the requests of the particular part of Namibian legislation[17] and make sense in order to attain the aims of the respective agenda.

The specific West Caprivi setting means that the conditions for the Khwe's economic and political development are different from those of other San communities in the country, e.g., the Jul'hoansi in the Nyae Nyae area, who lately have been said to take an "exemplary role" with regard to other San in the country (Biesele and Hitchcock 2000:307). The Jul'hoansi have not only got much more academic attention than other San, a fact often lamented in the Kalahari debate (e.g., Wilmsen 1989), but they have also received non-governmental support as early as the 1980s. At the time when the Jul'hoansi started to re-establish themselves on their home territories (n!oresi) after a period of population concentration around the regional centre and army base at Tsumkwe (Marshall 1991, Biesele 1993), the West Caprivi strip was still a military zone with restricted movements of people; inhabitants concentrated in and around the army bases at Buffalo, Omega, Doppies and Tcifume; and many Khwe employed by the South African Defence Forces. It is likely to not be by accident that, among the Namibian San, those with the most developed land rights and political organisation are also those who have received the most academic attention, the longest non-

---

[17] Another legal inconsistency that has been pointed out by different authors (e.g., Hitchcock 2000), but is not dealt with here, arises from West Caprivi's nature conservation status and concurrent settlement. Formally, the area falls under the jurisdiction of the Ministry of Environment and Tourism, but de facto other ministries have started projects or rearranged settlement in West Caprivi. These are the Ministries of Lands, Resettlement and Rehabilitation, of Agriculture, Water and Rural Development, of Defense, and of Prisons and Correctional Services. For a conflict arising from the activities of the latter compare Orth (this volume).

governmental support, and were allocated a homeland by the apartheid regime.

Chronicle of Events

This is not the place to detail the background of the Caprivi secessionist movement,[18] which was mainly supported by Mafwe people of East Caprivi and led by Mishake Muyongo, a member of the Mafwe royal family and former president of the opposition party Democratic Turnhallen Alliance (DTA). When a rally of armed activists of the CLA was discovered in Mudumu National Park in October 1998, searches and interrogations by Namibian Defense Force (NDF) soldiers were also carried out in Khwe villages in West Caprivi. On the 26th of October, the Khwe Chief Kipi George briefed a newspaper that "in recent days Namibian Defense Force soldiers, armed with AK 47 assault rifles and other automatic firearms, had been engaged in door-to-door searches, asking villagers to show them a clandestine military camp believed to be set up by pro-secessionists."[19] According to the newspaper report, the villagers were also "grilled on their alleged cooperation with Unita elements who have been crossing into the western Caprivi in recent weeks to barter ill-gotten game meat for mealie meal and other food stuffs." The soldiers came at nighttime and asked for identity documents. They warned the villagers that they better leave the place.[20]

The first Khwe to seek refuge in Botswana were 50 inhabitants of ǂQowexa (see map 1), a village close to the Botswana border, followed by most of the more than 600 villagers of Omega III. People were frightened to the degree that they left behind their livestock, hiding only pots and other household equipment in holes hastily dug in the ground. One of the only twelve villagers who stayed behind in Omega III reported in November 1998 that soldiers had shot over the heads of people and threatened to come back the next day in order to kill.[21]

The villages of Guixa and ǂQowexa were left completely abandoned; some of the villagers, however, shifted their homes to either Mashambo or Chetto. A considerable number of inhabitants of the latter two settlements

---

[18] Brief accounts are given in Wölle (1999) or Fisch (1999); see also Fosse (1996) and Kangumu (2000).

[19] The Namibian, 27.10.1998. *San flee from Caprivi raids.*

[20] Ibid.

[21] Field notes 27.11.1998.

also decided to seek refuge in Botswana. Comparatively small numbers of people from Omega and Mutc'iku left the scene, among them Chief Kipi George, who was reported missing[22] for some weeks before it became clear that he was at the United Nations High Commission of Refugees (UNHCR) camp in Dukwe[23] near Nata in Botswana, where most of the refugees from Caprivi had been brought. Up until then, his people were not aware of his fate and feared the worst as he had been expressively searched for by the Special Field Force (SFF) at his home in Mutc'iku as well as at his wife's place at Mashambo.[24]

After numerous arrests in East Caprivi and the exodus of many activists and sympathisers, the revolt seemed to have been crushed soon afterwards. Subsequently, the repatriation of refugees was envisaged and partly accomplished during the following months. By November 1998, the Namibian Prime Minister and the Botswana Deputy President agreed that the refugees would only be returned to Namibia on a voluntary basis. In the same month, the UNHCR, however, alleged that the refugees would face persecution if they returned home,[25] and in January 1999 there was still a continuing inflow of Namibians into Botswana.[26] Up until May 1999, a total of 2,232 Namibians were granted political asylum in Botswana,[27] the majority of them claiming to have nothing to do with the secessionist cause, but to have fled out of fear of security sweeps.[28] The number of Khwe at Dukwe was reported at about 600.[29] An additional unknown number had crossed the border and managed to stay with relatives in northern Ngamiland, unrecognised by Botswana officials.[30]

The repatriation process finally commenced in March 1999, after delegations from Namibia and Botswana led by the Home Affairs Ministers of both countries had promoted the idea of voluntary repatriation during a visit to the Dukwe camp in February.[31] A tripartite agreement was signed by

---

[22] The Namibian, 19.11.1998. *Khwe Chief Missing.*
[23] The Namibian, 21.12.1998. *Missing San Chief found.*
[24] Field notes 15.10.2000.
[25] The Namibian, 7.1.1999. *Caprivi refugee decision soon.*
[26] The Namibian, 27.1.1999. *More Caprivians flee*; 28.1.1999 *Caprivians fleeing daily.*
[27] The Namibian, 14.5.1999. *Refuge now granted to 2.232 Namibians.*
[28] The Namibian, 7.4.1999. *1,116 Namibians granted asylum.*
[29] Allgemeine Zeitung, 23.4.1999. *Ein abgeriegeltes Flüchtlingslager.*
[30] Field notes 21.7.1999, 23.11.2000.
[31] The Namibian, 7.4.1999. *1,116 Namibians granted asylum.*

the UNHCR, Botswana and Namibia, according to which a general amnesty was granted to those Namibians who fled to Botswana without having committed any crimes.[32] Up to the end of July 1999, the majority of the 600 Khwe refugees in Dukwe, along with several hundred East Caprivians, were repatriated. The number of Khwe remaining in Dukwe was reported to total about 40 to 60 by the repatriates.[33] Among them was Chief Kipi George, who apparently was intimidated by separatist hardliners in Dukwe and threatened to face a jail sentence or harassment on his return to Namibia.[34]

The repatriation process was stopped after an armed attack by CLA members on the Mpacha airport and the police and the broadcast stations in Katima Mulilo on the 2nd of August 1999. NDF troops in all of Caprivi were reinforced and a dusk-to-dawn curfew was established. The fears of the Khwe were again on the rise; however, another exodus only took place when Unita started its attacks on travellers, villagers and army bases in West Caprivi in January 2000. CLA was said to be backed by Unita[35] although the extent of Unita's support remains unclear (Möllers 1999). An unknown number of young secessionist fighters was trained in Angola (Fisch 1999), and, especially after the attack in August 1999, rumours circulated in West Caprivi that CLA and Unita planned a common attack to blow the Okavango bridge at Divundu in order to separate Caprivi at least logistically.[36] The rumours were substantiated by documents found with people arrested on the day of the attack (Fisch 1999). NDF officials, however, maintained that possible support by CLA members for Unita assaults on travellers on the Trans-Caprivi Highway was unlikely.[37]

From January 2000 onward, security standards in West Caprivi decreased even more and the Angolan army, Forcas Armadas Angolanas (FAA), and its civil war enemy, Unita, became players on the scene. At the end of 1999, the FAA had cut off the supply lines for Unita troops in southern Angola, and FAA units started to operate from Namibian soil, whereupon Unita guerrillas attacked and raided villagers and travellers in Namibia out of hunger and revenge. NDF and SFF personnel in West Caprivi were

---

[32] The Namibian, 12.7.1999. *600 Caprivians to return this week.* It has to be noted that an amnesty is normally granted to people who have committed crimes.

[33] Field notes 21.7.1999.

[34] The Namibian, 6.7.1999. *George given Govt guarantee.*

[35] CLA was also openly supported by the Barotse Patriotic Front (BPF) in West Zambia (Möllers 1999).

[36] Field notes 20.8.1999.

[37] The Namibian, 28.2.2000. *Horror weekend in the north-east.*

reinforced and army camps were set up every ten kilometres along the highway. In order to protect travellers, a military escort that crossed the area two times a day in both directions was established between the two checkpoints into Caprivi Game Park in late January 2000. Although the escort is praised for its safety, cars travelling without the escort as well as villagers continued falling victim to attack.

Within West Caprivi, more violent incidents occurred in the western part, in the Omega and Mutc'iku areas and on the road between them. A large number of attacks also took place further west in the Kavango Region, between Divundu and Rundu and beyond. Travellers, villagers, local officials, as well as soldiers and policemen, all fell victim to attacks or mine blasts. At least 100 people have been killed[38] and 130 maimed by mines[39].

The Khwe in West Caprivi do, however, not only fear the terror of war, but also the suspicion and harassment by security forces. In January 2000, almost every Khwe respondent in Mutc'iku had a story to tell how he or she had been threatened or harassed by security personnel. Some were unlawfully arrested and kept in custody for more than 48 hours without seeing the magistrate,[40] which is against Namibian law. Among them was the stand-in-leader of the Khwe, Acting Chief Thaddeus Chedau[41] and a Khwe police sergeant from Omega Police Station.[42] In July 2001, the Khwe man Hans Dikua was shot by NDF soldiers under circumstances that remain unclear.[43]

Human rights abuses such as the confiscation of identity documents, arbitrary arrests, summary executions, torture to extort confessions, handing over to the FAA, and enforced disappearances were repeatedly reported by the press,[44] but also by the National Society for Human Rights (NSHR 2001) and Amnesty International (2000) for all of northeastern Namibia.

---

[38] The Namibian, 10.5.2001. *Many lodges in north-east shut.*
[39] The Namibian, 29.9.2000. *Secret detention centre uncovered near Rundu.*
[40] Field notes 29.11.2000.
[41] Allgemeine Zeitung, 6.10.2000. *Mehr Kavango Razzien.*
[42] The Namibian, 9.10.2000. *Khwe living in fear.*
[43] The Namibian, 12.7.2001. *Soldiers accused for executing Caprivian*; 13.7.2001. *Facts of alleged Khwe execution still unclear*; 18.7.2001. *Shot Khwe man 'was trying to escape' – NDF*; 19.7.2001. *NDF alters version of how Khwe man died.*
[44] E.g., The Namibian, 25.2.2000. *Evidence of torture emerges in Kavango*; 18.10.2001. *NDF admits Unita suspects being held*; 13.11.2001. *NDF claims success in Angola.*

According to the reports, rights violations were committed by all armed forces in the area: Unita, FAA, SFF and NDF.

On a national and regional level, many voices[45] spoke out demanding that Angolan troops should no longer be allowed to stay in Namibia. Concerns were raised from an economic as well as an ethical perspective. Most effective seems to have been the demand made by the Regional Councillors of Kavango,[46] soon after which the FAA withdrew the bulk of their soldiers in September 2000.[47]

Local people as well have relied on political actions so as to better their fate. In June 2000, a Khwe delegation went to Windhoek in order to inform the Ministers of Defense and Home Affairs about strained relations between the Khwe and security forces personnel.[48] The same year in December, Khwe and !Xun people held a meeting in Omega to discuss political actions concerning the increased number of detentions and harassments. The meeting was facilitated by IRDNC, which also ended up under suspicion.[49] In January 2001, the Khwe met with the Ombudswoman in Omega, and in September 2001, another Khwe delegation went to see the Ombudswoman in Windhoek in order to raise the community's concerns.[50] Relatives of 15 Khwe men detained by the NDF in August 2000 applied to the Namibian

---

[45] Among them are the voices of the Council of Churches in Namibia, the parliamentarian opposition of DTA, UDF, MAG and DCN, the Swakopmund Chamber of Commerce, the Roman Catholic Bishops Conference, joined by the Lutheran churches and the National Council of Students (The Namibian, 10.2.2000. *Churches lobby Nujoma*; 1.3.2000. *Call for FAA to go rejected*; 6.3.2000. *Govt short-sighted in giving support to FAA*; 6.3.2000. *Nujoma denies increase in Unita attacks*; 31.8.2000. *Nacos calls for pull-out of FAA troops*).

[46] The Namibian, 23.8.2000. *Rein in the FAA*. It was pointed out by the press that all of the eight Kavango Regional Councillors are Swapo supporters.

[47] The Namibian, 1.9.2000. *Angolan troops start to pull back*.

[48] The Namibian, 9.6.2000. *Government to address Khwe concerns*.

[49] New Era, 15-18.1.2001. *Caprivians Caught Between two Fronts. President Invited to Help*. All three of permanent IRDNC staff in West Caprivi have been targeted by security forces. One was accused of high treason and arrested for more than a month, one ran to Botswana in fear of arrest after being warned that he was to be taken into detention, and the third one was arrested and held in custody by the army for a few days before being released (Rousset 2002).

[50] The Namibian, 7.9.2001. *Aggrieved Khwe meet with Ombudswoman*.

High Court against the government to release them.[51] Whereas the NDF claims that the 15 escaped from custody at the Bagani army base and their footprints were followed into Angola, their relatives fear that they have been executed. These fears were fuelled when two Khwe men, arrested in connection with a mine blast at Omega in January 2001, reported to have been threatened by a soldier that they would be taken to Angola and "killed like the others." People also said that a large fresh heap of earth just outside the fence of the Bagani army base was the place were the Khwe detainees had been shot and buried.[52] It is important to stress that these comments are not specified here in order to make a claim for their truth or untruth, but to give evidence of an atmosphere reigned by fear and mutual distrust. The government's claim that the detainees were left in an unlocked casspir, while at the same time being regarded as "agents of guerrilla warfare, destabilisation and crime,"[53] is, at the least, lax. When representatives of the LAC visited West Caprivi to collect affidavits from the relatives, SFF members said the meetings were illegal and twice shot over a vehicle taking witnesses home (Rousset 2002). Reservations also grew from the fact that one Khwe NDF soldier, who had stated to have seen some of the detainees in army custody after their alleged escape, did not appear before court as a witness. Further examination of the case was, however, put an end to by the Namibian High Court.

As a consequence of attacks and harassment by security forces, the number of Khwe refugees in Dukwe climbed to its former level during 2000 and 2001. In September 2000, Chief Kipi George was repatriated on humanitarian grounds, as he was seriously ill. He died on the 17th of December in the same year. On his return, George had stated that loyalist supporters of Mishake Muyongo were harassing other Namibians and preventing them from participating in the repatriation process.[54] Political

---

[51]   For details of the case see The Namibian, 20.2.2001. *18 missing in Caprivi*; 23.2.2001. *NDF dismisses report on Caprivi missing*; 10.7.2001. *Relatives demand release of 15 missing Caprivians*; 26.7.2001. *Fate of missing Khwe 15 in spotlight*; 27.7.2001. *Missing Khwe case delayed by no-show of key witness*; 17.9.2001. *Shock evidence in Caprivi case*; 18.9.2001. *Khwe disappearance case back in court in October*; 30.11.2001. *Judgement in missing Khwe case next week*; 6.12.2001. *Khwe case fails to resolve fate of missing 15*. Originally, the number of detainees was given as 18, but for the court case only 15 names were written down.

[52]   Field notes 23.11.2000, 19.1.2001, 23.1.2001.

[53]   The Namibian, 6.12.2001. *Khwe case fails to resolve fate of missing 15*.

[54]   The Namibian, 25.9.2000. *New scourge for refugees*.

tensions between groups of different ethnic origin among the refugees were also confirmed by an official at the camp.[55] In May 2001, negotiations between the Namibian Ministry of Home Affairs and the United Nations were taken up again in order to pave the way for repatriation. Many of those who want to return are Khwe,[56] but the process is blocked by the instability in West Caprivi due to Unita raids and security sweeps.[57]

Impacts on Khwe Economy

The tense situation has affected all areas of Khwe life. Settlement was rearranged, causing conflict about resources, among other things. Family life has been disrupted due to the high number of refugees. Education, health and transport facilities have deteriorated (Suzman 2001). My focus here, however, is solely on the impacts of recent developments on Khwe economy, their food security, as well as their aspirations for development.

Food Security

Scarcity in Khwe economy has to be regarded as the product of the historically induced lack of entitlements (cf. Sen 1981). Before 2000, Khwe economy primarily relied on agriculture on plots that were part of a resettlement scheme implemented between 1991 and 1996 in the villages of Mutc'iku, Omega, Chetto and Omega III by the Evangelical Lutheran Church in Namibia (ELCIN) on behalf of the Ministry of Lands, Resettlement and Rehabilitation (MLRR). The scheme was aimed at the former 'Bushmen soldiers' and meant to prevent an economic disaster among the Khwe and !Xun people in West Caprivi, who, to a great extent, had been economically dependent on the SADF before Namibian independence (Jansen, Pradhan and Spencer 1994). Without doubt it was also a measure to control settlement by former SADF soldiers in a nature conservation area. The fields in the plots of the resettlement scheme are, however, by no means a secure base for subsistence due to ecological as well as socioeconomic reasons. Rainfall in West Caprivi is highly variable (Mendelsohn and Roberts 1997) and does not provide sufficient harvests every year. Money for seeds and ploughing is often insufficient due to the

---

[55] Refugee Councillor Kue at Dukwe, pers. comm.; 21.10.2000.

[56] Field notes 21.10.2000.

[57] Recently, however, a new tripartite agreement between UNHCR, Namibia and Botswana has been signed for the repatriation of Namibian refugees (The Namibian, 12.4.2002. *Pact paves way for repatriation*).

lack of job opportunities. And the general poverty combined with the social value of, or pressure for, sharing may result in consuming grain that was meant to be kept as seed for the following year.

Agriculture was supplemented by gathering bushfood, animal husbandry, very few formal or informal jobs, and some income from crafts and tourism. Pension money for aged and handicapped people, as well as food supplies in times of need, are provided by the state. Even before the outbreak of the current conflicts many Khwe households had been struggling at poverty level, but almost each of their income opportunities suffered additional declines as a result of the state of insecurity.

In 2000 many people decided not to plough their fields for fear of striking mines.[58] At most, some millet was planted just around their houses.[59] In the village of Mashambo, where no mines have been detected so far, the uncertain revenues from invested work were brought forward as a reason not to plough and plant crops. People argued that they were not prepared to work in the fields only to have to leave the crops to wild animals or bandits,[60] because they may also have to flee to Botswana.

Villagers also refrained from taking to the bush in order to collect food and fuel supplies mainly for fear of being accused of using forays in order to support Unita rebels.

> There is a lot of food in the bush, but we cannot go. We are afraid of Unita and SFF. They will capture or arrest us. SFF will say that we give water and food to Unita and arrest us. They won't believe us.[61]

Many Khwe decided to slaughter their animals with the possibility of fleeing to Botswana. Thus, they stripped themselves of their capital, as domestic animals are primarily not owned for consumption, but to pay extraordinary costs, e.g., a healing session or court debts. From the more than 100 goats I counted in Mashambo in July 1999, only five were left in October 2000. The others had been slaughtered as people were always on the

---

[58] Mines were said to have been encountered mainly on paths and fields, not in the middle of the bush (Field notes 23.11.2000).

[59] Field notes 19.1.2001.

[60] Field notes 25.10.2000. Mashambo has not been included into the resettlement scheme. Fields lie at some distance from the village in the next dry river bed and not close to people's houses like in Mutc'iku.

[61] Field notes 22.1.2001.

go with the expectation that living conditions would worsen even more. As it would have been impossible to take the goats to Botswana, they were slaughtered and eaten or sold in order to be on the safe side and not leave them to Unita bandits or anyone else. This was to avoid the experience that people from Omega III had had, who, when repatriated in July 1999, found their livestock gone.[62] In Mutc'iku, people additionally reported an increased number of stock thefts together with the impossibility of following tracks and reclaiming losses.[63]

After the murder of three French juveniles on the Trans-Caprivi Highway in January 2000, tourism in the Kavango and Caprivi Regions steadily declined. Foreign governments, including those of the United States, France, Germany and Britain, advised their nationals that travelling to the Kavango and Caprivi Regions was not safe.[64] The Khwe Community Campsite at Nǁgoava-ca on the Okavango River near Popa Falls was abandoned and looted later on.[65] It was the only tourism enterprise from which the Khwe could gain profits. The financial loss may not be that great, as rates for camping had always been low and visitors rare so that the turnover was hardly enough to pay for personnel and maintenance. Staff members are now temporarily supported by IRDNC until tourism resumes (Rousset 2002). Much more importantly, however, is the loss of the campsite as a symbol of possible economic development, as well as of cultural self-esteem and the

---

[62] Field notes 25.10.2000.

[63] Field notes 23.11.2000.

[64] The Namibian, 6.6.2000. *Angolan war killing north-east tourism*. In order to rescue Namibia's tourism industry as a whole, the Tour and Safari Association of Namibia (Tasa) voted that tourists should be advised not to travel to the Kavango and Caprivi Regions, although Caprivi tourism was at the time only slowly recovering from declines in connection with the secessionist attack in August 1999 (The Namibian, 14.1.2000. *Tourism left reeling*). A governmental press release stated that important tourist attractions in the rest of the country were not affected by 'banditry' in the northeast (Allgemeine Zeitung, 10.1.2000. *Scharfe Dementi*). Tourist enterprises and taxi drivers protested against the warning as well as the military escort (The Namibian, 30.8.2000. *North-east tourism revival – reality or wishful thinking*). The warning was withdrawn in early 2001, although attacks and raids continued and the escort was still in place. By the end of 2001, tourism into northeast Namibia seemed to be recovering, as overland tour operators pulled in again. This, obviously, was an effect of the 'Go North Campaign' by the Deputy Minister of Tourism (The Namibian, 23.11.2001. *Tourism on the mend in NE*).

[65] Field notes 23.11.2000.

successful defending of Khwe rights and goals. The campsite represents one of the few Khwe success stories, because its planned closure by the Ministry of Prisons and Correctional Services in order to extend the Divundu Rehabilitation Centre was effectively prevented in 1998 (see Orth, this volume).

The Khwe craft industry was threatened because the site where palm leaves were collected for basket making[66] became a no access zone under military control. Again, IRDNC stood in by providing transport to an area about 150 km away in East Caprivi, where palm leaves could be collected in order to secure craft earnings, which have made a vital contribution to incomes of Khwe families during the past years. Discussions with NDF seemed to be promising that a military escort soon could be provided to allow basket makers to collect palm leaves in West Caprivi (Rousset 2002).

Patrols of the IRDNC-paid community game guards and community resource monitors were affected for obvious reasons. Limited patrols are still taking place. Some game wardens have been going on patrols with the army, or into areas south of the tar road where it was permitted by the army;[67] however, a number of game wardens and resource monitors reported to be no longer carrying out their duties.[68] IRDNC, nevertheless, continued to pay them, as the NGO felt an extraordinary responsibility not to withdraw from West Caprivi despite the instability in order not to put itself at the risk of loosing the community's trust in the organisation itself, as well as in aspirations of development.[69]

Least affected by the tense security situation were the salaries for formal jobs in government ministries such as teachers, nature conservation officers of the MET, etc., and pensions. There were even some new job opportunities as 25 Khwe men and women were employed by and received military training from the NDF in 2000. What was praised as a positive outcome from a meeting of Acting Chief Thaddeus Chedau with the Minister of Defense in Windhoek in June 2000[70] was more controversial at home in West Caprivi. Although more than 200 Khwe were ready to register for NDF

---

[66] For an account of Khwe basketry as a source of income and as an ethnic marker see Boden and Michels 2000, Boden 2001.

[67] Karine Rousset, IRDNC, pers. comm.; April 2002.

[68] Field notes 23.10.2000, 24.10.2000.

[69] Karine Rousset, IRDNC, pers. comm.; February 2001.

[70] The Namibian, 9.6.2000. *Government to address Kxoe concerns.*

employment in December 2000,[71] some of them seemed not really enthusiastic:

> There are lots of jobs in Namibia. Why can't they give opportunities for that? They put the Khwe only where death is. The SADF has put us in it. If you have a dog, you can take your best dog who runs fast and is a killer. The Boers did like that with us Khwe. Maybe because of that the Namibians say that we know how to kill. Now they turn to us and want that we join the NDF. They do the same like SADF. They give us the dog's work. I have registered myself, but I don't want to go. If they call me I will go. If I refuse they will say that I am Unita.[72]

Generally speaking, Khwe people have become more economically dependent in recent years. Dependency has increased on the generosity and support of IRDNC, on government institutions that were expected to give additional relief supplies, and on the Mbukushu.[73] Stripped of their main independent subsistence activities of agriculture and gathering, many Khwe resorted to doing 'ten-cent-jobs' for Mbukushu people,[74] mainly cleaning fields and cutting grass for roof thatching. The increased dependency on both the government and the Mbukushu is felt by the Khwe to be especially bad because both parties are supposed to be against them.

> When we asked for food from the Government they refused to give us any food saying 'you will take the food to Unita rebels.'[75]

> The Mbukushu discriminate us. They like to misuse the Khwe. They do not treat us like human beings. Whenever they want to do something they give piecework to Khwe. But they do not pay what they promised. The Mbukushu give piecework for only traditional beer. The old people can drink but the children

---

[71] Field notes 31.12.2000.

[72] Field notes 22.1.2001.

[73] Another form of economic dependency that has become more abundant during recent years was that of Khwe women and even school girls providing sexual services more or less voluntarily to the increased number of soldiers.

[74] The latter is not true for the inhabitants of Mashambo as there are no Mbukushu settlers in this village.

[75] The Namibian, 6.9.2001. *Khwe bemoan bushban.*

are suffering. The Khwe have to accept the piecework because they have nothing to eat.[76]

Mutc'iku Resettlement Scheme, November 1998

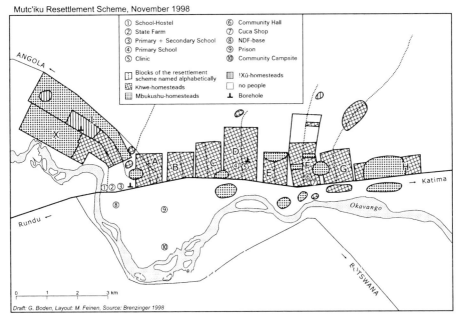

Map 2: Mutc'iku resettlement scheme, November 1998

Mbukushu people were able to provide such jobs because they continued to plant their fields. Although most Mbukushu who had lived on or between Khwe plots in the Mutc'iku resettlement scheme had shifted to safer places across the river due to security reasons, they continued to plant their fields, many of which are located between the river and the Trans-Caprivi Highway (see map 2) and thus in a safer area. The fields of the Khwe, in contrast, were confined to the area north of the tar road within the marked plots of the resettlement scheme. The heavier soils near the river are better suited for agriculture, but lie within the core conservation area of Caprivi Game Park (Brown and Jones 1994: map on page 64). The Khwe had already protested against the Mbukushu making fields between the road and the river being tolerated by MET officials while they themselves were kept out of the core area and restricted to the poorer land of the resettlement scheme.[77] In the

---

[76]   Field notes 17.01.2001.
[77]   Letter by Chief Kipi George to the Minister of Home Affairs Jerry Ekandjo, 15.11.1995.

current situation they even had to abandon that poor land along with their homesteads.[78]

Economic dependency taking the form of real enslavement or a patron-client relationship between Mbukushu and Khwe people has been well established during the 19th and the first half of the 20th century (Wilhelm 1954, de Almeida 1965, Köhler 1989). Similar relationships have been reported to exist between other San and Bantu people (e.g., Silberbauer and Kuper 1966, Osaki 2001) and other hunter-gatherers and peasants in Africa (e.g., Bahuchet and Guillaume 1982). They have been described as flexible and oscillating, with 'servants' relying on their masters in times of need, while living more independently in times when resources are abundant and readily accessible (Silberbauer and Kuper 1966). To return to an economic dependent relationship can therefore be regarded as a common strategy used by San people in cases of emergency. But even from a more general perspective, it can be said that, as a rule, people who are vulnerable anyway become more dependent in times of crisis.

Khwe feelings towards the people and institutions on which they have become more dependent during the last few years are not alike. While the NGO is said to be supportive and protecting,[79] the state and its representatives are judged as acting in an unfair or even hostile manner, and the Mbukushu are said to exploit the Khwe. It is striking that all reasoning concerning economic activities is substantiated in one way or another by foreign identifications the Khwe believe are held towards them by the government, the security forces or their Mbukushu neighbours. Such are the

---

[78] In October 2000, the blocks E, H and I of the Mutc'iku resettlement scheme (see map 2) had been abandoned completely. In other blocks, all those people who had occupied plots located at some distance from the tar road moved their homesteads and either joined people on plots closer to the road or shifted to a place south of it (Field notes 23.11.2000). In late 2001 all homes north of the road had been vacated (Matthias Brenzinger, University of Cologne, pers. comm.; December 2001). Although the area south of the road actually belongs to the core conservation area of Caprivi Game Park, some Khwe and Mbukushu homesteads had long been built there. This, obviously, was tolerated by the MET, as people reported not to have faced any measures from officials (Field notes 7.12.1998, 9.12.1998). The increased number of recent shifts across the road in the course of the years 2000 and 2001, was, however, encouraged and even openly requested by the SFF (Field notes 23.11.2000, 18.1.2001), thus adding to the uncertain legal status of people's lives.

[79] Field notes 25.12.2000.

feelings of people who lack the capital, properties and entitlement necessary to make an independent living.

Development Aspirations

The state of insecurity has also put a halt to Khwe development aspirations in connection with the proclamation of Bwabwata National Park and the realisation of measures planned to insure that the local community benefits from it (Suzman 2001). West Caprivi has a long history of nature conservation.[80] In 1963, the strip of land between the Okavango and Kwando Rivers was declared a nature park by the South African administration and in 1968, it was elevated to the status of a game park. In the 1970s, however, West Caprivi became a military zone, and nature conservation an issue of secondary concern. After independence, the game park status was confirmed and core conservation and multiple-use areas were identified (Brown and Jones 1994). With support of IRDNC, a local committee was established that worked out a constitution, one of the necessary prerequistes for a conservancy application. The latter was stopped by MET's plans to reorganise the status and the different use areas in the park. Local people faced a confusing number of different plans and prospects, and were forced to wait for a definite solution from the ministry. In the meantime, the cabinet has approved recommendations for the establishment of the Bwabwata National Park, which will incorporate the Mahango and West Caprivi parks, as well as the game-rich Kwando Triangle that was not declared before. The Mutc'iku and Omega areas will be de-proclaimed, and the residents of West Caprivi will be allowed to continue collecting bushfood in the park with a license from MET. The next phase before the new national park becomes reality is mapping the boundaries of the areas to be proclaimed and de-proclaimed. The plan also makes provision for communities living in areas adjacent to the park to develop some kind of tourism venture within its boundaries (MET n.d. [1999]). While the Khwe were waiting for the de-proclamation of parts of the park, some of the communities across the Kwando River had managed to establish conservancies there[81] and will probably be the first to benefit from it. The MET has already given permission to the Mayuni Conservancy to develop a

---

[80] The history of West Caprivi is dealt with in more detail in Orth (this volume); see also Brenzinger (1998).

[81] Kwandu and Mayuni conservancies were both registered in December 1999 with 1,800 and 410 members, respectively (MET 2001).

community campsite in the proposed Kwando core area, a fact that makes the Khwe feel additionally outmanoeuvred.[82]

Conservancies are the kind of institution contemplated by MET for generating community revenues from wildlife and tourism. Legislation does not, however, allow conservancies within the boundaries of a national park. Thus, only the de-proclaimed areas of Mutc'iku and Omega will be qualified to become conservancies. These two areas are those with the highest population density, in fact, the very reason why they were to be de-proclaimed. They are also the zones with the highest proportions of Mbukushu settlers, and the only tracts where cattle farming continued to be allowed after the outbreak of the cattle lung disease contagious bovine pleuropneumonia (CBPP) in Botswana in 1996. In contrast, cattle farming was prohibited in the rest of West Caprivi. Due to the contagiousness of CBPP through wildlife, the Mutc'iku and Omega areas will have to be fenced once they are de-proclaimed. Local villagers thus doubt that they will be able to benefit from wildlife within such conservancies, as there is little likelihood that there will be great numbers of wildlife inside the fenced areas (Rousset 2002). Khwe people have argued that allowing cattle farming only in those areas within the game park where most Mbukushu and also some Ovambo people live was a selective measure by the Namibian government to privilege members of these ethnic groups while discriminating against the Khwe.[83] Such feelings are aggravated by the notion that the inhabitants of the future multiple-use areas of the Bwabwata National Park, who are almost exclusively Khwe, will be excluded not only from cattle farming, but also from wildlife management. Khwe rhetoric, as well as San rhetoric in general, however re-inforced by academic and NGO staff it may be, claims a strong link between themselves and wildlife (e.g., Taylor 2000). To the Khwe, loosing access to wildlife by fencing and by the lack of legal right to establish a conservancy within the future park means discrimination targeted at them because of their very ethnic affiliation and an exclusion from development.[84]

There will still be a chance of benefiting from trophy hunting in West Caprivi. Trophy-hunting concessions are located in and around the Kwando Triangle and in the Buffalo Core Area. The local community in West

---

[82] Letter by a schoolteacher at Mashambo village to the Permanent Secretary of the MET, 18.4.2001. Mashambo is the Khwe village closest to the Kwando core area.

[83] Field notes 23.7.1999.

[84] Field notes 30.9.1999.

Caprivi, in contrast to communities in established conservancies elsewhere, will, however, not be able to negotiate with possible concessionaires and autonomously manage wildlife themselves. They will only be able to gain benefits via the ministry. MET officials have already explained to community representatives that trophy-hunting revenues can only be transferred to a legally recognised body and has called upon local people to establish an appropriate management committee (Rousset 2002).

Another segment of economy with the potential for yielding high returns in the future Bwabwata National Park is tourism. Local Khwe people plan to establish a tourism enterprise on a well-suited site near Popa Falls alongside the already existing low-grade Khwe Community Campsite at Nǁgoava-ca. However, the enterprise can only be started when the de-proclamation of the Mutc'iku area is finalised. Only then will the community be able to apply for a Permission to Occupy (PTO). But PTOs are the responsibility of Traditional Authorities in communal areas.[85] Here the issue of political representation again comes into play.

State Decisions as Catalysts for Ethnicity

In August 2001 President Sam Nujoma instructed the Minister of Regional, Local Government and Housing, Nicky Iyambo, not to formally recognise the chieftainship of the Khwe according to the Traditional Authorities Act. By doing so, the President accepted a recommendation of the Council of Traditional Leaders,[86] based on a Commission of Inquiry that had visited West Caprivi in March 1999. Although the cultural distinctiveness of the Khwe is recognised, they are denied their own leadership due to allegations that there is no history of chieftainship in the Khwe community and that the West Caprivi area historically belonged to the Mbukushu.[87] The latter argument definitely turns history around. West Caprivi was called 'Hukweveld' by the German colonial administration, in reference to the Hukwe (Khwe) inhabitants encountered by the geographer Franz Seiner (Seiner 1908). Also, Lt. Volkmann, when proposing the reconnaissance of Kavango and Caprivi and the establishment of a military post, writes that such an enterprise would be easy between the Okavango and Tschobe [Kwando, Linyanti, Chobe] Rivers as only 'Bushmen' were living

---

[85]   www.grnnet.gov.na/Nav_frames/Gov_launch.htm.
[86]   The Namibian, 4.9.2001. *Govt shuts out Khwe.*
[87]   Ibid.

in this area.[88] Ancestors of the Mbukushu first migrated to Kavango Region from upstream Zambezi through what is today Zambia, East Caprivi and southeastern Angola in the 19th century (van Tonder 1966). Moreover, there is abundant oral historical evidence that the Khwe themselves have had well-working institutions of leadership since remembered times. Most prominent were so-called *díxa-ǁ'áé-ǁùa* (owner-settlement-MASCULINE:PLURAL), best translated as 'responsible owners of settlements.' They granted and controlled access to land, water and other resources, settled conflicts within the community and represented the local community in conflicts with outsiders. Personal qualities and a good reputation were as important for legitimacy as a certain genealogical relationship to a predecessor. Some of these *díxa-ǁ'áé-ǁùa* had far-reaching reputations because of their conflict-solving abilities, and were consulted by other *díxa-ǁ'áé-ǁùa* in cases they could not settle themselves. Such outstanding people were called *ǁ'áxa*, a term later given to the office held by the Khwe representatives recommended by the administration of South West Africa during the 1950s. The first governmentally recognised Khwe *ǁ'áxa*, Martin Ndumba, resided at Mutc'iku and his vice, Kandunda Kaseta, lived at Bwabwata, another major Khwe settlement at the time. Today *ǁ'áxa* is translated as 'chief,' whereas the *díxa-ǁ'áé-ǁùa* were renamed *voormanne* in colonial times and *headmen* after independence. There is a strong feeling of continuity between yesterday's *díxa-ǁ'áé-ǁùa* and today's headmen in regard to the personal qualities required, as well as the duties to be performed (Boden 2002). Both are subject to permanent evaluation, discussion and contest, which can result in the replacement of one headman by another, a practice also experienced by NGO staff trying to set up a list of representatives for the offices provided for in the regulations of the Traditional Authorities Act.[89] In summary, although former Khwe leadership and rights to resources were organised on a more local level, they are nevertheless understood to have been self-defined and autonomous (Boden 2002).

In discourse, the Khwe used to substantiate their claim for government recognition of their own leadership in two ways: One was to stress historic autonomy from the Mbukushu, the other was to depict treatment by the Mbukushu as having been oppressive, thereby referring to the democratic constitution of independent Namibia and the equal rights granted to all its

---

[88] Letter of 23.5.1903; National Archives of Namibia: ZBU 1009 1, J XIIIb 4: 10.

[89] Axel Thoma, WIMSA, pers. comm.; October 2000. The Traditional Authorities Act makes provision for the offices of a Chief, four Senior Traditional Councillors, six Traditional Councillors and a Secretary.

citizens. To emphasise Mbukushu oppression is an ambiguous strategy in this context, because it risks being exploited in order to demonstrate the alleged Khwe subordination.[90] In the Khwe case, the powerful Mbukushu intruders have been recognised for what they were, and life was reconstructed around them, but there are also accounts of simple escape from Mbukushu oppression to areas in either Zambia or Botswana.

There also are some Khwe headmen who are known, or have been said, to have defected to the side of the Mbukushu Chief Erwin Munika Mbambo. Provided they proved to be capable conflict solvers, they are still approached and respected as judges in cases of conflict (Felton 1998, Boden 2002). At the same time, however, they are condemned for their collaboration with those whom the Khwe feel are their enemies and definitely are their opponents as far as land rights and political representative power are concerned. To malign individuals by maintaining they collaborate with Chief Mbambo is a common practice in order to deny the legitimacy of their headmanship. It seems to have been due to Kipi George's integration skills that some renegades temporarily parted with Mbambo. That, however, turned out not to be a stable turnover during the times of crisis that caused and followed Kipi George's escape.

Relationships between the Khwe and Mbukushu have taken different forms in the past, as they do today. History and tradition are the pools from which arguments are drawn for political discourse. The apartheid regime has expressively stressed ethnic distinctiveness and spatial separation. The Mbukushu were evicted from sites in West Caprivi (Brenzinger 1998), and the "natural hostility between the Bushmen and the Blacks" (Uys 1993) was exploited to promote military aims during the liberation war. Current group formation along ethnic lines is a political strategy to secure or gain access to resources and, above all, to development, and political representation in terms of 'traditional communities' is the key resource to all other resources.

Access to state power is essential for the welfare of its subjects, but such access has never been equally available (cf. Markakis 1994). Within the local context, the Mbukushu chief's much easier and effective access to

---

[90] Autonomy claimed by one group and subordination claimed by an opponent group do not necessarily need to be inconsistent. Osaki (2001) has argued that both can be true, as is the case with Tswana-Gǁana relationships in the central Kalahari in Botswana. While the Tswana claim that they dominated the San, San do not think they were dominated by Tswana, but perceived tributes as part of exchange.

power is alleged to exist not only in terms of institutional recognition, but also in terms of political party affiliation and personal connections. Whereas the late Khwe Chief Kipi George and most of his people used to vote for the opposition party, Democratic Turnhallen Alliance (DTA), Chief Mbambo is not only a well-known Swapo supporter, but is also said to have established powerful relations to the governing Swapo leadership while in exile in Angola during the struggle for independence.[91]

In 1998, the status of the land and the question of political representation were still undecided. Within this open situation the Khwe felt the absence of Chief Kipi George to be especially severe. As long as Kipi George was still alive, people continued being loyal to his chieftainship, even though he lived in exile in Botswana. This was attributed to his good performance as a chief on the local level, as well as on the national and international stage.[92] After his death in 2000, Kipi George was buried in West Caprivi at a site dedicated to be a graveyard from then on, although making graveyards has not previously been a Khwe practice. His burial on the land the Khwe regard as theirs has to be understood as a strong symbolic claim for recognition of the Khwe leadership and land rights in times when political action has not been successful.

Due to the instability in the region and the prohibition of large gatherings by security forces, the Khwe have not yet to this day been able to organise the election of a new chief. In January 1999, a stand-in leader was appointed, the Senior Councillor designate Thaddeus Chedau.[93] Soon afterwards Chedau felt the force of Chief Mbambo, who instructed government policemen to bring him to his court and intimidate him.[94] The need to have a strong leader, and thus be better represented in the political field is strongly felt by Khwe people:

---

[91] Mbambo's good relationships with the present Swapo leadership are also brought forward by the press when referring to the internal Mbukushu quarrel for chieftainship between government-recognised Mbambo and community-elected Mayavero (The Namibian, 12.6.2000. *Political cabal rejects Hambukushu chief*).

[92] Field notes 17.-23.1.2001; Kipi George had been the WIMSA chairman and a delegate to the 15th Session of the United Nations Working Group on Indigenous Populations in Geneva, 28.7.-1.8.1997. The success of the extrajudicial arrangement for the Khwe Community Campsite to stand its ground was ascribed by his people to Chief George's efforts (Field notes 28.11.2000, 19.1.2001, 23.1.2001).

[93] Field notes 20.1.1999.

[94] Field notes 11.2.1999.

The Khwe community should come together and choose a chief. We don't want an acting chief, but a true chief who can do his work. When we choose a chief and build our own head office even those who went to the Mbukushu will see that we are strong and turn again. When Kipi was still here everybody felt that we have a chief. Others are now pretending to be Mbukushu. They are no more on the Khwe side. That's what we hate. We wanted all our headmen to be on our side.[95]

The Traditional Authorities Act has made ethnic distinctiveness in terms of 'traditional' authority structures a key resource and therefore a matter of profile and competition. The Khwe embarked on a strategy to adapt their perceptions of leadership and authority based on the recommendations of the Namibian legislation in order to have their voice heard in the Namibian choir. This has been lobbied by NGOs, who expected them to make a quick transition to representational leadership (Biesele and Hitchcock 2000), and who themselves need representative bodies of the people they are mandated to work with. Not the least significant, the lack of recognition by the Khwe Traditional Authority or other legal bodies also renders dubious the legal base for consultations with development workers. When a Khwe delegation went to Windhoek for several meetings in September 2001, the MET was reluctant to grant the Khwe leaders an audience since they are not allowed to hold meetings with traditional authorities that are not recognised in terms of the Traditional Authorities Act. Finally, they accepted meeting with the delegation as "citizens and people of West Caprivi".[96] Government officials, as well as NGOs, have to rely on some community representatives. The latter's work may be highly appreciated, but by working with bodies not recognised by the state, they nevertheless risk loosing the fruits of their work, the trust of state officials, and, moreover, that of the people they work for, who may not understand why prospects do not come to fruition.

Competition for resources and the role the state plays in controlling their allocation have been identified as the two main objective factors that act as catalysts to endow ethnicity with the potential for political conflict in a given social setting (Enloe 1973, Markakis 1994). The Khwe case serves as a prime example. Orth (this volume) has exposed identity formation as a political strategy at a time when land rights and leadership recognition

---

[95] Field notes 20.1.2001.
[96] Letter from MET Permanent Secretary to the West Caprivi Traditional Authority, 31.8.2001.

seemed to be realistic objectives. The latest state decisions have made relationships with fellow citizens more tense and have intensified notions of ethnic difference, as did the recent armed conflicts in the region.

Armed Conflicts as a Catalyst for Ethnicity

With the recent armed conflicts in Caprivi, Khwe living conditions have become strained, and notions of enmity and subversiveness were increasingly attached to their visibility as an ethnic group. Khwe people explain their current stand by falling back upon past relations. The prevalent relationships in this respect are with two groups of people: security forces personnel as former enemies of war, and Mbukushu people as former slave-masters. Quite a lot has already been said about Khwe–Mbukushu relations in the past and present, among other things, about their different potentials for access to power due to party affiliation. Since independence, Swapo is the ruling party in Namibia, and a great number of former independence fighters are today's NDF and SFF personnel. Discrimination experienced by Khwe people is often expressed in terms of political party alliance:

> The SFF say that the Khwe's party is DTA and that it is the same party as that of Unita.[97]

Such identifications were felt all the more disappointing as many Khwe reported to have voted for Swapo during elections in December 1999, and viewed themselves as cheated because they had expected to profit from voting Swapo instead of DTA. Instead of becoming better, living conditions worsened after 1999 to the extent that many thought of joining the exodus and seeking a better life in Botswana. They refrained, however, from doing so, expressing strong feelings of relatedness to and the fear of loosing the land to the Mbukushu if they left.

> We are just crying 'why did we stay behind when others fled to South Africa or Botswana?' Our decision was stupid. Those who fled do not cry. We decided to stay because we were born in this place, it belongs to us, we cannot leave it open. Otherwise the Mbukushu will take it over.[98]

Thus, to stay meant demonstrating a claim to the land. Tension and distrust between Khwe and Mbukushu people were on the rise, as the Mbukushu (but also some Khwe) were blamed for having reported Khwe

---

[97] Field notes 23.1.2001
[98] Field notes 19.1.2001.

individuals to the security forces, thus exploiting the armed conflicts for their own interests within personal enmities.

> The Mbukushu are happy now. They say, the Khwe will suffer because they used to communicate with Unita. They give incorrect information to the SFF and report lies about us. For me it is difficult to live with Mbukushu and Kwanyamas. They neglect us.[99]

As pointed out above, the Mbukushu are also blamed for taking advantage of the disastrous Khwe economy, bringing to the surface older sentiments of enslavement.

> The Mbukushu gathered Khwe people and told them to clean their fields. Then they just drink *tombo* [traditional beer]. It is the only thing they give. If the parents work to drink, the children will suffer at home with hunger. In old days they started like that. They only gave us tobacco. It seems that they start again like that.[100]

Thus, the Mbukushu–Khwe divide is not only fuelled by recent state decisions, but also by the dangers and opportunities brought about for political and economic standing by the recent armed conflicts. Though not necessarily as individuals, the Khwe and Mbukushu have also become more opposed as ethnic groups as a consequence of the tense security conditions.

The Khwe expect mistreatment by security forces out of revenge or in order to settle old scores. Khwe people were convinced that SFF members in particular, the majority of which are Ovambo, were still plotting revenge against the Khwe for having fought on the side of the SADF during the liberation war. This is in gross contrast to what the late Chief Kipi George said in an interview in October 1996. The Chief then denied that the Namibian government held resentment towards the Khwe as former enemies of war (Boden 1997). Although he pointed to promises not kept by the government, he rejected the idea that his people were facing attitudes of revenge.[101] Since the outbreak of the secessionist movement by Caprivians in October 1998, it is hard to tell if interpretations have drastically changed or if the tense political climate has only brought to the surface what was not

---

[99] Field notes 17.1.2001.

[100] Field notes 19.1.2001.

[101] Author's interview with Chief Kipi George, 8.10.1996. For a more detailed presentation of pre-1998 conditions in West Caprivi see Orth (this volume).

openly stated before. Many Khwe perceived the developments not in terms of a crucial change, but as a consequent continuation of their everlasting suffering (Rousset, forthcoming) discrimination and victimisation.[102]

The Khwe are not the only Namibians who fought in the lines of the colonial forces during the war of independence. But, different from others, they are exposed to special distrust because of the very location and history of their settlement area. The colonial borders and the status of nature conservation rendered some important practices of their traditional lifestyle illegal. This is true for hunting as a main subsistence activity, as well as for mutual cross-border visits as a means of social reduction of stress and sharing of resources.

The international border to Botswana can be legally crossed by people in possession of temporary passports. But, due to the high cost of passports, which can only be issued in the regional capitals at Rundu or Katima Mulilo, many rely on illegal border crossings into Botswana. Repeated illegal actions are, however, not likely to enhance trust and good relationships between local people and state officials.

The border to war-torn Angola[103] implies the permanent co-existence of former enemies of war. In a border area that used to be crossed illegally by foreigners, identity documents have a special importance. In order to prove Namibian citizenship to security agents within the country, birth certificates are sufficient, but a great number of Khwe still do not have even these basic documents. As a result, they fall under additional suspicion from security forces. The dragging issuing of birth certificates is felt to be a discrimination against the Khwe ethnic group and an intended exclusion from Namibian citizen rights.[104]

Besides the fact that many Khwe were employed as soldiers in the SADF, the proposition that Khwe people are engaged in some kind of cross-border

---

[102] Field notes 17.1.2001.

[103] In 1994 President Sam Nujoma ordered the closure of the Angolan border, particularly in the Kavango Region, but Angolans can still officially enter Namibia at specific entry points for humanitarian purposes (The Namibian, 6.3.2000. *Nujoma denies increase in Unita attacks*).

[104] There are people of other ethnic origins in the border area who also do not possess identity documents. According to the Namibian Prime Minister Hage Geingob, 45 percent of the inhabitants of the Kavango Region had to register for the last elections using sworn affidavits (The Namibian, 25.2.2001. *Most Namibians have IDs – Ekandjo*).

relations with Unita-controlled southeastern Angola serves as an argument for suspicion. The two cross at the point that the SADF supported Unita in military and financial terms (Uys 1993).

As already stated, the Khwe settlement area was divided by the colonial borders. Border crossings were undertaken to meet Khwe and other Angolan relatives. Some Khwe within West Caprivi used to trade with Angolan border crossers coming in search of maize meal and other goods, such as, for example, tyres for their donkey carts.[105] Known Unita members, like other people in distress, were said to have been helped with food by both Khwe and Mbukushu in earlier years.[106] Angolans also came in order to look for work in Namibia, as well as to steal. For example, in February 1999, the Khwe acting leader, Thaddeus Chedau, had to report to the local office of the MLRR that the construction company repairing the floors of 25 stone houses built for individual plot-owners in the resettlement scheme had employed six Angolans, who had entered Namibia illegally and were consequently replaced by local workers.[107] In February 1999, a gang of Angolans stole a number of cattle belonging to Khwe people in Mutc'iku. Thereupon, one Khwe headman went to discuss the matter in Angola and managed to bring back at least some of the animals.[108] Such relations between Khwe and Angolans, as well as the border crossings in both directions, though definitely illegal, were not related to political or military aims.[109] Neither were these border crossings accompanied by the same extent of violence or the planting of mines before December 1999 as seen afterwards. Similarly, in other parts of the Kavango Region, the Namibian-Angolan border cut family ties, and border crossings have been a well-known practice, as have been cross-border raids, especially for cattle. Kavango people even used to seasonally farm in Angola.[110]

Whereas the Namibian government attributes attacks and raids to Unita and Unita's collaborators, others, including Khwe people, claim that FAA also has to be blamed for a number of attacks. Some Khwe maintained that FAA soldiers planted mines in order to 'prove' Unita's activities in the

---

[105] Field notes 26.11.1999.

[106] Field notes 23.1.2001.

[107] Field notes 25.1.1999.

[108] Field notes 7.12.2000.

[109] With the exception of seven Khwe who were said to have joined Unita in 1989, when the SADF left and more than 1,000 Khwe resettled to South Africa (Field notes 29.7.1999).

[110] The Namibian, 12.1.2000. *Namibian urged not to plow in Angola.*

region and thus justify their own presence in the area.[111] Other rumours even asserted that the NDF personnel themselves planted mines to legitimate their presence in West Caprivi and the continued involvement in the Angolan conflict to the Namibian public.[112]

The opinion that the Khwe are engaged in supporting Unita and possibly other enemies of Namibia is widely held. It was expressed, for example, by white businessmen in the region as an understandable "reaction to century-long suppression by the blacks,"[113] thus echoing the SADF's rhetoric. A number of local officials of the MET, MLRR and Ministry of Basic Education and Culture also considered Khwe collaboration with Unita to be irrefutable.[114] These others used to argue that the Khwe were clever and sneaky, and it could never really be known what they did out there in the 'bush', a realm to which notions of danger and obscureness are attached. Khwe people, on the other hand, used to bring forward their origin from the 'bush' in order to substantiate their ignorance and innocence concerning the recent conflicts.

> This Muyongo stays in Katima and we are staying here in the western Caprivi but people are putting the blame on us. We are just staying in the bush. People do not know anything about the new army.[115]

> When I asked them what wrong thing they have seen they accused us of having killed Hamukoto, of having planted the mine from which he died. We don't know where bombs are made. But they say we are clever, that we do know. But according to our tradition we don't know where to get a bomb and guns. Only the axe, the spear, the hooked probe and the arrow. That is all we know.[116]

---

[111] Field notes 29.11.1000.

[112] Karine Rousset, IRDNC, pers. comm.; April 2002.

[113] Field notes 28.11.2000.

[114] Field notes 28.11.2000, 5.12.2000.

[115] Kipi George cited in: The Namibian, 27.10.1998. *San flee from Caprivi raids.*

[116] Field notes 22.1.2001. Hamukoto was an Ovambo and the head of the local MLRR office in Omega. His car struck a mine in January 2001 when driving workers to the cotton fields of the Namibia Development Corporation (NDF) near Omega (The Namibian, 9.1.2001. *Landmine outrage. Three die as vehicle blown up*).

The 'bush' has been termed a "domain of ignorance" (Taylor 2000), because Khwe in Botswana like those in Namibia, and San in general, used to explain their powerlessness and underdevelopment as a consequence of their lack of education and being uninformed about important decisions affecting their lives. This in turn is attributed to their originating from 'the bush', a realm without schools, newspapers, radios and the like. It has been indicated above that to stress one's affiliation to the bush is, of course, at the same time a means to make a claim to the resources therein, especially wildlife and bushfood, but also trophy hunting and tourism revenues.

In addition to being a 'domain of ignorance', the 'bush' is represented as a 'domain of innocence' in the above quotations, a representation which is in blatant contrast to depictions of Khwe mercenaries by SADF personnel, who maintain that the Khwe were "the ideal warriors" (Uys 1993:4) and tended "to overdo the killing" (ibid:100). The Khwe claim of innocence and ignorance may be an effort to veil such 'overdoing', but to 'know nothing' also serves as a kind of shield in an atmosphere where to know something may easily turn into being found guilty. In April 2000, an Omega headman complained to the press that villagers who "[...] stumble upon Unita rebels in the surrounding bush are sometimes afraid to tell the security forces about their presence because they are usually interrogated by local security forces and asked 'why didn't they kill you?'"[117] One Khwe man had to walk in front of a team of soldiers to check the area for mines. They forced him to do so, alleging that he had helped plant the mines and thus knew where they were.[118] Serving as a human mine detector is, however, an experience well known to San soldiers from the time they worked for the SADF (Kangumu 2000).

The Khwe have repeatedly signalled their continuing loyalty to the Namibian government and dismissed claims that they are collaborating with Unita.[119] Proof of collaboration has not been presented, but members of the Khwe ethnic group, nevertheless, face general suspicion. The myth that the Khwe act as enemies of the state refuses to die. Far from being but rumours and opinions, it has to be taken seriously as it can easily result, and has

---

[117] The Namibian, 7.4.2000. *Terror strikes north-east.*

[118] Field notes 23.1.2001.

[119] The Khwe themselves are not free from making unproven accusations towards others. A Khwe headman, disclaiming that Khwe people were collaborating with Unita, said "it is not true, but there are Kavangos working with Unita" as they speak the same language (Allgemeine Zeitung, 9.10.2000. *Khwe Notschrei an Innenminister*; The Namibian, 9.10.2000. *Khwe living in fear*).

resulted, in political action. Obviously, this myth is even more deadly than the myth of the primordial San, which has to be rejected not primarily because it is false, but because it was used for the purpose of excluding people from development and other resources and denying them an equal position in society (Marshall 1991).

To be lumped with CLA and Unita rebels is understood by the Khwe people in just this way; namely, as not being accepted as Namibians with equal rights and status, or, worse, not even as human beings.

> We are also not living like other Namibians in an independent Namibia because we are being picked up and arrested randomly.[120]

> Mbukushu, like SFF, are talking about us that we are Unita. That we are clever. That we know how to kill someone. They are much afraid of us. It is very difficult to survive with Mbukushu. It seems we are not living in Namibia. Because there is much apartheid. It seems we are not human beings.[121]

People are also especially sensitive to unequal treatment according to ethnic affiliation.

> Since the SFF arrived they punish us for any mistake. They don't talk to us. I never saw that they talked. It seems that the SFF is also looking on us like slaves. You can beat your slave. You will not talk to a slave. You only talk to a human being. As the Boers treated the Ovambos, they are treating us now. I never saw them acting towards Mbukushu in the same way.[122]

Although Khwe maintain that they were the only ones harassed by security forces, while Mbukushu, Kavango and Ovambo people were spared such experiences, newspaper reports show that this is not altogether true. Not only were members of other ethnic groups victims of attacks and mine blasts,[123] but also of suspicion and reproaches of collaboration as well as harassment and rights abuses.[124]

---

[120] Field notes 17.1.2001.

[121] Field notes 23.1.2001.

[122] Field notes 19.1.2001.

[123] E.g., The Namibian, 13.3.2000. *Rundu in rocket near miss.*

[124] E.g., The Namibian, 17.5.2000. *Mine kills boy, injures brother.*

Khwe rhetoric describes their position in independent Namibia as victims of an apartheid attitude held by their fellow Namibians. They not only see and represent themselves as victims, but also ask others, e.g., reporters, NGO workers and cultural anthropologists, to represent them as victims in the national and international arena. In doing so they actively try to seek support from more powerful allies as making a wider audience aware of their fate is hoped to potentially raise their marginal status. In this they are seeking to compensate for their ethnic 'visibility' that makes them victims of security forces on the local level with visibility on the level of the international community that is hoped to provide protection. To speak of victims does not mean to deny them of being self-determined actors. Rather, in their current situation, the Khwe can be said as acting as victims. 'Victim' is a moral concept, and it is the moral dimension that the Khwe are referring to when putting the blame on the government and security forces, as well as requesting better living conditions from them. From a moral perspective, there is no doubt that Khwe and other San's human and legal rights have often been violated in the past and present. However, from a more theoretical perspective, the actions of Khwe people, like those of all other human beings, are constrained by facts and developments not under their control. They act in a self-determined way according to what they perceive and judge as being the best options. Such options, however, not only keep changing objectively, e.g. by the issuing of a new bill or the infringement of an armed conflict, but perceptions and judgements change as well due to, for example, education, crisis or just the experience of life and changing relationships.

Summary

The Khwe hopes of early 1998 have all been dashed by recent developments. The proclamation of Bwabwata National Park is still pending, and the establishment of a conservancy in the park is rendered impossible. The refusal to recognise the Khwe Traditional Authority has aggrieved people especially because it means that they are subjects of the Mbukushu chief. An appeal at the Namibian High Court is currently being prepared by the LAC.[125] The secessionist rebellion in East Caprivi has caused many Khwe to seek refuge in Botswana. Most of them were repatriated in July 1999, only to flee again due to the state of insecurity in West Caprivi caused by the overspill of the Angolan civil war since January 2000, in the course of which the Khwe were also exposed to Unita raids and to suspicion,

---

[125] Norman Tjombe, LAC, pers. comm.; March 2002.

harassment and even rights abuses by the Namibian security forces. The state of insecurity has had serious impacts on Khwe food security and the economic prospects for access to and control of resources. The latter depend on the implementation of planned measures to insure community benefits from resources in the Bwabwata National Park, which will replace the Caprivi Game Park. In order to enjoy prospected benefits, recognised institutions have to be in place. However, the establishment of such institutions is hindered by the state of insecurity in West Caprivi and, even more so, by the lack of governmental recognition of Khwe leadership.

The denial of state-recognised power correlates to the exclusion from access to resources controlled by the state. The matters of land rights, political representation and insecurity are intermingled to the extent that development of the Khwe in economic and political terms seems to be 'caught in the middle'. The state of insecurity hinders the prospects of the Bwabwata National Park, as well as the election of a new Khwe leader by the community. The absence of a strong Khwe leader weakens the Khwe stand with regard to encroachment by security forces, as well as other matters, not the least of which is in negotiations with government institutions about the community benefits of the planned Bwabwata National Park.

The Khwe interpret their present situation in Namibia by reverting to historic relationships with their fellow Namibians, above all, their former Mbukushu slave-masters and their former enemies of war. The ethnic conflict between Khwe and Mbukushu has been fuelled by recent state decisions. Mbukushu people are said to economically and politically exploit the overspill of the Angolan civil war. The conflict between Khwe and security forces is expressed in ethnic terms as well as in terms of political party. It is also due to the fact that West Caprivi is geographically located between two international borders.[126]

---

[126] Another conflict that will have impacts on the lives of Khwe people in the future could arise if plans to build a hydropower scheme at Popa Falls are realised. The Ministry of Mines and Energy has recently commissioned a feasibility study (The Namibian, 9.1.2002. *Rivers body raises Popa concerns*). The scheme would not only endanger the unique ecosystem of the Okavango Delta in Botswana, but consequently also the yearly 350-million-US-dollar-tourism business connected to it, and is therefore disposed to lead to an international conflict between both countries. Not only would it be the deathblow to the long-struggled for Khwe Community Campsite, but also, as Khwe live on both sides of the border, they easily could be worn down in a possible conflict.

In the current West Caprivi setting, competitors for resources increasingly group along ethnic lines. Although rival groups claim their own cultural distinctiveness and autonomy, ethnicity is not the reason for the conflict, but its ideological form, and memories of former mutual mistreatment are used to nourish contemporary hatred (cf. Fukui and Markakis 1994b). In the Khwe case, suffering, discrimination and victimisation are at the centre of their constructed commonality, which can, to a certain degree, be extended to all other San. Unlike other San groups in independent Namibia, however, development progress and the normalisation of the political environment, however small they may generally be among San (cf. Suzman 2001), have suffered an additional setback during recent years. The ceasefire in Angola may now open the door for progress and development. The Namibian state holds the key position for granting access to development. It mainly depends on how enabling and fair the state will act towards the Khwe whether, and to what extent, they will be able to take part in the development process.

References

Almeida, A. de
1965   The Black Bushmen (Zama or Kwengo). In: Tobias, P.V. and J. Blacking (eds.). *Bushmen and other Non-Bantu Peoples of Angola. Three Lectures by António de Almeida.* Johannesburg:13-22.

Amnesty International
2000   *Angola and Namibia. Human Rights Abuses in the Border Area.* AI-index: AFR 03/001/2000. web.amnesty.org/ai.nsf.

Bahuchet, Serge, and Henri Guillaume
1982   Aka-Farmer Relations in the Northeast Congo Basin. In: Leacock, E. and R.B. Lee (eds.). *Politics and History in Band Societies.* Cambridge: Cambridge University Press.

Biesele, Megan
1993   Land, Language and Leadership. Jul'hoan Bushmen Present a Model of Self-Determination, both before and since Namibian Independence. *Cultural Survival* Summer 1993:57-60.

Biesele, Megan, and Robert K. Hitchcock
2000   The Jul'hoansi San under Two States. Impacts of the South West African Administration and the Government of the Republic of Namibia. In: Schweitzer, P., Biesele, M. and R.K. Hitchcock (eds.). *Hunters and Gatherers in the Modern World. Conflict, Resistance, and Self-Determination*. New York and Oxford:305-326.

2002   Caught in the Crossfire. The Caprivi Strip *Cultural Survival Quarterly* 26 (1):30.

Boden, Gertrud
1997   *Jäger und Gejagte. Die Buschleute im südlichen Afrika.* Katalog zur gleichnamigen Ausstellung im Kultur- und Stadthistorischen Museum Duisburg 7.9.1997-4.1.1998. Oberhausen: Plitt.

2001   Falsche Buschleute – Echte San? Identität, kulturelle Diversität und materialisierte Kultur bei den Kxoe im West-Caprivi (Namibia). In: Eisenhofer, S. (ed.). *Tracing the Rainbow. Art and Life in Southern Africa*. Stuttgart: Arnoldsche:192-201.

2002   *Khwe Traditional Authority.* Unpublished Report to the Legal Assistance Centre. March 2002.

Boden, Gertrud, and Stefanie Michels
2000   *Kxoe Material Culture. Aspects of Change and its Documentation.* Khoisan Forum Working Paper No. 16. Cologne: University of Cologne.

Brenzinger, Matthias
1998   Moving to Survive. Kxoe Communities in Arid Lands. In: Schladt, Mathias (ed.). *Language, Identity, and Conceptualization in Khoisan*. Research in Khoisan Studies 15. Cologne: Köppe.

2000   *Report on the Situation of San Communities in Angola and Zambia for the Legal Assistance Centre, Namibia.* Windhoek: LAC.

Brown, C.J., and B.T.B. Jones
1994   *Results of a Socio-Ecological Survey of the West Caprivi Strip, Namibia: A Strategic Community-Based Environment and Development Plan.* Windhoek: Directorate of Environmental Affairs. Ministry of Wildlife, Conservation and Tourism.

Enloe, G.
1973   *Ethnic Conflict and Political Development.* Boston: Little Brown.

Erasmus, P.A.
1997   The Harmless People: From Stone-age Hunter to Modern Soldier. *South African Journal of Ethnology* 20 (4):165-170.

Felton, Silke
1998   *Report of the San Community Assessment Visit to West Caprivi (Mukwe Constituency) 2-6 June 1998.* Windhoek: Centre for Applied Social Sciences. University of Namibia.

Fisch, Maria
1999   *Hintergründe der Separatistenbewegung im Caprivi.* Windhoek: Namibia Scientific Society.

Fosse, Leif John
1996   *Negotiating the Nation in Local Terms: Ethnicity and Nationalism in Eastern Caprivi.* MA Thesis. University of Oslo.

Fukui, Katsuyoshi, and John Markakis (eds.)
1994a   *Ethnicity and Conflict in the Horn of Africa.* London: James Currey and Ohio University Press.

1994b   Introduction. In: Fukui, K. and J. Markakis (eds.). *Ethnicity and Conflict in the Horn of Africa.* London: James Currey and Ohio University Press:1-14.

Gordon, Robert
1992   *The Bushman Myth. The Making of a Namibian Underclass.* Boulder: Westview Press.

Hitchcock, Robert K.
1996   *Kalahari Communities: Bushmen and the Politics of the Environment in Southern Africa.* IWGIA Document 79. Copenhagen: International Work Group for Indigenous Affairs.

2000   *The Kavango Basin: A Case Study.* The Waterpage: www.thewaterpage.com/okavango_case_study.htm.

James, Wendy
1994   War and Ethnic Visibility: The Uduk on the Sudan-Ethiopia Border. In: Fukui, K. and J. Markakis (eds.). *Ethnicity and Conflict in the Horn of Africa.* London: James Currey and Ohio University Press:140-166.

Jansen, Ruud, Pradhan, Neville, and John Spencer
1994   *Bushmen Ex-Servicemen and Dependents Rehabilitation and Settlement Programme. West Bushmanland and Western Caprivi. Republic of Namibia. Evaluation. Final Report April 1994.* Windhoek: Evangelical Lutheran Church in Namibia and Royal Norwegian Embassy/NORAD.

Kangumu, Bennett K.
2000   *A Forgotten Corner of Namibia: Aspects of the History of the Caprivi Strip, c 1939-1980.* MA Thesis. University of Cape Town.

Köhler, Oswin
1989   *Die Welt der Kxoé Buschleute im südlichen Afrika. Eine Selbstdarstellung in ihrer eigenen Sprache.* Vol. I: *Die Kxoé-Buschleute und ihre ethnische Umgebung.* Berlin: Reimer.

Markakis, John
1994   Ethnic Conflict and the State in the Horn of Africa. In: Fukui, K. and J. Markakis (eds.). *Ethnicity and Conflict in the Horn of Africa.* London: James Currey and Ohio University Press:217-237.

Marshall, John
1991   Tödliche Mythen. In: Kapfer, R., Petermann, W. and R. Thoms (eds.). *Jäger und Gejagte. John Marshall und seine Filme.* Munich: Trickster:9-50.

Mendelsohn, John, and C. Roberts
1997   *An Environmental Atlas of Caprivi.* Windhoek: Directorate of Environmental Affairs.

MET, Ministry of Environment and Tourism
o.J. [1999]   *Conservation in Caprivi and the Vision for the Future. Backgrounder.* Unpublished Paper.

2001   *Conservation. The Importance of the Environment for Development in Namibia.* Special Edition. Windhoek.

Möllers, Hein
1999   Caprivi im Ausnahmezustand. *Afrika Süd.* Juli/August 1999 (4):2.

NSHR, National Society for Human Rights
2001   *Namibia: Human Rights Report. Summarised Version.* www.nshr.org.na.

Osaki, Masakazu
2001   Reconstructing the Recent History of the Glui and G‖ana Bushmen. In: Tanaka, J., Ichikawa, M. and D. Kimura (eds.). *African Hunter-Gatherers: Persisting Cultures and Comtemporary Problems.* African Study Monographs, Suppl. 26. Kyoto: The Center For African Area Studies:27-39.

Piek, Janine
1998   The Role of Traditional Authorities in Natural Resource Management. In: d'Engelbronner-Kolff, F.M., Hinz, M.O. and J.L. Sindano (eds.). *Traditional Authority and Democracy in Southern Africa.* University of Namibia: Centre for Applied Social Sciences:228-246.

Rousset, Karine
2002   *Report on West Caprivi Situation. January 2002.* Unpublished IRDNC report.

forthc. *To Be Khwe Means to Suffer: Local Dynamics, Imbalances and Contestations in the Caprivi Game Park.* MA Thesis to be presented at the University of Cape Town.

Schladt, Mathias (ed).
1998   *Language, Identity, and Conceptualization in Khoisan.* Research in Khoisan Studies 15. Cologne: Köppe.

Seiner, F.
1908   Ergebnisse einer Bereisung des Gebiets zwischen Okawango und Sambesi (Caprivi-Zipfel) in den Jahren 1905 und 1906. *Mitteilungen aus den Deutschen Schutzgebieten* 22 (1):1-111.

Sen, A.
1981   *Poverty and Famines. An Essay on Entitlements.* Oxford: Clarendon Press.

Sharp, J.
1994   *!Xũ Bushmen Leave the South African Army: "Culture" and Practical Anthropology in the New South Africa.* Paper read at the Annual Conference of the Pan African Association of Anthropologists. Douala, 7-10 August 1994.

Silberbauer, George B. and Adam J. Kuper
1966   Kgalagadi Masters and Bushman Serfs: Some Observations. *African Studies* 25:171-179.

Suzman, James
2001   *Regional Assessment of the Status of the San in Southern Africa. An Assessment of the Status of the San in Namibia.* Report No. 4 of 5. Windhoek: Legal Assistance Centre.

Taylor, M.
2000   *Life, Land and Power. Contesting Development in Northern Botswana.* PhD Thesis. Edinburgh: University of Edinburgh.

Tonder, Louis L., van
1966   *The Hambukushu of Okavangoland. An Anthropological Study of a South-Western Bantu People in Africa.* PhD Thesis.

Uys, I.
1993   *Bushman Soldiers. Their Alpha and Omega.* Germiston 1993.

Wilhelm, J.H.
1954   Die Hukwe. Mit einer Einführung, Anmerkungen, Schlußbetrachtung und einer Karte von F.R. Lehmann. *Jahrbuch des Museums für Völkerkunde zu Leipzig* XIII:8-44.

Wilmsen, Edwin N.
1989   *Land Filled with Flies. A Political Economy of the Kalahari.* Chicago and London: University of Chicago Press.

Wölle, R.
1999   Zündstoff im Caprivi. *afrika süd.* Januar/Februar 1999 (1):23; 26-27.

Zeller, Wolfgang
2000   *Interests and Socio-Economic Development in the Caprivi Region from a Historical Perspective.* NEPRU Occasional Paper No. 19. Windhoek: The Namibian Economic Policy Research Unit.

"We are looking for life.
We are looking for the conservancy"[1]
Namibian Conservancies, Nature Conservation
and Rural Development: The N‡a-Jaqna Conservancy

Thekla Hohmann

Introduction

Since the demise of colonial and Apartheid politics in Southern Africa, discussions around land and resource rights have been playing an important role in social, political and scientific discourse[2]. This discourses has been based on the fact that the Apartheid system has grossly discriminated against rural populations in terms of access to land and natural resources. Their decision making and use rights have been curtailed to a great extent. Suggestions on how this historical injustice should be compensated for in a suitable way in the new independent political setting, however, are manifold and sometimes conflicting.

Community-based natural resource management (CBNRM) is the primary approach currently employed by several national governments in the region to restore justice in terms of rights to natural resources. CBNRM programmes are designed to give rural-area dwellers conditional legal rights to manage and benefit from wildlife and tourism, with some of them recently also planning to incorporate plant resources. An important tool for CBNRM in Namibia is the conservancy programme. This chapter will first discuss the legislation regulating the establishment of conservancies in Namibia with its historical and motivational background. Secondly, it will analyse aspects of their practical implementation and discuss social and political effects of the implementation process on the local setting, and local actors' perceptions and reactions to conservancies. Finally, the conservancies' potential role in common property resource (CPR) management will be discussed. This chapter will focus on a case study of the planned N‡a-Jaqna Conservancy in

---

[1] Quote by a Jul'hoan woman in Tsumkwe District West during a conservancy planning meeting in 1998. Interview excerpts are presented in my own translation from Afrikaans to English.

[2] See recent publications on the issue; for instance: Cousins 2000; Rohde 1994; Ibsen and Turner 2000; and Meer 1997.

Tsumkwe District West, the former Homeland "Bushmanland," in northeastern Namibia[3].

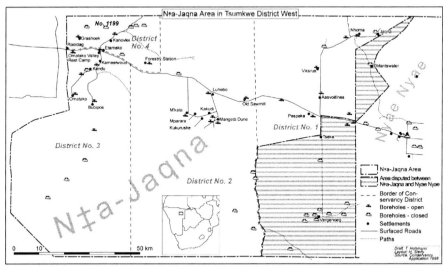

Map 1: Tsumkwe District West

By devolving proprietorship over resources and concessionary rights over tourism to rural populations, and thereby giving them the opportunity to benefit economically, CBNRM addresses the disparities in access and rights to natural resources imposed on them by colonial politics. The ideology of environmental protection that stemmed from the colonial period had led to the introduction of strict conservation regimes all over Southern Africa that were counterproductive to the interests of local populations, which Adams and Hulme term "fortress conservation" (Adams and Hulme 2001:10). Until today, the objective of protecting the environment and maintaining biodiversity has played a vital role in connection to CBNRM, especially among regional and international development agencies involved in implementing the concept. The rapid internationalisation of the related discourse has recently forced governments in Southern Africa to adjust their policies to propositions and guidelines created for CBNRM by external

---

[3]   The site of the field research will further be referred to as Tsumkwe West. It is adjacent to Tsumkwe East, where the Nyae Nyae Conservancy was granted approval in February 1998 as Namibia's first communal area conservancy (cf. table 1).

organisations, internationally received researchers[4], politicians and the media. As a consequence, the design of conservation policies has been modified immensely after the end of Apartheid. In addition to rural development and nature conservation, the CBNRM idea is frequently associated with the goals of empowering indigenous minorities worldwide and increasing their tenure security for land.[5] This is shown in recent strategies and programmes of an influential lobby, including organisations such as the United Nations, the World Bank, and some specialised international non-governmental organisations (NGOs).[6] In the majority of Southern African countries, the CBNRM approach has become the basis of projects currently being implemented with the assistance of national and international NGOs and CBOs (community-based organisations).[7] In these projects, contrary to former colonial policy, local actors with their resource management strategies are now conceived of as active stakeholders in environmental management. Local groups and their interests are meant to be incorporated as beneficiaries into the CBNRM strategy, an objective mentioned in policies and project proposals; however, this is sometimes questionable in practice. The CBNRM concept was developed by the state and, in most cases, is implemented by NGOs in Namibia's communal areas, whereby the state's and NGOs' aims are not always in accordance with local actors' aims or perceptions. The realisation of these aims depends on the

---

[4] See, for example, Hulme and Murphree 2001, Mehta 1999, and Thomas-Slayter and Sodikoff 2001.

[5] Most of the Namibian CBNRM projects are situated in areas inhabited by minority groups.

[6] Currently the World Bank's project database, for instance, lists six projects in operation and one in the works related to indigenous populations worldwide, with a total budget of 1067.95 million US$. One World Bank project with a total cost of 7.93 million US$ is in the field of community-based natural resource management and tourism in South Africa (http://www4.worldbank.org/s projects/).

[7] These are ADMADE (Administrative Management Design) in Zambia, CAMPFIRE (Communal Areas Management Programme for Indigenous Resources) in Zimbabwe, NRMP (Natural Resources Management Programme) in Botswana and LIFE (Living In a Finite Environment), which is implementing the communal area conservancy projects in Namibia, all of them funded by USAID (United States Agency for International Development). The CBNRM component of USAID's programme in Namibia in 2001 had a budget of 2.8 million US$. According to USAID, a total of ten international donors have provided more than 4 US$ million to support CBNRM activities in Namibia (http://www.usaid.gov/pubs/bj2001/afr/na/namibia_ads.html).

national social and political context and on the local setting in which CBNRM is implemented. Critical assessments of the CBNRM concept and its intended and unintended effects have increasingly been made in the social sciences during recent years, and doubts about the potential of CBNRM projects for generating tangible benefits for their participants have been voiced.[8] This chapter is to be understood as a critical contribution in this respect, taking into account the specific implications of the Namibian government's current conservation approach for the San population in Tsumkwe West[9].

Like all the other chapters in this volume, this chapter should also be understood as a contribution to San research in terms of a way to move beyond the Kalahari debate. The San described here, with their perceptions and actions, are not seen exclusively as isolated foragers, nor as members of a submerged underclass but as global actors participating in social networks and political action reaching much further than the Kalahari's boundaries. San groups in Namibia and Botswana have been deprived of their resources and positive self-image by colonial and post-Independence politics, among other things, in the name of nature conservation and are continuously affected by racist perceptions and the actions of outsiders. Sullivan (2001) has demonstrated such detrimental perceptions when referring to a newspaper quote by an unnamed Namibian government official who commented on the death of five Khwe due to starvation: "[t]o them it is a natural thing that at this time of year people should die of hunger" (Inambao 1998). Many San groups have embarked on CBNRM as they perceive it as one among extremely few chances to improve their situation in economic, but importantly, also in political terms.[10] It is one of the discourses in which

---

[8] Cf. Sullivan 1999; Sullivan 2000; Sullivan 2001; Taylor 2000:233-267; and Suzman 2001:13-16.

[9] The term "San" is used here when refering to the entire group of people with a foraging background and speaking Khoisan languages who live in Tsumkwe West. This population group consists of sub-groups having different languages and places of origin (as explained in detail in paragraph 4.). Where possible I will use the ethnonyms that actors use to refer to themselves. A lot of what is being said here however, refers to the entire group which is currently consolidating itself as such in order to achieve common political goals. In this context, the term San is the one used not only in Tsumkwe West by many of them as well as by NGO and government personnel (see also Widlok 1999:17).

[10] San constitute the majority group in three of the fifteen registered or planned CBNRM projects in Namibia, and many CBNRM initiatives in Botswana lie in areas in which the San constitute a part of or the majority of the population.

recently emerged political action and articulation of San groups on a regional and international level is manifest.

Methodology

The findings presented here are based on observations made and interviews conducted during 16 months of fieldwork, both scientific and developmental, in Tsumkwe West between January 1998 and November 2001. It resulted in the author's MA thesis (Hohmann 2000) and was connected to several consultancies carried out for two NGOs assisting the San community of Tsumkwe West in establishing the Nǂa-Jaqna Conservancy[11].

My involvement in social anthropological fieldwork on the one hand and development work on the other could be seen as a potential problem for the objectivity of the data. On the contrary, however, I see it as a great advantage to have had the opportunity to become part of local processes of conservancy establishment to some extent. It gave me the privilege to engage in participatory observation and to follow the discussion about CBNRM in the field from different angles. Through this I was able to take the different perspectives offered by local stakeholders, development agencies and government institutions into account.

CBNRM and the Namibian Conservancy Concept

For the purposes of this chapter, I will define CBNRM using Hulme's and Murphree's description of the concept of "community conservation" as one example of

> [...] ideas, policies, practices and behaviours that seek to give those who live in rural environments greater involvement in managing the natural resources (soil, water, species, habitats, landscapes or biodiversity) that exist in the areas in which they reside (be that permanently or temporarily) and/or access to benefits derived from those resources. (Hulme and Murphree 2001:4).

According to various policy papers and development programmes of NGOs and other agencies, CBNRM is meant to foster sustainable natural

---

[11] Namely, the Working Group of Indigenous Minorities in Southern Africa (WIMSA) and the Centre for Applied Social Sciences (CASS).

resource management by offering economic incentives to local people in order to protect their environment.

The agency responsible for nature conservation policy in Namibia is the Ministry of Environment and Tourism (MET), which formulated the aims of participatory planning of land use in a policy paper from 1994: "The Ministry recognises that the success of all development projects will rest on the extent to which local communities have participated in the planning of land use and have real decision making power" (MET 1994:2). In a second document, the MET mentions the following objectives of an "economically based system for the management and utilisation of wildlife and other renewable living resources on communal land":

    a. to participate on a partnership basis with this and other Ministries in the management of, and benefits from, natural resources;

    b. to benefit from rural development based on wildlife, tourism and other natural resource management;

    c. to improve the conservation of natural resources by wise and sustainable resource management and the protection of our biodiversity (MET 1995:1).

This quote shows the different levels of objectives the MET is pursuing through the CBNRM idea in accordance to the general objectives connected to this approach that I summarised above. Paragraph a. formulates the political objective of creating a "partnership basis" between administration and local population that can be seen firstly as a counteraction to the Apartheid political system, which had prevented any equal partnership between these two. Secondly elevating the local population to the level of partners in the management of their environment also benefits the national administration in that it can devolve responsibility for environmental protection to the local level. It must be critically mentioned here that this attempt to shift costs and responsibilities for conservation to the local level is accompanied by assumptions based on existing projects and calculations according to which CBNRM will yield very little additional income on the local level (cf. Sullivan 2001:18). The costs of wildlife conservation especially also include

    policing of people's activities in relation to wildlife; [...] the funding of community institutions designed to manage wildlife and related revenues; and [...] the day-to-day experience of living with large and sometimes dangerous mammals (Sullivan 2001:17).

Hill (1996:106) has hinted at some other interests that Southern African states have in CBNRM:

> The state uses conservation policies in much the same way as it uses taxation, investment, interest rate, or land resettlement policies; to establish and extend its own interests, in which in a relatively new and tenuous polity, centre on authority maintenance and extension.

Paragraph b. of the MET's policy document quoted above refers to the economic objectives linked to the CBNRM approach when talking of local groups benefiting from rural development. Both the envisaged "partnership" relation between administration and local population, as well as the economic incentives offered are meant to motivate people to manage natural resources sustainably. Finally, paragraph c. contains objectives connected to environmental protection when using terms like "conservation," "*wise* and *sustainable* resource management" and "protection of *our* biodiversity." This section seems to be aimed solely at the promotion of the Namibian CBNRM concept. The highly positively connoted terms I highlighted in italics remain completely undefined.

The amended nature conservation legislation of 1996[12] introduced the concept of communal area conservancies[13] defined in the Act as "a demarcated piece of communal land to which a group of persons, resident on this land, is being granted the right to sustainable use of game." The conservancy owns the huntable game, i.e., kudu, oryx, springbok, bushpig, buffalo and warthog, and holds exclusive concessionary rights to tourism within its area. Hunting quotas however, are worked out and awarded by the MET, thus, the state keeps the ultimate power over wildlife. While the legislation so far has only transferred ownership and management rights of wildlife and tourism to communal area conservancies, a similar concept for communal management of forest resources is currently being considered.[14] Conservancy projects have been planned and established in many locations,

---

[12] The Nature Conservation Amendment Act, 5 of 1996.

[13] By using the term conservancy I will further refer to communal area conservancies if not specified otherwise.

[14] As a consequence, forest resources have already been included into the management plan of the N‡a-Jaqna Conservancy in Tsumkwe West in 1998 because of their vital importance for the San's livelihoods.

especially in the Kunene and Caprivi Regions, as well as in Tsumkwe District. Since 1998 a total of fourteen conservancies have been gazetted and at least 30 more are in various stages of planning according to the MET[15] (see map 2). Altogether 38,500 km^2, i.e., approximately 5% of the Namibian territory and over 30,000 people, are formally involved in the conservancy programme[16].

Table 1: registered communal area conservancies[17]

	Name	Region	Biome	Date registered	Size (km^2)	registered members
1	Nyae Nyae	Otjozon-djupa	Woodland	02/1998	9 003	752
2	Salambala	Caprivi	Woodland	06/1998	930	3-4 000
3	Torra	Kunene	Desert	06/1998	3 522	450
4	#Khoadi //Hôas	Kunene	Desert / Savanna	06/1998	3 366	1 600
5	Twyfelfontein -Uibasen	Kunene	Desert / Savanna	12/1999	400	61
6	Doro !Nawas	Kunene	Desert/ Savanna	12/1999	4073	430
7	Kwandu	Caprivi	Woodland	12/1999	190	1 800
8	Mayuni	Caprivi	Woodland	12/1999	151	1 500
9	Wuparo	Caprivi	Woodland	12/1999	148	1 700
10	Puros	Kunene	Desert	05/2000	3 568	85
11	Tsiseb	Erongo	Desert	01/2001	8 083	950
12	Ehi-Rovipuka	Kunene	Savanna	01/2001	1 975	500
13	Marienfluss	Kunene	Desert	01/2001	3 034	121
14	Oskop	Hardap	Shrub Savanna	02/2001	95	20

---

[15] http://www.dea.met.gov.na/programmes/cbnrm/conservancies.htm#conslist
[16] http://www.dea.met.gov.na/data/publications/leaflets/1-wild.pdf
[17] (Source: http://www.dea.met.gov.na/programmes/cbnrm/conservancies.htm# conslist).

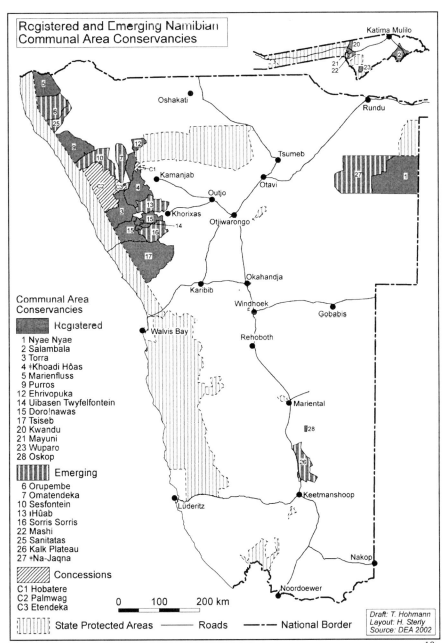

Map 2: Gazetted and planned Namibian communal area conservancies[18]

---

[18] Source: http://www.dea.met.gov.na/programmes/cbnrm/images/conserv.pdf.

Since the programme's beginning, CBNRM, in the form of communal area conservancies, has been considered a promising strategy to foster their aims by both local stakeholders and the Namibian government. In September 1998, the Namibian government was even the first country worldwide awarded with the international Gift to the Earth Award for the conservancy programme by World Wildlife Fund (The Namibian:28.09.1998). Although at first sight, the conservancy idea looks very successful in serving both national and local goals, it is not always easily applicable to the local setting, nor successful in ensuring both conservation and 'development' of local populations. Reasons for this have been the subject of a growing number of publications on different case studies[19]. Before summarising and analysing some of these reasons in detail, I will give a brief introduction to the local setting of Tsumkwe West, where the N‡a-Jaqna Conservancy that I will refer to in my analysis is situated.

Tsumkwe District West and the N‡a-Jaqna Conservancy – Ethnographical Background

Tsumkwe West, which encompasses approximately 9600 km^2, is situated in northeastern Namibia in the semi-arid Kalahari Desert in the eastern part of the newly formed Otjozondjupa Region. It is situated outside the former police zone that was proclaimed by the German colonial administration in 1906 and became Namibia's communal areas after 1990. It borders the commercial farm sector, with mostly Afrikaaner-owned private farms in the west and the Nyae Nyae Conservancy in the east. The district's borders as shown on map 1 have existed in their present way since the proclamation of the entire district as the Homeland "Bushmanland" in 1976. They had been earmarked and set aside for the Namibian "Bushman" population arbitrarily by the South African administration according to the so-called Odendaal-Plan of 1964. Bushmanland remained an administrational entity isolated to a large extent from its surroundings and administered from Tsumkwe town until Namibian Independence in 1990. Although its borders do thus not reflect particularly long-standing geographical or cultural borders, they have come to be perceived more and more as given facts by the district's population and by outsiders. The same holds true for the internal border between the west and the east areas of the district. Its history and present implications will be described in more detail in section 5.2. The former isolation, which must be perceived as part of the discriminatory Apartheid

---

[19] See, for example, Turner 1996; Mosimane 1996; Sullivan 1999, 2000, and 2001; and Jones 2001.

background and which resulted in the state's firm control of the San's resources, choice of economic strategies and lives, has also, as a consequence, resulted in the relative protection of the land from unwanted immigration by outsiders (as non-San were defined and restricted by the administration at that time). This relative security disappeared with Namibian Independence when the right to free choice of residence was granted to all Namibian citizens in the constitution. Today, this is often used as an argument by outsiders moving into Tsumkwe West against the express will of the local San majority and members of the !Kung Traditional Authority[20].

The high quantitative and spatial variability of the generally scarce rainfall – the average yearly rainfall is about 400 mm (Wiese 1997:42) – in the arid environment of Tsumkwe West determines the prevalence of natural resources such as surface and ground water, grazing, wildlife and plants. As a consequence, all of them are relatively scarce and variable. Throughout its history the district's population has applied flexible economic strategies based primarily on using wildlife and plant resources in a foraging lifestyle in order to adapt to such adverse and uncertain conditions[21].

For detailed population figures one will have to wait for the results of the 2001 national population census. Statements on population numbers and especially about the ethnic backgrounds in Tsumkwe West will probably have to remain estimations in the near future, as the population census unfortunately does not offer a differentiation between language groups. My estimates are based on different sets of data: census data from 1991, data from a field survey by Thoma and Piek in 1997, and the figures of people currently registered as N‡a-Jaqna Conservancy members (see table 1, page 217).

According to my own estimates, about 120 non-San and up to about 170 San have not registered for the conservancy in certain places partly due to opposition to the conservancy and partly because of absence during the time of registration. The majority of the region's population are San from various geographical origins and languages, i.e., !Xun both from the area around the

---

[20] A body of 11 elected San recognised according to the Traditional Authorities Act, 8 of 1997 as laid down in government gazette No. 307 of 1998. The general position and role of its members in the CBNRM endeavour in Tsumkwe West will be detailed further in section 5.4.

[21] For a detailed account of economic strategies used by the San in Tsumkwe West nowadays see Botelle and Rohde 1995:51-96.

Omuramba Omatako and from Angola – the latter ones are also called
Vasekela –, Jul'hoansi from the adjacent Tsumkwe East and the present
Khaudom National Park, and Mpungu – or alternatively termed Mahenge –
from the Kavango Region. Residents with other ethnic backgrounds
originally came from the surrounding areas inhabited mainly by Herero and
various groups from the Kavango and Caprivi. Some Damara and Ovambo
families have also moved to Tsumkwe West. The most recent immigrants
came for two major reasons, i.e., either to work as government employees in
the regional offices or to engage in livestock farming with their herds of
primarily cattle and goats[22]. The San make a living from a range of
economic strategies that they apply in a flexible and dynamic manner
depending on the spatial and seasonal availability of resources. These
include hunting and gathering, the production and sale of handicrafts, crop
and livestock farming, and in fewer instances, wage labour for communal or
commercial farmers, tourism projects or the regional state institutions.
Furthermore they acquire part of their income through state subsidies and
pension money. San have stated in interviews that nowadays land, plant and
wildlife resources have become too scarce to continue making a living from
hunting and gathering, their traditional economic strategy. Most of them
ascribe this to climatic conditions and/or the high population density, which
resulted from the influx of people in the 1970s (field notes 12.09. to
15.09.2001). Hunting and gathering does, however, still make a vital
contribution to household incomes so that access to and control of natural
resources are of great concern to the San. During Botelle's and Rohde's
survey interviewees ranked bushfood as the most important source of food
for households (Botelle and Rohde 1995:66-70). Hunting was ranked fifth
behind food aid, crops and store-bought food. The ranking of hunting in
interviews, however, is problematic because, as of this date, hunting in
Tsumkwe West is illegal.[23] On informal occasions as well as in interviews,
several San mentioned to me that they usually "also look for huntable game
when looking for bushfood," which some of the household members do
almost every day. In this light, the new CBNRM programmes are perceived
by many of them as an opportunity to, above all, increase and secure
resource rights in terms of hunting legally and owning the huntable game
and through that gain increased control over land.

---

[22] Most of the government employees engage in farming as a supplementary
economic activity.

[23] Cf. for the negative consequences of this ban by the state for Jul'hoansi in
Tsumkwe District East and their attitudes towards nature conservation as
promoted by the state: Biesele and Hitchcock 2000:320.

Table 1: population figures for Tsumkwe District[24]

Village	Conser-vancy mem-bers 1998	Conser vancy mem-bers 2000	Thoma/ Piek 1997	State Census 1991 Bushm an-land total	State Census 1991 Central and Western Bushma n-land
Aasvoëlnes	56	103			
Bubipos	31	54			
Etameko	5	24			
Grashoek	76	109	50		
Kameelwout	6	24			
Kandu	26	51			
Kankudi	23	41			
Kanovlei	101	119	107		
Kukurushe	0	0			
Luhebo	34	47			
Mangetti	81	99	200		
M'kata	102	130			
Mparara	50	53			
Nhoma	53	40	60		
Omatako	114	237	700		
Omatako Valley Restcamp	46	62			
Perspeka	19	25	70		
Rooidaghek	0	45			
Viksrus	12	12	40		
Total	**835**	**1275**	**1227**	**3851**	**2358**

---

[24] The differences between conservancy members in 1998 and 2000 arose because, after an initial registration process, amendments to the conservancy application became necessary and the opportunity was used to also conduct a second registration. The estimates of Thoma and Piek (1997) are based solely on the figures that interviewees from the respective villages mentioned themselves, and in addition to that, are incomplete as 12 of the 19 villages are not included.

The planning for N≠a-Jaqna Conservancy[25] in Tsumkwe West commenced in January 1998. At that time, the Southern African NGO Working Group of Indigenous Minorities in Southern Africa (WIMSA) and the Namibian Centre for Applied Social Sciences (CASS), on request by the San chief, sent me as a permanent field worker/researcher to the region. The chief, along with some community members, wanted to establish a community-based tourism and resource management project in the area. Planning for the conservancy went on intensively until a first draft application was submitted to the MET in September 1998. By that time its boundaries had been defined to encompass the entire Tsumkwe District West, a conservancy constitution had been written regulating membership, decision-making processes (e.g., meeting procedures), and the composition and election of a conservancy committee. Between one and three representatives were elected for the committee in all 19 villages and sent to committee workshops and a constitutional assembly. Currently there are 32 village representatives on the committee. As an appendix to the constitution, a resource management plan was formulated. It highlights the most urgent resource management issues in the region as assessed by the conservancy committee, as well as some potential strategies for their solution. These include "regulations regarding the number and grazing areas of cattle and other livestock," establishing "Community Resource Monitors and anti-poaching units dealing with wildlife, but mainly also forest resources that are being taken from the Conservancy by inhabitants of the surrounding regions," "the control of bush fires," the promotion of sustainable harvesting of forest resources like bushfood and wood," and "the control of cattle influx in culturally and economically valuable forest areas" (conservancy application:paragraph 16.1-16.3). The application was later modified three times on the basis of comments of the MET and consultancies commissioned by WIMSA and CASS. The finalised document was handed in to the MET by the end of 2000, but has not been approved to date.[26]

---

[25] The conservancy was named N≠a-Jaqna after two *omiramba* that border its territory in the west and the east: The dry river bed N≠a in the west of the district and the one in the east called Jaqna in the local !Xun dialect that form landmarks next to the conservancy's western and eastern boundaries have been used for the name by the San to symbolise their aim of incorporating the entire district into the conservancy project (field notes 05.08.1998).

[26] On the process of conservancy development see also WIMSA 1998, 1999 and 2000, as well as http://www.san.org.za.

San and employees of NGOs active in Tsumkwe West speculate that plans by the Namibian government, which became public at the end of 2001, to resettle around 18,000 Angolan refugees from their present location in Osire refugee camp to the central part of Tsumkwe West might be one factor presently keeping N‡a-Jaqna from being approved. Under these changed circumstances, not only the project's potential for approval, but also the pre-conditions for it to reach its aims of conserving natural resources and gaining economic benefits for its members have drastically changed. Since further developments, however, can presently not be predicted, especially in view of the latest events in Angola, this element will be left out of the analysis below.

The Conservancy Concept and its Practical Implementation

For the practical implementation of the conservancy concept, criteria had to be found by policy-makers and practitioners in the MET that any group wanting to apply for a conservancy has to fulfil in order to get the MET's approval. These criteria are defined by the revised legislation as follows:

- defined membership
- a representative management committee
- a legally recognised constitution, and
- defined boundaries
  (Website of the MET's Directorate of Environmental Affairs)[27].

The MET's toolbox for communal area conservancies mentions a plan for equitable distribution of the conservancy's benefits among its membership as an additional criterion.

The rights deferred to registered conservancies as specified by the MET are to:
- use, manage and benefit from wildlife on communal land,
- propose recommendations for quotas for wildlife utilisation and decide on the form of utilisation, and
- enter into agreements with private companies and establish tourism facilities within the conservancy boundaries.

Furthermore,

registered conservancies will be given ownership over huntable game and game birds, being bushpig, buffalo, oryx, kudu,

---

[27] http://www.dea.met.gov.na/programmes/cbnrm/cbnrm.htm

springbok and warthog. Applications can be made for permits to use protected and specially protected game. A conservancy which also registers as a hunting farm will be able to allow trophy hunting on its land
(Website of the MET's Directorate of Environmental Affairs)[28].

The requirements that the MET has identified and enacted in the nature conservation legislation belong in part to a number of criteria that have been described elsewhere as being crucial for common property resource management[29]. A question previously raised by researchers, which may have also played a direct role in shaping nature conservation policy in independent Namibia (Jones and Murphree 2001:52) and other Southern African countries, is whether models like the conservancies or similar CBNRM projects can serve as tools for the successful management of common property resources (CPRs).[30] This question is going to be taken up where applicable to the case study presented here in the following paragraphs. Furthermore, it will be critically assessed as to the extent that aspects of the above-mentioned requirements that local actors are confronted with in order to be granted the right to influence decision making with regard to the management of natural resources and tourism in envisaged conservancy areas can be valid and practicable for local social situations in general and especially for the case of Tsumkwe West. The ways in which people discuss and try to fulfil the requirements will be highlighted. It is notable that, as a consequence of all the processes required in order to be able to apply successfully for a conservancy, profound changes in the district's spatial and social order and in forms of decision making and political representation of the San have been initiated and partly laid down in the conservancy constitution. These will be discussed and summarised in section 6.

---

[28] http://www.dea.met.gov.na/programmes/cbnrm/cons_guide.htm

[29] For supposed criteria for a well-functioning common property regime see, e.g., Gibbs and Bromley 1989:26. For a comprehensive summary and description see Shackleton et al. 1998.

[30] See on this issue, for example, Turner 1996:28-38.

"Defined Membership" –
Conservancies and Their Social Boundaries

A problem caused by the conservancy legislation and its practical requirements is the "problem of defining 'community'[31]". The concept of communities as stakeholders and agents in development processes initiated by development agencies or national governments in South Africa has become popular, not only in the discourse about CBNRM, especially after the end of Apartheid. The definitional vagueness of the concept in general, the problem of suitable representation of a social group called community, and the resulting difficulty of applying it to CBNRM has recently been discussed increasingly by social scientists[32].

The comments on the conservancy legislation imply that a "group of persons" applying for a conservancy constitutes a social group called a "community," a term that is not clarified any further. The MET has made the definition of a social group with more-or-less clear and stable boundaries a necessary condition for groups of local people wanting to realise certain goals. It is also required that conservancy committees have to be representative of the community (an aspect which is further discussed in section 5.4).

The legislative requirement disregards that, especially in localities with highly mobile populations such as, e.g., Tsumkwe West, groups residing in a given area are marked by a high degree of flexibility and fluidity. This fact alone makes it difficult for them, the MET or implementing agencies to define reliable terms of conservancy membership and its representation by the conservancy committee. For the context of community conservation Barrow and Murphree define community as

> a principle manifest in social groupings with the actual or potential cohesion, incentive, demarcation, legitimacy and resilience to organize themselves for effective common pool natural resource management at levels below and beyond the reach of state bureaucratic management (2001:27).

---

[31] See an article with this title by Thembela Kepe (1998) referring to the land reform programme in South Africa.

[32] See for example Turner 1996:28-31; Hinz 1998:7; Barrow and Murphree 2001:24-27; and Berzborn 2001:passim.

The explicit definition of criteria that make a group a community however, is not a task usually carried out by the group of applicants in daily life and such criteria are not self-evident and visible.

The Southern African population has recently emerged from a period of discrimination on ethnic grounds promoted by state policies designed to create prejudice and dissociation between social groups. The negative impacts of such policies are obvious and, as a consequence, it is presently discouraged and disapproved of strongly by the Namibian government, as well as the wider public, to stress ethnic distinctions between individuals or social groups. However, some groups may themselves resort to ethnic categories in search of suitable criteria to define conservancy membership. It might be the only readily available strategy for local actors in order to fulfil the requirements set by the legislation. They might adopt this as an approach resulting from historical processes of identity formation. Incorporating into conservancy planning and operation all resident groups in an area which would comply with public opinion and the conservancy framework as intended by policy makers and effectively creating practicable tools for "community representation" can sometimes become very complicated. Such incorporation of perceived 'outsiders' can also be contrary to the aims a group actually attaches to the conservancy concept. As Sullivan has pointed out, it is a common attempt to try and use it as a means of striving for increased control over resources and, above all, over land: "This context of gross inequality in land distribution has fuelled local appropriation of conservancies in communal areas as the only existing forum in which claims to land can be made and contested, and access to land and resources permitted or denied" (Sullivan 2001:11). This issue is certainly a crucial one for all the San groups in Southern Africa who have recently embarked on a process of searching for suitable means of political representation in the context of independent nation states to protect and/or secure access to land and natural resources against outsiders.[33]

Such unintended effects of introducing the CBNRM agenda to local constellations of stakeholders' interests is reflected by the planning for the Nǂa-Jaqna Conservancy and its constitution. The conservancy committee's considerations of how conservancy membership should be regulated by it had the following result:

---

[33] It should be stressed once again how strongly these processes are influenced by one further group of outsiders, i.e., NGOs and development donors.

The members [...] shall include the following: All members of the community (i.e.: long-term, legal residents) [...]. Members of the community are defined as those individuals who either:
i) can demonstrate an ancestral claim to the area (i.e.: has relatives currently or in the past living permanently on one of the n!oresi); or
ii) has been granted permission to use the land and resources by the traditional authority and the conservancy committee [...]

On application from a prospective member who has been permanently residing on one of the n!oresi for five consecutive years [...].
A prospective member of the community is defined as:
i) the relative by blood or marriage of an existing member; or
ii) a person who has been granted permission by the traditional authority to use land and other resources in the Conservancy" (Nǂa-Jaqna Constitution:paragraph 10.1).

For prospective members it is thus possible to apply for conservancy membership once they have been residing in Nǂa-Jaqna with the consent of !Kung Traditional Authority and conservancy committee for a period of five consecutive years. It is apparent that the authors of the constitution (the conservancy committee in co-operation with the Traditional Authority and WIMSA, though being solely a San organisation) – in accordance with the legislative framework – have not based membership on ethnic principles. From local discourse, in interviews and during public meetings, however, a different picture emerges. In practice, the conservancy is frankly seen by most of its San members as a means to secure themselves resource ownership and land rights not only in reaction to former disempowering Apartheid policy, but also in reaction to resource and land claims by members of other ethnic groups. One sign of the ethnic bias of the conservancy initiative in Tsumkwe West is the composition of the committee, composed of 32 members elected from the 19 villages, which currently consists of 28 San and only four non-San[34]. It can be doubted whether the non-San who might apply for member status or be granted use

---

[34] Without meaning to stick to such ethnic categorisation per se or to ascribe ethnic identity to local actors myself, I am referring here to the mentioned committee members' own statements about their ethnic identity and to their San neighbours' perception of it.

rights on Nǂa-Jaqna's territory will be represented adequately by this managing body.

The main reason for the San's attempt to use the conservancy as a means to secure themselves greater control over resources and restrict outsiders' access is the pressure on vital resources most of them currently feel. This can be explained by their lack of alternative income opportunities, and at the same time, a rising number of non-San immigrating into the region. Namibian Independence opened the way for this development as all political initiatives to regulate property rights for the country's communal areas have so far remained fruitless. Instead, an open access situation has been created on communal land by granting the right to free movement in the Namibian constitution, which many immigrants are referring to when challenged. Most of them come primarily in search of the natural resources that the San subsist on. Immigrants arrive with herds of cattle or small stock, and some of them use forest resources like Mangetti (*Ricinodendron rautanenii*) fruits, the traditional staple of the San, for brewing *kashipembe* wine, as well as timber, or the medicinal plant devil's claw (*Harpagoqhytum procumbens*) for commercial purposes. Currently, access to such resources is regulated by the local MET offices, where harvesting permits have to be obtained. Permits have often been given without the San's consent and without consulting their Traditional Authority, whose duties and functions according to the Traditional Authorities Act include issues related to environmental protection (Felton 2000:26). In other cases, resources are harvested without valid permits. As a consequence, the San argue that apart from the Traditional Authority which is currently too weak institutionally and individually to protect the San's rights effectively, the conservancy is the only available means to curb the unwanted use of natural resources.

This became especially apparent in the case of a conflict around borehole No. 1199, situated between Grashoek and Kanovlei (see map 1), which had been ongoing for several months when it escalated in 1999. A group of Kwangali from Kavango had moved to their relatives' who served as government employees at Rooidag gate. They were planning to move to the borehole permanently with their cattle and had applied for permission from the relevant government institutions and the !Kung chief. Their plan was strongly opposed by the majority of San, especially in Grashoek, Kanovlei, Etameko and at the Omatako Valley Restcamp. In the dispute about the borehole, the conservancy was used as one of the strongest arguments against giving the borehole to the applicants. Members of the conservancy committee involved, though not yet officially recognised, featured prominently in the discussions in their role as committee members and represented the majority's opposition to the approval of the application during meetings and on informal occasions. They refused to give their approval to a transformation of the area around the borehole into pasture for cattle. The inhabitants of the surrounding villages complained that the borehole was situated in an area rich in plant resources they subsist on. They were also afraid of having to compete with cattle for the special type of grass they use for building. Additionally, during planning meetings, the committee had identified the borehole as a potential watering point for game in wildlife management.

> The question of the borehole touches Grashoek just like Kanovlei. Kanovlei's people do not want to give away this borehole, because in its vicinity there is food. This is why we do not want cattle there. In Kanovlei itself we do not find food. The members of the conservancy committee are here. If the conservancy gets approved, we want to use this borehole as a game water for the conservancy.
> (conservancy committee member from Kanovlei)

At first it seemed as if the chief, who was ready to give the borehole to the applicants, could not effectively be challenged by the conservancy committee, and the Traditional Councillors from Grashoek and Kanovlei as the latter did not interfere to actively take the side of the conservancy committee and their villages. A decisive meeting on 08.10.1999 ended with the chief granting the borehole to the Kwangali. But the discontent after the meeting continued to grow among committee members and villagers to such an extent that during a regional development meeting in Omatako on 24-25.10.1999, the chief was forced to withdraw his decision and the applicants were then denied access to the borehole.

Regarding the definition of the terms of membership necessary for the approval of a conservancy, the case study shows that this is not an unproblematic task for a given group of applicants, as cohesive groups interested in pursuing a common goal might not be readily available as part of their social reality. Suitable features to define the eligibility for benefiting from a conservancy's resources will not be self-evident in many cases, but have to be negotiated and can contain considerable potential for conflict, as has been seen in the borehole case. In cases in which groups of actors in envisaged conservancy areas get to fight for a concrete common goal in connection with natural resources, the conflicting parties and outside facilitators start to increasingly see such conflicts in the context of conservancy formation. The conservancy project gets used in their arguments to protect their interests more effectively. Even prior to its registration, the conservancy and related disputes also played a crucial role in this context in terms of forming cohesive groups identities among local actors. They can now refer to themselves as part of the larger 'we-groups' of conservancy members or committees beyond the scope of the parties involved in the actual disputes and use this identification to achieve their goals. Such groups are often formulateded regardless of ethnic boundaries that individuals formerly identified themselves with. One Mahenge participant in a conservancy planning meeting on 02.10.1999 in Mangetti intervened in this direction: "We fight too much among ourselves in the west. We will never manage to run a project like a conservancy in this way. In the east it is different. They are one people in the east. This [the conservancy] is not a Mahenge or Vasekela thing, but a community thing" (field notes). In Tsumkwe West, in the context of development initiatives like the conservancy, a common San identity begins to play a more important role than the identification with the various San groups such as !Xun, Vasekela or Mpungu.

"Defined Boundaries" –
Conservancies and Their Physical Boundaries

According to comments to the legislation, another necessary requirement for the creation of a conservancy are clearly defined geographic boundaries, which have to be marked. Map coordinates for conservancy boundaries should be provided where possible. "A description of a physical boundary marker is only acceptable if it is a permanent feature, e.g. hill, river, road, etc." (MET 1996b:2). This requirement, however, is sometimes hard to meet under local circumstances. In many cases no natural landmarks can be used to identify the boundaries, and the terrain may be too difficult to access in order to measure the boundaries and mark them with artificial beacons. Since the inception of Nyae Nyae Conservancy in Tsumkwe District East, for instance, its exact boundary remained unknown to the neighbouring communities in Tsumkwe West until the line was demonstrated to them by NGO personnel with the help of a map produced by the Nyae Nyae Conservancy. Such a map alone, of course, is not a practicable tool in daily life for a mostly illiterate population not used to such instruments. As not all of the border's sections have been physically marked, people from both sides who hunt in the vicinity of the border cannot be sure which territory they are on at a given time. Such conditions can cause local conflict involving resources and decision-making rights, especially in cases where two conservancies have a common border. Since the San of Tsumkwe West have commenced planning and applied for a conservancy in 1998, not only the problem of marking borders, but the mere fact that boundaries have to be clearly defined and thus to be negotiated with their neighbours, resulted in discussion and conflict that caused part of the delay in reaching approval. In the following paragraphs a boundary conflict between Nyae Nyae and N‡a-Jaqna Conservancies in Tsumkwe District East and West will be analysed as one exemplary case of conflicting views about a common conservancy boundary. It also serves as one more example of conflict in connection to the creation of a conservancy that fosters the formation of group identities among both arguing parties.

The conservancy initiative in the Nyae Nyae area, supported mainly by the Living In a Finite Environment (LIFE) programme from 1995 only encompassed the eastern part of the district. A division between the two districtss had already started to evolve earlier mainly because of differences in their recent historical development and demography. The western population as described above is far more heterogeneous than the eastern population, which consists primarily of Jul'hoansi who have lived in the area of Nyae Nyae or used it as seasonal hunting grounds for generations. In contrast, the current demographic composition of the western district is the result of voluntary or forced movements of San groups from various regions (the Grootfontein and commercial farm sector area, Mpunguvlei in former Kavangoland, Angola and the area of the Khaudom Game Reserve) to Tsumkwe District during the past three decades. The division has been deepened by the different engagement of the SADF (South African Defence Force) and ELCIN (Evangelical Lutheran Church in Namibia) in the two parts of the district. SADF army bases were almost exclusively established in the west, with the only exception in the east being Tsumkwe. Since 1974, the SADF recruited about 4000 San (ELCIN 1992) from Bushmanland's vicinity and from as far as southern Angola to the seven army bases where they became employed as soldiers and settled with their families, and where, in many cases, they remain until today. In 1989, 2000 of them accepted the SADF's offer to join them in moving to South Africa and be resettled in a camp at Schmidtsdrift, near Kimberley (Botelle and Rohde 1995:17). The army's activities in Bushmanland resulted in the different ethnic composition of the two parts of Tsumkwe District that one finds today. ELCIN concentrated its missionary and development activities on the western part from 1989 to 1995. Far more development initiatives were undertaken in the east, especially under the auspices of the LIFE programme, which resulted in the gazetting of Nyae Nyae Conservancy in 1998. These activities again did not encompass the west. Furthermore, the processes leading to the election of separate Traditional Authorities in both parts and ultimately to their official recognition in 1998 has certainly strengthened the perception among the local population of a division existing between them. The Traditional Authorities are labelled according to the majority of San groups from the respective districts, i.e., Jul'hoansi in the east and !Kung in the west. Of course, the differences in ethnic composition described by these terms are perceived more or less strongly by different people. The division expressed by them, however, sometimes becomes a factor they would refer to in their arguments, contrary to above-mentioned tendencies to form larger 'we-groups' above such a level, e.g., in the case of the boundary dispute.

During interviews, I received differing versions of how the boundaries of Nyae Nyae were identified by NGO staff with Jul'hoansi from Tsumkwe East and how they have been discussed with their western neighbours. Conservancy management staff of Nyae Nyae in Baraka, as well as the Jul'hoansi chief, have stated that, before their application had been handed in to the MET, people in the four villages closest to the border in the west had been consulted and agreed to the planned borderline (field notes 15.07.1999). He further elaborated that his ancestors used to have use rights of the disputed area south of the main road, while the only San group he remembers to have lived in the western part then was staying relatively far away around Omatako and Bubipos (ibid.). Even before the first version of the application for N‡a-Jaqna had been handed in it was clear that many San in the west were dissatisfied with the way that Nyae Nyae's boundaries had been established and gazetted by the MET in February 1998. They repeatedly complained that they were not consulted on the intended borders before the Nyae Nyae application was handed in. The submitting of the application in September 1998 then brought to the surface an open border conflict with Nyae Nyae. By the time the application was handed in, the western community and the !Kung Traditional Authority claimed that the Nyae Nyae Conservancy incorporated a piece of land that the eastern community of Jul'hoansi had unjustly declared as theirs (see map 3, following page).

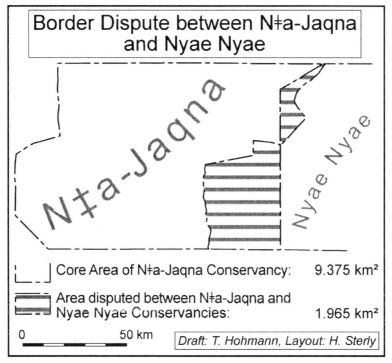

Map 3: Disputed area in the boundary conflict between Nyae Nyae and N‡a-Jaqna Conservancies

In the area south of the main road, presently not permanently inhabited by anybody, wildlife is known to be relatively plentiful so interest is high to create a wildlife management regime as part of a conservancy. People in the west led by the !Kung chief decided not to address this problem openly with people from the east, but to incorporate the said piece of land into their own conservancy application without informing Nyae Nyae. When it became known to the Nyae Nyae management, this led to local heated discussions of the issue. At the same time, the MET, who had to review the N‡a-Jaqna application to assess its potential for approval, became aware of the inconsistency and finally referred the application document back to the applicants in 1999 with the request to re-consider the boundary and seek discussions with Nyae Nyae in order to solve the conflict. After Nyae Nyae had been made aware of the problem by MET staff in Tsumkwe and representatives from N‡a-Jaqna, I facilitated discussions between members of the two conservancies as a consultant hired by WIMSA along with Nyae Nyae staff and officials of MET and the Ministry of Local and Regional Government and Housing (MLRGH) in 2000.

Two effects of the situation were new to the conflicting parties: For the first time a relatively big part of both groups, i.e., the respective conservancy members from east and west, numbering over 700 and 1200 people, respectively, had to make decisions as corporate, cohesive interest groups. In a situation of concrete conflict, they had to pursue common goals with a united opinion if they were to realise their aims. The dispute was about such a big part of land that no definable sub-group of either of the parties was attached to it, but the claim was made by both groups in their entirety. Arguments had to be found or created to substantiate such extensive claim. Effective and accepted means of representation had to be agreed upon, and thus individuals or a group of people vested with authority and trust to stand in for group claims far bigger than ever before, so that entirely new considerations about suitable representation became necessary. The claim was essentially for land with the wildlife on it and, again presumably for the first time, the two groups had to find plausible ways of proving their land rights, which led to the mention of several criteria they deemed suitable to do so. Above all, this took place in the still rather uncommon situation of a big public meeting, organised partly by NGO staff and chaired by government officials. Some facilitators had a considerable degree of influence on the direction and sometimes, on the outcomes of meetings. While some of them certainly intervened on behalf of the group they had worked with and merely took the part of supporting their arguments, others clearly had their own agendas and notions of what the outcome of the case should be. This especially holds true for government officials from the MET and the MRLGH, who had come from Tsumeb to chair the decisive meeting on 11.09.2000. One element of the decision later agreed upon by the San was already formulated by these officials among themselves before discussions commenced: The already gazetted boundaries of Nyae Nyae should not be modified.

During facilitated discussions at several meetings in 2000 and various conversations about the conservancy boundaries, I witnessed both parties on informal occasions in Tsumkwe West discussing the problem in connection to the conservancy framework, which focuses on the sustainable management of natural resources as a major aim. At the same time, it became apparent that they in fact indirectly discussed their claims to land and resources in political and economic terms

> [...] these places in the east are my area. So I want the border [border of Nyae Nyae as gazetted] to stay where it is. The border is now lying along the villages of G!an!ha, N!aye and N!u!xoe down to the border with Hereroland. These places are

my own. My village used to be ‖Habe [Vergenoug]. I used to
gather in that area, down to the south, at the veterinary fence.
(headman of Vergenoug, then residing permanently in Denǀui
on 11.09.2000).

To forward this interest, disputants resorted to arguments such as
customary claims to hunting and gathering grounds that their forebears had
used, longstanding claims of certain kin groups to some of the localities
where they had been residing or regularly visiting, alleged borders of
nǃoresi[35], and the perceived border between the east and west of the district,
which was described above.

I would like the conservancy border to be at the point up to
which I used to gather and hunt. Because when you do
something, you have to know precisely why you are doing
something like that.
(headman of Nhoma at the same meeting on 11.09.2000).

Members of the N≠a-Jaqna Conservancy Committee and the ǃKung
Traditional Authority argued that the course of the conservancy boundary
they envisaged went along a longstanding boundary between the district's
east and west commonly known by everyone in the region, which the San
from the east had purposefully violated with the establishment of the Nyae
Nyae boundary on western territory. Although some manifestations of a
division of present-day Tsumkwe District into east and west has arguably
existed since the establishment of Bushmanland as a Homeland, such a
boundary was never physically fixed nor described in any written document,
nor formally recognised otherwise. By using it as their argument, the western
representatives now moved in the direction of further affirming the area's
spatial order that looked advantageous to them.

Finally, however, it was agreed on 12.09.2000 and set out in writing in a
document signed by representatives of both Traditional Authorities and
conservancy committees that N≠a-Jaqna would accept the gazetted Nyae
Nyae boundary and pull back their western boundary contained in the
application document so that it would be identical with the border of Nyae

---

[35] Nǃore (pl.: nǃoresi): According to Wiessner (1982:62) "areas of landrights [..] the
right to exploit the resources of the land along with others who inherit similar
rights," according to Dickens' dictionary "territory, country, land (especially that
belonging to a village)" (Dickens 1994).

Nyae[36]. Once Nǂa-Jaqna is recognised, it is planned that the disputed area become an area of co-management for the two conservancies according to a management plan to be developed jointly with the facilitation of a suitable agency still to be identified. This is an agreement primarily to pave the way for Nǂa-Jaqna's approval, but certainly not an agreement to prevent all potential future conflict involving the territory in question, even if both sides manage to find a compromise suiting their interests and laid down in a management plan.

The example of Tsumkwe District is not the sole one in Namibia for territorial conflicts involving land and natural resources that seem to have arisen or escalated as a consequence of planning for a conservancy, as, for instance, the case of the planned wildlife reserve in Uukwaludhi illustrates (Sullivan 2001:12 and Turner 1996:22).

Such cases lead to the re-formulation of land and resource rights as neighbouring groups are forced to define and discuss their claims in an unprecedented manner. Through the conservancy, they try to use the opportunity to get formal recognition for some of their claims. In the process of disputing, new kinds of arguments are often found and individuals or institutions given authority to stand in for a group's claims. Evolving disputes in connection to conservancy projects thus contribute to the discussion and/or establishment of political institutions and spatial orders of parts of Namibia's communal areas on the background of the national CBNRM agenda.

Size and Composition of the User Group

According to CPR analyses, group size plays a vital role for the common management of a resource (see, e.g., Ostrom et al. 1999:279) as the costs for individuals to communicate and obtain the information necessary to take management decisions depend on it. In the case of communal area conservancies in Namibia, groups deciding to jointly apply for a conservancy have not necessarily had forms of communication in place before which joint decision making for sometimes vast resource and user units can be ensured. Management problems arise especially for conservancies that encompass large areas with groups of members who have not co-ordinated joint resource management over the entire area before. At the planning stage and when finally managing a conservancy, they engage in

---

[36] See final draft of conservancy boundaries as contained in the application marked on map 4.

the formation of co-ordinating processes often according to suggestions from outside facilitators.

In Tsumkwe West, for example, it will be relatively costly for resource users to obtain the necessary information and maintain the level of communication needed to ensure that decisions regarding the conservancy as a whole will be beneficial for the entire group of conservancy members and thus beneficial for resource management. During the planning process for N‡a-Jaqna from 1998 to the present, one of the obstacles for the San that could only be overcome with the assistance of NGOs has been the problem of transport. With 19 villages situated at a maximal distance of 150 km apart, with some roads in bad condition and virtually only one San participating in the planning work who was in possession of a car (the chief), it was almost impossible to organise the necessary meetings of people from different villages. Definitely the operation of a conservancy would require a far greater number of meetings for the conservancy committee to make informed decisions for the entire area, spread information among villagers and hold discussions with, e.g., the Traditional Authority or government institutions. Such constant contact also seems necessary if one of the committee's aims is to continue creating a community.

In the long run, the operation of an approved conservancy will remain complicated, especially for conservancies with a large membership where it is not clear to which extent the social group it represents is having common goals regarding the management of their environment and the necessary resources to engage in its communal management on the level of all the members. Turner highlights two game reserves, Salambala in Caprivi Region and Uukwaludhi on the border of Kunene and Omusati Regions, as two examples of such a situation (1996:32).

In Tsumkwe West, the entire group of co-users within the envisaged conservancy consists of smaller groups of resource users who are already currently using the resources of one area and co-ordinating their management decisions. The prospective conservancy members can be divided roughly into four partly overlapping local sub-groups, depending on the same resources, most importantly bushfood and game. These user groups are a consequence of the settlement pattern in Tsumkwe West, with four relatively dense clusters of villages, which has resulted from the settlement and resettlement of San at the time of the establishment of the SADF military bases and again when the SADF left the area.

Table 2: groups of co-users of natural resources in Tsumkwe West[37]

Group No.	Villages	Conservancy members per village	Total of registered conservancy members
1	Aasvoëlnes	103	180
	Nhoma	40	
	Perspeka	25	
	Viksrus	12	
2	Kankudi	41	410
	Kukurushe	40[38]	
	Luhebo	47	
	Mangetti	99	
	M'kata	130	
	Mparara	53	
3	Etameko	24	297
	Grashoek	109	
	Kanovlei	119	
	Rooidag Gate	45	
4	Bubipos	54	428
	Kameelwout	24	
	Kandu	51	
	Omatako	237	
	Omatako Valley Restcamp	62	

The existing four use-areas – sub-areas of the conservancy – are not marked by visible landmarks, nor manifest on people's mental maps with clear-cut borderlines. Use rights are flexibly defined by a combination of residence in a certain village and kinship bonds. As has been described for the Jul'hoansi in the Dobe and Nyae Nyae areas by Lee (1979) and Wiessner (1982), territorial boundaries are fluid and access rights adaptable to the

---

[37] Group numbers have been chosen randomly, in accordance with the numbers of the four districts of N≠a-Jaqna Conservancy. The division into the four groups is the result of the drawing of mental maps that I carried out with informants from all the villages in 1998 (cf. Hohmann 2000:30-31.) and from interviews and continuous observations of resource use.

[38] Not yet registered, my estimate.

demand structure. There are no management bodies that convene regularly to discuss communal resource management or allocation. The four groups (see table 2, previous page) are much larger in number than the user groups of the *n!oresi* described for Dobe and Nyae Nyae that were exploited by bands of 10 to 30 people (Lee 1979:54).At the time of compiling the first application with the conservancy boundaries and map, the idea had already emerged out of NGO staff considerations and been taken up by conservancy committee and Traditional Authority to form four conservancy districts (according to the user groups shown in table 2). These are planned to have district management committees of their own in order to reduce the need for the entire committee to meet and ease communication in the four management units. Decisions concerning a single district should only be taken by the district committees after meetings with the conservancy members in their villages. In this way, the size of the user groups that actually engage in co-management of resources and are required to take joint decisions is reduced, so that decisions might be easier to make and enforce. Decisions concerning the conservancy as a whole have to be discussed and agreed upon at the level of the conservancy committee.

The identification and assessment of local management institutions for conservancies by their members in order to make joint resource management of the entire area might possibly include elements described here for the N‡a-Jaqna Conservancy or other solutions in practice. It will always involve reconsideration of existing management structures and resource use patterns that can lead to transformations. It will be interesting in the years to come to analyse social and economic change in this regard initiated by CBNRM projects that have been in operation for some time.

Institutional Framework: Regulations and Authority

Regulations pertaining to the management of a conservancy – or any CPR – like the ones described in the last part of the previous section have to be embedded in some institutional framework, a structure underlying and sanctioning joint resource management. CPR management becomes more successful with an established institutional setup that has effective and recognised authority systems, shared rules and regulations, and clearly understood mechanisms of sanctions and punishment (adapted from Shackleton et al. 1998:38-40). Such a framework in the case of a conservancy has to be understood and respected at least by the project's core management, but must also be accessible to the rest of the members and even to outsiders, so that they can contribute to controlling and improving the decisions made by the managing body.

The committee managing a conservancy is required in the comments to the legislation to be "representative of the community residing in the area," a requirement which has to remain obscure to a great extent if the term "community" itself is unclear, as shown above; the term "representative" is not explained in detail either. The practical problems that ensue in the establishment of conservancy committees are meant to be eased by the following advice, based on the democratic values and understandings of participatory management processes by NGOs and MET:

> A simple guideline which can be used is to ensure that as many people as possible within a community had the opportunity to choose the committee members. Were public meetings held to discuss the conservancy and choose the committee? Were all sections of the people residing within the conservancy area included in theses meetings? Were women or people of minority ethnic groups excluded for example? Is the committee viewed as representative by the conservancy members in terms of their culture and traditions? (MET 1996a:2).

These rough guidelines about how representation, in the MET's sense, can be assessed leave the term's definition and its practical handling open to the respective groups of people.

Resource management in Tsumkwe West is currently not centrally co-ordinated at all and little institutionalised, which might at times prove counterproductive to the new conservancy structure. As described above, loose user groups exist that are formed around clusters of villages lying in the same use area, combined with use rights in other areas derived from kinship bonds. Direct discussions about resource use would usually only occur in concrete cases of conflict between individuals or groups over a certain area. People involved will first try to settle the dispute in discussions on the spot and sometimes threaten to make use of violence or report the cases to village headmen or members of the Traditional Authority. People would most likely resort to reporting a case when non-San are involved, or large amounts of resources or highly important resources are affected. This was the case, for example in 1999, with a group of San who cut about 70 trees to sell as timber in the vicinity of Omatako[39], and with a group of people originating from the Kavango who wanted to open a borehole for their cattle, a case already described above. Usually discussions end with the accused being warned not to make illegal use of the accuser's resources

---

[39] A detailed analysis of the case is contained in Hohmann (2000:59-61).

again, but apart from that, no other sanctions result, which makes it likely that contraventions will continue to occur at regular intervals and be silently tolerated in the same way.

Currently in Tsumkwe West, no organisational structure to make and enforce decisions concerning the entire group is in place apart from the relatively new Traditional Authority. The recently established !Kung Traditional Authority in its present form is a new institution, which explains its frequently observable lack of decision-making and sanctioning power. No such centralised authority has existed among the San or the different sub-groups in the region before. Although persons with locally recognised authority based on relative experience and age are certainly part of San societies, San groups in general have been described as having very little centralisation and being relatively equal[40]. Local leaders in Tsumkwe West have their influence on smaller groups of people who are mostly the inhabitants of one village. Usually they are the eldest men in the village. I would term them "headmen" after Lee, who described such local leaders for the !Kung bands in the area of Dobe (Lee 1979:350). The chief, traditional councillors and senior traditional councillors elected as the !Kung Traditional Authority by the majority of the San, and equipped with duties and rights according to the regulations in the Traditional Authorities Act, 8 of 1997, and exist in part alongside the headmen and in part, the two positions are vested in the same person. The centralised power structure has been established by the community very much as a result of NGO advice, which has included leadership training and information on the Traditional Authorities Act. But up to now, the meaning of the structure and the obligations and rights of the holders of the new positions are open to negotiation and dispute by the San. There are hardly any established and clear-cut regulations or traditions in this regard that the chief and his nine councillors, as well as their community can rely on to fulfil their positions, maintain them in relation to others, and to control and assess it. This holds true for questions regarding natural resource management as for any other issue under the influence of the Traditional Authority. Presently, the chief and councillors are sometimes consulted about some questions of natural

---

[40] A local political institution which existed for a certain period if time during the South African administration has been the Bushman Advisory Council, established at the same time as the Homeland Bushmanland in 1976. According to Jul'hoansi informants however, the San elected for this body were mainly a liaison between the San and the Apartheid government, serving its interests rather than the local San (cf. Biesele and Hitchcock 2000:313).

resource management and tourism by community members, but also by the MET and some individuals interested in private commercial activities in the area. This, however, is not regularly done, as none of the parties involved seem to be clear about how far-reaching the decision-making rights of the Traditional Authority are concerning the natural resource base of their area. Some of its members are not widely accepted among the community, which is known to many of the outsiders interested in exploiting natural resources or establishing tourism enterprises in Tsumkwe West and which makes the leaders' position more problematic and weak. This has been seen, e.g., in the borehole dispute described above where a ruling of the chief was ultimately, fundamentally changed because of the dissatisfaction of a large group of community members. So the people most affected in the dispute received what they wanted, but at the same time demonstrated the weakness of the highest political authority in their place.

During the course of conservancy planning in 1998, a second new organisational structure was created in form of the conservancy committee, which has the special purpose of making decisions relating to natural resource and tourism management. Thus, regional political power was the subject of further diffusion as three different structures – the Traditional Authority, the headmen and the conservancy committee – are now in place that will certainly cause ambiguousness about the division of authority among them and potential competition between them for some time to come.

Just like the Traditional Authority in its present form, the conservancy committee is uncommon to the area's inhabitants so it might not be as effective as some stake holders in the conservancy project – especially NGOs and San themselves – expect. Furthermore, it might be contested by other stake holders interested in maintaining their particular spheres of influence and power. This might also hold true for the Traditional Authority itself, fearing to loose power and still not entirely clear themselves about their rights and obligations. In the debate around borehole No. 1199, the !Kung chief voiced his fears directly by saying: "I am afraid for the conservancy right now because the decisions on the land rest with the chiefs, but the decisions on natural resources rest with the committee" (field notes 08.10.1999). At the same time, co-operation between the Traditional Authority and the conservancy committee is a principle contained in the constitution of N‡a-Jaqna, which will indeed be vital for the conservancy's functioning.

Recently, CBNRM initiatives have caused local political transformation through the establishment of new local organisations, power structures and differing interests in the realm of natural resource and tourism management.

Existing systems of political representation and decision making can be integrated or expanded into the changing setting where local actors are ready to do so. As the case of the San in Tsumkwe West has shown, however, such structures are not necessarily in place. In this case, as in the case of other Southern African San groups, recent political change and mobilisation has led to the establishment of the Traditional Authority and of a conservancy management structure while the rules and functions of both of them are widely unclear and subject to negotiation and mutual competition. The outcome remains to be seen, but will certainly have, at least in part, profound changes in the political organisation of such groups as a result.

Conservancies and Gender Relations

Throughout anthropological literature, the entire group of Southern African San is depicted as an egalitarian society, including the lack of centralised power structures and relative equality of women and men. Such general depiction can be critically questioned, and social changes in the recent past have partly brought men into a prominent position in representation towards, e.g., the colonial administration and employers like commercial farmers or the military. Still, according to my observations in Tsumkwe West in regard to the use of natural resources, women and men are largely equal in decision making and access rights with wildlife and hunting belonging more into the male sphere.

Gender relations and the different influence that women and men exert on planning and potentially on the operation of conservancies are a crucial issue for CBNRM projects depicted by some NGO approaches and discussed by social scientists[41]. In these approaches and discussions, questions such as how perceptions of gender relations can affect CBNRM projects on the one hand, and how gender relations can be transformed by CBNRM initiatives on the other are prominent. Equal participation of both sexes in CBNRM projects is seen by the implementing agencies as vital for their sustainability and success as both women and men play their part in resource use and management. Equal rights of men and women are promoted as part of NGO agendas that are based on western models of democratic processes and emancipation:

> However, the sustainability of any CBNRM initiative is
> founded on the notion of equity *within* the community. That is,
> the opportunity to benefit from CBNRM should be the same for

---

[41] E.g. Gujadhur 1997; Sullivan 1999 and 2000; and Nabane 1994 and 1998.

all community members, irrespective of their ethnic group, how
they make a living, age, or whether they are men or women.
(Cassidy 2001:6, italics in the original).

At the same time, however, there are aspects of local relations and
resource knowledge meaningful for women's role in natural resource
management that remain hidden to or disregarded by facilitators as Sullivan
has repeatedly emphasised (cf. Sullivan 1999:21). One can argue that the
western models of democracy and emancipation contained in the CBNRM
agenda through the legal requirements set for it by the state and the
implementation process mostly carried out by NGOs sometimes create
conditions under which it becomes more difficult for women to actively
participate in decision making in resource management. It has become
apparent in a number of CBNRM projects in Southern Africa that women's
representation, and especially of those from female-headed households, in
decision-making bodies such as elected committees remains weak because of
cultural values and household obligations that keep them from being elected
or from running for these positions at all. Furthermore, their participation in
certain management and training activities, which often include travelling to
workshops or meetings, is inhibited by the fact that "the women were being
put under pressure by *men*, who did not trust their wives to sleep away from
them. They also found it difficult to leave their household responsibilities"
(Cassidy 2001:11, italics in the original).

During the planning for the Nǂa-Jaqna Conservancy, there was a
considerable gap between the intentions of the actors involved and the
outcomes in terms of participation and representation of women. From the
outset, the decision of the Traditional Authority, which was again
encouraged by NGO staff, to elect – if possible – a proportion of 50% of
women to serve on the conservancy committee seemed to some extent
unrealistic. Only one of nine members of the Traditional Authority is a
woman, and women are generally by far underrepresented in the kind of
public discussions and decision making that has recently evolved among
others through the CBNRM approach. Thus, the goal turned out hard to
reach. It was agreed from the beginning that each village should elect at least
one woman as a conservancy committee member, and villagers were
repeatedly encouraged to do so during conservancy meetings. Initially,
committee members were only elected in 16 out of a total of 19 villages.
This initial committee consisted of a total of 30 members, eight of whom
were women. In 2001, when committees had been established in all of the 19
villages, out of the 32 members only six were women. When approached on
this unequal proportion, men and women gave different reasons: Some men

frankly regarded women as incapable of such a task, because of fears of speaking up during meetings and to articulate themselves in Afrikaans or English. Others referred to the lack of women in their village who were willing to be elected for such a post. Women themselves sometimes claimed to be afraid of the tasks that would be expected from them and of the attention that the position would have as a consequence. Several interviewees, women and men, mentioned an obstacle to be the husbands' jealousy in case their wives should engage in working with other men at far away places, possibly involving staying away from their home and outside their control for some time. Potential absence from home was also stated to be problematic for the maintenance of households.

> If we elect a woman, we have to elect her husband as the second committee member. Otherwise it would be impossible for her to participate in meetings, especially in other villages or outside Bushmanland. Her husband would be against this, he would be jealous and would not agree if she took part in meetings with other men. We elected Josef /Kunta, but his wife does not want to join the conservancy committee, because one of them also has to take care of food and children. So we will elect a second man.
> (Nhoma villagers during a conservancy meeting on 22.04.1998)

It was obvious that by serving in the conservancy committee it would remain hard for women to get an equal say on the level of decision making and managing the conservancy's affairs. At the same time, their participation in planning meetings on the village level was by far not equal to the men's input on such occasions either.

It has often been shown elsewhere[42], and is apparent from my own fieldwork, that many San women have a rich knowledge of local plants used as food or traditional medicine and have indirect, but sometimes also direct, impact on wildlife management, which is otherwise often described as part of the male sphere[43]. Their knowledge enables women to make important contributions to CBNRM projects. It seems, however, that acknowledging and encouraging such contribution requires methods expressly designed to

---

[42] See for !Xõ ethno-botanical knowledge Heinz and Maguire 1974; and for female contributions to male hunting success: Biesele and Barclay 2001.

[43] For problems concerning women's participation in Southern African CBNRM projects resulting from their focus on wildlife see Sullivan 2000.

enhance women's participation[44]. Otherwise, the demands of participation and emancipation according to western values connected to the new CBNRM agenda seemingly cannot be met by women. Most of them remain reluctant to speak out publicly during occasions in the context of CBNRM implementation, refrain from taking responsibility for endeavours of wider public concern and from serving in official positions. As a consequence of women's difficulties to actively participate, by resorting to official meetings and offices as the main planning and management devices, CBNRM facilitating agencies in many cases enforce gender inequality instead of preventing it.

During conservancy planning in Tsumkwe West, women usually turned up in low numbers at meetings and hardly played an active role in the discussions. From the seating arrangements that they chose themselves (see photo 1), it was obvious that they did not plan to get involved, make comments, nor air their views. The few exceptions to this rule were women who seemed to individually have a more outspoken and fearless character. They sometimes made statements such as the one by the only female member of the Omatako Valley Restcamp committee when interviewed on her perceptions of the successes and failures of the camp endeavour in 1999: "The problem is that women have not been participating a lot in the project. This is why things do not work. Had the women had a say from the very beginning, it would have functioned better" (cf. Weicke 1999:72).

What was more common with women than the few direct comments that sometimes challenging male dominance were lively and occasionally heated discussions among themselves during which they assessed the events they witnessed in and outside meetings or the statements they heard from local men, NGO representatives and administrative officials. These discussions sometimes went on during the meetings to the extent that they became irritating and disturbing to the rest of the participants. Most often the women were then called to order so that they had no chance to fruitfully contribute their opinions. They would mostly discuss and critically assess the planned

---

[44] E.g. the Namibian NGO Integrated Rural Development and Nature Conservation (IRDNC) assisting conservancy planning in West Caprivi during the 1990s provided positions as "Community Resource Monitors" exclusively to women, an approach which has been both successful for sustainable resource management and empowering women (IRDNC 1997:6-7). In the Nqwaa Khobee Xeya Trust in Botswana women's participation in hunting activities was ensured by hiring one woman each for the member villages' escort guides to record the details of the hunt (cf. Cassidy, Bowie and Jones 1998).

conservancy in the private sphere of households and village communities. Here the degree of impact they can have is not as obvious as in the public sphere, but might be far more influential. During many informal gatherings and conversations I observed, especially at the Omatako Valley Restcamp, in Etameko and Omatako, women often appeared to be very interested in the discussions that took place next to the houses and were thus more easily accessible to them. Although they hardly expressed their views openly on such occasions, they at least received as detailed information as the other participants and had the chance to discuss them again later on among themselves in order to draw their own conclusions. Thus, despite the fact that the public sphere of disputing and decision making in relation to CBNRM in Tsumkwe West seems less open to women than to men, women can use the private sphere and their personal networks to influence discourse and decisions in a manner that can be rather significant, too.

Photo 1: Seating arrangements during a conservancy planning meeting

Closer analyses of the mutual influence of gender relations and the CBNRM agenda are still called for in the case of the N≠a-Jaqna Conservancy project and other Namibian conservancies. The role this plays in establishing and the subsequent running of CBNRM projects would surely yield interesting insights for both social science and development or state agents implementing the CBNRM concept.

The Conservancy as a Source of Local Change

The implications of the CBNRM approach in terms of its ideological background, formal foundation and the international, national and local aims that different stakeholders connect to it have been shown. Essentially, they can be summarised to be the conservation of the natural environment, rural development and the empowerment of local populations. In combination and in how they are applied in local settings, they result in different aspects of social and political change in the project areas. The outcome is sometimes different from the above-mentioned aims than the CBNRM agenda has intended locally, as well as unintended effects on a social, political and economic level. These transformations began after the end of Apartheid in the context of the general political mobilisation of San groups regionally, and their search for advantageous options to further their aims of political emancipation and economic improvements.

Processes of change include the re-formulation of individual and group identities. Through the CBNRM agenda, state politics, among other things, is promoting a decline in the importance of ethnic boundaries and identities per se as they are seen to be counterproductive to the aim of nation building and reconciliation. NGO tactics and their impact, on the other hand, aim for the strong promotion of the category 'the San' as a larger 'we-group' having a different identity and culture than other population groups because this is seen an effective means to lobby for San interests. This often rather one-sided strategy, however, does not take into account the fact that conflicts with non-San groups might be further aggravated by it. Conflicting interests and perceptions of their own identity within the envisaged group of 'the San' are often ignored by NGOs, as these do not fit the image of a cohesive, united group. In Tsumkwe West, a group identity according to NGOs' imagination beyond the boundaries of the four existing San groups is currently emerging. It looks promising to the groups involved as a strategy to increase their negotiation power and is perceived necessary to obtain recognition of the envisaged conservancy. Former boundaries between different San groups are thus loosing importance in the context of CBNRM, whereas the ethnic category of 'the San' on the other hand is playing an increasing role. Thus, it remains questionable whether the state's aim of decreasing the importance of ethnic categorisation can be realised in CBNRM.

Current tendencies of change are also apparent in the political field. Individual actors who have not been part of local power structures before try to increase their political influence by striving for positions in the newly established management institutions for CBNRM and using CBNRM goals as their arguments in claims for land or resource control. Competition arises between those individuals (often young educated men), the also newly established Traditional Authority and the mostly elderly men who function as village headmen. The political system of the social group related to an envisaged conservancy territory becomes re-organised. New institutions and positions of power emerge that are widely legitimised by their relations to outside factors such as NGOs, state agencies and the state laws. Western democratic values form the basis of development interventions among the San by international NGOs and donor agencies. These are not consistent and easily reconcilable with traditional political structures and processes which influence the attitudes and behaviour of local actors. Their previous approach in conjunction with the newly emerging one may thus lead to transformations which are only partly intended and beneficial. The rights and obligations of the new local political offices are still in the process of formulation. Such are the concrete expectations the 'community' has from them.

Furthermore, the spatial order of envisaged conservancy territories has become the subject of negotiations in an unprecedented manner. Territorial and resource boundaries have to be re-defined or defined for the first time, including their discussion in public meetings with government officials and NGO staff, and their codification in written documents. Disputes are arising or coming into the open and taking a new course as a consequence of the need for definition and clarity. Those cases further stress the frequently complex question of who has the necessary authority and power to take enforceable decisions. In this context, local San resort to the CBNRM concept to seek new opportunities to ensure secure resource or land ownership status and reliable mechanisms to exclude outsiders.

Apart from development and donor agencies, the state is playing a central role here. The transformation of the national political system after the end of Apartheid has had several wanted and unwanted consequences for the San in Tsumkwe West and elsewhere. As the case study presented here illustrates, several moves by the Namibian government all have their influence on current processes of social and political change among San groups. The right to free movement guaranteed in the Namibian Constitution results in increasing immigration of cattle herders into the area, which the San are trying to curb by instrumentalising the CBNRM concept with the assistance of NGOs. The Traditional Authorities Act laid the foundation for a new political representation and mobilisation among the San, which they also try to use as a means to increase the control over their territory. Finally, the conservancy initiative was made possible through national nature conservation policy and is seen by the San in Tsumkwe West as one more factor in their quest for emancipation.

Conclusion

Profound changes for many Namibian rural groups have commenced with the country's independence in 1990, which enabled different state politics and increased the influence of development agencies. Under the influence of development organisations, the San have embarked on a regional struggle for political representation and unity, and against political and economic discrimination resulting from colonial history, which, according to their view, is still embodied in state policies today.

The Namibian state – as most other Southern African states – has embarked upon the CBNRM agenda as a means to ensure their aims in both nature conservation and rural development. Local populations are, in most cases, confronted with this approach by facilitators from NGOs, who identify their own aims that they hope to achieve by promoting CBNRM. These include the empowerment of local groups on the one hand, but also growing prestige and continuous influence in the development scene on the other. They will also identify certain means through which they hope to realise these goals and act accordingly. Local people often receive CBNRM as one of the few opportunities to obtain rights to natural resources, gain income opportunities through tourism projects and increase their control over land. CBNRM is discussed, implemented and utilised against this background in ways which depend on the local social and political situation and which again lead to transformations of this situation. Some aspects of local constellations and processes have not been part of the state's and implementing organisations' considerations on the formulation of the Namibian CBNRM policy, and, furthermore, the interests that state agencies, NGOs and local actors pursue by it, sometimes diverge. As a consequence, the social and political processes initiated during CBNRM planning and operation locally can be unintended and hard to fit to the formal requirements for conservancy approval set by the MET. Successful management of a group's common resources in terms of increased economic opportunities through CBNRM projects often remains difficult to achieve.

The San in Tsumkwe West have been assisted with their intention to improve their political and economic situation by NGOs that identified major strategies for this area to be the promotion of centralised political representation in the form of a !Kung Traditional Authority and of CBNRM in the form of community-based tourism projects and a conservancy. Local actors take up these strategies and try to adapt to NGO discourse and methods. In the process, their facilitated action has initiated local change regarding assertions of individual and group identities, power relations in a new institutional set-up, the regulation of territorial and resource boundaries, gender roles in natural resource management, reactions to claims to the area's natural resources by non-San immigrants, and the role ascribed to outsiders like NGO facilitators, consultants and government officials. Considerable conflict among the group and with outside parties has been part of the process and can still be expected to result from the San's struggle for a CBNRM project that will fit their intentions. This process is not yet finished and remains subject to factors on a larger level, most prominently expressed in the MET's current hesitation to approve the N‡a-Jaqna Conservancy and the government's plans to resettle the Osire refugee camp with about 18,000 Angolan refugees in Tsumkwe West, which is feared to be detrimental to the area's resource base. Thus, it remains an open question in how far the desire expressed by a San woman participating in a conservancy planning session in 1998 to achieve a conservancy in order to achieve life as quoted in the heading of this chapter will be realised.

References

Adams, William and David Hulme
2001   Conservation and Community. Changing Narratives, Policies and Practices in African Conservation. In: Hulme, David and Marshall Murphree (eds.). *African Wildlife and Livelihoods. The Promise and Performance of Community Conservation*. Oxford: Heinemann:9-23.

Application for the N‡a-Jaqna Conservancy 1998. Windhoek.

Barrow, Edmund and Marshall Murphree
2001   Community Conservation. From Concept to Practice. In: Hulme, David and Marshall Murphree (eds.). *African Wildlife and Livelihoods. The Promise and Performance of Community Conservation*. Oxford: Heinemann:24-37.

Berkes, Fikret, David Feeny, Bonnie J. McCay, and James M. Acheson
1989   The Benefits of the Commons. *Nature* 340:91-93.

Berzborn, Susanne
2001   *Landrechtsprozesse und gesellschaftliche Transformationen in Post-Apartheid Südafrika. Das Problem der „community" im Landrechtsprozeß Richtersveld.* Paper presented at the ESSA conference "Recht, Rechtswirklichkeit und Rechtsräume", 10. to 12. May 2001, in Bonn.

Biesele, Megan and Robert Hitchcock
2000   The Jul'hoansi under Two States: Impacts of the South West African Administration and the Government of the Republic of Namibia. In: Schweitzer, Peter, Megan Biesele, and Robert Hitchcock (eds.). *Hunters and Gatherers in the Modern World. Conflict, Resistance and Self-Determination.* New York: Berghahn Books:305-326.

Biesele, Megan and Steve Barclay
2001   Jul'hoan Women's Tracking Knowledge and its Contribution to their Husbands' Hunting Success. In: Tanaka, I., M. Ichikawa, and D. Kimura (eds.). *African Hunter-Gatherers: Persisting Cultures and Contemporary Problems.* African Study Monographs Suppl. 26. Kyoto: Center for African Studies:67-84.

Bollig, Michael, Robert Hitchcock, Cordelia Nduku and Jan Reynders
2000   *Evaluation of KDT Kuru Development Trust Ghanzi and Ngamiland districts of Botswana.* Bonn: EED.

Botelle, Andy and Rick Rohde
1995   *Those Who Live on the Land: Land Use Planning in the Communal Areas of Eastern Otjozondjupa: A Socio-Economic Baseline Survey.* Ministry of Lands, Resettlement and Rehabilitation (MLRR) and the Social Science Division (SSD), Windhoek: University of Namibia.

Bromley, D.W. (ed.).
1992   *Making the Commons Work: Theory, Practice, Policy.* San Francisco: ICS Press.

Cassidy, Lin
2001   *Improving Women's Participation in CBNRM in Botswana.* CBNRM Support Programme Occasional Paper No. 5. Gaborone: CBNRM Support Programme.

Cassidy, Lin, H. Bowie and B. Jones
1998   *Living for Tomorrow: Evaluation Report of the KD/1 – Thusano Lefatsheng CBNRM Project.* IUCN for SNV. Gaborone: SNV.

Constitution of the N‡a-Jaqna Conservancy 1998.

Cousins, Ben
2000   *At the Crossroads. Land and Agrarian Reform in South Africa into the 21ˢᵗ Century*. Belville: PLAAS.

Critchley, W. and Stephen Turner (eds.)
1996   *Successful Natural Resource Management in Southern Africa*. Windhoek: Gamsberg Macmillan.

Dickens, Patrick
1994   *Englisch-Jul'hoan, Ju/'hoan-English Dictionary*. Quellen zur Khoisan-Forschung. Bd. 8. Cologne: Köppe.

Evangelical Lutheran Church in Namibia (ELCIN) 1992. *Annual Report*.

Felton, Silke
2000   "We want our own chief" – San Communities Battle Against Their Image. In: Le Beau, Debie and Robert J.Gordon (eds) *Challenges for Anthropology in the 'African Renaissance': A Southern African Contribution*. Windhock: University of Namibia Press.

Gibbs, Christopher J.N. and Daniel W. Bromley
1989   Institutional Arrangements for Management of Rural Resources: Common-Property Regimes. In: Berkes, Fikret (ed.). *Common Property Resources. Ecology and Community-Based Sustainable Development*. London: Belhaven Press:22-32.

Gujadhur, Tara
1997   The Impact of the Community Based Natural Resources Mangement Project on Jul'hoansi Women in |Xai|xai. In: SNV Botswana. *|Xai|xai Project Review*. Gaborone: SNV.

Heinz, Hans Joachim and B. Maguire
1974   *The Ethno-Biology of the !Kõ. Their Ethno-Botanical Knowledge and Plant Lore*. Botswana Society Occasional Paper No. 1. Gaborone: University of Botswana.

Hill, Kevin A.
1996   Zimbabwe's Wildlife Utilisation Programmes: Grassroots Democracy or an Extension of State Power? *African Studies Review* (39) 1:103-122.

Hinz, Manfred O.
1998   *Conservancies and Indigenous Law*. Paper presented at the SASCA conference "Southern Africa: Anthropology and the 21st Century", 10./11.09.1998 in Pretoria.

Hohmann, Thekla
2000   *Transformationen   kommunalen   Ressourcenmanagements   im Tsumkwe   Distrikt   (Nordost-Namibia).*   Unpublished   MA   Thesis. University of Cologne.

Hulme, David and Marshall Murphree (eds.)
2001   *African Wildlife and Livelihoods. The Promise and Performance of Community Conservation.* Oxford: Heinemann.

Hulme, David and Marshall Murphree
2001   Community Conservation in Africa. An Introduction. In: Hulme, David and Marshall Murphree (eds.). *African   Wildlife   and Livelihoods.   The   Promise   and   Performance   of   Community Conservation.* Oxford: Heinemann:1-8.

Ibsen, Hilde and Stephen Turner
2000   *Land and Agrarian Reform in South Africa. A Status Report.* Bellville: Programme for Land and Agrarian Studies.

Inambao, Crispin
1998   *San "Starving to Death".* In: *The Namibian* 8 June 1998. Windhoek.

Integrated Rural Development and Nature Conservation (IRDNC)
1997   *Community-based Natural Resource Management in Caprivi: A 21-Month Grant.* Unpublished Project Proposal. Windhoek: IRDNC.

Jones, Brian
1999   *Community Management of Natural Resources in Namibia.* IIED Issue Paper No. 90. London: International Institute for Environment and Development.

2001   The Evolution of a Community-based Approach to Wildlife Management at Kunene, Namibia. In: Hulme, David and Marshall Murphree (eds.). *African Wildlife and Livelihoods. The Promise and Performance of Community Conservation.* Oxford: Heinemann:160-176.

Jones, Brian and Marshall Murphree
2001   The Evolution of Policy on Community Conservation in Namibia and Zimbabwe. In: Hulme, David and Marshall Murphree (eds.). *African Wildlife and Livelihoods. The Promise and Performance of Community Conservation.* Oxford: Heinemann:38-58.

Kepe, Thembela
1998   *The Problem of Defining "Community". Challenges for the Land Reform Programme in Rural South Africa.* Bellville: Programme for Land and Agrarian Studies.

Lee, R. B.
1979   *The !Kung San. Men, Women, and Work in a Foraging Society.* Cambridge: Cambridge University Press.

Meer, Shamim (ed.)
1997   *Women, Land and Authority. Perspectives from South Africa.* Oxford: Oxfam.

Mehta, Lyla
1999   *Exploring Understandings of Institutions and Uncertainty. New Directions in Natural Resource Management.* IDS Discussion Papers 372. Brighton: Institute of Development Studies.

Ministry of Environment and Tourism
1994   *Land-use Planning: Towards Sustainable Development. Policy Document.* Windhoek: MET.

1995   *Wildlife Management, Utilisation and Tourism in Communal Areas – Policy Document.* Windhoek: MET.

1996a   *Interpretative Guide to the Legislation and Regulations which Make Provision for Communal Area Conservancies and Wildlife Councils.* In: *A Toolbox for the Establishment of Communal Area Conservancies.* Windhoek: MET.

1996b   *Notes on Developing a Communal Area Conservancy Constitution.* In: *A Toolbox for the Establishment of Communal Area Conservancies.* Windhoek: MET.

Mosimane, Alphons Wabahe
1996   *Community Based Natural Resource Management in East Caprivi: A Case Study of the Choi Community.* SSD Discussion Paper 16. Windhoek: University of Namibia.

Nabane, Nontokozo
1994   *A Gender Sensitive Analysis of A Community Based Wildlife Utilization Initiative in Zimbabwe's Zambezi Valley.* CASS Occasional Paper Series – NRM. Centre for Applied Social Sciences. Harare: University of Zimbabwe.

252 Thekla Hohmann

1998 *Proceedings of the Regional Conference on Gender Issues in Community-Base Natural Resource Mangement CBNRM. Cresta Lodge, Harare:24-27 August 1998.* CASS Occasional Paper – NRM Series. Centre for Applied Social Sciences. Harare: University of Zimbabwe.

Ostrom, Elinor et al.
1999 Revisiting the Commons: Local Lessons, Global Challenges. *Science's Compass. Review: Sustainability,* 9 April 1999, Vol. 284:278-28.

Republic of Namibia
1996 *Nature Conservation Ammendment Act, 5 of 1996.*

1997 *Traditional Authorities Act, 8 of 1997.*

1998 *Government Gazette No. 307 of 1998.*

Republic of Namibia,
National Planning Commission, Central Statistics Office
1991 *Population and Housing Census, Vol. 1.* Windhoek.

Rohde, Rick
1994 *Tinkering with Chaos. Towards a Communal Land Tenure Policy in Former Damaraland.* SSD Discussion Paper No. 8. Windhoek: University of Namibia.

Shackleton, Sheona, Graham von Maltitz and Jeremy Evans
1998 *Factors, Conditions and Criteria for the Successful Management of Natural Resources Held Under a Common Property Regime: A South African Perspective.* Bellville: Programme for Land and Agrarian Studies.

Sullivan, Sian
1999 Folk and Formal, Local and National – Damara Knowledge and Community Conservation in Southern Kunene, Namibia. *Cimbebasia* 15 (1999):1-28.

2000 Gender, Ethnographic Myths and Community-Based Conservation in a Former Namibian 'Homeland'. In: Hodgson, Dorothy L. (ed.). *Rethinking Pastoralism in Africa. Gender, Culture and the Myth of the Patriarchal Pastoralist.* Oxford: James Currey:142-164.

2001 How Sustainable is the Communalising Discourse of 'New' Conservation? The Masking of Difference, Inequality and Aspiration in the Fledgling 'Conservancies' of Namibia. In: Chatty, Dawn and

Marcus Colchester (eds.). *Displacement, Forced Settlement and Conservation*. Oxford/New York: Berghahn Books:158-187.

Taylor, Michael
2000   *Life, Land and Power. Contesting Development in Northern Botswana.* Unpublished PhD Thesis, University of Edinburgh.

Suzman, James
2001   *Regional Assessment of the Status of the San in Southern Africa. An Introduction to the Regional Assessment of the Status of the San in Southern Africa.* Windhoek. Legal Assistance Centre.

Thoma, Axel and Janine Piek
1997   *Customary Law and Traditional Authority of the San.* Centre for Applied Social Sciences Paper No. 36. Windhoek: CASS.

Thomas-Slayter, Barbara and Genese Sodikoff
2001   Sustainable Investments. Women's Contributions to Natural Resource Management Projects in Africa. *Development in practice,* 11:45-61.

Turner, Stephen
1996   *Conservancies in Namibia. A Model for Successful Common Property Resource Management?* SSD Discussion Paper No. 13. Windhoek: University of Namibia.

Weicke, Inga
2001   *Präsentation und Partizipation der San Namibias in touristischen Projekten.* Unpublished MA Thesis. University of Cologne.

Wiese, Bernd
1997   *Afrika. Ressourcen, Wirtschaft, Entwicklung.* Teubner-Studienbücher der Geographie — Regional, Bd. 1. Stuttgart: Teubner.

Widlok, Thomas
1999   *Living on Mangetti. "Bushman" Autonomy and Namibian Independence.* Oxford: Oxford University Press.

Wiessner, Polly
1982   Risk, Reciprocity and Social Influence on !Kung San Economics. In: Leacock, Eleanor and Richard Lee (eds.). *Politics and History in Band Societies.* Cambridge: Cambridge University Press:61-84.

Working Group of Indigenous Minorities in Southern Africa
1998   *Working Group of Indigenous Minorities in Southern Africa: Report on Activities April 1997 to March 1998.* Windhoek: WIMSA.

1999   *Working Group of Indigenous Minorities in Southern Africa: Report on Activities April 1998 to March 1999.* Windhoek: WIMSA.

2000   *Working Group of Indigenous Minorities in Southern Africa: Report on Activities April 1999 to March 2000.* Windhoek: WIMSA.

'Wilderness', 'Development', and San Ethnicity in Contemporary Botswana

Michael Taylor

Introduction

This chapter examines the place of San in contemporary Botswana, with particular reference to conservation and tourism, popular perceptions of San ethnicity, and government development programmes aimed at the San. It is based on ethnographic research on the periphery of a conservation area in northern Botswana; Moremi Game Reserve. San who had previously lived in this area were removed from Reserve when it was created in 1964.

Moremi Game Reserve is situated in the Okavango Delta, an inland marsh in the northern Kalahari, which attracts multitudes of tourists for its scenic beauty and large wildlife populations. It is a sparsely populated area, and contains only three villages; Khwai, Mababe and Gudigwa. The majority of each of these villages are San; Bugakhwe in Khwai and Mababe, and Ts'ega in Mababe. Their proximity to the waterways of the Okavango Delta, for the residents of Khwai in particular, has given them the label 'River Bushmen', distinguishing them from San who live in the drier areas of the Kalahari Desert.

The removal of San from Moremi Game Reserve was the first of a number of such relocations. The most recent such removals were in February 2002, when the government of Botswana grabbed international attention by cutting off all services to the residents of the Central Kalahari Game Reserve (CKGR) in an effort to make the final remaining residents leave, most of whom were San. Their efforts were largely successful. Three months later only a handful of stalwarts remained within the reserve, the rest having moved outside to government-created settlements.

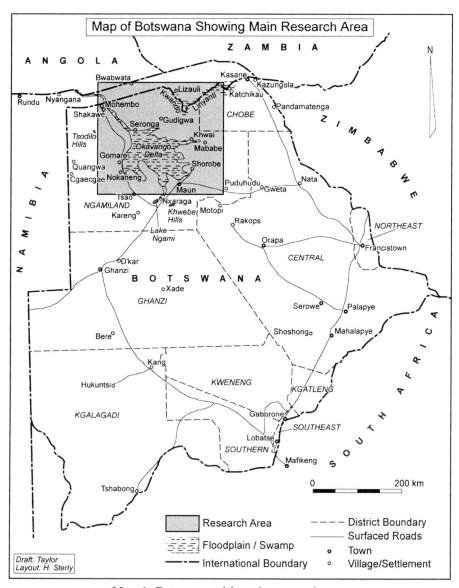

Map 1: Botswana with main research area

When the Central Kalahari Game Reserve was declared by the British colonial government in 1963, it was specifically meant to provide an alternative livelihood for San who had lost their land seventy years previously in the Gantsi farms, on the western border of Botswana. When it was created, an estimated 4,000 people lived within its boundaries. Nonetheless, in 1987 the Botswana government declared its intention to relocate the Reserve's residents outside the Reserve. Domestic and international protest ensued, and these plans were put on hold until 1997, when 1250 of the estimated 1600 people still living in the Reserve were relocated. Some of these returned over the next few years, and 350 people were again relocated in March 2002. It is unlikely that many residents will now return, with the cessation of all services within the reserve, and restrictions imposed on entry by former residents.

Various reasons have been put forward to explain the dogged determination of the government to remove the residents of CKGR, including the discovery of diamonds, depleting wildlife populations, and the expense of providing services to such remote locations. Whatever combination of reasons may have prompted the relocations, there was an underlying inevitability about the removals. San – particularly those remaining within the reserve – present an anathema as people who are seen by many within Botswana as 'backward' in a country that prides itself on its rapid economic and social development since independence.

San Ethnicity and Inequality

Despite being known as 'hunter-gatherers', the most starkly felt commonality of many San today is not a lifestyle of hunting and gathering, but a feeling of shared dispossession and subordination at the hands of those with economic and political power. Rather than framing San in terms of cultural patterns associated with a hunting and gathering past, this chapter explores the contemporary experiences of ethnic categorisations in Botswana, and the locally ascribed values and meanings associated with carrying the label 'Mosarwa'.

The label *Basarwa*, or its singular form *Mosarwa*, is not simply descriptive of a group of people who display – or have until recently displayed – socio-economic systems and practices associated with a foraging lifestyle, such as sharing, egalitarianism and nomadism. More importantly today, this label defines political spaces of policy and negotiation, or lack of such political spaces, and the power relations within these spaces. In other words, the values and practices associated with being Mosarwa, which could include practices such as foraging (and it becomes inconsequential that some of these may no longer be practised), structure relations between San and others in an environment where 'Mosarwa' is a highly value-laden term.

I argue that in a large part ethnicity has structured the relationship between San and those with political power, being the central logic in maintaining, and challenging, various forms of domination. Ethnicity is also the lens through which problems – and their solutions – are often codified locally, thus making it a key axis of difference.

As with 'first peoples' worldwide, the external domination of San is increasingly structured by the state (Hitchcock and Holm 1993, cf. Albert 1997). However, following Barth (1994:20ff), this analysis of ethnic and social processes pays explicit attention to micro, median and macro levels at which they work. Apart from the Botswana government (macro), this paper takes as its main subjects the interests of local and international tourism and conservation bodies (macro and median) and the perceptions and interactions of wider Setswana society (median and micro). Through each of these interconnected levels, I examine the structural relationship between San and the various people and institutions that have attempted to define and shape both them and the landscape in which they have lived. Although of a very different nature, these contemporary relationships have their roots in the violent subjugation of San in the second half of the nineteenth century (cf. Morton 1994).

In examining the ways in which power and authority are exercised with respect to the situation of San in Botswana, I focus on the power inherent in a variety of discourses or practices that do not appear to be formally part of the institutions of government, rather than on the coercive and explicit means that such institutions may use. One of the most important of these is the ways in which San are represented in dominant discourses, which becomes an essential means of attempting to wield control over them. These discourses are often produced in the context of talking about 'development' interventions, in which the state and other dominant institutions become the producers and possessors of legitimate knowledge; of history, of collective representations of identity, of what is legitimate and what is not. Such claims to knowledge and attribution of ignorance bring to the fore the forms of power that development creates and sustains. For example, representing certain people as 'underdeveloped' or backward and childlike allows them to be treated as such by legitimating intervention in the form of 'development' (cf. Hobart 1993). Development thus becomes, in part, an attempt to produce governable subjects, largely by asserting norms by which a society can be understood and regulated (cf. Watts 1996:48; Ferguson 1990; Escobar 1995, 1996; Scott 1998).

The analysis begins by considering Western views of the place of San in the landscape of the Okavango Delta. Conceptions of nature and the African landscape are integral to this analysis, as these have influenced the place that people have in it, and thus policy and practice in conservation and tourism. I go on to examine how San are imagined by their non-San neighbours, and the discursive frameworks through which Sesarwa ethnicity in Botswana is moulded. Lastly, I examine how these views have contributed towards defining development interventions, particularly the Botswana government's Remote Area Development Programme (RADP).

Imagining Wilderness

Integral to dominant perceptions of San have been conceptions of the landscape in which they have lived. As a sea of waterways in an otherwise parched semi-desert environment, the Okavango has long captured the imagination of Western visitors. Take, for example, the lyrical description penned by Hauptmann Streitwolf, a German visitor to the Delta in 1911:

> High leafy trees wooded the island banks and mirrored their hanging greenery in the water. Lotus lilies and water-plants of all sorts covered the unruffled water surface. Countless waterfowl sat motionless on the pools and trees, amongst the deep green of which often showed forth the dazzling white of the heron. Duck, geese, 'snake-neck' birds [cormorant], did not dare to disturb the silence of this secluded region. It is a beautiful world, this swamp region! Practically uninhabited except for a few Makuba [Bayei] engaged in catching fish, shut off from the outer world and difficult of access, it has retained its virgin charm (translated and quoted by Stigand 1923:403).

Streitwolf's vision of the Okavango as a wilderness where nature rules supreme has proved pervasive, especially within the context of the expanding tourist industry. Today, the Okavango Delta continues to attract foreign tourists seeking its 'virgin charm', and fuels Botswana's fastest-growing industry; tourism, growing in economic terms by an average of over ten percent per year through much of the 1990s.

Many tourists to Botswana end up staying at one of the Okavango Delta's sixty or so lodges or hotels. The first of these was Khwai River Lodge, built in 1967, four kilometres downstream from the present site of Khwai village. The residents of Khwai were moved out of Moremi Game Reserve when it was created in 1964, to their present position on its northern border. Nonetheless, Khwai village is itself a hub of tourist activity. Situated at the North Gate of the Reserve, Khwai is the transit point between Moremi and Chobe for overland visitors, and in close proximity to two other upmarket lodges in addition to Khwai River Lodge; Mochaba and Tsaro (Map 2). Clients of these lodges arrive by light aircraft to an airstrip several kilometres east of the village, where they are picked up by a guide in open-sided safari vehicles, and taken to relax and refresh before a game drive. One of the lodges, Tsaro, lies to the west, beyond Khwai village. Clients on the way to Tsaro, however, are usually taken on a specially constructed circuitous route to avoid the village of Khwai, one example of how 'nature' is carefully 'staged' for tourists seeking the 'authenticity' of a wilderness experience.

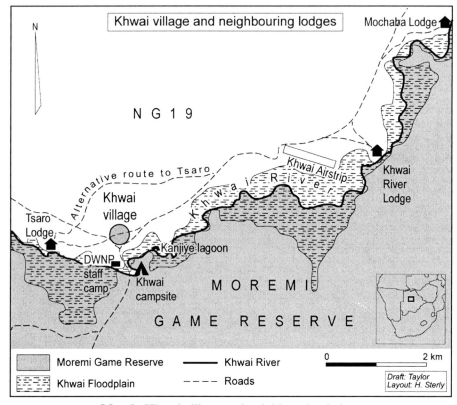

Map 2: Khwai village and neighbouring lodges

Selling and Consuming Nature in the Okavango Delta

'We are living a dream to be here', Dick, a retired professor from New York, told me as he savoured his first evening at Machaba Lodge, echoing a comment that continually surfaced in the well-filled pages of all three of the lodges' guest books. The dream that their hosts carefully cultivate, despite the presence of Khwai at North Gate, and Mababe on the route between

Moremi and Chobe, is one in which people have little place. Take, for example, Gametrackers'[1] brochure:

> You find yourself harmonising with a different, timeless place, remote from cities, beyond ordinary history [...] and the realisation dawns that you are fortunate and privileged to be in one of the last corners of the planet *under the total governance of nature* (emphasis added).

Photo 1: Tourists in the Okavango

An analysis of the publicity brochures from fifteen lodges and camps in the Delta by Damm et al. (1998:8) reveals that fourteen make no mention whatsoever of local population or culture. Three do mention 'Bushmen', but in a generic sense as an unthreatening part of the prehistoric landscape, such as the claim by Kanana Safaris that 'this is where the Bushmen have stalked game for untold generations'. The brochure from Xugana lodge, (on the land lived on by some residents of Gudigwa until the 1980s), gives the same message:

---

[1]   Gametrackers is a subsidiary of the international leisure group Orient Express Hotels, which owns Khwai River Lodge.

> There was a time when the ancient Bushman would kneel down
> to drink from the promised water of the Xugana lagoon, a lake
> formed by the timeless meanderings of the Okavango Delta's
> waterways [...]. Today 'Xugana' means more than 'kneel down
> to drink'. You will now find a lodge on an island nestling
> within a forest of wild ebony and *garcinia* trees [...]. Xugana
> has awaited your arrival for millenia (ibid:8-9).

Few of the photographs that generously cover these glossy brochures
show contemporary local people, apart from eager servants within the
confines of the camp. This is a world not only consumed by people from
outside Africa, but also one that – up to now – has to a large extent been
produced and controlled outside Africa as well.

People in Nature

'Landscape', Mitchell (1994:1-2) suggests, 'doesn't merely signify or
symbolise power relations: it is an instrument of cultural power'.
Representations of landscape can act, in much the same way as an ideology,
to naturalise a social construction of wilderness; an external nature that can
be dominated, conquered or protected by a human society that exists as
separate from it. Neumann (1998:9) refers to this as the 'national park ideal',
which he describes as the 'the notion that "nature" can be "preserved" from
the effects of human agency by legislatively creating a bounded space for
nature controlled by a centralised bureaucratic authority'. From its inception
with Yellowstone National Park in 1872, this particular ideal has provided a
model for national parks throughout the world, not least those in Africa. The
African landscape has been particularly prone to Western constructions as a
special kind of Eden (Anderson and Grove 1987:4-6), thus begging
'protection' as national (and more recently, international) heritage, for
consumption by modern society.

Needless to say, these 'pristine' environments were not untouched by the
hand of man prior to the arrival of tourists. Promotional material for Xugana
makes no mention of virtually the only known and excavated prehistoric
archaeological site in the Delta – about ten metres from the present bar area
(Damm et al. 1998:9) – nor of the more contemporary habitation by
Gudigwa residents. The Okavango Delta thus represents (as Neumann
[1998:31] characterises national parks in general) a harmonious, untouched
space of nature, which masks colonial dislocations and obliterates the history
of those dislocations.

Closely associated with the concept of the unique and mysterious wilderness of the Okavango Delta has been the idea, in the second half of the twentieth century, of a mystical and unknown people hidden in its depths. For some, the wilderness of the Okavango constituted the final frontier beyond which the last 'undiscovered Bushmen' might be found. Four expeditions were mounted between the 1940s and 1960s to attempt to 'discover' the 'remnants' of the River Bushmen: Balsan (1950); Van der Post in 1958 (1986); Cowley (1969); and Heinz (1969). 'Mystery and ignorance hang over the reedbeds of the swamps', wrote Heinz (1969:743) in introducing his journey. 'Some say that remnants of Bushmen tribes live hidden away on inaccessible islands here and that the River Bushmen who have been seen are tall and dark, totally unlike their small, light skinned desert cousins'. In true expeditionary fashion, Cowley and his men set off from Maun in 1966 with 150lb of leaf tobacco, 40lb of trinkets and a locked tin trunk of instruments for taking anatomical measurements, looking for 'Swamp Bushmen [who] were said to be the purest survivors of the Old Yellow Race' (1969:3). He had already faced the disappointment of visiting Khwai in 1960 and finding them 'hybridised'. He therefore aimed to find out what he could 'before the fabled tribe of swamp Bushmen was swallowed up in the racial hodgepodge of the Okavango Swamps' (1969:61). Needless to say, each of these expeditions did not find the pure exemplars they had hoped for. Constrained by a fantasy of 'pure Bushmen', protected by a 'pure nature' from being tainted by non-Bushmen, it was inevitable that they would come to a similar conclusion as Seiner (1910:31-2) had half a century earlier; that Swamp Bushmen were, 'relics in a rapid process of assimilation into the dominant culture, and that in a few years it would be impossible to describe them unequivocally as Bushmen'.

Narratives of racial purity and of natural purity form parallel discourses based on the same presuppositions. They rely on the essentialisation of a pure form of nature, and a pure form of humanity (in this case 'Bushmen') subject to it. Such people exist in contradistinction to others (both white and black) who have subordinated and tainted nature. This has been the essence of the remarkably pervasive van der Postian myth of Bushmen as the archetypal 'noble savages'. Like wilderness, 'Bushmanness' is seen as fragile and easily lost. 'It is very difficult to refer to [the residents of Khwai] as San because they are not true San anymore, they are too mixed, and their features are different... the Bushman gene is a very weak gene and disappears quite quickly', I was told by one of the original tourism operators in the Khwai area. Such constructions of nature and 'Bushmanness' are more than academic arguments. Once Bushmen cross the conceptual line between nature and culture, their presence in a 'wildlife' area becomes an anathema. The very real implications of this worldview and consequent policy have been repeated not only in the Central Kalahari Game Reserve, but also the Etosha Game Reserve in Namibia, from where Hai//om Bushmen were evicted in 1954 (see Dieckmann, this volume). Justifying its actions, the commission argued that Hai//om 'assimilation had proceeded too far', so that it would not be 'worthwhile to preserve the Heikum [sic] as Bushmen' (Schoeman n.d.:14, quoted in Widlok 1999:25).

Photo 2: "no hunting" sign produced in 1961 for Botswana's game reserves

Casting San in the Okavango Delta as inimical to the aims of the proposed Moremi Game Reserve was therefore an essential strategy to their eviction, a characterisation in common with general characterisations of African hunting by conservation advocates as cruel and wasteful slaughter (Neumann 1996). June Vendall-Clark, a prime initiator of the reserve, alleged that, 'Masarwa Bushmen in some areas routinely surrounded herds of red lechwe antelope and deliberately broke the legs of as many of them as they could so that the flesh of the still-living beasts would stay fresh for longer' (1990:223). Tourism operators questioning the ongoing settlement at Khwai use arguments in the same vein. 'But they are not even pedigree Bushmen'[2], one of the lodge managers complained to me about Khwai, and another argued that most of Khwai's residents are only there because of the job opportunities in the area. Both these assertions carry the implication that their 'transformation' from Bushman to proletariat delegitimises their continued presence in a 'wildlife area'.

Contestation over access to land in the Okavango therefore becomes a contestation over ideas of nature and culture, and where (literally) to draw the boundary between them (cf. Neumann 1998:11). Damm et al (1998) use the rustic wooden bridge at North Gate (Plate 4), which spans the Khwai River – the northern border of Moremi Game Reserve – as a metaphor for the crossing between nature and culture. While this is true in a legal sense, in that Khwai village is permitted to exist on the north bank, and its inhabitants are excluded from the south bank (unless in transit or as guides), in reality priority is given on *both* sides to nature. Although none of the three lodges have been granted concessions to land beyond their immediate vicinity, their extensive use of the land outside the park for game viewing contributes to its *de facto* status as a wildlife area. About half their game drives are conducted outside the reserve, as the reserve is not fenced, allowing the wildlife to move freely either side of the shallow river. The construction of Khwai as a 'nature' area means that attempts by the lodges to present an image of corporate responsibility to their potential clients are framed with reference to the environment, rather than local people. For example, a brochure of Gametrackers boasts, 'We maintain a respectful relationship with a fragile environment and pride ourselves on harmonising with the ecological balance; the wellbeing of all natural inhabitants is paramount'. The brochure contains no acknowledgement of local human inhabitants. Most operators would simply prefer Khwai and Mababe not to be there, and in the words of one operator to a consultancy team gauging opinion on Community Hunting Areas around the Okavango, their greatest need is 'birth control' (OCC 1995:A39).

---

[2] Her use of a word normally reserved for animal breeds betrays the conceptual categories in which 'Bushmen' are often placed by observers. While few would explicitly adhere to the implications of such a statement, the use of terms normally reserved for animals in discourses about 'Basarwa' is remarkably pervasive (Damm 1999:3).

The land on which Khwai is situated is designated as a Wildlife Management Area, which permits existing settlements to remain, but places restrictions on land use, such as the creation of new settlements, or the keeping of domestic stock. Nonetheless, Khwai's position in an area sold to tourists as 'wilderness' has prompted efforts by various government departments to relocate them elsewhere. These are efforts that Khwai has so far resisted, agreeing to relocation only if it is back to their previous location *within* the reserve, thus challenging its designation as a 'nature' area. 'They don't know there are people here', was an exasperated comment I often heard in Khwai, referring to the priority the government and tourist industry gives to nature over people in their area. The invisibility of San is not a new phenomenon. Early censuses of the Okavango area tended to ignore San, such as the 1921 census which noted 'a good number of River Bushmen', but failed to enumerate them because of the 'impossibility of catching and numbering the wild River Bushmen' (Stigand 1923:412). This census completely ignored San in the sandveld (the ancestors of those now in Gudigwa), and, still today, the villages of Khwai, Mababe and Gudigwa are omitted from many official maps. Nonetheless, although the autonomy that this invisibility afforded may have been valued, San in the northern sandveld today face a struggle to make their presence felt in an environment that is predominantly regarded as one in which people have little place.

I now turn from predominantly Western ideas about their landscape to ideas about San themselves within Botswana, and the conceptual place San occupy in the worldviews of their neighbours.

Imagining San

The nature of dominant stereotypes of San in contemporary Botswana is an issue that, as Hitchcock and Holm (1993:314) have pointed out, academic discussion has tended to avoid – perhaps a function of most such research being done under the auspices of official programmes. There is no doubt that San are imagined in a particular manner by many of their neighbours, but the forms that these take are open to various interpretations. To illuminate the place of San in the wider conceptual landscape of Botswana, I recount two everyday interactions between San and non-San, chosen from a multitude of similar interactions that I have observed.

The first occurred as I sat next to a dusty road with the two San men I had started chatting to, as we whiled away the time waiting for a lift. During our conversation, a non-Mosarwa man sauntered over and started chatting to one of the men. Without a hint of malice, he asked, 'Where are the *namagadi* [female ones], I want to grab their backsides'. The Mosarwa man fended off his question, and they continued to make small talk with each other, holding each other's hands as many men do in friendly conversation. *Namagadi* is a Setswana word meaning 'female', but it is usually reserved for animals. Viewing the reproductive nature of *Basalagadi,* or female San, as equivalent to that of animals or livestock, has a long history. Chapman (1971[1868],1:74, quoted in Morton 1994:226), for example, said of the Bangwato that they 'hold the Bushmen as beasts, term them bulls and cows, heifers and calves. In speaking of a female they say she has calved'. Yet, as Gordon (1992:212-3) argues with reference to constructions of Bushmanness by white settlers in Namibia, their 'inhumanity' was only one in a series of stereotypes used to justify actions against them, and did not load the use of San women for sexual services with the taboos of bestiality. That the question about *namagadi* did not elicit visible offence hints at the pervasive and socially acceptable structures of society in Botswana that govern social interaction between San and non-San.

The second example is taken from a visit to a small Jul'hoansi village in Western Bushmanland, Namibia, by a group from Khwai, Gudigwa and Mababe. The non-Mosarwa driver we were with turned to some of the group, and commented on the children going to fetch water: 'If only they went to school, they would be people'. This perhaps gets closer to the nature of dominant attitudes to Sesarwa ethnicity; that it is not always so much about San *per se* (as the comment was made to people who called themselves San as well), but about a 'backward' lifestyle that many San are seen to represent. This is a lifestyle associated with the bush and a lack of 'civilisation', which makes the civilising project of development particularly potent when aimed at San.

The relegation of San to beyond the realm of civilisation is illuminated by the conceptual model governing Setswana land use. It consisted of a pattern of concentric circles around the sphere of sociality, the village (*motse*). As one moved outwards, through arable land (*masimo*), then cattle posts (*meraka*) and finally no-man's land – the bush (*naga*) – one moved from the realm of society to that of nature and wilderness. Although the function of the bush, especially around the Okavango, has changed, becoming for some a lucrative site of production through expanding cattle ranches or tourism, the stereotype remains that San are of the realm beyond society, of the bush. As San are seen to lack the civilisation that comes from sociality, they also represent a way of life that we all come from; they are *people of the past.* This stereotype is reproduced (and thus enforced) through local representations, such as school textbooks that tend to present San living very much as their predecessors 20,000 years ago (Motzafi-Haller 1995).

Several observers have commented on local representations of San as people of the bush (Suzman 1997) and of the past (Motzafi-Haller 1995, Saugestad 1998:60, Damm 1999). There has, however, been little comment (with the exception of brief mentions by Kuper [1970:45,66,91]) on perhaps the most important aspect of this; that they are thus people without *molao* – without 'law'.

Being seen as people without *molao* has two important implications for their relationship with the contemporary state. The first arises from the view that those who lack *molao* are anarchic, and do not submit to the norms and codes of conduct of society. Take, for example, the description a non-Mosarwa inhabitant of the Delta periphery gave me of San:

> San of the sandveld are unfamiliar with other people, and run away when you approach them. If you come across them alone they will kill you, or else they will see your tracks, follow you and kill you. If they see you, the first thing they ask you for is *motokwane* [cannabis]. You had better give them what you have, and leave quickly before they kill you.

For individuals, such stereotypes make San unpredictable neighbours. For the state, San become unpredictable subjects, as San, being beyond the reaches of *molao* (i.e. governability), become seen as separatist. In a review of the RADP, its originator, Liz Wily noted that one of its major stumbling blocks was the fear that San living in the bush are being separatist (1982:302). A decade later, this was still in evidence, with the reaction to calls for greater access to land by a delegation of San to the government. A spate of reports in national newspapers followed, claiming that San were being separatist and demanding self-rule (*Daily News* 21.05.92, *Mmegi* 22.05.92, *Botswana Guardian* 22.05.92., all quoted in Saugestad 1993:40).

The second implication, which follows closely from the first, is that San need to come under *molao* [law/civilisation]. Bringing San under *molao* is an essential step in increasing their 'legibility' (Scott 1998) to their neighbours and the state. Until the 1980s, some government officials used the unfortunate – though accurate from their point of view – term for their consequent policy; that San should be 'domesticated' (Gulbrandsen, in Saugestad 1998:113). 'Integration into mainstream society' has since become the more acceptable buzz-phrase for policy towards San. Behind this aim lies the assumption that San will gradually absorb dominant norms, values and customs, submit themselves to existing authority structures and, in short, become more governable subjects. Integration is justified by constructions of San as backward. 'How can you have a Stone-Age creature continue in the age of computers?' Festus Mogae – then vice-president of Botswana, and now president – was reported by the New York Times to have asked (Daley 1996). Presenting a similar viewpoint, the outgoing president, Sir Keitumile Masire, commented in Ghanzi, as he gave his farewell tour, on the relocations of San from Xade in the Central Kgalagadi Game Reserve (CKGR), as reported in the government-produced *Daily News*:

> He said the government did not want to see certain tribes in the country remaining primitive. He blamed some anthropologists and sociologists from Europe for a misinformation campaign on the relocation programme. He said such people wanted San to remain primitive for research purposes. He described such people as '*bo marata helele*' [loosely translated as 'those who enjoy a spectacle'] who did not want to see San enjoying the fruits of this country like the rest of Batswana (Shabani 1998:1).

The President presents San (presumably *all* San, although his statement is in the context of Xade) in a similar manner to the way they are commonly represented, especially in development discourse; by the attributes that they *lack* (Motzafi-Haller 1995, Saugestad 1998). In this case they lack the position to 'enjoy the fruits of the country', but it could be any number of things; *molao*, civilisation, money, jobs, or skills. The problem is defined as one of culture, that their culture – rather than systematic dispossession by their neighbours – is to blame for their material poverty. This is not a new thought, it echoes the sentiment of a German traveller through the Kalahari almost a century earlier, who commented on the unequal relationship between San and Batswana: 'Inevitably the oppressed bear the major blame. Their inability to accept cultural imperatives, to rise to the cultural level of their suppressers is their own fault' (Passarge 1997[1907]:128). These representations of the problem beg a clear solution; that for 'progress' to be achieved, San must adopt a way of living that conforms to that of the majority.

The conception that San represent a 'primitive' way of life is widely held. To most people in Botswana, as well as the government, San represent an inappropriate continuation of 'the primitive' in a country that has prided itself on its rapid economic growth and social change since independence. While this view of San is not too different from popular Western notions, it has very different connotations; rather than constituting a romantic alter ego of their own society, they are an embarrassment. San, therefore, generally occupy a space in the conceptual landscape of contemporary Botswana that is different not only from Setswana-speakers, but also other minorities as well. Although San are not alone in carrying a legacy of subjugation, they face the double disadvantage of also being placed conceptually in a very different category from other minority groups; being people of the bush, and people who lack the constraints of *molao.*

The State, (Non)ethnicity and Development

Botswana achieved independence in 1966, surrounded by white-ruled states that were in the process of entrenching their power through ethnic ascription and division. Although this initially provided a powerful motivation to develop, in contrast, a 'healthy *non-racial* democracy' (Khama 1969:point 29), the policy of disavowing an ethnic discourse has remained, despite the magnitude of political changes in its neighbours. This policy has proved expedient beyond its time, as a means of maintaining the image of a culturally homogenous state. Rather than being non-ethnic, it is decisively *mono*ethnic, preserving the *de facto* hegemonic status of Setswana language, culture and political power (cf. Saugestad 1998:71).

About sixty percent of Botswana's 1.6 million citizens are ethnically Batswana. However, there is a deliberate blurring of the distinction between being a citizen of Botswana (labelled *Motswana*), and being ethnically a member of one of the dominant Setswana-speaking tribes (also labelled *Motswana*). Dominant discourses tend to conflate these two meanings of the root -*tswana*, so that if you are a *Motswana* (citizen), you are expected to reflect the traits that are associated with being a *Motswana* (in the ethnic sense), such as speaking *Setswana* (the language of the ethnic majority), or holding to its pastoralist values. Conflation of the two meanings is so pervasive that it is often even apparent in the narratives of non-Batswana (in the ethnic sense), such as the unnamed Mosarwa who told a team of consultants researching policy issues on wildlife, 'I am now a Motswana [citizen]. Therefore I must own cattle [associated with the pastoralist values of ethnic Batswana]' (Cooke et al 1992:11).

The state's aversion to recognising ethnic particularities in its policies is nonetheless challenged in two respects. Firstly, by the distinct position that San occupy conceptually, including in the minds of many officials, in the social landscape of Botswana. This is reflected, for example, in the tendency for the press to refer to 'Basarwa' in reports that concern Basarwa, although they do not use ethnic labels in reference to other people in Botswana. The second challenge is a more direct one, arising from some donors and researchers, and more recently from the rise of San interest groups, such as First People of the Kalahari. Along with occurrences such as the second regional conference for San held in Gaborone in 1993, and the CKGR removals, San have gained a higher profile within Botswana. The treatment of San has become a political issue, taken up by local organisations, such as Ditshwanelo (The Botswana Centre for Human Rights), and some opposition politicians. For example, Ephraim Setshwaelo, the head of the newly formed *Bosele* UAP party, denounced the CKGR removals at a public rally in March 1998 (as reported in *Mmegi* 06.03.98):

> 'It is barely conceivable that residents of such a village as Serowe or Ramotswa [large Batswana villages] could be uprooted from their ancestral land'. He dismissed as false government claims that Basarwa had moved voluntarily. 'I personally visited the Basarwa and what they wanted to know was when Batswana will cease their dictatorial hold over them'.

When the particular (or others on behalf of the particular) assert themselves and challenge their situation, this poses a dilemma for the state, forcing it to acknowledge the particularity of San, despite espousing a non-ethnic discourse. An example of this is in the issue of research permits, stipulated by the Anthropological Research Act of 1967 as a requirement for all social research undertaken in Botswana. Most research permits issued since 1996 have carried the proviso that the research 'does not cover Basarwa at all. At no point during data collection will the issue of Basarwa people be touched upon, nor will there be any research involving this population group'. Despite contradictions such as this, San nonetheless face a development apparatus that is explicitly aimed at *dissolving* local difference, subjecting them to a universal development plan that does not take into account local histories. This is most clearly reflected in the Botswana government's Remote Area Development Programme (RADP).

RADP and the Depoliticisation of Inequality

The RADP's overwhelming focus since its introduction in 1974 has been on service provision, which has become an essential element in facilitating the bureaucratic management of San. Hitchcock and Holm (1993:325) have argued that the programme of creating settlements with essential services have been, above all, a carrot to induce San to congregate at locations where the government can establish its authority and encourage assimilation, especially of children through formal education.

'Development', or its commonly used Setswana equivalent, *tlhabololo*, thus becomes a path of modernisation in which 'they' are made like 'us' (and thus more governable). In Setswana, the most common use of the word, which literally means to 'improve' or 'renew', is as a verb, sometimes in the passive sense, *go tlhabologa* (to be developed), but most often in the active *go tlhabolola* (to develop). Both these senses imply a process involving a subject (usually the government) doing the development, and an object (in this case San) being developed. Conceptually, therefore, San are seen as passively being developed – and thus assimilated – by the government, as commented to me by a Department of Wildlife and National Parks official in Maun:

> If we keep them with Special Game Licenses, how are we going to develop (*tlhabolola*) them? They must go to developments where they can have tar roads, clinics, roads, and the like. Basarwa here are different because they already have fields, so it is easier to make them leave a hunting and gathering way of life. We can entice them out by providing services and showing them another way of life is better and easier.

Through all its formulations and reformulations, the RADP has consistently failed to involve San themselves in setting its agenda. This is symptomatic of a more general attitude of officials to San where, in the estimation of Selolwane (1995:9):

> Botswana continues very much as during the pre-independence era when Basarwa were regarded as minors who were incapable of making or implementing decisions of their own [...] . The perception of those responsible for encouraging and nurturing [the] democratic culture has been that Basarwa could not usefully gain from such knowledge and practice.

Despite being staffed by generally sympathetic officers, its assumedly apolitical nature is evident from its failure to address anything beyond welfare and training. For example, the RADP officer responsible for Khwai and Mababe (who had recently been transferred from Central District) found herself frustrated by what she saw as the lack of co-operation with her attempts to introduce 'development' projects. After an offer to fund an orchard in Mababe that met with little enthusiasm, she complained to me:

> To be honest, people here are lazy. They don't want to work, and they don't want to co-operate. They are different from Basarwa in Central District. They waste my time [...] . I used to take money they earned to the bank and give them half and

> make them save the rest. Here they won't let me touch their money. They won't even tell me how much they are earning [...] Why don't they just move? Basarwa in Central District moved into the [government-created] settlements. Then they would be given what they want.

Well-meaning in her intentions, she was genuinely frustrated that her initiatives provoked such a feeble response. Predictably, this was blamed on their culture, rather than the patronising and non-participatory nature of RADP initiatives, and their attempts to provide technical solutions to deeper, underlying, political problems.

Unsurprisingly, the prime consequence of RADP has been judged to be the 'clientification' of San (Saugestad 1998:231). It would be more accurate to say that the RADP has constituted the logical continuation of a process of clientification that has characterised relations between San and their neighbours for almost two centuries. In the same way that during hard times in the past, San appealed to the 'goodwill' of their Bantu-speaking neighbours through providing occasional agricultural labour, many now appeal to the state to provide their basic needs – the difference being that now this no longer a mutual process. 'The government oppresses Basarwa', Mogodu, an elderly man from Mababe, complained to me, 'because it doesn't give us enough food and clothes'. Far from being a passive recipient of government handouts, Mogodu held down a job with a taxidermist company in Maun, while at the same time maintaining one of the largest fields in Mababe. Although he was not as dependent on government welfare as many elderly people, government policy has fostered a widespread attitude among San that the government should provide their daily needs. (see Bollig, this volume). Paine (1977:3) uses the term *welfare colonialism* to refer to the perpetuation of domination of 'indigenous' people by the state through such relations of dependency. The relationships are characterised as liberal rather than repressive, solicitous rather than exploitative, but nonetheless function to maintain political and economic control in the hands of the state.

Conclusion

In a continuation of the paternalistic relations that grew historically to characterise relations between Bantu-speakers and San, the Botswana government oversees a contemporary form of welfare colonialism over its indigenous populations. Its programmes aimed at San, particularly the RADP, are dressed in the language of concern and benevolence, but function to retain, even extend, political and economic control over San. Such development interventions are underpinned by (to use Fraser's [1989:6] words), the hegemonic 'power to construct authoritative definitions of social situations and legitimate interpretations of social need'. Dominant constructions of San as people who lack skills, material goods, civilisation – in short, 'development' – function to invite the 'normalisation' and standardisation of their reality, legitimating bureaucratic intervention and control over their lives.

San in the 'wildlife' areas of Okavango face the double challenge of making themselves visible in an environment which is constructed as one in which people have no place, as well as attempting to resist aspects of the universalising tendencies of the Botswana government. They therefore find themselves in a landscape that has little space for real people, and in which they and their desires become invisible.

Dominant discourses often characterise San as hunter-gatherers whose poverty is a product of their culture. Their culture, and the technical solutions needed to solve their problems, provide a powerful external motivation for 'development' by a concerned government that is able to benevolently provide what San lack. The removals from Central Kalahari Game Reserve were thus framed in terms of providing San with the opportunities that all other citizens enjoy. 'Ethnicity' remains as a central logic in dominating San. This may be through the corrupting influence they exert on a 'pristine' environment as devolved hunter-gatherers, ethnocentric constructions of the implications of their ethnicity in popular discourse in Botswana, or the strongly mono-ethnic discourse of the contemporary Botswana government. Within this framework of understanding, the poverty of San remains a product of their culture, and questions of wider power and inequality in Botswana, which implicate the powerful in the poverty of San, remain taboo.

References

Albert, Bruce
1997   'Ethnographic Situation' and Ethnic Movements: Notes on Post-Malinowskian Fieldwork. In: *Critique of Anthropology* 17(1):53-65.

Anderson, David and Richard Grove
1987   Introduction: the Scramble for Eden: Past, Present and Future in African Conservation. In: David Anderson and Richard Grove (eds.). *Conservation in Africa: Peoples, Policies and Practice.* Cambridge: Cambridge University Press.

Balsan, F.
1950   *L'étreint du Kalahari: Première Expédition Francaise au Desert Rouge, 1948.* Paris: Boivin.

Barnard, Alan
1992   *The Kalahari Debate: a Bibliographic Essay.* Occasional Paper No 35, Centre of African Studies, University of Edinburgh.

Barth, Frederik
1994   Enduring and Emerging Issues in the Analysis of Ethnicity. In: Hans Vermeulen and Cora Govers (eds.). *The Anthropology of Ethnicity: beyond Ethnic Groups and Boundaries.* Amsterdam: Het Spinhuis:11-32.

Chapman, James
1971 [1868]   *Travels in the Interior of South Africa* (2 vols). Cape Town: Balkema.

Cooke, H.J., L.D. Harris, A.U. Pfister, T. Tietema and P Wramner
1992   *Environmental Management in Botswana: Preliminary Report of Findings from a Fact-finding Mission, January 19th-28th 1992, Regarding National Policy Issues Concerning Wildlife and Environmental Conservation in Botswana.* Unpublished report submitted to Department of Wildlife and National Parks, Gaborone.

Cowley, Clive
1969   *Fabled Tribe: a Journey to Discover the River Bushmen of the Okavanago Swamps.* London: Longmans.

Crush, Jonathan (ed.)
1996   *The Power of Development.* London: Routledge.

Daley, Suzanne
1996   Botswana Pressuring Bushmen to Leave Reserve. In: *New York Times*, Sunday 14th July.

Damm, Charlotte
1999   *A People of the Past – but without History? Representations of Basarwa in Botswana.* Unpublished paper, University of Tromsø, Norway.

Damm, Charlotte, Paul Lane and Maitseo Bolaane
1998   Bridging the River Khwai: Archaeology, Tourism and Cultural Identity in Eastern Ngamiland, Botswana. In: Andrew Bank (ed.). *The Proceedings of the Khoisan Identities and Cultural Heritage Conference, 12-16 July 1997, South African Museum, Cape Town.* Cape Town: Institute for historical research, University of Western Cape:344-350.

Escobar, Arturo
1995   *Encountering Development: the Making and Unmaking of the Third World.* Princeton: Princeton University Press.

1996   Imagining a Post-development Era. In: Jonathan Crush (ed.). *The Power of Development.* London: Routledge:211-227.

Ferguson, James
1990   *The Anti-Politics Machine: Development, Depoliticisation and Bureaucratic State Power in Lesotho.* Cambridge: Cambridge University Press.

Fraser, N
1989   *Unruly Practices: Power, Discourse and Gender in Contemporary Social Theory.* Cambridge: Polity Press.

Gordon, Robert
1992   *The Bushman Myth: the Making of a Namibian Underclass.* Boulder: Westview Press.

Hasselring, Sue
1997   *A Sociolinguistic Survey of the Okavango Region.* Unpublished report for the Botswana language use project, Bible Society of Botswana, Gaborone.

Heinz, H.
1969   Search for Bushmen Tribes of the Okavango. *Geographic Magazine* 41:742-50.

Hitchcock, Robert K. and John D. Holm
1993   Bureaucratic Domination of Huntergatherer Societies: a Study of the San in Botswana. In: *Development and Change* 24:305-38.

Hobart
1993   Introduction: the Growth of Ignorance? In: Hobart (ed.). *An Anthropological Critique of Development: the Growth of Ignorance.* London: Routledge:1-30.

Khama, Seretse
1969   *Address to the General Assembly of the United Nations, September 1969.* Gaborone: Government Printer.

Kuper, Adam
1970   *Kalahari Village Politics.* Cambridge: Cambridge University Press.

Lee, Richard
1992   Art, Science or Politics? The Crisis in Hunter-gatherer Studies. In: *American Anthropologist* 94:31-53.

Mitchell, W.T.J. (ed.)
1994   *Landscape and Power.* Chicago: University of Chicago Press.

Morton, Barry
1994   Servitude, Slave Trading and Slavery in the Kalahari. In E. Eldredge and F. Morton (eds.), *Slavery in South Africa: Captive Labour on the Dutch Frontier.* Boulder: Westview:214-250.

Motzafi-Haller, Pnina
1995   Liberal Discourses of Cultural Diversity and Hegemonic Constructions of Difference: Basarwa in Contemporary Botswana. In: *Political and Legal Anthropology Review* 18(2):91-104.

Neumann, Roderick P.
1996   Dukes, Earls and Ersatz Edens: Aristocratic Nature Preservationists in Colonial Africa. In: *Society and Space* 14(1):79-98.

1998   *Imposing Wilderness: Struggles over Livelihood and Nature Preservation in Africa.* London: University of California Press.

OCC (Okavango Community Consultants)
1995   *Management Plans for Controlled Hunting Areas Allocated to Communities in Ngamiland Wildlife Management Areas.* Unpublished report prepared for the Ministry of Local Government lands and Housing, 31.03.95.

Paine, R.
1977   *The White Arctic.* Newfoundland Social and Economic Papers, No 7. Newfoundland: University of Toronto Press.

Passarge, Siegfried
1997 [1907]   The Bushmen of the Kalahari. In: Edwin N. Wilmsen (ed.). *The Kalahari Ethnographies (1896-1898) of Siegfried Passarge: Nineteenth Century Khoisan- and Bantu-speaking peoples.* Cologne: Köppe:127-218.

Saugestad, Sidsel
1993   Botswana: The Inconvenient Indigenous Peoples. In: *Indigenous Affairs* (2):36-41.

1998   *The Inconvenient Indigenous: Remote Area Development in Botswana, Donor Assistance, and the First People of the Kalahari.* Faculty of Social Science: University of Tromsø.

Scott, James
1998   *Seeing Like a State: How Certain Schemes to Improve the Human Condition Have Failed.* London: Yale University Press.

Seiner, F.
1977 [1910]   Die Buschmänner des Okavango and Sambesigebietes der Nord-Kalahari. From: Globus. Illustrierte Zeitschrift fur Länder-und Völkerkunde (trans. Helga Esche). *Botswana Notes and Records* 9:31-6.

Selolwane, O.D.
1995   *Ethnicity, Development and the Problems of Social Integration in Botswana: The Case of Basarwa.* Unpublished paper presented at the University of Botswana Basarwa Research Committee Workshop, 24-25th August 1995.

Shabani, Thamani
1998   Criticism on Relocation of Basarwa Community: Botswana Will Not Be Intimidated. In: *Daily News* Feb 12 (#28):1.

Stigand, A.G.
1923   Ngamiland. In: *Geographical Journal* 62:401-19.

Suzman, James
1997   *Things from the Bush: Power and Colonialism in the Making of Ju/'hoan Identity in the Omaheke region of Namibia.* Unpublished PhD thesis, University of Edinburgh.

Taylor, Michael
2001   Narratives of Identity and Assertions of Legitimacy: Basarwa in Northern Botswana. In: *Senri Ethnological Studies* 59:157-181.

Taylor, Michael
2002   The Shaping of San Livelihood Strategies: Government Policy and Popular Values. In: *Development and Change* 33(3):467-488.

Van der Post, Laurence
1986   *Lost World of the Kalahari.* Harmandsworth: Penguin.

Vendall-Clark, June
1990   *Starlings Laughing: A Memoir of Africa.* London: Doubleday.

Watts, Michael
1996   A New Deal in Emotions: Theory and Practice and the Crisis of Development. In: Jonathan Crush (ed.). *The Power of Development.* London: Routledge:44-61.

Widlok, Thomas
1999   *Living on Mangetti: "Bushman" Autonomy and Namibian Independence.* Oxford: Oxford University Press.

Wilmsen, Edwin
1989   *A Land Filled with Flies: a Political Economy of the Kalahari.* Chicago: University of Chicago Press.

Wily, Elizabeth
1982   A Strategy of Self-determination for the Kalahari San (the Botswana Government's Programme of Action in the Ghanzi Farms). In: *Development and Change* 13:291-308.

Between Welfare and Bureaucratic Domination: The San of Ghanzi and Kgalagadi Districts

Michael Bollig

Introduction

Two developments have profoundly changed San communities in the Ghanzi and Kgalagadi Districts of western Botswana over the course of the last twenty years. Since the late 1970s all through the region, San, who had lived on unfenced farms and at the fringes of communal grazing lands while frequently maintaining a band-like social organisation, were concentrated in so-called Remote Area Dweller (RAD) settlements. The forced removal of San from the Central Kalahari Game Reserve in 1997 is probably one of the last moves of San bands to planned settlements (see contribution Taylor, this volume; also Hitchcock 2001, Ikeya 2001). The inhabitants of RAD settlements have been largely dependent on governmental and non-governmental welfare programmes since their inception. Other subsistence strategies such as hunting and livestock herding have been limited or abolished altogether by government regulations (Hitchcock and Masilo 1996, Hitchcock 2001). Ecological constraints make agriculture highly risky. In areas almost totally devoid of resources to support income-generating activities, sedentarisation has led to localised populations who are unable to maintain their subsistence. At the same time, San communities in western Botswana have been organised by and politicised through various development projects, connecting them with the wider economy and national society (Bollig and Berzborn 2002).

This paper undertakes to show how local economies and societies in villages and settlements occupied by San in western Botswana have developed. The data originate from three short periods of fieldwork done in the region; all three were aimed at producing consultancy reports (Bollig et al 2000, Bollig 2001, Bollig and Hohmann 2001). Additionally, a great deal of unpublished literature, such as reports, project documentation and government publications, were analysed. It is significant that, due to the Botswanan government's nearly total embargo on anthropological research with San communities, little anthropological literature focusing on the household and village level has been available. While this study definitely lacks in anthropological depth, it discloses trends in the development of San communities on a regional level. The first section of the paper gives a rough outline of the history of state involvement with the San of Kgalagadi and Ghanzi Districts and the rise of non-government organisations (NGOs) among the San since the 1980s. Then, characteristics of RAD settlements are described, mainly addressing their short history, population dynamics, household structures, as well as the overall economic situation. Two settlements, Grootlagte (Ghanzi District) and Zutshwa (Kgalagadi District), are described in more detail. The following section contains data on the economy of settlements. Various sorts of welfare programmes as well as income-generating activities by development projects are assessed. The final section outlines social change in the settlements. The basic assumption underlying all chapters is that, since the early 1980s, San in both districts were fully captured by the welfare state. While in 1976, Alan Barnard could still maintain that "changes do not yet amount to a basic transformation of the society" (Guenther/Barnard 1976:132), today San societies have changed profoundly. These changes, however, have been highly ambiguous: Next to utter poverty and a terrible dependency on hand-outs, there are opportunities for generating income through tourism, artwork, and the absorption of development funds and project-related work. At the same time, communities have been rapidly integrated into a global system with institutional actors who offer aid to minorities and hope to contribute to their political emancipation.

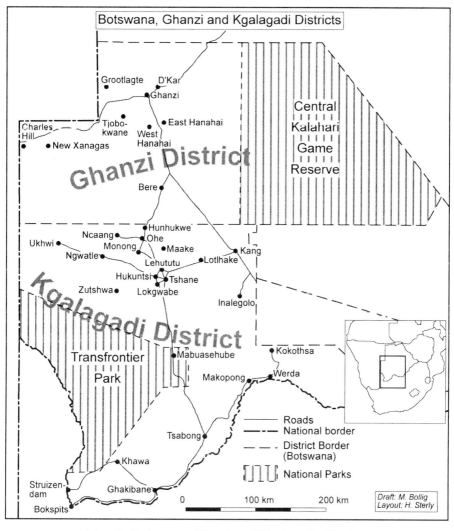

Map 1: Botswana, Ghanzi and Kgalagadi Districts

The San of Western Botswana and Development

The San in western Botswana have been the target groups of administration and governmental aid for almost a century. Since the early 1980s, administrative efforts have been accompanied by the attempts of non-governmental organisations to combat rural poverty and to foster political emancipation.

Government Programmes

Government concern with San communities began in the 1920s, when the League of Nations conducted an investigation into slavery. Several reports were issued by the Protectorate Administration, and a so-called "Masarwa Commission" was installed (Russell 1976:180*f*). The aim was to describe the conditions under which Sarwa were employed by Batswana and to clarify the degree of corporal punishment meted out against Sarwa (the Setswana term for San) serfs. One outcome of the commission was the establishment of two settlement projects in the Ghanzi District. A settlement approach had already been advocated earlier by officials in the Ghanzi farm region as a way to combat stock theft and the setting of bushfires (Hitchcock and Holm 1993:317). Both settlements founded in the 1930s were short-lived and abandoned only two years after their foundation (pers. comm., R. Hitchcock). Not until the 1950s, did the Betchuanaland Protectorate government again turn to what was termed the "Bushman Problem." A study by Silberbauer, then employed as the Bushman Development Officer, lead to the establishment of the Central Kalahari Game Reserve (CKGR) as an area where local foragers, as well as the unique habitat, of the Southern Kalahari could be protected. The Bushman Survey Report (Silberbauer 1965), which laid the foundation for development work with the San in early independent Botswana, singled out education and economic development as the most important trajectories of a positive transition. Silberbauer recommended that promising San farmers should be supplied with livestock and bore-holes to pave the way for economic development. In 1974, the Bushman Development Plan put forward empowerment, self-reliance, participation and acculturation into the national society as major goals (Hitchcock and Holm 1993). Land allocation became a major issue, as the implementation of the National Policy on Tribal Lands (TGLP) excluded San from even applying for land with the Tribal Land Boards (Wily 1979a:33; for a critical documentation of TGLP, see Hitchcock 1990). In the mid-1970s, settlements at the margins of the commercial farm block were envisaged in Ghanzi District as a new home ground for San. While some villages had already been established by the government (D'kar in 1964, Bere in 1968, Ka/gae in 1973; see Hitchcock and Holm 1993:319), a greater number of them was founded in the late 1970s in a concerted effort to solve the so-called Bushman problem. The District Officer for San at that time proposed specific settlement sites (Wily 1979b). The plan was implemented with the help of foreign donors, and by the early 1980s most San not resident on farms had been moved to one of the settlements. In the Kgalagadi District, settlements were founded mainly during the early 1980s in a move to bring development to San and Kgalagadi communities. Development efforts in the settlements were coordinated by the Remote Area Dweller Office (RADO), a reformulation of the Bushman Development Office launched in order to prevent any ethnic bias. Accordingly, the settlements came to be known as Remote Area Dweller, or RAD, settlements. Many households in the settlements remained dependent on hand-outs by the government and heavily subsidised income-generating activities run by development projects. Alcoholism, internal conflicts, unemployment and illiteracy were rampant (Hitchcock, Ebert and Morgan 1989:318-320).

Non-governmental Organisations in Western Botswana

Since the mid-1980s, non-governmental organisations accompanied government initiatives. The work of NGOs in the region is hardly conceivable without the establishment of RAD settlements. In order to organise and mobilise people, they have to be concentrated together and sedentary. NGOs had the explicit aim of developing communities economically, but also to empower them politically and culturally. Especially since the early 1990s, the political mobilisation of San communities through NGOs (especially in the Ghanzi Distict) has been significant.

The First People of the Kalahari (FPK, *Kgeikani Kweni*) was founded in 1993 as an NGO explicitly working for the political emancipation of San. FPK is the only NGO operating in Botswana that was founded by San, according to the publications of the organisation (IWGIA 2000). However, John Hardbattle, the charismatic leader of the organisation through its first years, was the son of a British man and a Nharo woman and was schooled mainly in England. FPK today works from Ghanzi Town and for several years has been mainly concerned with stepping up opposition against the forced removal of San from the Central Kalahari Game Reserve. The Kuru Development Trust, operating from the church-owned farm D'kar in Ghanzi's farm block since the early 1980s, has offered various income-generating activities as well as literacy and cultural programmes. Since the 1990s, the organisation has expanded its services to most RAD settlements in the Ghanzi District, whereas its activities targeted at San living on farms has remained limited. The Working Group on Indigenous Minorities in Southern Africa (WIMSA) has organised San in the entire South African region since the middle of the 1990s. WIMSA facilitates the exchange between San communities across national borders and connects community-based organisations to international indigenous rights movements. Permaculture and Thusano Lefatseng, two NGOs working on the national level, were mainly engaged in small-scale agricultural projects. Both NGOs are devoted mainly to small-scale agricultural developments in Botswana's peripheral areas and do not have any ethnic focus. In contrast to government programmes, which viewed the acculturation of San communities to Batswana national society as a major aim, NGOs have generally stressed cultural emancipation and advocated a peculiar San identity that found its expression through specific economic and cultural activities.

NGOs operating in western Botswana can be roughly grouped into those with a national agenda (Permaculture, Thusano Lefatseng), those with a regional agenda (Kuru Development Trust, Ghanzi Craft, First People of the Kalahari), and those with a local agenda (Maiteko Tshwaragano Development Trust). The activities of Kuru Development Trust and Maiteko Development Trust will be presented here in more detail. All NGOs depend on foreign donor money to a large extent. A major difficulty for NGOs was the definition of the target group: Did they want to focus on the entire settlement population, on the poorer part of the population, or on the San? Different NGOs found different solutions. While FPK and the Working Group of Indigenous Minorities in Southern Africa have been founded as advocacy organisations of and for San, Kuru Development Trust has projects aimed at San and others aimed at a wider population. Maiteko Tshwaragano Development Trust, Thusano Lefatseng and Permaculture, on the other hand, de-emphasise the importance of ethnicity in their activities and reports.

Kuru Development Trust (KDT)[1]

Kuru Development Trust was founded in 1986 as a charitable organisation for San occupying the church owned-farm, D'kar, with the support of the Reformed Church of Botswana. In contrast to other RAD settlements, the D'kar community developed on a private farm owned by the church within the Ghanzi farm block. People settling on D'kar came from both neighbouring farms and from farther away. Significantly, the population at D'kar is only half San (most of them are Nharo speakers), while the population in the neighbouring settlements is made up of over 70 percent by San. Despite the ethnic heterogeneity of D'kar, KDT has maintained a focus on the San and even the Nharo since its inception. In 1999, there were about 900 people living in D'kar. For a decade, the Kuru Development Trust concentrated on D'kar residents in developing a full-fledged programme with, for example, an education component, a handicraft

---

[1] Kuru comes from the Nharo word "to do or to create" (Cassidy 2000:48).

section, an agricultural component and an arts section. Throughout the 1990s, KDT was very successful in gaining support from international donors. Development agencies of Lutheran churches in Scandinavia and Germany, as well as Dutch donors, financed large parts of KDT. Since the mid-1990s, KDT expanded from its focus on D'kar to render assistance to the communities of the RAD settlements surrounding Ghanzi farm block and to communities in the district of Ngamiland. KDT has assisted in the foundation of community-based organisations in several RAD settlements (Grootlagte Village Organisation, West Hanahai Village Organisation, Tshobokwane Village Organisation, and Huiku Trust, which combines activities of the RAD settlements Grootlagte and Qabo). In the late 1990s, more than ten expatriates had offices in D'kar to run the various sub-branches of the project. Due to internal organisational problems and continued discrepancies between the aspirations of the incipient, mainly Nharo-speaking, D'kar-based elite and the project's aim to reach as many San communities as possible, KDT broke up into seven independent branches in 2001. Major parts of the programmes were relocated to Maun, Ghanzi, and Shakawe in Ngamiland District

KDT defined itself as an indigenous development organisation committed to the "development of the San ... in the Kalahari Desert" (KDT Annual Report 1997). The NGO tried to focus its efforts on the San community, not withholding that occasionally non-San were beneficiaries of the programme. Income-generating activities were seen as a stepping stone for political and cultural empowerment of the San. Cultural projects (literacy, art, oral tradition, preschool projects) have made up a major part of KDT's programme. Some care was taken to maintain it as an organisation steered by the community. The Board, for example, has been occupied solely by San. However, this does not preclude that the NGO is still operated mainly by expatriates and is largely dependent on donor money.

Maiteko Tshwaragano Development Trust (MTDT)

The starting point for the development initiative that later lead to the establishment of Maiteko Tshwaragano Development Trust (MTDT) in Zutshwa, a RAD settlement in Kgalagadi North, was the identification of the great potential of Zutshwa's saline groundwater for salt production. Salt extraction in Zutshwa was started by the Botswanan NGO Rural Industrial Innovation Centre (RIIC) in October 1989. MTDT was founded in 1990 to coordinate development initiatives in Zutshwa, and its Deed of Trust was registered in 1992. Its membership was open to all adult inhabitants of the village and the board of trustees has since been elected during an annual general assembly. SNV – Netherlands Development Organisation, a Dutch volunteer organisation – got engaged in the project early on: It seconded a volunteer to the project and has offered considerable project support. Additional income-generating activities apart from salt production have been incorporated into MTDT.

The Remote Area Dweller Settlements
of Ghanzi and Kgalagadi Districts

Today, almost all San of western Botswana either live in RAD settlements, on commercial farms, or in towns. While there is little anthropological and sociological literature on RAD settlement populations, there is even less information on the San who live in towns and on farms. I will first address the situation of settlements in the Ghanzi District, singling out the community at Grootlagte and then turn to the situation in Kgalagadi District, where the settlement at Zutshwa will be taken as a case study. The section will mainly portray structural parameters such as demographic structures and economic and social organisation.

Ghanzi District Settlements

In the 1890s, a group of Boers was allotted farms by the British Protectorate Administration in Ghanzi. Since then, commercial farms have become firmly established in the district. These farms remained unfenced well into the 1960s, and San communities, mainly Nharo, moved between farms while subsisting on farm work and hunting and gathering. Alan Barnard (1980:139) has pointed out that San probably saw white farms as just another resource that could be exploited temporarily if natural resources did not yield sufficiently to sustain living standards. Commercial ranching and subsistence foraging apparently co-existed on the same ground for decades (for similar co-existence of land management systems in northern Namibia, see Widlok, this volume). After commercial farms in the Ghanzi District were fenced in the 1960s and 1970s in an attempt to modernise ranching, many San were expelled from these farms. Barnard (1980) summarises the changes as: (1) fencing and engine-pump bore-holes diminished the overall amount of work needed to be done, (2) the introduction of better quality livestock required skilled labour, (3) remuneration of employees gradually changed payment in kind to payment in cash, which made farm labour interesting for migrant labourers, and (4) the increase of livestock numbers and the introduction of high-velocity guns diminished the supply of plant food and huntable game. Farmers reduced the number of workers on their farms and frequently replaced unskilled San herdsmen with better qualified migrant labourers. The Botswanan government tried to alleviate the problems of San forced to leave commercial farms by founding formal settlements around the commercial farms. The sedentarisation and concentration of San in settlements was seen as a pre-condition for acculturation and integration into the Botswana national society (Childers 1976). The settlements were allotted land units of 40,000 ha each, an area meant to be sufficient for local livestock keeping. All settlements were fitted with some formal housing, a school and a health station. Detailed information on the economic status of settlements is lacking, and, in particular, the social aspects are not well described. For some settlements, only population numbers could be obtained (Table 1).

Table 1: Ghanzi District communities

Place	Popula-tion 1991	San popula-tion (%)	Settlement type	Land use zone
D'kar	1079	50	RAD Settlement	CLF
West Hanahai	628	90	RAD Settlement	WMA
East Hanahai	733	85	RAD Settlement	TG
Grootlagte	477	95	RAD Settlement	WMA
Qabo	200	75	RAD Settlement	WMA
Bere	282	90	RAD Settlement	WMA
Xade, New Xade	ca. 800	100	RAD Settlement	Game Reserve and WMA
New Xanagas	ca. 490	75	RAD Settlement	TG
Tshobokwane	318	95	RAD Settlement	TG
Kuke	1209	50	Informal Settlem.	CLF
Kagcae	484	90	RAD Settlement	WMA

Abbreviations are CLF = Commercial Livestock Farming, TG = Tribal Grazing, WMA = Wildlife Management Area. Source: Cassidy et al. 2000:A2-A19.

Most settlements are located either in Wildlife Management Areas or on tribal grazing lands. This indicates that either land boards and/or the Directorate of Wildlife and National Parks have an important influence on decision making on economic strategies. While none of the settlements is inhabited exclusively by San, they constitute the majority population in most settlements. Settlement populations range between 280 and 1000 people. Today, approximately 4200 San live in Ghanzi's RAD settlements, 5700 live on Ghanzi's commercial farms, and another 1000 live in Ghanzi township (Guenther 1979, Barnard 1980:143 ff., Barnard and Widlok 1996; Russell, 1976, describes living conditions of San in the Ghanzi District mainly for the 1970s).

Case Study: Grootlagte

The site of the Grootlagte settlement had already been chosen in 1976 by the Bushman Development Officer Childers as part of the district development scheme. But only after potable water was struck in 1982 did people settle there. Due to a food distribution programme, Grootlagte became a very attractive place to settle. In December 1993, a population of 403 people was counted: 217 males and 186 females, organised in some 75 households. The average household size was 6.5 people per household. Only 5 households were headed by females. Of the 75 households, 70 were Sarwa households and 5 were Bakglagadi. Some 86 people were counted as absentees: of these, 56 were employed mainly on the Ghanzi farms; 17 were visiting farm settlements.

Thirty-six households (48%) owned cattle or goats. In total, some 131 cattle and 46 goats were owned by Grootlagte's 75 households in 1995. Most cattle originated from donations by the RAD programme: prior to 1992, 47 households were given two heifers each. Two bulls were shared by the community. Twenty households received 15 goats each in another donation by the RAD programme. These figures seem to indicate that (1) most livestock herded by San stem from donations and that (2) quite a number of families who had originally obtained livestock did not succeed in establishing herds. According to the RADO/VA in Ghanzi, not only the 131 cattle owned by community members were herded on Grootlagte community land. In total, some 500 cattle were grazed around Grootlagte, pointing at the fact that large numbers of cattle from outsiders were either herded on a loan basis or herded for minimal salaries. Shepherding was of considerable importance in other settlements as well. In addition, cattle from farms bordering Grootlagte were driven seasonally onto the settlement pastures. The heavy use of settlement pastures by outsiders hindered the establishment of locally owned herds. Resources were mainly used to feed the herds of people coming from outside the settlements.

In 1989-1990, a 3.5-ha woodlot and vegetable garden was established at Grootlagte by the NGO Permaculture Trust. Production from the community garden increased with the improvement of the water supply over subsequent years. Vegetables were produced for participating residents and the school food programme. Only eight households (11%) reported having ploughed and planted maize/sorghum and melons in the 1994 rainy season on private fields. Although the allocation of arable land has increased in the area since the late 1990s, most of the new allocations have not been fully developed. As the Botswanan government compensates farmers for crop losses due to drought according to the acreage of the fields, farmers occasionally clear fields more with the perspective of gaining revenues from compensation funds later on than to plant them.

Grootlagte has been a reserve of cheap labour for commercial farmers in Ghanzi. There are camps on at least five farms near the settlement where members of Grootlagte community stay with employed relatives and friends while working as casual workers for farmers. Besides farm work, there is very little employment nearby. The volatility of agriculture and the lack of employment are conducive to great dependence on drought relief and destitute programmes. Over the last decade, Grootlagte has seen several drought relief projects. These projects included brick moulding, construction of housing and woodlot watering. Welfare in the form of destitute rations is of great importance for Grootlagte households. There were 69 destitutes obtaining food rations in Grootlagte in 1995: 35% of the population over 16 years.

Since the late 1990s, Grootlagte and the neighbouring settlement at Qabo have come together to form a CBNRM Trust, the so-called Huiku Trust. As a registered trust, they are eligible to be allotted a game quota, which can either be hunted or sold to a hunting safari company. Additional economic gains can be made by charging for camping sites and the sale of handicrafts to tourists. In late 1999, however, the trust had not yet succeeded in setting up any infrastructure for tourists, let alone in attracting any well-paying tourists to the settlements.

Kgalagadi District

Unlike Ghanzi District, the development of Kgalagadi District has not been shaped by the introduction of a colonial ranching economy. Until the 1980s, many Qgoon (also !Xo and !Xoon, according to the literature) and Balala[2] seem to have subsisted between foraging, labour contracts mainly on Namibian farms, and occasional labour mainly for local Kgalagadi, but also for Tswana and Herero agropastoralists (Silberbauer and Kuper 1966; for

---

[2] Balala are variously described in literature as a San group or as former slaves of the Kgalagadi (Hitchcock 1996).

ethnographic descriptions of Qgoon, see Heinz 1979, and for information about their colonial history, see Ikeya 1997). The San population of the district is concentrated in the northern area. Only during the late 1970s and 1980s was the population amalgamated into settlements. At the same time, large-scale cattle farming by commercialised cattle farmers from the Hukuntsi region extended further into the Kalahari, which diminished the Qgoon hunting territories. Today, there are about 2900 San living in the Kgalagadi District's settlements. In most settlements, San live with Balala and Ngologa, a subgroup of the Kgalagadi. About 850 San live in the major settlements of the Masheng villages (Hukuntsi and Lehututu), where they constitute a minority.

Table 2: San settlements in Kgalagadi District

Place	Popula-tion 1991	San popula-tion %	Settlement type	Land use zone
Ukwhi	430	67	RAD Settlement	WMA
Ncaang	191	12	RAD Settlement	WMA
Ngwatle	135	100	RAD Settlement	WMA
Monong	105	95	RAD Settlement	WMA
Maake	325	71	RAD Settlement	WMA
Zutshwa	365	78	RAD Settlement	WMA
Pudhuhudu	365	14	RAD Settlement	*TG*
Inalegolo	270	97	RAD Settlement	WMA
Hunhukwe	455	12	Village	
Khokhotsha	535	36	RAD Settlement	Around settlement, residential
Ohe	ca. 20	100	Informal Settlem.	TG
Kang	3289	9	Village	TG
Hukuntsi	3464	10	Village	TG
Lehututu	2070	10	Village	TG

Abbreviations are CLF = commercial livestock farming, TG = tribal grazing, WMA = Wildlife Management Area. Source: Cassidy et al. 2000:A52-A57.

The settlements of the Kgalagadi District are somewhat smaller than settlements in the Ghanzi Distict: they roughly number from 200 to 500 inhabitants. Livestock holdings are limited, and where there are substantial numbers of cattle, they usually belong to Kgalagadi. However, many San herd goats and maintain gardens (for comparable information on San goat herding and farming, see Ikeya 1993, 1996).

Case Study: Zutshwa

Zutshwa, located 65 km southwest of Hukuntsi, is situated in a Wildlife Management Area and today is the only settlement in the controlled hunting area KD2.[3] Groundwater in Zutshwa is extremely saline (six times the salinity of sea-water).

Zutshwa Pan had been a temporary rainy season settlement site of mobile San hunters for many generations. It was the presence of several fresh-water wells that attracted mobile populations. During dry seasons, the productivity of local sip-wells decreased the need for people to move on to other wells (Van der Jagt 1996:89). The first Ngologa Kgalagadi to use the resources of the pan arrived by the end of the 19th century. From their Hukuntsi base, they used Zutshwa as a cattle post during the rainy season to make use of the good pastures in the vicinity, while the pan was filled with rain water. It was from these times that Ngologa families claim dominance over Zutshwa's resources, viewing it as "their cattle post." Balala families, the third ethnic component of Zutshwa, obviously only started to make use of Zutshwa's resources since the 1950s. Until about 1980, however, Zutshwa Pan was only used seasonally: While Ngologa families moved between Hukuntsi and Zutshwa Pan with their cattle, the San moved between Zutshwa Pan and several other minor pans in the surrounding area. Like other settlements in Kgalagadi North, Zutshwa was founded as a RAD settlement in the early 1980s. The concentration of mobile populations at the settlements was partly a result of a conscious move by the government to deliver services (school, health services, etc.) to marginal populations and partly a spontaneous move by the San and Ngologa families to settle down. Zutshwa was attractive, as it offered a health post and a supply of relief food. Originally, only some San families and a few Ngologa families settled in Zutshwa. During the late 1980s and early 1990s, they were joined by more Ngologa families from Hukuntsi. In addition, the Botswanan government settled several Balala families, who were straddling the Namibian/Botswanan border in the 1980s and frequently did not have adequate personal documents, in Zutshwa.

A report from the late 1970s (KGDC 1978) stated that during the wet season, some 58 people lived in Zutshwa, while only 29 people lived there in

---

[3] Botswana's Wildlife Management Areas (WMAs) are organised in controlled hunting areas. For these controlled hunting areas game quotas are registered.

the dry season. The 1981 census gives the population for Zutshwa as zero. Ten years later, some 203 people were counted in Zutshwa, in 1996 van der Jagt established a population of 365, and in 2001 we estimated the population at about 450 (Bollig and Hohmann 2001).

The 365 inhabitants counted in 1994/1995 belonged to 44 households, putting the average household membership at 7.9 people. An astounding 44% of all households were female headed. Ethnically, the population fell into three segments: 52% claimed San or Qqoon, 22% Ngologa, and 26% Balala identity. Most of Zutshwa's inhabitants over the age of 18 were illiterate. Of the population in the sample between the ages of 7 and 18 years, all persons reported that they visited the local school at least for some years.

Van der Jagt (1996:94) states that, by far, most food consumed in Zutshwa is bought in shops. There are no cattle allowed in Zutshwa due to its status as a Wildlife Management Area. The few Zutshwa residents who own cattle (all Kgalagadi) keep them in the Hukuntsi area. Goats, however, are acceptable and quite a number of people own at least a few. In 1994/1995, the number of goats was estimated at 500, and about 60% of all households were accounted for as owning at least some small stock. While about half of Zutshwa's households owned donkeys, only ten households owned horses. Both were important for hunting. Almost all households in Zutshwa owned dogs.

Hunting has been of varying importance for Zutshwa's residents over the last decade: Traditionally, all Sarwa families relied on hunting for their livelihood at least seasonally. While subsistence hunting had long been acknowledged by the government, in the late 1980s, reports on dwindling game numbers and an environmentalist and tour-operator lobby growing in political significance urged the government to reconsider its stand on subsistence hunting. In the early 1990s, this led to the issuance of so-called special game licences (SPGLs), which allowed individual hunters to kill a specific number of animals. The SPGLs were aimed at legitimising hunting by the poorest members of the community (Hitchcock and Masilo 1996). The new system, however, abolished the legitimacy of subsistence hunting by groups of people. The licences were issued and controlled by the wildlife department in Hukuntsi. In 1994, only 28 SPGLs were issued to Zutshwa residents, most of them to San. However, the decline of wildlife numbers remained a problem in the area, and due to considerations on local development and wildlife conservation, the SPGL system was revoked in 1997. Since then, a quota management system has been installed, whereby the community is given a quota that can be hunted during the hunting season.

About half of Zutshwa's households practise some agriculture, cultivating fields between 0.5 to 1.5 hectares. With an average annual rainfall of about 200 mm, however, the risk of crop failure is very high. Most households mainly plant beans and pumpkins in heavily fenced gardens.

Zutshwa's household economy has been completely influenced by welfare programmes and the impact of MTDT over the past ten years. The project has offered income through jobs in salt production and through selling crafts made by local producers. Van der Jagt assumed that craft production forms the mainstay of the local population; the majority of craft producers are San and Balala.

Settlement Economies

Today, welfare contributes significantly to the income of most settlements. Heavily subsidised income-generating activities of various development programmes add another important component to household incomes. Craft production, agricultural programmes and community-based natural resource management have opened new venues for income. Livestock herding in RAD settlements is marginal, and many settlement dwellers would rather herd the cattle of outsiders than their own. Hunting, and especially gathering, are still of seasonal importance in some settlements (especially in Kgalagadi,) but are heavily regulated by governmental policies. Poaching is severely prosecuted, and many San in the region have been fined or even jailed for years for violating hunting laws.

Welfare Economy

Pension money, destitute rations, drought relief aid and labour intensive public works are of crucial importance for RAD settlement economies. By the 1980s, food relief was essential in many RAD settlements. Gulbrandsen (1986:23) estimated that up to 90 percent of the population in RAD settlements were dependent on food relief for their subsistence.

Pension Money and Destitute Rations: Since 1996, the state of Botswana pays pension money to all citizens over 65 years of age. From 1996 to 1998, the amount was 100 Pula (P) per month, and in 1998 it was increased to 110 Pula. Pensioners are also eligible for destitute rations (see Table 3 for the monthly basket ration), and as figures for Zutshwa show, a number of pension recipients also receive destitute rations. Out of 64 households in Zutshwa, 18 received both destitute aid and pension money, and a further eight households received destitute rations. Cassidy (2000:A-59) presented figures based on survey data from the end of the 1990s suggesting that, in total, 43 people in Zutshwa received destitute aid. People who are destitute are identified by village development councils (VDCs), which are present in every settlement. They report to the Remote Area Dweller Officer, who in turn facilitates the donation of food aid through the Ministry of Welfare. Destitute aid is meant to insure physical health at a very basic standard and is paid in the form of a monthly basket containing food and other basic consumer goods (for a critique of the food basket destitute aid, see Good 2000:36).

Table 3: destitute aid in 2001

10.5 kg mealie meal	1 packet of coffee
10 kg sorghum (mabele)	1 cake of washing soap
2 kg corn	1 cake of bathing soap
2.5 kg sugar	1 bottle of vaseline
1 kg beans	1 bottle of oil
1 packet of soup	1 packet of salt
1 packet of powdered soap	1 packet of matches
1 tin of powdered milk	2 candles
1 packet of tea	baking powder
2.5 kg bread flower	

Table 4 indicates that in several settlements, more than 10 percent of the population is over 60 years of age. Most of these people are eligible to receive pension money. Why older people concentrate in some settlements is not clear: While in Ukhwi, only 1 percent of the population is over 60, in neighbouring Ncaang, 15 percent are over 60 years of age. Ghanzi District's RAD settlements, D'kar and Bere, seem to be frequented by elderly people. The number of people in each community who receive destitute rations is enormous. Table 4 shows the number of recipients of destitute aid per community and contrasts it with the number of households. This is suggestive, however, as we do not know if, in some instances, one household pooled the destitute rations of several recipients. Nevertheless, a majority of households in several settlements seems to have access to destitute rations.

Table 4: destitutes and pensioners in some settlements in Kgalagadi and Ghanzi Districts

Settlement	District	No. registered destitutes	No. households	People 60+ (%)
Ukhwi	KG	39	50	1
Ncaang	KG	13	34	15
Ngwatle	KG	29	16	5
Monong	KG	14	21	3
Maake	KG	35	35	11
Zutshwa	KG	43	46	8
Phuduhudu	KG	22	?	?
Inaglegolo	KG	43	44	6
Khokhotshaa	KG	76	109	7
Kuke	GH	74	ca. 70	7
D'kai	GH	26	ca. 125	15
Grootlagte	GH	43	ca. 45	4
Qabo	GH	33	?	?
New Xanagas	GH	29	ca. 100	4
Chobokwane	GH	27	?	?
East Hanahai	GH	36	ca.90	5
West Hanahai	GH	46	ca. 70	9
Bere	GH	39	ca. 40	12
Kagcae	GH	58	Ca. 60	8
Xade, New Xade	GH	238	160	12

Abbreviations are KG = Kgalagadi District, GH = Ghanzi District.
Source: Cassidy et al 2000:A-9, A-12, A-59.

Rations to children under five years of age: Besides pension money and destitute rations, families with children under five years of age are also given aid. This aid is paid irrespective of the parents' income. There is a provision to double the rations if the health worker in charge establishes that a child is malnourished. In addition, rations are given to pregnant mothers, nursing mothers, and TB patients. In Zutshwa, 23 children aged 4-18 months, 26 children aged 19-36 months, and 27 children aged 37-60 months received such aid. No data was available on this kind of aid for other settlements.

Table 5: food donations to under five-year-old children

Age	Food Item	Malnourished
4-18 months	5 kg tsabana	10 kg tsabana
	750 ml oil	1.5 l oil
19-36 months	7.5 kg tsabana	15 kg tsabana
	750 ml oil	1.5 l
3-5 years	5.5 kg mealie meal	11 kg mealie meal
	1 kg dried milk	2 kg dried milk
	900 mg beans	1.2 kg beans
	750 ml oil	1.5 l oil

Note: Tsabana is a mixture of beans and maize.

Labour Intensive Programmes offered by the RAD Office: There are no comprehensive data that show the relevance of labour intensive programmes run by the Remote Area Dweller Office (RADO) in the settlements. Van der Jagt (1996) states that labour-based relief projects were of considerable importance in Kgalagadi District, bringing direct benefits to about eight percent of the RAD settlement population in the mid-1990s. In Zutshwa, it was found that the RADO regularly conducted labour projects from which many residents profited (Bollig and Hohmann 2001). In August 2001, there were 36 people producing bricks for a local school building. People working within these labour projects received eight Pula per day (six working hours) for three months.

Infrastructure Provision: In all RAD settlements, the water supply and public building maintenance are paid for by the state. Water supply is an especially serious and costly problem in many RAD settlements. Zutshwa is an extreme case in point. There have been several attempts to provide water to the community locally. A water catchment was set up in the early 1990s in order to provide water to livestock. Due to gross mismanagement and the destruction of fences and equipment the water catchment was soon defunct. It had worked only as long as an expatriate meted out strict control over the resource. The highly sophisticated reverse-water-osmosis plant, which provided water from a bore hole some 10 kilometres away from Zutshwa, worked occasionally between 1994 and 1998 and then fell into disuse. Since the settlement was established in the early 1980s, most of the time water has been brought in from Hukuntsi (60 km from Zutshwa). In the early 1990s, some 10,000 litres were brought to Zutshwa on a monthly basis. Today, a water truck drives all the way from Hukuntsi to provide several thousand litres of water to the settlement on a daily basis. The government supplies the settlement with its most needed resource at tremendously high costs without charging even a minor sum of money or demanding any other contribution for the delivery of water.

Fig. 1: Zutshwa welfare economy: an assessment of the contribution of state and NGO contributions to Zutshwa's general income

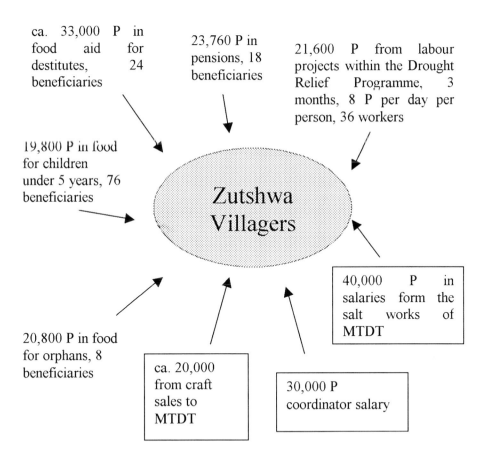

ca. 33,000 P in food aid for destitutes, 24 beneficiaries

23,760 P in pensions, 18 beneficiaries

21,600 P from labour projects within the Drought Relief Programme, 3 months, 8 P per day per person, 36 workers

19,800 P in food for children under 5 years, 76 beneficiaries

Zutshwa Villagers

20,800 P in food for orphans, 8 beneficiaries

ca. 20,000 from craft sales to MTDT

30,000 P coordinator salary

40,000 P in salaries form the salt works of MTDT

*Employment and Income-generating Activities
through Development Projects*

All development projects in the region have components that focus on generating income. Craft production is one important activity in three NGOs (KDT, MTDT, and Ghanzi Craft) operating in the region. Agricultural activities are fostered as well: from livestock husbandry to community gardens and attempts at exotic cochineal farming. On a local level at D'kar, art production, leather working and tailoring have been other important activities. All these activities have been highly subsidized through development projects. Recently, CBNRM activities have opened new venues of income for RAD settlements. However, only Ukhwi seems to have made any gains through CBNRM projects up to the year 2000, but many others hope to welcome well-paying game hunters and photo safaris in the coming years. Lastly, salaries paid through development projects have also been of great importance in the entire region.

Craft Production

Handicraft production is of great relevance in many San communities in Namibia and Botswana. "Bushman crafts" have become emblematically related to San communities. Most craftwork produced is for sale to the tourist industry. San usually produce simple beadwork (necklaces, belts, etc.) usually made of materials deemed "traditional," such as ostrich eggshells and seeds. They also make leather bags, and other utensils produced from veld products and hides and skins (see also Bollig et al. 2000).

Kuru's annual report for 1996/1997 notes "For most Ncoakhoe[4], the making of crafts as activity is still the only form of income in most settlements." Dekker (1999:29) states that craft production is the most important source of cash income with KDT project participants. According to project documents, 76 craft producers in various settlements work more or less regularly. Once a month, the KDT extension team visits settlements to buy crafts. Producers are paid immediately and may instantly buy a supply of new beads and ostrich eggshells. Handicrafts only have to meet minimum quality standards, and the loss of quality was deplored by the project staff in charge of handicraft acquisition both in the settlements of Ghanzi District and D'kar, as well as in Zutshwa. Given the projects' practice of highly

---

[4] Ncoakhoe is the name Nharo give themselves. In a rough translation, Ncoakhoe means "the real people."

subsidising craft acquisition, it is apparently more worthwhile to produce a lot of objects than to produce high quality objects.

In Zutshwa, craft production was part and parcel of MTDT from its early years. While craft production has always been secondary to salt production, it has been a consistent project activity since 1992. Aid in craft production was seen as a development strategy that fit very well into the Zutshwa context. "Support of the craft producers was, and is an extremely appropriate way to promote economic integration within the mainstream economy: income is directly related to production, income is for the most part used to ensure food security, women's economic self-reliance is assisted, and since traditional values and skills have a distinct relevance in the new cash economy, elements of culture and identity are strengthened." (MTDT 1995:20). In the early and mid-1990s, crafts were bought from the residents of Zutshwa twice a month. At the moment, MTDT buys crafts once a month. Each time, crafts are bought for sums totaling between 2,000 and 4,000 Pula.

Table 6: handicraft sales to MTDT between January and July 2001

Date	Women	Men	Not known	Total	Average amount of money obtained per person (in Pula)
26/02/01	31	4	2	36	60.4
20/03/01	55	18	2	75	36.5
30/04/01	63	19	1	83	53.4
29/05/01	32	5	1	38	44.6
26/07/01	40	2	2	44	58.5
Total	221	48	8	277	50.7

Women are the main beneficiaries of the craft sales programme (see Table 6). They account for nearly 80 percent of all craft producers. Given the very high number of female-headed households in Zutshwa, this figure is quite significant: Craft production offers income to the most vulnerable sector of Zutshwa community. While most formal employment is taken by men or schooled women, illiterate women can thus have a minimal but reliable income. Although the amounts of money actually obtained are fairly low – they averaged ca. 50 Pula/month (about half of the monthly paid pension) – the money is a significant contribution to household income. Taking Zutshwa's inflated prices for consumer goods as a basis, one could buy, for example, some 12 kg of bread flower or about 6 kilos of rice with the money. Although no one would claim that they could live on money obtained from craft production at this time, the sale of handicrafts offers a modest additional income to about 55 people per month. There is a wide spread of income from craft sales, and many households in Zutshwa profit from it.

Crafts are usually produced at home. Working on crafts is combined with other duties, such as tending children and caring for gardens. Children frequently assist women in producing necklaces from ostrich eggshells. Producing a long-string necklace takes about a week: After buying the necessary eggshells at MTDT, the shells are broken into small pieces. Then holes are drilled into these pieces and the rough beads are put on a string. After that, the beads are smoothened by rubbing along a stone. A long necklace sells for about 34 Pula. The costs for making the necklace were given at 2 Pula (eggshells bought at MTDT), plus about seven days of work.

The marketing of crafts is beset with various problems. The most important of those is that the "Bushman craft market" is nearly overflowing. In order to overcome the problem that several NGOs are competing on the narrow market for Bushman crafts, strategic alliances have been forged. MTDT was lucky to strike a deal with Kuru in 1999: Since then, Kuru buys crafts worth 30,000 Pula per year, and in addition, pays one of the two women working in MTDT's craft department (7,200 Pula per annum). Another problem of craft production is having access to materials, especially ostrich eggs and eggshells. Because of the Botswana government's Ostrich Policy (Republic of Botswana 1994), it is very difficult to obtain ostrich eggshells. Only during the hunting season may Zutshwa's residents roam the veld in order to look for hatched ostrich eggs. This, however, is in no way sufficient to maintain craft production at any level and only very little craft is produced from eggshells found locally. Today, ostrich eggs (for painting) and broken ostrich eggshell pieces are bought on an ostrich farm in Lobatse once a month by the coordinator. Ostrich eggs are then sold for 10 P to locals and subsequently bought back for 25 P once they are painted (resulting in a net profit of 15 P for the painter). The eggs are finally sold in curio shops for more than 100 P. Broken eggshells pieces are sold for 1 Pula per cup. The majority of Zutshwa's craftwork is produced from broken ostrich eggshells. Necklaces made with seeds or porcupine spikes, items that San living in Ghanzi's settlements frequently use for their craft products (Bollig et al 2000:40), are not used by Zutshwa's craft producers. Handicraft production is fully dependent on the supply of ostrich eggshells from outside the area. If this link were cut, there would be no craft production in Zutshwa. In general, craft making largely relies on subsidies from development organisations, and as yet there is little evidence that a self-sustainable mode of home production is developing.

Agricultural Activities

While agricultural activities are not the major source of income in the settlements, they add directly or indirectly to household food security. Agricultural activities are fostered by various NGOs and government institutions and are highly subsidised.

Livestock Husbandry: The RAD office assists villagers in building up their own livestock herds. The RADO stocking programmes have not been consistent throughout the region. In Kgalagadi District, each needy villager was entitled to 10 goats and 5 head of cattle. However, as Zutshwa lies within a Wildlife Management Area, the Department of National Parks and Wildlife rejected villagers from receiving cattle donations. In 2000, however, so-called destitutes were given three to five goats each. In Grootlagte, the RAD office distributed two heifers to each household in the early 1990s. During a later round of livestock distributions, 15 goats were supplied to each household. Given the highly subsidised state of livestock husbandry in the settlements, it is astounding that herds did not increase more rapidly.

Table 7: livestock holdings in D'kar and other communities[5]

Place	Cattle	Goats and Sheep	Horses	Donkeys
D'kar	-	714	-	-
West Hanahai	536	108	41	98
East Hanahai	558	79	22	103
Grootlagte	ca. 500	337	-	-
Qabo	-	87	-	-
Bere	232	175	30	81
Xade	528	-	-	-
New Xanagas	-	286	-	-
Tshobokwane	-	98	-	-
Kacgae	76	108	18	45
New Xade	218	75	40	96

---

[5] Source: veterinary Service Ghanzi, figures for 1998 and 1999. Unfortunately information on livestock holdings was not obtainable for all settlements.

Many cattle kept on RAD settlement pastures are owned by non-settlement dwellers, who employ local San to herd their cattle. In Grootlagte, ca. 140 cattle were owned by inhabitants of the settlement, while about 500 cattle were recorded there by the Veterinary Service. An interesting indication of this tendency is the ratio between cattle and goats in the settlement. In most settlements, many more cattle were recorded than goats. While goats in settlements are almost all owned by the local population, cattle are, to a large extent, owned by outsiders.

The Regional Assessment of the Status of San in Botswana (Cassidy et al. 2000:10) deplores that in many instances San "enter serf-like relations with the cattle owners, without being able to develop the means to become cattle owners themselves." The cases presented here underline this argument. In ethnically heterogeneous settlements, San own less livestock than members of other ethnic groups: In Grootlagte numerous cattle owned by non-community members were herded by locals; the same was found to be true in East and West Hanahai. In Zutshwa, cattle herding is prohibited and only resident Kgalagadi owned cattle, which they herded outside the Wildlife Management Area.

Cochineal Farming: In the mid-1990s, KDT embarked on an exotic project: local farmers would grow a type of insect that produces a natural dye used for cosmetics in the first world. The project was heavily subsidised by the United States Agency for International Development (USAID) and other donors. Cochineal insects are used to procure red dye for lipsticks and food. While a wild variety occurs in Botswana, the variety that produces red colour is foreign.[6] Cochineal insects dwell on cactus plants, thus, their production necessitates the prior establishment of cactus fields. By the late 1980s, a missionary in New Xanagas had experimented with cochineal without successfully going into production. In 1994, the project was introduced by KDT. The USAID-funded Natural Resource Management Project promised finances for the early steps of cochineal production. The KDT evaluation of 1993 had commented favourably on the prospects of cochineal production (KDT Evaluation 1993:26) and had pointed out that the project may give San access to land and render a source of long-term sustainable income. Today one wonders at the overtly optimistic prospects that were delineated for the production of a completely alien "crop." And not was only the crop alien, but so was the mode of production: private, fenced

---

[6] At this time most of the world's cochineal production comes from Peru.

fields; structured and at times intensive work input; heavy work inputs long before any benefits can be reaped.

The project started in D'kar in 1993, and in 1994 cochineal production expanded efforts to other settlements. During 1996/1997, the second and major phase of field expansion 90,000 pear cladodes (cactuses) were imported from South Africa. They were distributed to all settlements. By the end of the year, a total of 187 ha was under cactus plantation. The land board at Ghanzi allotted plots to local project participants, most of them San. However, there was no agreement on the supply of water to the plots. By the end of 1996, one hectare was allotted to each project participant. The plots of four families were placed together and fenced with the help of KDT. KDT paid about 1900 Pula per fenced plot, while the participating families were volunteering the work to establish the fences. For the first time, San were allotted permanent plots by the land board. Cactuses were soon planted on all fields to provide the basis for cochineal production. This took place on a food-for-work basis in the beginning. Food worth 80 Pula was made available to each project participant every month throughout 1996. In 1997, the system was changed: 60 Pula were paid out in food, while 20 Pula were paid in cash. This money was put into a project-driven savings account for each participant and not paid out. In 1998, the form of payment was changed again: now project participants were paid 80 Pula each for their work on their (own) fields. It soon transpired that additional arrangements had to be made with the land board for water to be supplied. In this respect, the project did not succeed in every aspect. In 1999, convincing arrangements for the supply of water were still lacking, for example, for West Hanahai and Tshobokwane, Grootlagte and East Hanahai, and cactus plantations there deteriorated drastically or were given up on altogether. Meanwhile, the insects were only kept at D'kar, but even there, no production of dye of any size took place.

While the cochineal project never delivered any marketable product, it supplied settlement dwellers with limited funds. In 1999, the cochineal-production project involved the most participants: About 180 people in eight settlements worked in the project (Dekker 1999:3). For comparison: the crafts group involved 76 people, the project's game farm had 21, leather working had seven people, and the silk screen group involved only two people.

Fig. 2: members of the cochineal project in settlements of the Ghanzi District

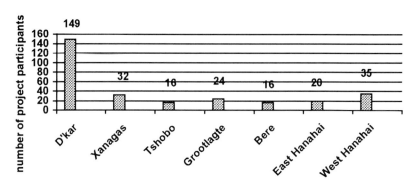

KDT has been experimenting with other agricultural programmes. Garlic production was started in 1999 on a low level. From funds made available from the U.S. Embassy (20,000 Pula), twenty participants received donations of garlic cloves (KDT Progress Report Jan-June 1998:5). Through this donation, KDT was able to sell cloves at highly subsidized prices to farmers. Although some farmers occasionally over-irrigated the garlic plants, production generally was successful, and plans were made to expand these efforts in the next growing season.

Several projects connected to agricultural efforts in a broader sense were in a planning stage in 1999. In 1998, an economic assessment study was done on processing donkey meat. Given that donkey numbers are fairly high and that poor people in the settlements own donkeys, considerations to make use of donkey meat are evident. The study, however, showed that a project would not be viable in the absence of a clear export market, requiring perhaps bulk transport through the Botswana Meat Commission. In the same vein, a study was conducted into the possibility of growing mushrooms in rural communities. In East Hanahai, the possibility for backyard fruit production for household consumption has also been envisaged. One common denominator of these projects is that they are mainly based on foreign technologies and need a major amount of external input and expertise at least in the beginning stage. High subsidies and food-for-work-like payments to project participants in initial phases are typical. Obviously, it is this direct remuneration that makes such projects attractive to farmers and their future prospects.

Community-Based Natural Resource Management (CBNRM)

Community-based natural resource management has become an important option for development in western Botswana's San communities since the mid-1990s (Rozemeijer 2001, Rivers 2001). The combination of conservation and rural development makes this initiative attractive both for international donors, local NGOs, and corresponding parts of the official administration. A well-defined group of people (usually dubbed "a community") who share access to and management of specific natural resources are given the right to manage a clearly defined land unit (see Republic of Botswana 1998). This includes that the community is given predictable and exclusive rights to land and that sustainable practices of management are agreed upon between different stakeholders and facilitated through development projects. The Directorate of Wildlife and National Parks (DWNP) allots a game quota to a trust.

Table 8: quotas and fees for hunting in KD2, |Xai|xai and KD1, Ukhwi for 2000. Source: SNV Brochure.

KD 2 quota	Fee per head in |Xai|xai [7]	Total	Fee per head in Ukhwi (KD 1) [8]	Total
25 Duiker	30 P	750 P	100 P	2,500 P
100 Steenbok	25 P	2,500P	100 P	10,000 P
93 Springbok	400 P	37,200 P	500 P	46,500 P
100 Gemsbok	800 P	80,000 P	1,000 P	100,000 P
78 Ostriches	300 P	23,400 P	400 P	31,200 P
5 Kudu	800 P	4,000 P	1,000 P	5,000 P
2 Eland	1,500 P	23,000 P	1,750 P	3,500 P
Total		70,850 P		198,700 P

---

[7] Minimum bids that have to be made to Cgaecgae Thlabololo Trust in |Xai|xai by safari companies.

[8] Fees as tendered in KD 1, for 2000.

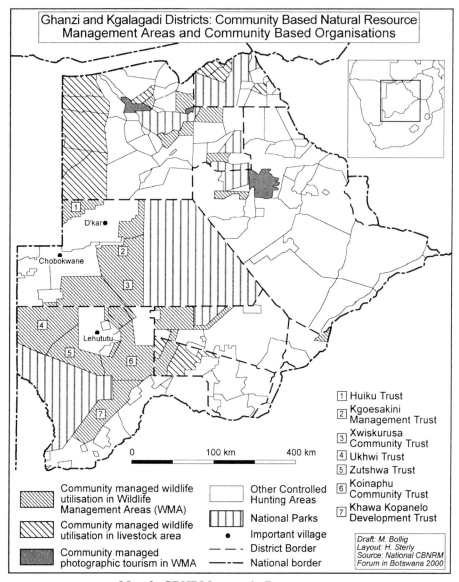

Map 2: CBNRM trusts in Botswana

A trust's quotas may be hunted by community members or they can be sold to hunting and photo safaris. Table 8 shows the quotas for two CBNRM trusts and the respective market value of animals when sold to a hunting company. In both communities, part of the quota was hunted by the community, while the remaining part of the quota was sold to the private sector.

Especially within the realm of Botswana's NGOs, the CBNRM approach is seen as ideal for promoting the tenure security of marginalised populations like the San. Both USAID and the Dutch SNV gave substantial aid to CBNRM initiatives. Map 2 shows that, in fact, the majority of trusts lies in areas occupied by ethnic minorities, mainly San. Trusts are formed or are in a planning stage in many RAD settlements in western Botswana.

In 1998 in the Ghanzi District, the settlements of Grootlagte and Qabo formed the Huiku[9] Trust, which was to manage an area of ca. 4,000 km². However, until 1999 no income had yet been earned through tourism. Similar conditions prevailed for the Xwiskurusa Community Trust (RAD settlements in East and West Hanahai, Kacgae) and Tshobokwane Community Trust. Interviews in Grootlagte disclosed that there was a wide array of ideas about what could and what should be done. While everybody asked was clear about the broad prospects for tourism, there were few realistic ideas about how to tap this resource. Planning for community-based natural resource management started in Zutshwa in 1993, but never resulted in a programme. The closeness of the Kgalagadi Transfontier Park made development through tourism an option in the eyes of many development planners. Planning for a CBNRM initiative was finally started anew in March 2001, when the German Volunteer Service seconded an expatriate advisor to restart and coordinate local CBNRM activities. While there have been no agreements with tour operators yet, Zutshwa has been allotted a game quota that can be hunted by community members. Due to internal quarrels with the expert the programme has come to stand still once again. Other community-based organisations in Kgalagadi, the Koinaphu Trust and the Khawa Trust are not yet active.

---

[9] Huiku comes from Nharo "to help each other" (Bollig et al. 2000:63). Typically, community trusts have names referring to solidarity and community spirit.

Table 9: CBNRM trusts in Kgalagadi and Ghanzi Districts and their activities.

	Ngwaa Khobee Xeya	Maiteko Tshwa-ragano Deve-lopment Trust	Koina-phu Commu-nity Trust	Khawa Kopa-nelo Deve-lopment Trust	Huiku	Xwisku-rusa
Size	12,180	7,002	?	?	?	1,248
Popula-tion	750	350	ca. 1,500	450	300	
Villages	Ukhwi, Ncaang, Ngwatle	Zutshwa	Koko-thsa, Inalego-lo, Phuduhud u	Khawa	Groot-lagte, Qabo	East and West Hanahai, Kagcae
Joint venture agree-ment	Yes, Safari Botswa-na Bound	None	None	None	None	None
Revenue 2000: hunting rights and photo-conce-ssions[10], quota fees	258,800 P	None from CBNRM	None	None	None	None
Other trust income	ca. 40,000 P	None from CBNRM	None	None	None	None
Donor income	246,000 P	None from CBNRM	None	None	None	None
Employ-ment	75 guaran-teed by safari compa-nies	None from CBNRM	None	None	None	None

NRM and other activities	Subsistence hunting, craft production, tourism venture, veld products	Selling salt, and crafts, quota hunting	Quota hunting	Quota hunting	Quota hunting, Crafts sales	Quota hunting, Crafts sales

Source: Proceedings of the First National CBNRM Forum in Botswana, 30 and 31 of May 2000, and CBNRM Status Report 1999/2000.

Until today, only the Ngwaa Khobee Xeya Trust at Ukwhi, Kgalagadi District, and the CgaeCgae Tlhabololo Trust at ǀXaiǀxai, Ngamiland District, have made progress with community tourism. In both instances, heavy investment by Dutch development aid has guaranteed some success. The trust at Ukhwi was registered in 1998. Since then, a joint venture agreement has been finalised with the private tourism sector. In 2000, the trust earned about 260,000 Pula from selling hunting rights, photographic concessions and obtaining quota fees. Another 40,000 Pula were obtained through the social development fund from the government, craft production, and entrance and camping fees. In addition, about 250,000 P of donor money was given to the trust. Unfortunately, there is very little information about how money was distributed internally. Obviously, major amounts of money were ploughed back into tourism infrastructure. CgaeCgae distributed parts of the money to the community's households. Trust members benefited directly from employment with tour companies and the trust.

The establishment of CBNRM trusts creates, by necessity, a problem concerning the collective-good in RAD settlement communities. Ethnically, heterogeneous and poverty-stricken settlement dwellers have to make decisions about collective activities without gaining direct remuneration. As the experience of Zutshwa and Grootlagte/Qabo shows, this is difficult and members are frequently only convinced to contribute to the common goal when they receive direct benefits. While the government offers direct payments from a social development fund, currently the costs of organising CBNRM trusts are almost totally carried by the NGOs and GOs involved. Ukhwi, the only functioning CBNRM trust in the two districts discussed

---

[10] In photographic concessions, the tour operator pays a lump sum to the trust for photographs taken by his clients.

here, has had an expatriate on site to organise the community and arrange contracts with the private sector. The recent decision made by the Botswanan government to first pool trust incomes with the district administration and then later to pay out to the communities involved in order to prevent financial mismanagement may already signal the end of community autonomy in CBNRM activities.

The Social Situation

While project reports contain quite some information about the economic situation of settlements they usually say very little about the social situation. This probably is due to the fact that (a) in-depth research into social change would require longer periods of fieldwork and that (b) the survey research done for development projects does not yield detailed descriptions of social organisation. Hence, little is known about social organisation in detail, but there is some information available about the basic changes that have occurred in household structures, ethnic heterogeneity, conflict management and stratification.

Household Structures

How has the basic unit of social organisation – family and household – changed over the last decades? There are earlier descriptions of Qgoon and Nharo social organisation (Heinz 1979, Guenther 1976) that demonstrate the importance of band organisation and the flexibility of social groups. Sedentarisation has changed the fundamentals of social organisation. Van der Jagt (1996) offers some information on households in the RAD settlements of Kgalagadi district. He presents quantitative data on the number of households per community and the overall population number, and from this, extrapolates the average size of households. Unfortunately, household-related figures are not differentiated according to ethnic status or wealth status, so that differences in household and composition remain unclear.

The average size of households in 10 settlements was 7.1 people, with a range of 4.4 to 12.2 members. Why average household sizes vary to such a large degree remains unexplained. For example, in Maake, Kgalagadi District, the average household size is 12.2 people. Van der Jagt (1996:108) alleges that "the reason for it is that unlike in other settlements, extended families seem to function more as a single household unit than as separate households who occasionally share food, tools, and labour among each other." Ncaang, on the other hand, only has an average household size of 4.4

people, but at the same time, it has the highest population of elderly people (15 percent over the age of 60).

Table 10: households, household size and female-headed households in Kgalagadi District

Place	Population	No. households	Average size	Female-headed (%)
Ukwhi	430	50	7.4	64
Ncaang	151	34	4.4	57
Ngwatle	135	16	6.8	25
Monong	105	21	5.1	38
Maake	275	24	12.2	40
Zutshwa	365	44	7.9	44
Pudhuhudu	n.i.	n.i.	n.i.	n.i.
Khawa	ca. 540	63	8.7	25
Inalegolo	ca. 270	44	6.3	11
Kokotsha	535	109	4.9	n.i.
Hunhukwe	455	61	7.5	n.i.
Average	326,1	46,6	7.1	38

Source: Cassidy 2000: A 52; Khawa 85% Bathlaro, no San; data on female headed households from van der Jagt 1996
n.i.: no information

The percentage of female-headed households per settlement averaged 38 percent with a range from 11 to 64 percent. This is an extremely high value and probably indicates profound changes in familial organisation.

Local Conflict Management

Several RAD communities are ridden with internal conflict. While short accounts on strained internal relations were recorded for several settlements, a clearer picture emerges only for Zutshwa.

From the beginning in the early 1980s, Zutshwa villagers have found it difficult establishing a community. Comments on the lack of community spirit run like a red thread through piles of development literature on Zutshwa (reports, evaluations, position papers, etc.). Two quotes illustrate the problem: There is "[...] little experience in the community of effectively organising at a group level to achieve a common goal"; and, "Despite our intensive efforts geared at building a strong community group that is able to withstand destabilising forces from both outside and within the community, we do not feel that this objective has yet been met." (Grant 1995:28 and 29). There are several obstacles standing in the way of community formation that are named again and again. Zutshwa is inhabited by three different ethnic groups: San, Balala and Kgalagadi (Ngologa subgroup). The two dominant factions, the San and Kgalagadi, especially, are constantly striving for control, although it is not clear what type of resources they are trying to control.

However, most violent conflicts take place within the San community. In 2000, an astounding number of 135 cases of assault were reported to Hukuntsi police from Zutshwa (with a population of some 450 people) according to one well-informed informant. Most of the cases were apparently attributable to violence within the San community. The health worker at the small village hospital also bemoaned the high degree of violence. Frequently he has to stitch up or plaster wounds from fights. Violence clearly has a gendered face: Frequently, men beat up their wives for alleged offences against some rule of conduct. Jealousy is given as a major reason why men react violently. During group interviews several people named violence as *the* major problem of the community, before poverty and landlessness. Most people asked attributed the high incidence of violence to the high degree of alcohol consumption: People (especially men) become violent when they are drunk. Others attributed the high incidence of violence to weak leadership and the lack of sanctioning of violent behaviour. Zutshwa, once planned as a village, is now hardly recognizable as a settlement. The San households, especially, live far apart from one another. They are spread around Zutshwa Pan, sometimes with several hundred metres between huts. Informants commented that they found it very difficult to live near each other as jealousies and violence frequently erupted between neighbours. When asked what could be done to restrain violence, many people voiced the opinion that a local police post would be of help. However, most people thought that a strong chief with authority could do a lot about the problem.

Generally, leadership functions are weakly developed in San societies. Traditional levelling mechanisms seem still to be at work here: Leaders have to cope with disobedience and constant criticism. In several settlements, the chief (*kgosi*) of the village was Kgalagadi or Herero, while the majority of the population was San. In cases where the chief was San (as is the case in Zutshwa), he was the target of criticism and a source of ridicule by the local community.

Increasing Economic Stratification

For several settlements there is evidence of an increase in economic stratification. Factors underlying increased stratification are differences in income and access to productive resources. Income is usually derived from employment with the government or, more frequently, with one of the many development projects. Generally, part of the income is invested into the establishment of a household herd. The capacity to sell livestock occasionally improves the economic status of a household considerably. Increased stratification expresses itself through better housing, cars and bikes, better clothing and improved educational options. Usually, local elites have a major share in decision making within local projects and are well represented on diverse boards and committees. Zutshwa and D'kar will be taken as case studies.

A wealth-ranking was conducted in Zutshwa with three informants deemed to be knowledgeable about the 67 households of the village. They were asked to sort the households into different wealth categories. Interestingly, they developed a fairly homogenous view of wealth differences within the village. The rich households (8) of the village consisted of some seven businessmen, all of them Kgalagadi. The only San in this category is the councillor, a political functionary with a fairly high salary.

Fig. 3: Wealth Categories in Zutshwa

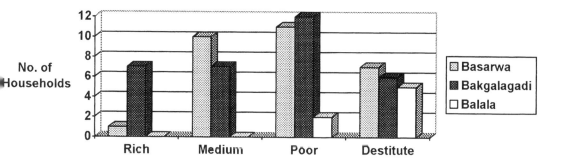

Thus, business is the basis for wealth in the village. Traders – most are Kgalagadi – invest part of their income in farmsteads in the Hukuntsi area, where they maintain their cattle herds. A mixed group of "medium" households (17) is made up of Kgalagadi and San. Many of those sorted into the middle category obtain some stable income from salaries; about 10 are employed by MTDT in one form or another. A numerous group of poor households (25) consists mainly of San. Many of them own a few goats. Rarely are herds larger than 10 to 20 animals. Most own one or two donkeys and perhaps even a horse. Some of them receive pension money and destitute aid. Out of a group of 18 destitute households, which were said to own neither donkeys, horses nor goats, eight received destitute aid. Interestingly, most pension earners were classified as poor and not as destitute because the 110 Pula per month was regarded as a reliable income. The wealth rank does have a clear ethnic profile only in specific aspects: The group of very rich people are Kgalagadi traders. Medium, poor and destitute categories are made up of both Kgalagadi households and San households. Balala households were all sorted into the categories "poor" and "destitute."

In a survey of D'kar, Mathias Guenther (1998:5) found large discrepancies in housing in the village: "In size dwellings range from small and cramped to quite large and spacious and in comfort, solidity and serviceability from leaky, wind-blown and skewed, shreds-and-patches hovels to well built, structurally sound houses." Walls made out of dung or even brick were preferred to walls made from waste products such as pieces of plastic, feed sacks, cardboard or flattened tins. Guenther says that the majority of well-built houses is owned by non-San. However, a minority of well-to-do San live in better housing conditions. Access to salaried income is the major venue of wealth in D'kar. Most people with an income work for the Kuru Development Trust. While 34 percent of all San households could rely on salaries, 56 percent of the non-San households earned incomes. While Guenther mainly stresses the ethnic basis of stratification, the figures for livestock holdings of San households (Guenther 1998:31f.) shows that there are considerable differences as well. Out of 55 households, two (3.6 percent) owned 29 percent of all cattle (households No. 5 and 6 in Guenther's list) and another two households (No. 1 and 2) owned 26 percent of all sheep and goats. While 18 (33 percent) of the San households owned cattle, 37 households (67 percent) owned none. Table 11 shows that holdings of smallstock are highly skewed in all settlements of Ghanzi District.

Table 11 smallstock holdings and their distribution within the community in Ghanzi settlements (1998)

Place	Total number of smallstock	Total TLU	Total number of owners	10% of the richest livestock owners own X% of total TLU
D'kar	705	88,13	16	62,55
Bere	286	35,75	11	29,37
West Hanahai	504	63,00	11	26,38
East Hanahai	79	9,90	8	25,28
New Xade	481	60,13	16	39,29
Grootlagte	333	41,63	12	25,23
Qabo	85	10,63	2	54,11
Tshobokwane	94	11,75	3	61,7
New Xanagas	286	35,75	6	29,37

Source: veterinary extension, 1 goat, 1 sheep equivalent to 0,125 TLU, for east Hanahai I had to rely on data for 1999

Increasing economic stratification in communities of western Botswana has been frequently dealt with as a matter of ethnic stratification: San were rendered as poverty stricken and dominated by other ethnic communities, such as Tswana, Herero or Kgalagadi. The preliminary insights show that, in fact, only a few San have established themselves as wealthy community members. Nevertheless, San are increasingly entering leading positions in their communities. At the same time, the poor of a community are not only San, but members of other ethnic communities also belong to the lowest economic strata and are as dependent on welfare as many San are. The ethnic lens through which anthropologists, as well as project workers, frequently view target communities tends to hide processes of increasing stratification rather than disclose them.

Traditional Leaders and Committees

All over the region, new forms of political participation are being experimented with. Government as well as NGO development initiatives are creating specific community structures in order to run their programmes. All settlements have Village Development Councils (VDCs) with a board and a chairman. At the same time, specific development projects have their own boards and chairmen. Maiteko Tshwaragano Development Trust and the situation in Zutshwa, as well as the regional Kuru Development programme, may be taken as examples here.

MTDT has existed as an organisation since the early 1990s. As far as can be seen from the documents, the organisational structure has not changed much over time: A board was meant to steer the organisation and supervise its major issues. The day-to-day activities were to be handled by a coordinator (an expatriate all through the 1990s) and his local counterpart. Board, coordinator and counterpart were in charge of the various programmes of the organisation, such as salt works, handicrafts, etc. The current organisational set-up of MTDT includes a steering board consisting of six to eight locally elected members and a smaller group of ex officio members. The elected members of the board change every year. According to MTDT's constitution, the board functions as a governing body that has overall responsibility for policy formulation and management. During the short period of research, the board had six members (two women and four men) and a chairperson who was also a MTDT staff member. Three members of the board were regarded as youths.

There were several government initiatives and NGO-like organisations operating in Zutshwa, and all have their own board to steer their activities. When asking questions about membership in other boards, it became clear that some of those members were also youths. Interestingly, very poor people stood a good chance of being selected for the board; at least, they did not have less of a chance than the rich and influential of the village. Women were present on all boards. To some extent this has implications for the redefinition of gender roles and remains an interesting question of further research.

The organisation of KDT has been a different matter, as KDT has been an organisation comprising several settlements, since at least the middle 1990s. In order to care for the many institutional problems of a rapidly growing organisation, the institutional set-up of KDT's management structure has been frequently redesigned. In 1999, a board with 16 members formally governed the organisation. Each of the settlements participating in the project delegated two members each to the KDT board (i.e., 14 members). D'kar, the settlement from which KDT was initiated, named a further five board members (three of these were chosen by the church and two others by the community). The board had regular monthly meetings and could be called upon when necessary. Furthermore, the secretary of the organisation and the programme coordinator were *ex officio members* of the board. While the board members from the settlements were the majority, according to informants, the D'kar board members still set the tone in most meetings. More versatile in matters pertaining to development and also more dominant in their community, they heavily influenced decision making by the board.

The dominance of D'kar members was underlined by the fact that, in 1998, an action committee was formed to liase between the board (as representation of the target group) and project staff. It had been found that the enlarged board as a body was too large and too dispersed to be really in charge of day-to-day decision making. Consequently, the action committee was institutionalised as a "task force" of the board. It is significant that all four action committee members were from D'kar, and out of four members, three were church council members, too. Thus, in respect to the overall board, the action committee formed, as much a task force that was responsible to the board as a decision making elite within the board and the village D'kar.

Committees and boards have become important institutions for local decision making. However, it remains unclear to what extent these new forms of political representation and decision making factually implicate changes in the political life of communities. Are these just experiments in social change set in place by development projects, or are these newly founded institutions already cornerstones of a decentralised village administration? To what extent are boards as elected representatives of a community able to create and mange collective goods such as community gardens, communal water-points or wildlife quotas? In the absence of strong traditional authorities, boards and committees may fulfil the function of lowering transaction costs of communal decision making as they limit the people eligible for decision making, go along established procedures to make decisions and through democratic elections at the village level have some legitimisation.

Summary

State welfare and development projects have come to determine the fate of San communities in western Botswana. While hunting and gathering have been severely curtailed by government regulations, local livestock husbandry as well as handicraft production is largely dependent on programmes decided upon in Gaborone or even in metropolises of the first world. San economy and society have changed rapidly: (a) Subsistent strategies are replaced by welfare, project-related employment, various income-generating activities and revenues from tourism, (b) local economies are largely dependent on input from the outside, (c) household and familial structures change with a definite trend towards the fragmentation and isolation of households, with a strong increase of a new type of household, i.e. the female headed household, (d) egalitarian bonds are gradually replaced by incipient stratification, project employment being one venue to upward social mobility, (e) leadership functions are more firmly instituted and local activists become specialists for the interaction with the development world, and (f) new forms of local administration based on elected boards, sometimes with strong female representation and frequently with strong representation of youths are probably changing internal decision-making structures. These concurrent trends produce a peculiar form of economic dependency and hegemony, which is created and reinforced in the institutions, social relations, and dominant ideas of the society.

The change has been comprehensive and, as yet, it is unclear what place San communities will have in the society of western Botswana in the future. There is evidence that San communities have developed into a class-like community and arguments are warranted that something like a class consciousness is evolving. However, there are also strong arguments against this view. On the one hand, a pan-San consciousness is developing rapidly and is being featured by NGOs and donors alike. Politically active San nowadays see the global system and strategic links to support organisations abroad as a major device to influence national politics in their favour. Exclusive forms of international tourism (e.g., trophy hunting) and anthropo-tourism add to this global perspective. On the other hand, dependence on welfare and subsidy is increasing rather than decreasing. Development projects in the region should be warned that targeting self-sufficiency and sustainability in RAD settlements is a vain effort. Economically, many settlements are nonviable under the present legislation (e.g., lack of legal means to ensure exclusive user rights for inhabitants of the settlement). Under favourable economic conditions, it is likely that folkloristic enclaves designed for tourism will come into being, with a limited amount of jobs, but major revenues generated through fees and contracts with tour operators. Under unfavourable conditions, human misery will accelerate. The tremendously high rates of HIV/AIDS infection will almost by necessity change not only demographic parameters, but also social and economic organisation; however, in what direction is not yet clear.

References

Barnard, Alan
1977   From Hunters to Squatters: Social and Cultural Change among the Farm San of Ghanzi, Botswana. In: Lee, R. and I. de Vore (eds.) *Kalahari Hunter-Gatherers: Studies of the !Kung San and their Neighbours*. Cambridge: Cambridge University Press:121-134.

Barnard, Alan
1980   Sarwa Settlement Patterns in the Ghanzi Ranching Area. *Botswana Notes and Records* 12:137-149.

Barnard, Alan and Thomas Widlok
1996   Nharo and Hai‖om Settlement Patterns in Comparative Perspective. In: Susan Kent (ed.), *Cultural Diversity Among Twentieth Century Foragers: An African Perspective*. Cambridge: Cambridge University Press:87-107.

Bollig, Michael
2001   *Risk Management in a Hazardous Environment. A Comparative Study of Two Pastoral Societies. (Pokot NW Kenya and Himba NW Namibia)*. Habilitationsschrift Phil. Fak. Universität zu Köln.

Bollig, M. and Jan-Bart Gewald
2000   People, Cattle and Land. Transformations of a Pastoral Society. In: M. Bollig and J.B. Gewald (eds.) *Herero Societies*. Cologne: Köppe:3-57.

Bollig, Michael and Susanne Berzborn
2002   *The Making of Local Traditions in a Global Setting. Indigenous Peoples' Organisations and their Effects on the Local Level in Southern Africa*. In preparation.

Cassidy, L. et al., 2000. Regional Assessment of the Status of the San in Southern Africa. An assessment of the status of the San in Botswana, Legal Assistance Centre, Windhoek

Childers, G.W.
1976   *Report on the Survey/Investigation of the Ghanzi Farm Sarwa Situation*. Gaborone. MLGL.

Guenther, Mathias
1979   *The Farm Bushmen of Ghanzi District*. Stuttgart. Hochschulverlag.

Guenther, Mathias
1998   *Kuru Household Survey and Survey on Qae Qare Game Farm.*
       Waterloo. Manuscript.

Gulbrandscn, O. et al
1986   *Remote Area Development Programme.* Gaborone, Botswana:
       Government Printer.

Heinz, H.J.
1979   The Nexus Complex among the !Xo Bushmen of Botswana. In:
       Anthropos 79 (3/4):465-480.

Hitchcock, Robert
2001   "Hunting is our heritage": The Struggle for Hunting and Gathering
       Rights among the San of Southern Africa. *SENRI* 59:139-156.

Hitchcock, R.K., Ebert, J.I., and Morgan, R.G.
1989   Drought, Drought Relief and Dependency Among the Sarwa of
       Botswana. In: R. Huss-Ashmore and S.H. Katz (eds.). *African Food
       Systems in Crisis. Part One: Microperspectives.* New York: Gordon
       and Breach: 303-336.

Hitchcock, R. and J. Holm
1993   Bureaucratic Domination of Hunter-Gatherer Societies: A Study of
       the San in Botswana. In: *Development and Change*, Vol. 24:305-
       338.

Hitchcock, Robert and Rosinah Rose B. Masilo
1996   Subsistence Hunting and Resource Rights in Botswana: An
       Assessment of Special Game Licences and Their Impacts on Remote
       Area Dwellers and Wildlife Populations. *Botswana Notes and
       Records* 28:55-64.

Hohmann, T.
2002   "We are looking for life. We are looking for the conservancy".
       Namibian Conservancies, Nature Conservation and Rural
       Development: The Case of the N‡a-Jaqna Conservancy. In:
       Hohmann, T. (ed.). *The San and the State*:205-254.

Ikeya, Kazunobo
1993   Goat Raising among the San in the Central Kalahari. *African Study
       Monographs* 14:39-52.

Ikeya, Kazunobo
1996   Dry Farming among the San in the Central Kalahari. *African Study
       Monographs*, Sppl. 22:85-100.

Ikeya, Kazunobo
2001 Some Changes among the San under the Influence of Relocation Plan in Botswana. *SENRI* 51:183-198.

IWGIA
2000 *Recognition of the Bushmen's Land Rights, Human Rights and Cultural Rights in Botswana.* Lincoln. Nebraska. (compiled by R. Hitchcock, Report from Review made in January 2000.).

Kuru Development Trust
1997 *Annual Report 1997/97.* Unpublished Report. D'kar.

1998 *Survey on Participants.* Manuscript. D'kar.

National CBNRM Forum in Botswana
2000 *Proceedings of the First National CBNRM Forum Meeting in Botswana 30ᵗʰ and 31ˢᵗ of May 2000 and CBNRM Status Report 1999/2000.* Gaborone: National CBNRM Forum in Botswana.

Republic of Botswana
1998 *Community Based Natural Resources Management Policy.* Government Paper No. 19. Gaborone.

Rivers, Roberta
2001 The Political Status of San in Botswana. In: Cassidy, L. K. Good and Isaac Mazonde (eds.) *An Assessment of the Status of the San/Sarwa in Botswana.* Windhoek: LAC:41-58.

Rozemeijer, Nico
2001 *Community-Based Natural Tourism in Botswana. The SNV experience in three community-tourism projects.* Gaborone: SNV.

Russell, Margo
1976 Slaves or workers? Relations between Bushmen, Tswana and Boers in the Kalahari. *Journal of Southern African Studies* 2:178-197.

Silberbauer, George
1965 *Report to the Government of Bechuanaland on the Bushman Survey.* Gaborone.

Silberbauer, George and Adam Kuper
1966 Kgalagari Masters and Bushmen Serfs. *African Studies* 25 (4):171-179

Taylor, Michael
2001 Narratives of Identity and Assertions of Legitimacy: Sarwa in Northern Botswana. *SENRI* 51:157-182.

Van der Jagt, C.
1996 *Kgalagadi District. Socio-economic baseline survey.* Unpublished manuscript. Gaborone.

Wily, E.A.
1979a *Official Policy Towards San (Bushmen) Hunter-Gatherers in Modern Botswana: 1966-1978.* Gaborone. Botswana: National Institute of Development and Cultural Research.

Wily, E.A.
1979b *Settlement as a Strategy for Securing Land for Nomads: An Examination of the Botswana Government's Current Programme for Settling the Kalahari San.* London: Agricultural Administration Unit. Overseas Development Office.

"Ek is 'n Nama, want ek praat die taal"
The Richtersveld and the National Language Policy in South Africa[1]

Susanne Berzborn

Introduction

For a long time, the Republic of South Africa has suffered from a repressive regime with a legislation that did not allow the majority of people to exercise basic individual rights and deprived them of resources. The society was divided along racial lines, with race, language and ethnicity being the main pillars of the Apartheid ideology. After the collapse of the system and the first democratic elections in 1994, a new era began. The 'New South Africa' is based on values like equality, human dignity and the advancement of human rights and freedoms for everyone. As the majority of African and Coloured[2] people had always rejected the state-imposed classification of ethnic groups, all people of South Africa should now have the right to development and self-determination, irrespective of their ethnic affiliation.

The government of the new South Africa recognises the cultural diversity of the country, however, it strives to build a united South African Nation.[3] The efforts to unite a nation while recognising its diversity and referring to its Khoekhoe and San roots are symbolised in the new South African coat of

---

[1] The research conducted in South Africa was sponsored by the German Research Council within the framework of the special research unit "Arid Climate, Adaptation and Cultural Innovation in Africa". I would like to thank Gertrud Boden, Michael Bollig, Matthias Brenzinger and Levi Namaseb for comments on earlier versions of this paper. My special thanks goes to the people in the Richtersveld who supported my research.

[2] In South Africa, people were classified as 'Black, White or Coloured'. I will use these labels when referring directly to the respective historical context. The same applies to terms like 'Hottentot' or 'Bushmen'. For the sake of legibility, these labels will be used without quotation marks, but it goes without saying that I reject this kind of labelling and classification of people.

[3] There are countless studies and essays about nation building in the new South Africa in an environment that is strongly shaped by the divisions created by colonialism and apartheid. See, e.g., Adam (1995), Alexander (1995), Maharaj (1999), Palmberg (1999), Kriger and Zegeye (2001), and Zegeye (2001).

arms, launched in April 2000. Among other elements, it contains rock art usually associated with San populations. The motto is written in the extinct Khoisan language of the |Xam people: "!Ke e: |xarra ||ke", literally meaning: diverse people unite. The official website presenting the coat of arms explains the meaning as follows:

> The Khoisan, the oldest known inhabitants of our land and most probably of the earth, testify to our common humanity and heritage as South Africans and as humanity in general. The figures are depicted [...], symbolising unity. This also represents the beginning of the individual's transformation into the greater sense of belonging to the nation and by extension, collective Humanity. [...] The figure embodies the spirit of the African Renaissance. [...] San rock art is one of the great archaeological wonders of the world – it is a mirror in which reflects the glories of the African past.[4]

Through this coat of arms, the government demonstrates the recognition of African, and especially, Khoekhoe and San roots by the modern nation state and outlines the model of a united nation that is comprised of different people and respecting all languages and cultures.

For historical reasons, ethnicity remains a sensitive issue in post-Apartheid South Africa. However, people are again referring to their ethnic affiliation and do have options to fill the concept 'ethnicity' with other and more positive contents. Whereas ethnic affiliation used to be a stumbling block for Non-Whites in South Africa and ethnicity was highly affiliated with detriments, it has now become a resource. People are re-discovering their tradition and choose which traditions they want to revitalise. They can now express them more openly and shape their ethnic identity. This process of identity formation is influenced by external actors (see Bollig and Berzborn 2002). Ethnic identity can be used as a resource not only to gain self-esteem, but also to attain more material aims such as access to land or income from ethno-tourism.

In South Africa, the people who speak Khoisan languages are amongst the groups that are pursuing to regain recognition in the nation state and reclaim indigenous identity.[5] Part of this movement is the revitalisation of

---

[4]   http://www.gov.za/symbols/coatofarms.htm and
      http://www.gov.za/symbols/lintonpanel.htm

[5]   Nama, !Xun and Khwedam are the Khoisan languages spoken on a daily basis in South Africa. In addition, there are some speakers of N|u, Gri (Xiri) and Koranna (!Ora) (Crawhall 1999:36).

their indigenous languages by promoting their use, enhancing their social status and bringing Khoisan languages into South African schools. The revitalisation of identity is usually coupled with the interest in indigenous languages as language often serves as one indication and expression of the speaker's identity (see Giles 1977; Kamwangamalu 2000; Kotzé 2000). Arguing along these lines, people are deprived of their identity and their self-esteem if they are deprived of their language.

This article will examine the actions taken by different stake-holders to promote Khoisan-languages in the broader framework of South Africa's constitutional provisions and actual language policy. The focus of the case study will be the Richtersveld in South Africa, where the Khoisan language Khoekhoegowab[6], also known as Nama, is spoken. The knowledge and language choice of Nama and Afrikaans in the Richtersveld will be analysed, and the actions taken by the people to promote the 'ancient tongue'[7] discussed. How and why did people start to regain interest in Nama, and how were they supported and constrained by the state South Africa? What impact did provisions made by the new government have on the local level?

Under Apartheid, the Nama people were classified as Coloureds and their language was marginalised. Recently, they have started to re-emphasise their original mother tongue as part of an emerging trend to stress their Nama identity. "Ek is 'n Nama, want ek praat die taal" is Afrikaans and means "I am a Nama because I speak the language." This statement is very popular in the Richtersveld and shows the close link between language and identity. Because of historical reasons, Afrikaans has become a 'second mother tongue' in the Richtersveld, and this statement is very often made in Afrikaans, a sign of the hybrid bilingual situation people live in.

---

[6] In Nama, *khoi* or in modern orthography, *khoe,* means "human being", *khoekhoe* "human human being/real people", *gowab* "language" (pers. comm. L. Namaseb). There are attempts to always call the language Khoekhoegowab, and the people Nama. As the Richtersveld people mainly referred to themselves and their language as Nama, this will be done in the following as well.

[7] One could argue that Nama itself is a construct, consisting of different central-Khoisan dialects classified as 'Nama' by missionaries and linguists.

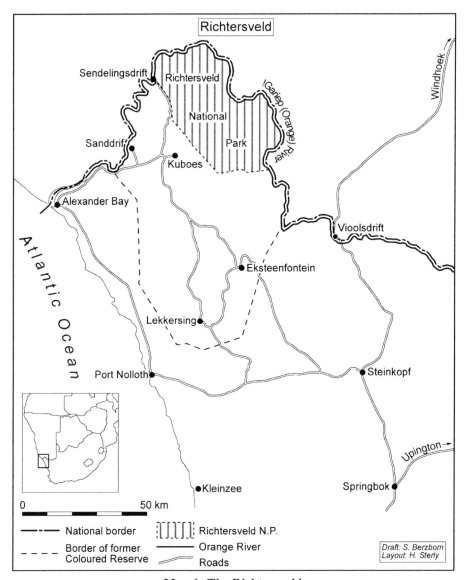

Map 1: The Richtersveld

Endangered Languages

Most Khoisan languages in southern Africa are endangered, and some have become extinct over the last centuries. This corresponds to the worldwide phenomenon that many indigenous languages are minority languages that are under threat.[8] Linguists tackling this phenomenon used to talk about language death (Brenzinger 1992; Crystal 2000) or even linguistic genocide (Skutnabb-Kangas 2000)[9]. Today, the term 'endangered languages' is widely used in scientific and policy discourse, and refers to languages that lose speakers. Undoubtedly, languages have continually vanished throughout history, but the loss of languages has accelerated recently (Crystal 1997). However, there are different opinions of how to assess this fact. Some people hold the view that it does not really matter if there is less language diversity in the world as they are not convinced that language death is followed by cultural loss (see Crystal 2000:27-32). But in the international discourse of today, there is usually the tendency to stress the immense value of every language and to point out that a whole body of inherited knowledge is lost when a language becomes extinct.[10] This latter view also predominates the debate on the decline of Khoisan languages. Speakers of Khoisan languages, especially San, attract a lot of interest in the international community, and with non-governmental organisations (NGOs) and donor organisations (Robins 2001; Bollig and Berzborn 2002). Analogous to this trend, their languages are seen as worthy of preservation as they are seen as a key to immense indigenous knowledge and the representation of a view of the world that is shared by no other.

Different measures have been taken to safeguard Khoisan languages in southern Africa. Linguists aim at documenting endangered languages, and activists and policy makers try to create options to prevent them from dying out. Besides intellectual arguments for preserving endangered languages, the

---

[8]   Almost half of the approximately 6,000 languages spoken in the world are endangered or dying, and are likely to disappear in the foreseeable future, which will lead to less language diversity in the world (Wurm 2001). Experts consider a community's language to be 'endangered' when at least 30% of its children no longer learn it (UNESCO 2002).

[9]   Skutnabb-Kangas holds the view that there is no 'natural death' of languages, but that languages are killed or people let them die.

[10] See the UNESCO's attempt to incorporate 'intangible heritage' such as languages into the concept of Cultural Heritage (UNESCO 2000). Further, there are worldwide projects and efforts to document endangered languages like the UNESCO Red Book of Endangered Languages (http://www.tooyoo.l.u-tokyo.ac.jp/Redbook/index.html), the Endangered Language Fund (http://sapir.ling.yale.edu/~elf/), the Foundation for Endangered Languages (http://www.ogmios.org/) and the Documentation of Endangered Languages of the Volkswagen-Stiftung (http://www.volkswagen-stiftung.de/foerderung/index.html).

value of language for identity is stressed as well, and language rights are more and more seen as human rights. To achieve the aim of promoting Khoisan languages, governmental language policy and planning is crucial, in addition to incorporating their use in the arenas of life, such as TV and radio broadcasting. Possibly the most important element for preserving endangered languages is found in the local perceptions of the language. As is the case for many endangered languages, Khoisan languages often were and are considered to be useless. The Khoekhoe and San cultures were derogated by the colonial and the Apartheid states, and their languages, as markers of ethnicity, became synonyms for backwardness. Many people disclaimed their origins and were ashamed to speak their language, for example, Nama. Besides raising awareness, it would, therefore, be essential to foster a positive attitude in the community towards their language, as languages can only be safeguarded by the speakers themselves (see Crystal 2000; Brenzinger 2002). If the people themselves do not want to keep their language alive, it is nearly impossible to prevent it from dying out.

Ethnic Terms and Classifications:
Coloured, Khoisan, Khoekhoe, Khoe and San

The people this research is concerned with were classified as Coloured under the Apartheid regime. The colonial and the Apartheid governments of South Africa formed a hierarchy among people based on 'racial' classifications that distinguished Whites from Coloureds and Blacks. The term Coloureds goes back to the early 19th century when white colonists started to distinguish themselves from "people of colour", a category that included Khoekhoe, free Blacks and people of mixed descent (Saunders and Southey 2001) whose mother tongue became Cape Dutch/Afrikaans. By the end of the 19th century, a more distinct Coloured identity developed within this heterogeneous group of people.[11] Coloureds had an intermediate position in the racial hierarchy, being not as inferior as Blacks but also not belonging to the superior white group. During Apartheid, they had to endure severe restrictions, and with the Population Registration Act of 1950, ancestry and not mere skin colour stipulated who belonged to which racial category. In contrast to Blacks, Coloureds, as a mixed category, did not have any peculiar

---

[11] This identity was and still is an extremely fluid and ill-defined one. For a more detailed analysis of the development and shape of a Coloured identity see, e.g., Pickel (1997), Erasmus and Pieterse (1999) and Martin (2001).

ethnic identity or affiliation and no 'culture'. Under this act, Nama, Griqua[12] and San were forcibly classified mainly as Coloureds, their identity was denied and their languages were suppressed by the government. They became de facto invisible, merged in the Coloured category and were forced to adopt a Coloured identity, which included the use of Afrikaans. However, due to the negative connotations related to 'being Nama/San' and some advantages 'being Coloured' offered within the Apartheid system, many speakers of Khoisan languages adopted a Coloured identity voluntarily. Only recently, these Coloureds have had the opportunity to promote their identity as Nama or San openly, others, however, still choose to identify themselves as Coloured.

There is some confusion around the terms Khoisan, Khoekhoe, Khoe and San, which have also become a political/activist issue since the emergence of different identities in the group of people formerly classified as Coloured. This relates mostly to the fact that the terms can be, and are, used in anthropological, linguistic, or political contexts. People whose languages are closely linguistically related to each other can belong to different groups and form different identities. Further, these terms are used as external attributions to groups of people or as self-identification of the respective people. To complicate matters even more, the distinction between Khoe and San is not at all clear (see Barnard 1992:10; Jolly 1996).

The term Khoisan was used first in 1928 by the physical anthropologist Schultze to refer to a racial commonality between Hottentot[13] and Bushmen. These names where given to the people of the Cape by Europeans in the 17th century. Referring to different economic strategies and physical features, early travellers and settlers called the cattle-herding Khoekhoe "Hottentots" and the people living off the veld "Bushmen" (Boonzaier, Malherbe, Smith, and Berens 1996:2). Khoekhoe is an emic term for pastoral people of the Cape region, comprised of different groups, most of which are now extinct. The colonists generally called people without cattle Bushmen, irrespective of the fact that they might not consider themselves as a homogenous group with

---

[12] Griqua were pastoralists of Khoekhoe and mixed descent. They were the first Khoekhoe-speakers who adopted Afrikaans, the language Griqua is regarded as extinct.

[13] The origin of the term Hottentot is unknown, probably it is referring to a greeting of the Khoekhoe which the colonists transformed into Hottentot. The notion that it refers to the language resembling stuttering seems to be false (Klocke-Daffa 2001:4). Others explain it as an onomatopoeic transcription of dancing Khoekhoe chants (Barnard 1992:9).

a corporate identity and that Khoekhoe who lost their stock also lived a hunter-gatherer lifestyle. The cultural anthropologist Isaac Schapera used the term Khoisan in his book "The Khoisan peoples of South Africa" (Schapera 1930) and went even further by stating that Hottentot and Bushmen form a racial, cultural *and* linguistic unit.

The linguist Greenberg (1963) then popularised the label Khoisan. Within the language family Khoisan, he identified Northern, Central and Southern Khoisan, each consisting of several languages. Among linguists, Greenberg's classification is controversially discussed.[14] However, according to Güldemann and Vossen (2000), Greenberg's work was a turning point in Khoisan linguistics because it was grounded on purely linguistic features and did not take anthropological or economical attributes into account. He classified Nama, the language of a Khoekhoe group, and Khwedam, the language of a San group, in the same branch because of linguistic commonalities, even though the speakers showed different physical and cultural features and used different economic strategies.

In cultural and social anthropology, Khoisan became a general term for indigenous populations in Southern Africa that share common features of territorial organisation, gender relations, kinship, ritual and cosmology across economic, cultural, linguistic and 'racial' boundaries (Barnard 1992). Barnard states that the Khoisan peoples are "the Khoekhoe (Hottentots), the Damara, the Khoe-speaking Bushmen, and the non-Khoe-speaking Bushmen of southern Africa" (Barnard 1992:11).

The term San was thought by anthropologists to replace the older pejorative term Bushmen from the 1970s onwards, but this term was met with reservation on the part of other anthropologists as it is both a pejorative Khoekhoe term and refers primarily to Khoekhoe people (Günther 1986). According to Namaseb (pers. comm.), in Nama, San refers to "people who speak a different language" and is a neutral term. There is no agreement among scholars which term is the best to be used (Gordon 1992; Widlok 1999, see also introduction this book), but, because San representatives, in stressing a common identity, decided that the collective name of the different

---

[14] Languages of the respective branches indeed share a genetic relationship to a certain degree, but Greenberg's hypothesis that all the languages summarised under Khoisan are genetically related to each other is highly questionable as they differ to a high degree from one another (Güldemann and Vossen 2000).

groups should be San[15], this term will be used in the following as referring to people also known as Bushmen. When talking about a specific group, the respective names, such as !Xun or Khwe, will be used.

On a political level, the label 'Khoisan' is again being debated. Some Coloureds have recently started to identify themselves as Khoisan in order to stress their Khoekhoe or San roots, to claim being indigenous, and First People of South Africa. At a National Khoisan Consultative Conference, a resolution was released stating that the 'National Khoisan Council' should speak on behalf of indigenous people of South Africa.[16] This National Khoisan Council was founded in May 1999 after year-long consultations between various communities who view themselves as indigenous and the Department of Constitutional Development. Even if San are represented on this council, which accommodates Nama, San, Griqua, Koranna and Revivalist Khoisan groups, there are voices that call of the foundation of a separate body for the representation of San as they claim a different identity "from the Khoi who don't share [their] culture"[17]. However, there is an understanding between San and Nama (read Khoekhoe) who share similar experiences and have a similar marginal status in South Africa. Both reject the notion that all people who claim an indigenous identity in Southern Africa should be called Khoisan. Nama and San activists see their heritage annexed by Coloureds who dominate this Khoisan movement and fear becoming marginalised again by the much more powerful and well-organised Afrikaans- and English-speaking people living in urban areas, who now claim Khoisan ancestry. They are concerned about the activities of Revivalist Khoisan groups and, especially relating to language issues, are suspicious of others claiming to be San or Nama. Nama and San in South Africa have formed an alliance to regain language rights, improve their marginal status and work on the representation of traditional authorities on

---

[15] This decision was made on the Consultative Conference on Communal Land Administration, held in Windhoek, Sept. 1996, by the Working Group for Indigenous minorities in Southern Africa (WIMSA), a network organisation of different San groups (Thoma 1997 in Hohmann 2000).

[16] The National Khoisan Consultative Conference was held in Oudtshoorn, South Africa, in 2001. It was facilitated by Prof. Bredekamp, Institute for Historical Research, University of the Western Cape, Cape Town. For representation of Khoisan in the Internet see e.g.: http://www.garib.co.za/index.html.

[17] Weekly Mail & Guardian, April 26, 2001. *The Khoi don't share our culture, say San. Delegates reject the idea of a Khoisan people at a conference in Windhoek.*

governmental level. In this context, Afrikaans serves as a lingua franca between Nama and San.

Governmental documents and the constitution have always referred to "Khoe and San languages", which, linguistically, does not make sense, because, as stated above, San languages do not form a linguistic unit. In this context, 'Khoe and San' is rather meant in a sociopolitical sense, stressing the ethnic affiliations of the different groups involved. The tendency to separate speakers of Khoisan languages along ethnic lines has to be seen in the broader context of revitalisation of ethnic identities in southern Africa and the people's objective to establish distinct identities. However, it would be correct to speak of 'Khoisan languages' as a language family, as will be done in the following when talking about the languages as a whole. Pursuant to the emic use of the term in the Richtersveld, 'Nama' refers in the following to the language as well as to the ethnic group.

It became clear from the above discussion that groups were often constructed and that the different labels prescribed to people or even used by themselves are rather flexible. They were and are instrumentalised and reflect the spirit of the respective age and the intentions of the speakers.

Khoisan Languages and Language Policy in South Africa

The Nama language used to be widespread in the Cape region, but it was maintained only in some areas, such as the Richtersveld, where quite a few speakers of Nama can be found today. Before colonisation, Khoisan languages were spread all over the Cape, which was inhabited mostly by Khoekhoe and San. But today, many Khoisan languages are regarded as endangered, and others have became extinct. This is related to the fact that speakers of Khoisan languages were either assimilated into a Cape Coloured community, which included the use of Afrikaans, or they fled from the colonists and settlers to remote areas. The decline of their languages was further aggravated by Apartheid and its education system.

As the dominant paradigm of Apartheid, racial segregation shaped education, which was strictly controlled by the government and designed to cultivate the separate identity and culture of each group to prepare its members for 'their place' in the economy of South Africa. As early as 1951, the UNESCO drafted a position that people should have the right to education in their mother tongue, but in South Africa it was used to support Bantu education (Sigrühn and Hays 2001). Children were excluded from the white English and Afrikaans school system. Further, values of the Apartheid government should be transported through the 'Christian National

Education'. Speakers of Khoisan languages were classified as Coloureds, and therefore fell under the Coloured Education Act of 1963, which codified the syllabus for Coloured schools. As the language of Coloureds was Afrikaans, Nama and San could not receive an education in their mother tongues, but in Afrikaans.[18] This resulted in the marginality of Khoisan languages and the dominance of Afrikaans. The negative implications related to 'being Nama' in an Apartheid setting led people to disclaim their origins. As their language identified them as Nama, they were ashamed to speak Nama, which became a synonym for backwardness. There are no exact figures of Nama speakers, but it is estimated that today there are 5,000 to 10,000 Nama-speaking people living in the Northern Cape (ILO 1999).[19] As a language, Nama is not endangered as it has many speakers in Namibia. In South Africa however, Nama is today spoken only in some remote areas and can be regarded as endangered as it is losing more and more speakers.

Constitutional Provisions Today

In May 1996, the first democratically elected government of the Republic of South Africa passed a constitution aimed at overcoming the inequalities created by the Apartheid regime. In the course of writing the constitution, language rights were seen as an important part of democracy. After long negotiations it was decided to choose eleven official languages. As only the official languages of the old South Africa were granted official status, Khoisan languages are not recognised as official languages.[20]

For a long time, the Apartheid government had ignored the existence of the Khoekhoe and San, and their languages. But even after the end of the

---

[18] Under the Bantu Education Act of 1953, there was an emphasis on African indigenous languages as a medium of instruction for Blacks, at least on primary school level. Whereas the education standards for Blacks were inferior to those of Whites and even Coloureds, at least the nine official *Bantustan* languages persisted under this policy.

[19] Nama is spoken as a home language by at least some people in the following Namaqualand and Bushmanland villages: Kuboes, Sanddrift, Lekkersing, Eksteenfontein, Port Nolloth, Steinkopf, Springbok, Matjieskloof, Henkries, Goodhouse, Vioolsdrift, Witbank, Pella and Riemvasmaak (Crawhall 1997). There exist no older figures of Nama speakers.

[20] The high number of official languages is almost unique in the whole world. The languages recognised in South Africa are the nine African languages that had official status in the former Bantustans on a regional level, plus the former official national languages Afrikaans and English (du Plessis 2000).

Apartheid era, there was no official awareness of Khoisan-speaking people; they were regarded as extinct. Even as late as 1996, on the occasion of the adoption of the new constitution, the Deputy President of the ANC government at the time, Thabo Mbeki, stated in his "I am an African" speech that today there are no Khockhoe and San in South Africa:

> I owe my being to the Khoi and the San whose desolate souls haunt the great expanses of the beautiful Cape, they who fell victim to the most merciless genocide our native land has ever seen, they who were the first to lose their lives in the struggle to defend our freedom and dependence and they who, as a people, perished in the result. (Mbeki 1996)

This statement caused a lot of protest from different communities who regard themselves as descendants of the Khoekhoe and San. But even though Mbeki's speech denied the actual existence of the Khoekhoe and San people, their languages are mentioned in the Founding Provisions of the Constitution that was adopted when he made his speech:

> The Pan South African Language Board[21] must
>
> a. promote and create conditions for the development and use of
>   - all official languages;
>   - the Khoi, Nama and San languages; and
>   - sign language.
>
> b. promote and ensure respect for languages, including German, Greek, Gujarati, Hindi, Portuguese, Tamil, Telugu, Urdu, and others commonly used by communities in South Africa, and Arabic, Hebrew, Sanskrit and others used for religious purposes.
> (Constitution of the Republic of South Africa of 1996, 6 [5])

Hence, the constitution differentiates between (a) official languages, (b) Khoisan and sign languages, and (c) so-called heritage languages commonly spoken in South Africa. South Africa's constitution is the first one that actively aims at promoting Khoisan languages[22], and even if they do not

---

[21] This board was established in 1995. See below for further information.

[22] In Namibia, children have the right to an education in their mother tongue for the first three years of schooling. For example, Nama and Jul'hoan are recognised as mother tongues, and are therefore used as a language of instruction at primary school level. However, there are often obstacles for doing this, as e.g., not all children in a class speak the same mother tongue. The choice of Nama as a subject at school is often hindered by the fact that high schools only accept

have the status of an official language, they are no longer invisible and good options exist for development.

Nevertheless, one has to bear in mind the difference between the provisions made by the constitution and the actual language policy. The legal framework for a multilingual South Africa exists, but regulations for the use of the official languages and the promotion of the other languages are subject to actual language policy and impose a great challenge for government. The Department of Arts, Culture, Science and Technology (DACST), with its Directorate National Language Service, is responsible for national language policy and has to oversee the implementation of a policy grounded on the provisions made by the constitution (Mkhulisi 2000). In 1995, a Language Plan Task Group (LANGTAG) was commissioned to work on a National Language Plan, while also tackling the language needs of Khoe and San communities (Crawhall 1997). There are drafts of a Language Policy and Plan and a Language Policy for South Africa Bill, expected to be submitted to Parliament in 2001 (Burger 2001), but which has not yet happened.

In addition to implementing language policies, capacity building is needed as well. It might be difficult for people who have been marginalised for decades, if not centuries, to enact their language rights as they usually do not have the power and the capacity to do so or do not even know their rights. For example, most of the complaints on alleged violations of language rights were from Afrikaans speakers; only very few came from African-language speakers (Marivate 2000), which indicates that there is a need to educate people about their rights and to build the capacity among all people to enact language rights.

PANSALB and the Khoe and San National Language Body

Because the interim constitution of the Republic of South Africa of 1993 (Act 200 of 1993) recognises the principle of multilingualism, the Pan South African Language Board (PANSALB) was established in 1995 (Act 59 of 1995, amended in 1999) as an advisory body to make recommendations to the state with regard to language policy and planning to promote an awareness of multilingualism as a national resource and to provide for the development and equal use of previously marginalised languages. The

---

pupils who have had English and Afrikaans at school. In addition to the schools, the church was also instrumental in teaching Nama/Damara. Further, there is a Nama/Damara broadcast on the radio and news on television.

provisions made for PANSALB referred mainly to the official languages, but PANSALB considers other languages as well. There are different categories of languages; Khoisan languages are one of those that shall actively be developed. PANSALB may be approached by any person or institution to lodge a complaint concerning violations of language rights, and it is the board's task to try to resolve and settle any dispute. Furthermore, translation and interpreting services have to be developed. There is a subcommittee, "Language in Education", which concentrates on the use and status of languages in education. It was approached by speakers of Khoisan languages, among others, requesting recognition of their languages in South African schools (Marivate 2000). In a discussion document on its position on the promotion of multilingualism PANSALB states that

> [...] for a language to survive, it must be used for a wide range of functions otherwise it begins to wither and die [...] We have seen this happen to many of the Khoe and San languages and their extinction is a loss not only to the communities, which used them, but it is a national disaster [...] When a language dies, very often a whole body of knowledge dies with it. (PANSALB 1998)

PANSALB faces great challenges and its mandate is quite complex, as the board has to develop languages, undertake or finance research, investigate language rights violations and advise the government on language matters (Marivate 2000). Therefore, PANSALB is supposed to establish several bodies to advise it on any particular language. Inter alia, 14 National Language Bodies (NLBs) are to be established to advise PANSALB on language issues concerning these languages.[23] They comprise 13 members from across the country belonging to one language group. The Khoe and San National Language Body (KSNLB) was the first – and until today the only – NLB to be established. It was launched in Upington, Northern Cape, in August 1999, and its first meeting took place in October 1999. The KSNLB should, among other tasks, (1) promote, develop and extend the use of the Khoe and San Languages, (2) advise PANSALB on these languages, (3) assist PANSALB in promoting multilingualism, (4) conduct surveys in communities where the languages are spoken, and (5) liase with other professional bodies that can help to expand the Khoe and San Languages (PANSALB 1999).

---

[23] It is envisaged that National Language Bodies for the 11 official languages, for Khoe and San languages, for sign language and for heritage languages will be established.

The Nama of the Richtersveld are one group participating in the KSNLB. From the ten members, four represent Nama (three from Richtersveld, one from Riemvasmaak), two members represent ǂKhomani (from the Kalahari), and four represent !Xun and Khwedam (from Schmidtsdrift). The NGO South African San Institute (SASI), was instrumental in the formation of the KSNLB by making PANSALB aware of the violation of Khoe and San rights and by facilitating a dialogue between the communities and governmental bodies (Crawhall 1997:4).

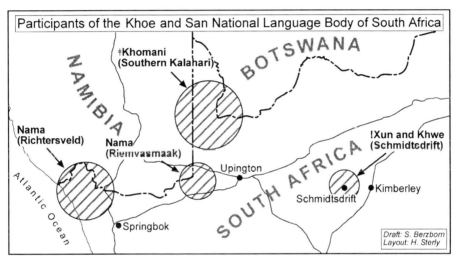

Map 2: Participants of the Khoe and San National Language Body of South Africa

In May 1999, PANSALB and the Department of Arts, Culture, Science and Technology (DACST) conducted interviews in Upington with people from different Northern Cape communities where Khoisan languages are spoken to select appropriate members for the KSNLB. Future members should be speakers of the respective language and have a vital interest in promoting the language. The process of selection was criticised by several people. Critics were concerned with how and to whom invitations were given and how transport to Upington was arranged. Not all the invited people came to the appointment, in part because they did not have transportation, and partly because they did not get the invitation letters; instead, others who were not invited showed up. Griquas and members of other groups were not invited because they do not speak an 'indigenous language'; Griqua is regarded as extinct. But some Griqua representatives wanted to be on the KSNLB, came to Upington and were very dissatisfied, as they could not participate in the interviews. Speakers of Khoisan languages applying for membership at the KSNLB agreed fully with PANSALB not to admit Griqua as they did not see the necessity for them to be on that board. Some even see their heritage annexed by the Griqua, with one representative from the Richtersveld stating:

> We have our language, our culture, we preserved it, it's them [the Griqua] who do not have a language, not us, and now, now they want to have our language![24] (13.10.2000)

In the beginning, the KSNLB had mainly conducted strategic planning and budgeting exercises with the support of SASI. Today, there are quite a few other activities performed by the KSNLB. There are numerous workshops and meetings aimed at capacity building for the members, establishing communication between the different communities, liasing with other indigenous and marginalised groups of Southern Africa, and working on a plan to promote the Khoisan languages in South Africa. The KSNLB is to push for the translation of the Namibian Nama-English dictionary (Haacke and Eiseb 1999) into Nama-Afrikaans, to foster the development of reading material, to help to write orthographies for the languages that do not yet have proper ones, and to push for the changing of Afrikaans place names on official maps to the original Khoisan names. The KSNLB is supported in its activities by PANSALB, the Northern Cape Department of Education, and SASI.

One major aim is to enforce the introduction of Nama now, and later, other indigenous languages into schools. The South African educational system was originally stamped by missionary societies and churches, and later by the segregation along Apartheid lines, which implied unequal access to education and an inferior education for Blacks and Coloureds. The new South Africa's vision is to integrate the diverse linguistic and cultural heritage into the formal educational system (Sigrühn and Hays 2001). The Bill of Rights, 1996, states that

> [...] everyone has the right to receive education in the official languages or languages of their choice in public educational institutions where that education is reasonably practicable (Bill of Rights 29 [2]).

The Northern Cape Department of Education has the objective, among other things, "to create an environment in the province where the concept of

---

[24] The interviews where conducted in Afrikaans, I translated the quotations into English. To ensure anonymity, all names have been changed.

African Renaissance can thrive"[25]. In keeping with the Curriculum 2005, the department tries to fulfil this objective by giving greater support to the development of indigenous African languages and encouraging the cultural heritage of African learners in all schools. It plans on introducing indigenous languages in the schools of the Northern Cape. At the moment, Afrikaans and, to a lesser extent, English are the only languages of instruction. However, there are differences in language proficiency between children in Nama-speaking communities and San communities. In Nama-speaking communities, such as Richtersveld, children usually speak Afrikaans as their first language and do not have language problems at school, whereas in San communities, children's mother tongue is often not Afrikaans, which is one reason for high drop-out rates and poor educational standards (especially for San education see Crawhall 1997; Sigrühn and Hays 2001; Robins, Madzudzo, and Brenzinger 2001). Hence, introducing indigenous languages has a twofold objective: to increase the ability of non-Afrikaans-speaking children to follow the classes, and secondly, to help indigenous people regain pride in their endangered language. The Northern Cape Education Department, stimulated by requests from the community and the school principal, started a pilot project in Kuboes, Richtersveld, and introduced Nama as a subject at the primary school. The teacher's salary was sponsored by the Trans Hex Mining Company[26] and later by the department.

Case Study Richtersveld[27]

The Richtersveld is situated in Namaqualand, Northern Cape, in the northwest corner of South Africa and has a semi-arid climate. Archaeological evidence shows that the area has been inhabited by pastoralists for at least 2,000 years (Webley 1997). Due to its remoteness, it served as a refuge for Khoekhoe and other groups who fled from European settlers in the Cape during colonial times. In December 1847, Namaqualand was incorporated into the Cape Colony, and only then did white settlers

---

[25] http://www.northern-cape.gov.za/departments/education/edsite/

[26] Trans Hex is a private enterprise. It gives 4.5% of sales revenues generated by its Namaqualand mining operations to the Trans Hex "Namaqualand Diamond Fund Trust". This money is used to support projects in the Namaqualand communities, such as the Nama teacher at Kuboes.

[27] Between February 1999 and November 2000, I conducted 18 months of ethnographical fieldwork in the Richtersveld. The information used in this paper was obtained through interviews and participant observation mainly in Kuboes. Interviews were conducted in Afrikaans.

came to stay there. Missionary work in Namaqualand was done from 1805 onwards, first by the London Missionary Society, and later by the Rhenish Mission Society. In 1842, the Rhenish Mission Station Richtersveld was established, around which the village Kuboes developed (Strassberger 1969). Mission stations established in the 19th century were granted 'tickets of occupation' for the surrounding lands to be used by local people exclusively. With that, the pastoral Nama had the opportunity to graze their stock on the communally used land, which was not possible in many other areas of the Cape because they were occupied by white settlers. This land was later transformed into 'Reserves'. In 1930, a certificate of reservation was issued, reserving the Richtersveld for the use of the 'Hottentots, Bastards and other Coloureds' Under the Population Registration Act and the Group Areas Act of 1950, the Richtersveld people, who are originally predominantly of Nama descent, were forcibly classified as Coloureds. People were restricted to reside in the 'Richtersveld Coloured Reserve', which was one of six 'Coloured Reserves' in Namaqualand. However, due to the Richtersveld's remoteness and comparably minor external contact, the transformation from a Nama to a Coloured identity remained ambiguous and incomplete. Today, there are four villages in the Richtersveld; the former mission station Kuboes is the main village. The approximate 3,500 inhabitants of the Richtersveld live mainly from wage labour in diamond mines in the area, stock farming and old-age pensions provided by the state.

Languages in the Richtersveld

Languages commonly spoken in the Richtersveld are Nama and Afrikaans, and knowledge of English is still limited. The Richtersveld is an area where many people have preserved their original language Nama in spite government repression, but everybody speaks Afrikaans as well. The following will examine how Afrikaans, at the cost of Nama, gained significance in the area and under which circumstances interest in the indigenous language Nama has recently re-emerged.

The original inhabitants of the Richtersveld only spoke their indigenous language Nama. With the colonists, settlers and missionaries, Cape Dutch came into the region. After their arrival at the Cape, German missionaries learnt Cape Dutch before starting work in Namaqualand or other areas (Strassberger 1969). The missionary Hein, who worked in the Richtersveld, struggled to convert people because of communication problems. In the beginning, the people did not understand Dutch and he did not speak Nama. Church services held in Dutch were translated into the indigenous language as possible. In a report, one missionary wrote that Hein only made progress in his work when he obtained a Nama translation of the Luke gospel from another missionary and read it for the people. When they heard the words of the bible in their own language, some of them wanted to become Christians (Meyer and von Heerde 1944).

Missionaries were instrumental in imposing a Coloured Afrikaans Christian identity on the people in the Richtersveld, and did, for example, not use the Nama bible, which was available and used in Namibia, but instead promoted the use of Afrikaans. Under the influence of the restrictive Apartheid government, Nama was even more systematically suppressed, chiefly through education policy, and it started to diminish. The tendency to speak Afrikaans with children, caused by suppression and permanent disparagement of the indigenous language Nama, lead to its decline.

In the 1930s, Nama was still prominent at school and at least one teacher held classes in Nama.[28] According to informant statements from Kuboes, Afrikaans became the dominant language in the 1940s. The teachers who came from the Cape region did not speak Nama and physically punished the children if they spoke their mother tongue. Not only was Afrikaans the language of instruction, the use of Nama was even prohibited on school premises, as well as outside the classroom during breaks. Elderly people tell about huge problems at school, as they did not speak a single word of Afrikaans and were punished for speaking Nama. That induced parents of this generation to speak Afrikaans to their children. They did not want them to suffer from ignorance of Afrikaans at school as they did, and therefore they taught them Afrikaans as the first language. Countless studies show that children learn best in their first language, an argument that is usually used to support education in the mother tongue (Sigrühn and Hays 2001). Ironically, parents behave in a manner consistent with these research results: As they could not change the language of instruction, they changed the mother tongue.

Nama was not only forbidden on school premises, but also in the workplace. It was banned from the public sphere, and people were ashamed to speak this 'backward and uncivilised' language, which had so many negative connotations outside the reserve. Many people assimilated to the norm of Afrikaans as a dominant language and they themselves suppressed Nama by not speaking it anymore. They adopted the negative attitude towards Nama and lost knowledge of and interest in their original language. However, Nama was always spoken in the Richtersveld in the private and

---

[28] PAE 49 CMS 110/67, Cape Town Archives.

also the public sphere. People report that they spoke Nama at work even though the *baas*[29] did not want them to do so, and they spoke Nama outside the reserve even if other people derided their language.

Attitudes towards Nama

In the Richtersveld, the attitudes towards Nama vary to a high degree. Some people have a negative view of Nama as being backward and embarrassing, others are indifferent and not interested in Nama; they feel that it is a waste of time and energy to promote this "old language which is of no use anymore". They would prefer their children to get better education in English instead, a language that they consider to be more important in the new South Africa than Nama. Children themselves sometimes referred to Nama as a backward language, which is just another subject at school.

However, I often also encountered people taking much pride in Nama and expressing their love of the language, and children being keen on learning the language. Some people passionately wanted to promote Nama in order to prevent it from dying out, as they considered their traditions and, as a consequence, their 'Namaness', dying out as well. "The home language is Afrikaans now, not Nama, therefore the traditions go out." (P.J., 8.5.1999) They were satisfied and very content that their language was honoured and that they could speak it with pride again. The negative notion it had had for a long time was substituted by the status of being a language of people who have a history, people who have a tradition, and people who can claim ancestral roots. For the people in the Richtersveld, there is a close link between language and identity. They feel they have an identity because they have a language. Hence, the possibility to openly display the indigenous language is closely related to an expression of this identity, and language serves as a marker for identity.

People often related having their own language to being a nation and having a territory; interestingly enough, this notion of the relation between language and nation goes back to the Apartheid ideology. To give only one example of many statements along these lines:

> For me, it is very important to have my language, every nation has its language, you, the Germans, they have Germany, the English, they have England, I am a nation, and I have my language Nama, we have Namaqualand. The white people

---

[29] Afrikaans for "boss". In South Africa, Coloureds or Blacks had to use this term to address a white man.

wanted to have our land, that is the reason why they wrote Coloured in our IDs, because Coloureds, they do not have land, where is 'Colouredland'? They do not have land. Then they took our land. (J.J., 26.5.1999).

The majority of people in Kuboes belong to the latter category wishing to promote Nama. This might be related to the fact that they are known as being 'traditional' in general, claiming the status of being the main and oldest village; the heart of the Richtersveld. This is also the only village in South Africa that has Nama as a subject at school (see below).

Knowledge and use of languages vary in the Richtersveld, and there are different factors determining both. The two southern villages, Eksteenfontein and Lekkersing, are more Afrikaans dominated than the northern ones, Kuboes and Sanddrift, which is derived from history. In 1949, in the course of resettlement by the Apartheid government, an Afrikaans-speaking group of 'Bosluis Basters' came to the area and settled predominantly in Eksteenfontein, but also in Lekkersing. Furthermore, in the 1960s and 1970s, the principal of the Lekkersing school, a descendant of the missionary J. F. Hein, was very rigid in promoting Afrikaans and banning Nama at his school. In Kuboes and Sanddrift,[30] the Nama population is more numerous, their language is spoken and many people at least understand Nama. Afrikaans never totally replaced Nama as the language spoken at home. Even though children were brought up mostly in Afrikaans, Nama was spoken at home as well, in some households more than in others.

Due to a lack of education in the old mother tongue, there is almost no Nama literacy in the Richtersveld, and until very recently, Nama was never taught at school. Just a handful of elderly people are able to write and read Nama. They were either in contact with people from Namibia or taught themselves by cross-reading a Nama bible, which they also obtained from Namibia, and an Afrikaans one. Since Nama has started to be taught at school in 1999, the literacy rate will increase in the future.

Levels of Language Proficiency

In general it can be stated that all the elderly and many adults speak Nama, whereas knowledge of Nama among the youth varies greatly. Elderly persons grew up speaking Nama at home, even if Afrikaans became

---

[30] In addition to the Nama/Coloured population, a group of Xhosa-speaking people arrived in Sanddrift in the early 1990s. Their dominant languages are Xhosa and English, but they speak Afrikaans as well.

dominant in the public sphere later on. Their children, today adults, grew up in a much more Afrikaans-dominated environment and the language switched to Afrikaans in many households, but nevertheless, most of them are at least passively bilingual, and many speak Nama as well. There are households where one parent may be not able to understand Nama, mainly if he/she came to the Richtersveld through marriage from an Afrikaans-speaking background. This has obviously had an impact on the choice of language in their households, and therefore on their children's command of Nama.

People under the age of 20 years or so are often only passively bilingual, if they speak Nama at all. The knowledge of Nama depends heavily on the setting in which a child grew up. There are children and young adults who do not understand Nama because they come from a background where Nama is not spoken at all. But people who grew up in households where Nama is spoken regularly have a good understanding of the language. This is usually the case when they lived with their grandparents in a bilingual environment. The grandparents approach the children in Afrikaans, but speak Nama to each other.

Some adults were of the opinion that the children and young adults can speak Nama, but they just do not want to. This leads to the (incorrect) impression that they are unable of speaking Nama. One reason for the refusal to speak Nama is that children consider Nama old-fashioned. Adults complained about these children, who do not understand that it is important to prevent Nama from dying out:

> [...] they do not want to speak Nama, they do not understand, only the children who went to Turkey, they understand, they went to Turkey as Nama, they saw. (7.6.1999, P.W.).

These interviewees are referring to children who went to Turkey in April 1999. A group of pupils participated in the "21st International 23 April Children Festival" in Ankara, Turkey, where more than 600 children from 28 countries came together. They performed traditional Namastap dance and song, and represented the 'Nama culture' in Turkey. Many children do want to learn Nama, and those participating in the dance group or a Nama choir at school proudly displayed their traditions on many occasions.

In addition to language proficiency, the mix of languages should to be mentioned. Many informants express sadness that they do not speak the "real pure Nama" like the people from Namibia, but a Nama that is strongly influenced by Afrikaans. They use, for example, Afrikaans numbers, and some words, such as 'sugar' or 'thank you', are borrowed from Afrikaans. In contrast, Namibian Nama use Nama numbers and, according to some people from the Richtersveld, their vocabulary is more elaborate.

People attributed not being able to speak Nama correctly to having a lot of contact with Afrikaans-speaking people and that Nama was not taught at school. One elderly man even said:

> [...] we do not have any proper language at all: we do not speak Afrikaans properly, we do not speak the 'high' Afrikaans, as our education was poor, and we also do not speak the correct Nama like the people from Namibia (W.J., 2.3.1999).

The perception of not being able to speak 'the correct Nama' is based, for example, on the experience Richtersveld people have when listening to the Namibian Nama/Damara radio. They have to struggle to understand everything that is said. One woman explained this by saying: "We don't speak the correct Nama, because actually, we are Coloureds" (K.S., 19.6.1999). However, according to the linguist and Nama/Damara-speaker L. Namaseb, the Richtersveld people do speak Nama correctly, just a different dialect. The broadcasts on the radio are made by various people, whose dialects differ. Therefore, there is always vocabulary not understood by everyone. The Namibian Nama/Damara-speakers also have the same problem as Richtersveld people (pers. comm., Namaseb). However, Richtersveld people often perceive their Nama as inferior. The Namibian Nama seems to be the standard, as it is a developed language in Namibia with its own learning materials, some literature and dictionaries, and broadcasts on the radio.

Choice of Language

Sociolinguists differentiate three perspectives from which choosing between languages can be approached (Appel and Muysken 1990). First, there is the concept of 'domains', which takes social organisation as its basis and focuses on overall social norms. Factors such as group membership, the situation and the topic of the conversation are factors that can influence language choice. Second, there are more person-oriented approaches, which tackle the problem of language choice through the model of a decision tree. The topic of the conversation or the ethnicity of the interlocutor are factors that determine language choice. Further, according to an approach within social psychology, interpersonal relations have to be taken into account, in addition to situational factors. Third, there is a model that tries to integrate the other approaches by focusing on the functions of language and the intentional use of languages by a speaker. In the following, a person-oriented approach is chosen and the function of language will be considered.[31]

In the Richtersveld, there are different factors that determine the choice of language in informal contacts and the public sphere: Namely, the speaker's age and proficiency in Nama, the other people present, the type of household, the setting in which the conversation takes place, the topic, and not least, the attitude and the intention of the speaking person (see Fig. 1).

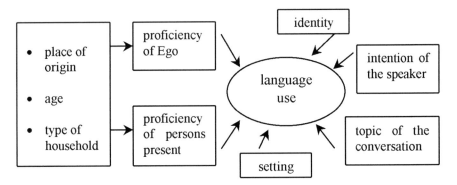

Fig. 1: Factors determining the choice of language

First, the proficiency and age of the persons participating in the conversation is considered. It goes without saying that knowledge of the speaking person determines the use of the language, and knowledge of the persons present is almost as important. Language can be a tool to include or exclude other people (see Allan and Burridge 1991; Appel and Muysken 1990). If Nama-speakers do not want non-Nama-speakers to follow the conversation for whatever reason, they switch to Nama.[32] But if there is no reason, which is usually the case in day-to-day conversations, people switch to Afrikaans if there are non-Nama speakers present, to include them.

Public meetings held by the local government, the church, the school, NGOs or any other institutions are always attended by some people who do

---

[31] There exists extensive socio-linguistic literature on the alternative use of several languages in one conversation. This phenomenon is called "code-switching" (see e.g. Milroy and Muysken 1995; Auer 1998). Richtersveld people switch between languages, but this will not be tackled here as it requires much more detailed socio-linguistic research.

[32] These reasons include talking about secrets and slander.

not have command of Nama. Therefore, these meetings are generally held in Afrikaans. Some elderly people even complained when NGOs wanted to translate contributions in a meeting into Nama because they felt that this is unnecessary, because they all understand Afrikaans properly.[33] It was insulting for them that these people assumed they could not speak Afrikaans properly, especially because some of the organisers of the meeting were Coloureds from the Richtersveld. In this case, it was not necessary to demonstrate Namaness by speaking Nama; quite the contrary, people did not want to seem uneducated and not able to understand Afrikaans. Only at meetings, for example, of the Nama Cultural Group or the Nama Choir, where only Nama-speakers are present, does Nama dominate public conversation.

Table 1: General trends in the use of Nama and Afrikaans as a contact language between different age groups

↓ Speaking persons	Approached persons →			
	Elderly	**Adults**	**Young adults**	**Children**
Elderly	1	2	3	3
Adults	2	3	3	4
Young Adults	3	4	4	4
Children	4	4	4	4

1 = Nama   3 = more Afrikaans than Nama

2 = more Nama than Afrikaans   4 = Afrikaans

Age group is an indication of the level of proficiency in Nama, as elderly persons always command Nama.[34] See Table 1 for general trends in language use. Elderly persons prefer to speak Nama with each other and other adults, and Afrikaans with children. Adults speak Nama or Afrikaans with each other, and Afrikaans with the children, whereas children speak

---

[33] This meeting held at Kuboes by two NGOs dealt with changes in the municipal structure and a community land claim. The people of the Richtersveld claim diamond-rich land which is at the moment occupied by the state-owned mine Alexkor.

[34] An exception is the people who have married into Nama-speaking families and come from an Afrikaans background, which is rarely the case.

Afrikaans to everybody; some of them have no, or only a passive, understanding of Nama, others are able to speak as well.

Many households can be considered bilingual, with the proportion of Nama/Afrikaans spoken dependent on various factors. There are households where Nama is usually spoken, even if the head of the household is not an elderly person. These households are generally more involved in stock farming, have close contact with elderly persons, and further associate themselves with a Nama identity. The dominance of Afrikaans in a household is usually due to the fact that at least one parent is not able to speak Nama properly. However, it can also be an expression of identity, stressing the association to the group of Coloureds.

Nama is commonly spoken at stockposts. Even young people will switch to Nama as soon as they arrive at the stockpost. One reason for this is the topics tackled in the conversations. People talk about stock farming, movements of the herd, state of the grazing, water, illnesses, decisions where to go next or which goat should be slaughtered. These are topics related to the traditional economic system that people have followed over the last centuries, at a time when they used to only speak Nama. There are plants and bushes that do not have Afrikaans names in the Richtersveld, and place names are very frequently only known in Nama, with no equivalent in Afrikaans. However, it is not only the topic, but also the setting that seems to influence language choice, as people often used Nama at the stockpost as well if they spoke about migrant labour, unemployment or news from the village. Afrikaans is used on stockposts only if there are persons present who do not understand Nama or when younger children are approached.

As noted earlier, the growing interest in the indigenous language of many people in the Richtersveld, as well as the whole of South Africa, is related to emerging identities. As people revitalise their culture and their identity, they also rediscover esteem for their indigenous language and regain interest in Nama. Informants have noted that Nama is much more present in the public sphere today than ten years ago. In a general survey conducted by myself in Kuboes, 95.6% of the interviewees related being Nama to being able to speak the language.[35] They had very strong feelings about the language and considered Nama a very important part of their identity. The very first

---

[35] In a random sample of 100 households, 65 informants related Nama identity to language, 3 stated that Nama (identity and the language) does not have any importance, 32 are missing. Generally, the head of the household or his wife were interviewed.

answer to the question if they were Nama was almost always: "I speak Nama." They are Nama because they are able to speak Nama. Along the same lines, they were of the opinion that people who do not speak Nama cannot be Nama, and people who speak Afrikaans are Coloureds. People indeed stress their association to the group of Coloureds by speaking Afrikaans, strongly rejecting the notion of being Nama.

People referred to themselves as Coloureds even if they could speak Nama, because this was written in their identity document (ID), and sometimes still is, as people have not organised new Ids for themselves. They do not see the necessity of identifying themselves as Nama and do not understand the hype of other people who suddenly stress their 'Namaness'. Many people would oppose this statement, refusing to be called Coloured and passionately rejecting this label. They remember with grief their forced classification as Coloured and stress:

> [...] people cannot be coloured, clothes can be coloured, many
> colours, your skirt is coloured, but not me, my skin, my skin is
> brown. (W.J., 6.3.1999)

Hence, in addition to the mere interest in the language, one can observe that languages are chosen strategically as an expression of identity and self-image according to the respective situation. On public occasions especially, Nama is used to demonstrate an indigenous identity. Just to name a few:

In 1989, a national park was to be established in the northwest corner of the Richtersveld. The local people who herded their goats and sheep inside this area were to be expelled and no consultations with the broader community took place. Therefore, an interdict was handed in to stop the establishment of the national park. Supported by NGOs and other external actors, community representatives engaged in negotiations. At the first meeting to take place after the interdict, community members only spoke Nama for 20 minutes (pers. comm., Henk Smith). By demonstrating that the National Parks Board officials did not understand them, they wanted to show that consultations with the community had not taken place. This was the first time Nama was used strategically. The negotiations resulted in a contract in 1992 between the National Parks Board and community representatives that ensures co-management and further use of the pasture inside the national park under certain restriction. The Richtersveld National Park was the first National Park in South Africa to be co-managed by the community and South African National Parks (SANP). The celebration of Nama traditions was part of the opening ceremony of the park, which was to be held in part in Nama. Being successful in resisting a national park on land where they used to communally graze showed the people from the Richtersveld that their history and traditions could be used as a resource and the fight against a national park without the local population represents the starting point for the emergence of a Nama identity (see also Sharp and Boonzaier 1994; Robins 1997).

At public meetings that are related to cultural issues, but on other occasions as well, the beginning and/or closing prayers are held in Nama. At the official opening of a new plant at the Trans Hex Mining Company at Baken (close to Sanddrift), one woman from Kuboes was asked to recite a praise-song in Nama in honour of the Minister of the Northern Cape, Mr. Manne Dipico, who was present as well.[36] The Trans Hex employee responsible for community liaison provided the woman with an English version of the Minister's vita, to be translated first by a Kuboes teacher into Afrikaans and then by the woman into Nama. She was approached to do this praise-song because she is one of the people who is very engaged in the promotion of the tradition, and is also member of the KSNLB. The Richtersveld community is claiming rights to land and is currently engaged in negotiations with Trans Hex. In my view, Trans Hex wanted to stress the good relations with the local community and to demonstrate its recognition of the Nama culture.

The most spectacular case of using Nama in the public sphere was in October 2000 in the Land Claims Court of South Africa, Cape Town. The Richtersveld community claimed land along the southern banks of the !Gariep (Nama name for the Orange River) and along the Atlantic coast, which includes the state-owned diamond mine Alexkor. In archival sources and accounts by early travellers and government officials (Alexander 1838; Backhouse 1844; Bell 1854; Melville 1890; Cullinan 1992; see also Hoernlé 1985 [1913]), the people originally living on this land were identified as Nama (Hottentots). At an earlier court hearing at the Magistrate's Court in Wynberg in 1999, Richtersvelders had already bid in Nama before the beginning of the case, which was very moving (pers. comm., Henk Smith). At the Land Claims Court in 2000, several community members were heard as witnesses to present their oral traditions about the occupation and usage of the land and their eviction. They had the opportunity to testify in Nama. This was the first time a Nama testimony was heard in front of a South African court. Due to the fact that there was no qualified professional interpreter

---

[36] It is a Nama tradition to recite praise songs in honour of any person. According to Richtersvelders, this old tradition is also on the decline.

working at the court, a Namibian-born Nama, who is a teacher in Cape Town, was sworn in as an official translator for the hearing. The witnesses not only talked about their relation to the claimed land, but by speaking Nama they also established a link to the indigenous inhabitants who stayed there. They gave living evidence of the continuity between themselves and the Nama who lived on the respective land, which supported their claim to the land. The reason to testify in Nama was twofold: On the one hand, the main witnesses (ages 59 and 89) were more fluent and confident in Nama than in Afrikaans, especially as they provided information about traditions, former places of occupation and their Nama names. As the previous sections have shown, people usually talk about these topics in Nama. On the other hand, however, the use of Nama was also to be viewed as a statement and was used strategically to emphasise the claim.

Impact of Actions to Promote Nama

The South African national language policy and the actions undertaken by PANSALB had a positive impact on the local level insofar as creating awareness for language issues. People realised that the government is interested in developing Nama and other indigenous languages, and they were pleased that somebody had started to care about their language.

With the formation of the KSNLB, people in the Richtersveld felt they were being taken seriously by the government in their endeavour to promote their language. Representatives from the community were put in charge of communicating the respective needs of the community to people in the political arena. Subcommittees were founded to work in the community and promote the use of the language. The outcomes of the KSNLB's work are twofold: On the individual level, members of the KSNLB have the opportunity of participating in workshops, strengthening their own capacities, and being able to get in touch with government officials and indigenous people from other areas. But the community as a whole also benefits from the KSNLB, as it helped to allocate money to the school and raise general awareness for language issues in the public eye. However, there was also discontent concerning the KSNLB. Complaints were lodged about how people were selected to work on the KSNLB, as the procedure was not totally transparent. And indeed, only those people who had contacts with NGO members or other external actors got the opportunity of being selected in the first place and then to travel to Upington to attend the interviews conducted by PANSALB. More serious, however, were complaints about the representatives not reporting to the community on their activities, not trying to get the mandate for decision making and not implementing practices that would promote the language. For example, adults were interested in improving literacy in Nama and demanded evening classes to give them the opportunity to learn to read and write. It was expected that the KSNLB should fund a teacher, which did not happen because of constrains imposed by the structure of KSNLB. These occurrences led to disappointment in the community, as they considered that the KSNLB worked to slowly. But one has to bear in mind that this structure has only been working for a short time.

The KSNLB has established a good working relationship with the school in Kuboes, and the striving to promote the language is always combined with the call to introduce Nama into the school. The Richtersveld was designated as the location for the first school to have a Khoisan language be introduced into the curriculum: Firstly, Nama is a written language and extensive learning materials already exist in Namibia, and secondly, there are many Nama speakers in the area.

Nama has been taught as a subject at the Kuboes primary school since 1999. Due to the lack of a qualified teacher, a formally unqualified man from Riemvasmaak came to the Richtersveld.[37] Later on, he received educational training in Namibia, and he is now teaching Nama for all pupils from grades 1 to 7 at the school in Kuboes. He has been supported by a second man from Riemvasmaak since mid-2001. Only in the beginning were there problems relating to the dialect he speaks. Children argued with their parents about 'correct' Nama, as the teacher taught them a slightly different Nama than what is spoken by the adults in the Richtersveld. One problem the teachers face is the lack of teaching material for Nama as a second language. The only existing learning material (to be imported from Namibia) has been designed for Nama as the first language, as it is taught there at that level. However, as the mother tongue of children in the Richtersveld is Afrikaans, this material has to be adapted. Even if Nama sounds familiar to the children, many of them have to learn it as a foreign language.

Most of the people in Kuboes have positive feelings about Nama at school and see its introduction as a part of the broader aim to revitalise Nama culture in Kuboes. The growing community interest in the traditional

---

[37] There was another teacher from Namibia before him, but she only stayed for a very brief time. Riemvasmaak is situated further up the !Gariep, Northern Cape. People were forcibly removed to Namibia in 1974 and came back to South Africa in 1995. As Nama is used in Namibian primary schools, people from Riemvasmaak could become literate in Nama there. The only qualified Nama teacher in South Africa also comes from Riemvasmaak.

culture and language manifests itself not only in the project to introduce Nama as a school subject, but also in the large number of other activities at the school level, thanks to the commitment of the school principal and community members. The school has become one place where pride in the traditional culture is sustained and promoted. Children learn about the Richtersveld in history classes, they do traditional handicrafts, and they have the opportunity to join the Nama choir or the *Namastap* Dance Group. As early as 1994, two women started training pupils in the traditional Namastap dance to send them to perform at the Golden Gate National Park, South Africa. The Nama culture is on display in other areas as well, and children travel a lot in South Africa, Namibia and even Turkey to present their culture to other people. They identify themselves with being 'Nama', which was not the case ten years ago. Therefore, the revival of a Nama identity has led to the demand to introduce Nama as a subject at school, but vice versa, the commitment of the school to promote Nama has further reinforced the pride in the traditional culture.

However, it has to be noted that this 'traditional culture' is, to a certain degree, constructed. People in the Richtersveld choose the elements they want to stress as typical Nama and that they consider will 'sell'. These markers of Nama ethnicity are language, special clothes, crafts, dance, music and songs or initiation rites, performed for tourists and film-crews. One young woman in Kuboes criticised this simplification of tradition and rejected being Nama, as in her view there are no Namas anymore:

> I am not a Nama, and they aren't Nama either, there are no Namas anymore, these people who today say they are Nama, they aren't, the great old Nama are extinct. If they want to be Nama, why don't they stay in mat-houses like the old Nama? If they are Nama, why do they cook on a gas stove? They don't want to live this old lifestyle. They just dance and wear these patchwork skirts, and then they think they are Nama, no man! (E.C., 8.6.1999)

Conclusion

Nama is an endangered language in South Africa due to a long history of suppression that began in colonial times and was aggravated by the Apartheid doctrine. The languages of Khoisan-speaking people were considered useless or nonexistent by the state, and the people themselves adopted a negative attitude towards Nama and saw some advantages in 'being Coloured' and speaking Afrikaans. They rejected the use of Nama in favour of Afrikaans. Recently, this decline in the use of Nama seems to be reversed as the language regains status and people rediscover their Nama identity. People are regaining interest in and promoting their languages, which are used as a marker and proof of identity: By speaking Nama, people establish their affiliation to the group and prove their authenticity as aboriginal inhabitants of South Africa. Identity is constructed primarily with reference to language, and by being Nama, people have options for gaining self-esteem and recognition in the state and to get access to resources.

There are various factors involved that led to the promotion of Nama and other Khoisan languages in South Africa. On the one hand, the political framework in which language policy and identity formation takes place plays an important role. In the aftermath of Apartheid, South Africa has undergone major changes towards being a state based on equality, human dignity and human rights, and the options for language policy changed dramatically. Language rights are seen as human rights, and documents released by PANSALB and DACST stress the value of languages and multilingualism as a resource, with the view that languages retain knowledge that is lost if the language dies out. However, in South African political language debates, there is also the position that multilingualism is a problem. Some people favour a monolingual solution and choose English as a dominant language. In fact, English is already dominant at least at the governmental level and also in the media (see du Plessis 2000; Strydom and Pretorius 2000; Maphalala 2000; Alexander and Heugh 2001). The hegemony of English is related to the fact that it is a language that enables international communication. Further, it has the connotation of being the 'language of liberation' favoured by the leadership of the oppressed people in South Africa.

On the other hand, it is the speakers themselves who promote Khoisan languages, both supported and constrained by the political framework. In the end, they are the only ones able to prevent their languages from being endangered. On the local level, many people in the Richtersveld have started to revitalise and promote Nama as part of a broader movement to stress their Nama identity and to regain esteem for their traditions and their history. From the 1990s, Nama identity has re-emerged in the Richtersveld. People have started to perform traditional dances and music and try to attract public interest; tourists and film-crews being their main audience. They speak and promote Nama, and have succeeded in having it taught at one school as a second language. However, the 'traditional Nama culture' that is on display now is a combination of selected elements of culture, some of which are practiced in everyday life, others only on special occasions. In addition to language, profound knowledge about the environment, sustainable land use practices, initiation rites, crafts and traditional dances and dress are such selected parts of 'traditional Nama culture'. But even if Nama proficiency varies in the community, and, in fact, many children are only passively if at all bilingual, the language and other elements of culture have never vanished. There is continuity, even if some elements were hidden, or de-emphasised and not shared by everybody.

Reasons for the promotion of Nama language and identity have different dimensions. On the one hand, there are material ones. The language can be strategically used to express an ethnic identity, and thus to claim rights as an indigenous group and to get access to resources. Richtersveld people were, for example, successful in acquiring the co-management of the Richtersveld National Park by referring to their Nama roots and the sustainability of their traditional land use practices. They are further engaged in an aboriginal land claim to diamond-rich land in the Richtersveld region, referring to continuity between themselves and the dispossessed inhabitants of the area. They are trying to get resources for additional teachers who can teach Nama to children (and adults). Applications are made for subsidies to cover expenses for children and adults to travel to cultural events. Richtersvelders aim at attracting tourists by displaying 'typical Nama culture' to generate income. But on the other hand, the revival of the language combined with the revitalisation of other elements of 'traditional culture' also have a psychological effect on the well-being of the people. Their self-esteem is much higher and most of them are very content that they, as a people, are recognised by the government and are no longer invisible. The introduction of Nama in the Kuboes school and the formation of the KSNLB were symbols for success in regaining recognition and revitalising Nama identity.

However, stressing Nama identity does not mean rejecting a national identity as South Africans. People in the Richtersveld, as everywhere, oscillate between multiple identities, depending on the context and purpose. They are Nama when they want to re-establish self-respect, to claim access to resources, to promote language rights or to attract tourists. They are Richtersvelders when they claim rights to land. They are marginalised indigenous people when they form alliances with other speakers of indigenous languages not recognised by the South African constitution in order to claim official status for their languages.[38] They are South Africans

---

[38] There was, e.g., a Conference on Language Rights for Marginalised People, held in Kimberly in March 2000, organised by SASI. Representatives of Khoisan languages, sign language and non-official Bantu languages attended this conference.

when they stress their citizenship, get welfare payments from the state or travel to other countries. People change identities and so they switch between languages that are an instrument to express group affiliation.

References

Adam, Heribert
1995   The Politics of Ethnic Identity: Comparing South Africa. *Ethnic and Racial Studies* 18(3):457-475.

Alexander, Neville
1995   'The Moment of Manoeuvre': 'Race', Ethnicity and Nation in Post-Apartheid South Africa. *South Asia Bulletin. Comparative Studies of South Asia, Africa and the Middle East* 15(1):5-11.

Alexander, Neville, and Kathleen Heugh
2001   Language Policy in the New South Africa. In: R. Kriger and A. Zegeye (eds.) *Culture in the New South Africa. After Apartheid – Volume Two.* Cape Town and Maroelana: Kwela Books and SA History Online:15-39.

Alexander, Sir James Edward
1838   *An Expedition of Discovery into the Interior of Africa, Through the Hitherto Undescribed Countries of the Great Namaquas, Boschmans, and Hill Damaras in Two Volumes.* London: Henry Colburn.

Allan, Keith, and Kate Burridge
1991   *Euphemism and Dysphemism. Language as Shield and Weapon.* New York: Oxford University Press.

Appel, René, and Pieter Muysken
1990   *Language Contact and Bilingualism.* London: Edward Arnold.

Auer, Peter (ed.)
1998   *Code-switching in Conversation. Language, Interaction and Identity.* London, New York: Routledge.

Backhouse, James
1844   *A Narrative of a Visit to the Mauritius and South Africa.* London: Hamilton, Adams and Co.

Barnard, Alan
1992 *Hunters and Herders of Southern Africa. A Comparative Ethnography of the Khoisan Peoples.* Cambridge: Cambridge University Press.

Bell, Charles D.
1854 *Report of the Surveyor-General Charles D. Bell on the Copper Fields of Little Namaqualand, 19 December 1854.* Cape Town.

Bollig, Michael, and Susanne Berzborn
2002 *Global Indigenous Peoples' Movements and Their Effects on the Local Level. The Influence of NGOs on Ethnicity and Land Rights in Southern Africa.* Paper presented at a Symposium on "Local Vitality and the Localisation of the Global", Bayreuth, June 2002.

Boonzaier, Emile, Candy Malherbe, Andy Smith, and Penny Berens
1996 *The Cape Herders. A History of the Khoikhoi of Southern Africa.* Cape Town & Johannesburg: David Philip.

Brenzinger, Matthias
1992 *Language Death. Factual and Theoretical Explorations with Special Reference to East Africa.* Berlin, New York: Mouton de Gruyter.

2002 *Safeguarding Endangered Languages.* Paper presented at the International Mother Language Day, February 2002. UNESCO, Paris.

Burger, Delien
2001 *South Africa Yearbook 2000/2001:* STE Publishers.

Crawhall, Nigel
1997 *Results of Consultations with San and Khoe Communities in Gordonia, Namaqualand and Bushmanland. South African San Institute's Third Submission to the Pan South African Language Board,* pp. 52.

1999 San and Khoe Rights, Identity and Language Survival in South Africa. In: G. Maharaj (ed.) *Between Unity and Diversity. Essays on Nation-Building in Post-Apartheid South Africa.* Cape Town: Idasa:33-57.

Crystal, David
1997   Vanishing Languages: When the Last Speakers Go, They Take With
        Them Their History and Culture. *Civilization (Library of Congress)*
        Feb-Mar:40-45.

2000   *Language Death*. Cambridge: Cambridge University Press.

Cullinan, Patrick
1992   *Robert Jacob Gordon 1743-1795. The Man and his Travels at the
        Cape*. Cape Town.

du Plessis, Theo
2000   South Africa: From Two to Eleven Official Languages. In: K.
        Deprez and T. d. Plessis (eds.) *Multilingualism and Government.
        Belgium, Luxembourg, Switzerland, Former Yugoslavia, South
        Africa*. Pretoria: Van Schaik Publishers:95-110.

Erasmus, Zimitri, and Edgar Pieterse
1999   Conceptualising Coloured Identities in the Western Cape Province of
        South Africa. In: M. Palmberg (ed.) *National Identity and
        Democracy in Africa*. Pretoria: Human Sciences Research Council of
        South Africa and Mayibuye Centre at the University of the Western
        Cape:167-187.

Giles, Howard (ed.)
1977   *Language, Ethnicity and Intergroup Relations*. London: Academic
        Press.

Gordon, Robert J.
1992   *The Bushman Myth : the Making of a Namibian Underclass*. Conflict
        and Social Change Series. Boulder: Westview Press.

Greenberg, Joseph
1963   *The Languages of Africa*. The Hague: Mouton.

Güldemann, Tom, and Rainer Vossen
2000   Khoisan. In: B. Heine and D. Nurse (eds.) *African Languages. An
        Introduction*. Cambridge: Cambridge University Press:99-122.

Günther, Mathias
1986   'San' or 'Bushmen'? In: M. Biesele, R. Gordon, and R. Lee (eds.)
        *The Past and Future of !Kung Ethnography: Critical Reflections and
        Symbolic Perspectives. Essays in Honour of Lorna Marshall*.
        Hamburg: Buske:27-51.

Haacke, Wilfrid H.G., and Eliphas Eiseb
1999   *Khoekhoegowab-English. English-Khoekhoegowab. Glossary/Mîdi Saogub*. Windhoek: Gamsberg Macmillan.

Hoernlé, Winifred
1985 [1913]   Richtersveld: The Land and its People. In: P. Carstens (ed.) *The Social Organization of the Nama and other Essays by Winifred Hoernlé*. Johannesburg: Witwatersrand University Press:20-38.

Hohmann, Thekla
2000   *Transformationen kommunalen Ressourcenmanagements im Tsumkwe Distrikt (Nordost-Namibia)*. Unpublished M.A. Thesis.

ILO, International Labour Office
1999   *Indigenous Peoples of South Africa: Current Trends. Project for the Rights of Indigenous and Tribal Peoples*, pp. 47. Geneva: ILO.

Jolly, Pieter
1996   Between the Lines: Some Remarks on 'Bushmen' Ethnicity. In: P. Skotnes (ed.) *Miscast: Negotiating the Presence of the Bushmen*. Cape Town: UCT Press:197-209.

Kamwangamalu, Nkonko M. (ed.)
2000   *Language and Ethnicity in the New South Africa. International Journal of the Sociology of Language*. Berlin and New York: Mouton de Gruyter.

Klocke-Daffa, Sabine
2001   *„Wenn du hast, mußt du geben" – Soziale Sicherung im Ritus und im Alltag bei den Nama von Berseba/Namibia*. Studien zur sozialen und rituellen Morphologie, Bd. 3. Münster: LIT.

Kotzé, Ernst F.
2000   Sociocultural and Linguistic Corollaries of Ethnicity in South African Society. *International Journal of the Sociology of Language* 144:7-17.

Kriger, Robert, and Abebe Zegeye (eds.)
2001   *Culture in the New South Africa. After Apartheid – Volume Two*. Cape Town and Maroelana: Kwela Books and SA History Online.

Maharaj, Gitanjali (ed.)
1999   *Between Unity and Diversity. Essays on Nation-Building in Post-Apartheid South Africa*. Cape Town: Idasa.

Maphalala, Jabulani
2000   Public Policy and African Languages: the Case of isiZulu. In: K.
       Deprez and T. du Plessis (eds.) *Multilingualism and Government.*
       Belgium, Luxembourg, Switzerland, Former Yugoslavia, South
       Africa. Pretoria: Van Schaik Publishers:148-156.

Marivate, Cynthia
2000   The Mission and Activities of the Pan South African Language
       Board. In: K. Deprez and T. d. Plessis (eds.) *Multilingualism and*
       Government. *Belgium, Luxembourg, Switzerland, Former*
       Yugoslavia, South Africa. Pretoria: Van Schaik Publishers:130-137.

Martin, Denis-Constant
2001   What's in the Name "Coloured"? In: A. Zegeye (ed.) *Social*
       Identities in the New South Africa. After Apartheid – Volume One.
       Cape Town and Maroelana: Kwela Books and SA History
       Online:249-267.

Mbeki, Thabo
1996   *Statement of Deputy President Thabo Mbeki, on Behalf of the*
       African National Congress, on the Occasion of the Adoption by the
       Constitutional Assembly of "The Republic of South Africa
       Constitution Bill 1996", Cape Town, May 8, 1996.

Melville, S.
1890   *Report on the Lands in Namaqualand Set Apart for the Occupation*
       of Natives and Others, 1890. Cape Town.

Meyer, G., and G.L. von Heerde
1944   *Johan Frederik Hein en die sendingsgemeente Richtersveld.* p. 8.

Milroy, Lesley, and Pieter Muysken (eds.)
1995   *One Speaker, two Languages. Cross-disciplinary Perspectives on*
       Code-Switching. Cambridge: Cambridge University Press.

Mkhulisi, Nonhlanhla
2000   The National Language Service and the New Language Policy. In:
       K. Deprez and T. d. Plessis (eds.) *Multilingualism and Government.*
       Belgium, Luxembourg, Switzerland, Former Yugoslavia, South
       Africa. Pretoria: Van Schaik Publishers:121-129.

Palmberg, Mai (ed.)
1999   *National Identity and Democracy in Africa.* Pretoria: Human
       Sciences Research Council of South Africa and Mayibuye Centre at
       the University of the Western Cape.

PANSALB
1998   *PANSALB's Position on the Promotion of Multilingualism in South Africa. A Draft Discussion Document*, p. 10. Pretoria.

PANSALB
1999   *Khoe and San Reclaim their Linguistic Dignity.* PANSALB News. Vol. September 1999.

Pickel, Birgit
1997   *Coloured Ethnicity and Identity. A Case Study in the Former Coloured Areas in the Western Cape/South Africa.* Demokratie und Entwicklung; Bd. 28. Hamburg: LIT.

Robins, Steven
1997   Transgressing the Borderlands of Tradition and Modernity: Identity, Cultural Hybridity and Land Struggles in Namaqualand (1980-94). *Journal of Contemporary African Studies* 15(1):23-43.

Robins, Steven
2001   Citizen and 'Bushmen': The ‡Khomani San Land Claim and the Politics of Citizenship and 'Community' in the Kalahari. *Journal of Southern African Studies* 27(4).

Robins, Steven, Elias Madzudzo, and Matthias Brenzinger
2001   *An Assessment of the Status of the San in South Africa, Angola, Zambia and Zimbabwe.* Regional Assessment of the Status of the San in Southern Africa. Report Series. Report No 2 of 5. Windhoek: Legal Assistance Centre.

Saunders, Christopher, and Nicholas Southey
2001   *A Dictionary of South Africa History.* Cape Town & Johannesburg: David Philip.

Schapera, Isaac
1930   *The Khoisan Peoples of South Africa. Bushmen and Hottentots.* London: Routledge & Kegan Paul Ltd.

Sharp, John, and Emile Boonzaier
1994   Ethnic Identity as Performance: Lessons From Namaqualand. *Journal of Southern African Studies* 20(3):405-415.

Sigrühn, Amanda, and Jennifer Hays
2001   *Implementation Plan for Pilot Projects for the Khoe and San Languages in Schools in the Northern Cape Province. Report for the Northern Cape Education Department.* pp. 45.

Skutnabb-Kangas, Tove
2000   *Linguistic Genocide in Education – or Worldwide Diversity and Human Rights?* Mahwah-New Jersey: Lawrence Erlbaum Associates.

Strassberger, Elfriede
1969   *The Rhenish Mission Society in South Africa. 1830-1950.* Cape Town: C. Struik Ltd.

Strydom, Hennie, and Loot Pretorius
2000   On the Directives Concerning Language in the New South African Constitution. In: K. Deprez and T. d. Plessis (eds.) *Multilingualism and Government. Belgium, Luxembourg, Switzerland, Former Yugoslavia, South Africa.* Pretoria: Van Schaik Publishers:111-120.

UNESCO
2000   *World Culture Report 2000 Calls for Preservation of Intangible Cultural Heritage. UNESCO Press release No. 2000-120.* Paris.

UNESCO
2002   *Linguistic Diversity: 3.000 Languages in Danger. UNESCO Press Release No. 2002-07.* Paris.

Webley, Lita
1997   Jakkalsberg A and B: The Cultural Material from Two Pastoralist Sites in the Richtersveld, Northern Cape. *Southern African Field Archaeology* 6(1):3-19.

Widlok, Thomas
1999   *Living on Mangetti: 'Bushman' Autonomy and Namibian Independence.* Oxford Studies in Social and Cultural Anthropology. Oxford: Oxford University Press.

Wurm, Stephen A.
2001   Atlas of the World's Languages in Danger of Disappearing. Paris: UNESCO.

Zegeye, Abebe (ed.)
2001   *Social Identities in the New South Africa. After Apartheid – Volume One.* Cape Town and Maroelana: Kwela Books and SA History Online.

NGOs, 'Bushmen' and Double Vision: The ǂkhomani San Land Claim and the Cultural Politics of 'Community' and 'Development' in the Kalahari[1]

Steven Robins[2]

This article focuses on the ambiguities and contradictions of donor and NGO development discourses in relation to local constructions of 'community', cultural authenticity and San identity. It deals specifically with the cultural politics of the successful 1999 ǂkhomani San land claim in the Northern Cape Province of South Africa. The study investigates local responses to state, NGO and donor discourses on indigenous identity and 'cultural survival'. It shows how strategic narratives of community solidarity, social cohesion and cultural continuity, were produced by claimants and their lawyers during this process. In the post-settlement period, however, social fragmentation and intra-community conflict between 'traditionalists' and 'western bushmen' became increasingly evident. These conflicts drew attention to the difficulties of creating community solidarity and viable livelihood strategies in a province characterised by massive

---

[1] The editor would like to thank the editors of the Journal of Southern African Studies for their kind permission to reprint Steven Robins' article of 2001: 'NGO's 'Bushmen' and 'Double Vision': The ǂKhomani San Land Claim and the Cultural Politics of 'Community' and 'Development' in the Kalahari. *Journal of Southern African Studies* Vol. 27 (4):833-853. See for further reading the journal's homepage: http://www.tandf.co.uk.

[2] I wish to thank Professor Ben Cousins, Director of the Programme for Land & Agrarian Studies (PLAAS) for his unstinting support in the research and writing process. The contributions of the UWC-Bergen Universities Admin South Africa Project, the Acacia Project, Cologne University, and the African/Caribbean/Pacific-European Union (APC-EU) are also hereby acknowledged . Thanks to Roger Chennels and Nigel Crawhall for friendship, insights and conversations in the field, and to James Suzman, Shula Marks, Bruce Kapferer, Ciraj Rassool, Andrew Bank, Lauren Muller, William Ellis, Jattie Bredenkamp, John Sharp, Michael Bollig, Bill Derman, Jocelyn Alexander, and the anonymous reviewers for their support, editorial interventions, and comments on earlier versions of this paper. Thanks also go to Dawid Kruiper and Petrus Vaalbooi and numerous other ǂkhomani San members for generosity and hospitality to yet another anthropologist in a long lineage of inquisitive, and at times intrusive, researchers.

unemployment and rural poverty. The paper suggests that these divisions were also a product of the contradictory objectives of NGOs and donors to provide support for traditional leadership, San language and 'cultural survival', and to inculcate modern/western ideas and democratic practices. Furthermore, despite the thoroughly hybridised character of contemporary San identity, knowledge and practices, San traditionalists appeared to stabilise 'bushman' identity by recourse to notions of a 'detribalised Other' – the 'western bushmen' living in their midst. It is evident, however, that the 'traditionalist' versus 'western bushman' dichotomy is itself at the heart of donor and NGO development agendas. Consequently, the donor double vision of the San – as both 'First Peoples' and modern citizens-in-the-making – contributed to these intra-community divisions and conflict.

Introduction

During the ǂkhomani San land claim process of the mid-1990s the San claimants appeared in the media as a highly cohesive and consensual community with a common cultural heritage and continuity. Media representations of the San land claim process comprised a series of stereotypical images of timeless and primordialist San 'tribes' reclaiming their ancestral land. Deputy President Thabo Mbeki's speech on 22 March 1999 at the Human Rights Day celebration of the signing of the historic land restitution agreement was optimistic that the return of the land to the ǂkhomani San would heal the wounds of the past. Mbeki spoke of the dreams of a return from exile for the ǂkhomani San claimants, who had been scattered across the Northern Cape, living in rural ghettos and in poverty in communal areas and on white farms:

> We shall mend the broken strings of the distant past so that our dreams can take root. For the stories of the Khoe and the San have told us that this dream is too big for one person to hold. It is a dream that must be dreamed collectively, by all the people. It is by that acting together, by that dreaming together, by mending the broken strings that tore us apart in the past, that we shall produce a better life for you who have been the worst victims of oppression.[3]

---

[3] Statement of then Deputy President Thabo Mbeki, on behalf of the African National Congress, on the occasion of the adoption by the Constitutional

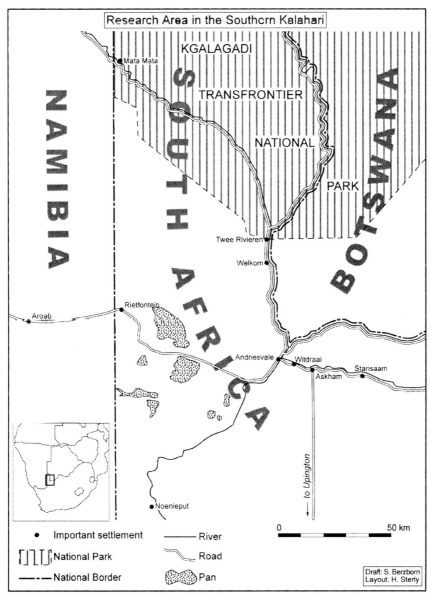

Map 1: Research area in the Southern Kalahari

Assembly of the Republic of South Africa Constitutional Bill, Cape Town, 8 May 1996 (see Hadland and Ratao 1999:154).

Subsequent to the successful resolution of the land claim in 1999, these optimistic 'bushman' images and narratives were replaced by front-page Cape Times reports of conflict, homicide, suicide, alcohol abuse, AIDS, and social fragmentation at the new San settlements adjacent to the Kalahari Gemsbok National Park, Northern Cape Province.[4] Reports also focused on allegations of financial mismanagement by the ≠khomani San Communal Property Association and divisive leadership struggles.[5] A striking aspect of these conflicts was the emergence of intra-community tensions between the self-designated 'traditionalists' and the 'western' bushmen at the new settlement area. This divide drew on markers of cultural authenticity that included genealogies, language, 'bush knowledge', bodily appearance, clothing and so on. These tensions, only a year after the land signing ceremony, raised a number of troubling questions. Why had what was widely perceived to be a cohesive and 'harmonious' San community so quickly come to be seen as a deeply fractured group of individuals struggling to constitute themselves as a community? Was the notion of San community and solidarity a strategic fiction fashioned by the San and their NGO allies during the land claims process? What happened in the post-settlement phase to unleash processes that undermined this prior appearance of solidarity? In other words, how could one explain the dramatic shift from media celebrations of a pristine and consensual hunter-gatherer culture in March 1999, to the more sober, and at times quite grim, journalistic descriptions of the Kalahari San settlement a year later. Finally, why did local constructions of a 'great divide' between 'traditional' and 'western' bushmen emerge when they did? In attempting to answer these questions I became increasingly interested in the roles of NGOs in local political processes, in mediating representations of the San, and in brokering global discourses on 'civil society', 'cultural survival' and indigenous people's rights. Fieldwork encounters in the Kalahari San settlement in 1999 drew my attention to the effects of these donor and NGO discourses on local constructions of 'community', cultural authenticity and identity in the Kalahari. It appeared that, despite these local constructions of a 'Great Divide' between 'traditionalists' and 'western bushmen', none of the Kalahari San fitted the mould of indigenous people untouched by modernity, neither were they modern citizens completely moulded by discourses of western democracy and liberal individualism. Instead, San identities, local knowledge and

---

[4] Cape Times, 5 May 2000.
[5] Cape Times, 5 May 2000.

everyday practices were com-posed of hybrid discourses. This begged the question as to how this 'Great Divide' had emerged.

This line of inquiry raised further questions concerning the impact of the contradictory objectives of NGOs and donors to provide support for traditional leadership, San language and 'cultural survival', and to inculcate modern/western ideas and practices of democratic decision-making, proceduralism and accountability. It began to appear as if the 'traditionalist' versus 'western bushman' dichotomy in the Kalahari was itself partly a result of this contradiction and ambiguity at the heart of donor and NGO development agendas. Could these donor double visions of the San – as both 'First Peoples' and citizens-in-the making – be a catalyst for these intra-community divisions? The article investigates how these global discourses on indigeneity and democracy are brokered by an NGO, the South African San Institute, and reappropriated and reconfigured 'from below' by San communities. It draws attention to the ambiguities and contradictions embedded within these development discourses on San tradition and civic citizenship, and examines how this contributed towards intra-community divisions and leadership struggles within a hypermarginalised ‡khomani San community. These leadership struggles and divisions also draw attention to the problematic ways in which notions of San tradition and 'First People' status can be deployed as strategies of exclusion that promote intra-community division. It appeared that, despite the thoroughly hybridised character of contemporary San identity, knowledge and practices, San traditionalists sought to stabilise bushman identity through recourse to notions of a 'detribalised Other', the 'western bushmen' living in their midst. These socially divisive processes draw attention to the problematic colonial legacy of the dichotomy between modernity and tradition. Within this dichotomous framework, modernity continues to be associated with progress, development, 'the West', science and technology, high standards of living, rationality and order, while tradition is associated with stasis, stagnation, underdevelopment, poverty, superstition and disorder. Although the divisions and conflicts referred to above seemed to be shaped by these binary conceptual grids, the everyday practices and experiences of the San did not . t the neat dichotomy of 'modern' and 'traditional'. In other words, their knowledge and practices could not be reduced to the modern, western and scientific, nor could they be simply deduced on the basis of indigenous knowledge alone. The hybridised conditions of everyday life in the Kalahari include 'local' knowledge, practices and identities as well as San access to 'exogenous' cyber-technologies, fax machines, cellular phones and

international indigenous peoples' conferences and conventions in Europe
and North America. This hybridity draws attention to the existence of what
some scholars refer to as indigenous modernities[6] that implode traditional
versus modern dichotomies. This paper aims to bring these theoretical
debates to a growing literature on San historics and identities in southern
Africa,[7] and on anthropological studies of indigenous people, NGOs and
'civic society' in Africa.[8] It also aims to contribute towards studies of the
cultural politics of land restitution in South Africa after apartheid.[9] The
cultural politics of 'indigenous' identity discussed in this paper only became
publicly visible in South Africa in the 1990s. Unlike the situation of
indigenous groups, such as the Pan-Mayan Movement in Guatemala, where
about 60 per cent of the population are said to have an indigenous
background, San and Nama 'ethnic revitalisation' has been confined to
relatively small numbers of people, mostly from the Northern Cape
Province.[10] The South African San Institute (SASI) was established in the
early 1990s as the first, and only, NGO in South Africa dealing with
indigenous issues. SASI was established by a human rights lawyer, Roger
Chennels, who, in the late 1980s, became involved in attempts to negotiate
improved labour conditions for San farm workers at the Kagga Kamma
'bushman' tourist village at Ceres, a few hundred kilometres from Cape
Town.[11] Chennels soon realised that the ‡khomani San community was in a
strong position to succeed in a land claim. Since the San had been forcibly
removed from the Kalahari Gemsbok National Park (KGNP), as a direct
result of racial legislation implemented after the 1913 cut-off date, their

---

[6]   Gupta 1998; Povinelli 1999; Povinelli 1999; and Sahlins 1999.

[7]   There is a vast literature on San communities in Namibia and Botswana that
addresses similar issues to the South African situation. Examples of this
extensive literature include Lee 1979; Lee 1984; Wilmsen 1989; Gordon 1992;
Hitchcock 1982; and Hitchcock 1987. This paper, however, will be restricted to
the case of a specific San community in the Northern Cape Province in South
Africa. The following references draw attention to a burgeoning literature on
Khoi and San issues in South Africa: Boonzaier 1992; Boonzaier and Sharp
1994; Rassool 1999; Rassool and Hayes 2001; Robins 1997; Sharp 1984; Sharp
1994; Sharp and Douglas 1996; and White 1995.

[8]   Garland 1999.

[9]   James 2000a; James 2000b; and Robins 2000.

[10] The concept of 'ethnic revitalization' appeared in Anthony Wallace 1956.

[11] See White 1995.

claim would be taken seriously by the Commission for Land Rights and Restitution. The preparations for the land claim initiated a process of San cultural 'revitalisation' that was later to be spearheaded by SASI. During the 1980s, anti-apartheid activists and rural NGOs had focused on populist class-based forms of political mobilisation and popular land struggles rather than 'cultural' struggles.[12] These NGOs were often af. liated with the United Democratic Front (UDF) and formed part of a broad Left coalition of trade unions and civic organisations. Intellectuals in the popular Left tended to be dismissive of 'cultural' struggles and ethnic mobilisation strategies, which were regarded as playing into the hands of apartheid 'divide and rule' policies. From the perspective of many Left intellectuals in the universities,[13] labour unions, and political organisations such as the Unity Movement, the South African Communist Party (SACP), Pan Africanist Congress (PAC) and the African National Congress (ANC), ethnicity and 'tribalism'[14] constituted forms of 'false consciousness' promoted and abetted by Pretoria's architects of the 'homelands' and 'Separate Development' policies. The end of apartheid, along with the retreat of socialism and class-based mass mobilisation, meant that there was virtually no opposition from the Left, or from the state for that matter, to the 'cultural' struggles of San people in South Africa. In fact, ethnicity and race had come to replace class as the keywords of the new official political discourse. There was no significant state opposition to SASI's intimate involvement with international donors, NGOs and indigenous organisations that actively promoted self-determination and cultural rights for indigenous peoples. It was within this dramatically changed political landscape that 'indigenous' Nama, San and Griqua ethnic revitalisation movements took place. The 1990s ushered in new intellectual and political challenges to Left-leaning anthropologists who subscribed to Marxist arguments about the primacy of class. The rise of post-structuralist and post-colonial theory, cultural studies and 'the literary turn', strengthened Marxist and post-Marxist arguments concerning 'the relative autonomy of culture' (and identity). This challenged notions of the base/superstructure dichotomy and the idea that ethnicity could be reduced to 'false consciousness', or the mere superstructural reflection of the underlying material base. However, as Shula Marks correctly points out, not all South African Marxists subscribed to a crude

---

[12] See Warren 1998.

[13] See Magubane 1973; Mafeje 1971; and Boonzaier and Sharp (eds.) 1988.

[14] See Mafeje 1971.

vulgar materialism during the apartheid era.[15] Many historians and anthropologists, for example, drew on the work of Raymond Williams, E. P. Thompson, Maurice Godelier and Shula Mark's own work to interrogate class essentialism and material reductionism. It was within the distinctly 'post-Marxist' intellectual milieu of the 1990s that a number of South African anthropologists began to write about the 'new' Khoi and San ethnicities. This interest in 'new ethnicities' and the 'politics of difference' raised a number of ethical and political conundrums concerning the appropriate roles of anthropologists. Although anthropologists were tempted to deconstruct all essentialist claims to Khoi and San cultural continuity and authenticity, or interpret them as 'staged ethnicities' self-consciously choreographed in order to gain access to material resources, it soon became apparent that such deconstructivist strategies were too instrumentalist, rationalist and reductionist, as well as being unlikely to serve the interests of these marginalised communities (Robins 2000:56-75). These were similar dilemmas to those facing anthropologists working with indigenous peoples and ethnic revitalisation movements elsewhere in the world. Kay Warren encountered similar problems while working with Pan-Mayan cultural nationalists in Guatemala (Warren 1998:69-85). Whereas Warren felt obliged, as a savvy North American anthropologist, to deconstruct essentialist Pan-Mayan claims of cultural continuity to pre-Columbian cultural ideas and practices, the Mayan activist intellectuals that she worked with wanted her to assist them in doing research in order to strengthen these claims. Rather than simply deconstructing the Pan-Mayan project, Warren recognised the political imperatives of critically engaging with these tactics of strategic essentialism in order to further 'Mayan' struggles for language and cultural rights and the increased visibility of indigenous people in Guatemalan public life. This approach was also deemed necessary in order to draw attention to the pervasiveness of deeply embedded forms of Ladino racism, and the fact that 'Mayans' constituted a hyper-marginalised subaltern group within a monocultural and monolingual Ladino-dominated nation-state. Warren also had to contend with Left critics of Pan-Mayan cultural nationalism who claimed that the movement comprised an elite group of intellectuals who were dodging the 'real' political issues and therefore not representing the impoverished masses. Instead of engaging with the popular Left's class-based political mobilisation, they were seen to be involved in 'cultural' struggles and essentialist constructions of Mayan

---

[15] Marks, personal communication.

identity that contributed to 'Orientalist' conceptions of exotic 'Indians' (Warren 1998:41-45; 201). Both the Left and Right in Guatemala were also profoundly sceptical and suspicious of the political objectives of Pan-Mayan cultural nationalism, which were seen to encourage 'ethnic separatism' that would ultimately undermine Guatemala's precarious state of national unity and encourage 'Balkanisation'. As an anthropologist studying Pan-Mayan public intellectuals, Warren was deeply enmeshed in these complicated webs of political and intellectual argumentation. Kay Warren's strategic engagement with the troubling questions raised in public debates in Guatemala resonate with some of the dilemmas of anthropologists working with 'indigenous' communities in South Africa. Although the situations of the San and Pan- Mayan intellectuals differ from each other in many respects, they are intimately connected through co-participation in international forums and conferences on indigenous peoples. They also participate in common donor circuits and academic and NGO networks. However, unlike the Mayan case, the hyper-marginalised San do not yet have their own university-trained linguists and public intellectuals who are able to engage on equal terms in public debate with their critics. Unlike the Pan-Mayan intellectuals, the San have also not encountered critics from the Left and Right who argue that ethnic mobilisation constitutes a threat to national unity and the integrity of the nation-state, and neither is the ANC and 'the Left' openly critical of San cultural revitalisation for not addressing the 'real' material concerns of poverty and access to land. Despite these significant differences, it is worthwhile drawing on the comparative dimensions of indigenous movements. The following discussion of the micro-politics of cultural authenticity draws attention to problems faced by indigenous groups whether they are in Guatemala or South Africa. It also draws attention to issues relating to the strengths and weaknesses of arguments for or against strategic essentialism (see Robins, 2000).

The Politics of Authenticity: The 'Real Thing' or Just 'Faking It'

On 1 July 1999, only a few months after the signing of the land agreement, Roger Friedman and Benny Gool reported in the Cape Times that 'fake bushmen' were being employed at the internationally renowned 'bushman' tourist village at Kagga Kamma Nature Reserve. In an article entitled, 'Fake San on Show: The Great Bushman Tourist Scam', Friedman accused the Kagga Kamma management of 'passing off non-bushmen as the "genuine article" for the gratification of tourists'.[16] What also emerged from the article was a deepening schism between 'western' and 'traditional' bushmen at the new San resettlement adjacent to the KGNP. I too had heard NGO workers and community members refer to the growing 'western'/'traditional' bushmen divide during my visits to the Kalahari in early 1999.

The 'Great bushman tourist scam' uncovered by Friedman and Gool took place only a few months after the successful conclusion of the land claim. Following the hand-over ceremony, the ‡khomani San had decided to leave Kagga Kamma and settle at Welkom, a small settlement adjacent to the Park. After a decade of involvement in bushman tourism at Kagga Kamma they planned to establish their own tourism initiatives at their newly acquired farms. In response to the departure of the 'bushmen', the Kagga Kamma management had brought in a number of new 'bushmen' who, according to Friedman and Gool, were in reality 'coloureds' from neighbouring farms. Isak Kruiper, the ex-leader of the Kagga Kamma group and traditional head of the ‡khomani San, told the Cape Times that it was "very hurtful that the owner of Kagga Kamma is continuing to display 'bushmen' [even though] they are not there [...]. Kagga Kamma must close down or be honest with tourists and tell them that the people are coloured."[17] While the Kagga Kamma tour guide had initially told the Cape Times reporter that they had '100% pure bushmen', the owner, Heinrich de Waal, later conceded that he had offered employment to coloured farm workers, some of whom were married to 'bushmen'. According to de Waal, although it was not ethical to tell people they were 'bushmen', 'there is no such thing as a "100% bushmen"'. He justified the employment of coloured people on the grounds that the Kruiper family had left Kagga Kamma and they urgently needed to keep the bushman business running. Friedman also solicited the views of members of SASI in his quest to get to the bottom of the Kagga Kamma scandal. SASI's director accused the Kagga Kamma management of violating fair trade agreements in their use of 'fake bushmen', and Chennels stated that Kagga Kamma's use of 'pretend bushmen' was insulting to both the San and the public. However, during my numerous conversations and interviews with Chennels it became clear that he recognised the difficulties and inconsistencies that surfaced when attempting to define the exact

---

[16] Cape Times, 1 July 1999.
[17] Ibid.

boundaries of the ǂkhomani community. In fact, he pointed out that even the term ' ǂkhomani San' was being questioned in the light of recent linguistic and historical research. This concern with bushman authenticity is, of course, an age-old preoccupation that goes back to the first arrival of Europeans on African soil. The problem of classifying 'bushmen' created considerable anxiety amongst European travellers, scholars and administrators. Attempts to resolve this problem generally took the form of scientific inquiry into whether these people were 'pure products', 'fakes' or hybrids. Language, genealogies, bodily features and livelihood strategies have gone into such classificatory exercises. However, the cultural hybridity of 'bushmen' has posed enormous problems for those seeking neat and unambiguous classifications. One of the responses to such classificatory quagmires has been the anxious repetition of bushman stereotypes. Such stereotypes continue to frame images of 'bushmen' in popular culture, museum dioramas and tourist spectacles at Kagga Kamma and the San settlement near KGNP. The colonial stereotype of the pure and pristine bushman hunter and gatherer has also been embraced and articulated 'from below'. The Kruiper clan, for example, appear to have strategically deployed bushman stereotypes in order to draw a clear line between themselves as 'traditionalists' and the 'westernised' 'bushmen' in their midst.[18] This representational strategy feeds international donor conceptions of 'bushman' authenticity and it is likely to continue to influence San struggles over access to scarce resources such as land, traditional leadership offices and donor funding. It is also being used as claimants are being called upon to define the exact boundaries of the beneficiary community at their new settlement area.

Whereas donors, fly-by-night consultants and development tourists may view the ǂkhomani San as the 'pure product', as pristine hunter gatherers, NGO fieldworkers and consultants such as Roger Chennels and Nigel Crawhall[19] of SASI have a far more nuanced and complex understanding of

---

[18] Ibid.

[19] Nigel Crawhall, a socio-linguist , has been instrumental in identifying the few remaining ǂkhomani San-speakers in the Northern Cape Province. Along with the anthropologis t and . lmmaker Hugh Brody, Crawhall is currently involved in the audio-visual documentation of the language and life histories of these San speakers. Crawhall and Brody believe that these language projects, oral histories and accounts of San cultural practices are invaluable local resources that can translate into social capital. They can also function as inter-generational sources

this community. Chennels' direct interactions with the San over a period of more than a decade has allowed him to recognise the ambiguities, hybridities and contradictions of San identities and local constructions of tradition and community. Although, as their lawyer, he recognised that the land claim process required coherent and consistent narratives of cultural continuity and belonging,[20] Chennels and the San now have to grapple with the problem of competing claims regarding who is ‡khomani San and who is not. These are pragmatic questions that will determine who may or may not join the ‡khomani San Communal Property Association (CPA) and gain access to land and state resources. Chennels expects the boundaries of the ‡khomani San community to remain unstable and contested, and openly acknowledges the fraught nature and fragility of current attempts at creating a sense of community.[21] He also recognises the troubling implications of these problems for the development of viable livelihood strategies at the new San settlements. Chennels' intermediary position as a cultural broker between the San claimant community and the donors becomes apparent when he points to the difficulty of explaining this complexity to funders. Whereas donors expect to find 'real bushmen' when they visit the Kalahari, Chennels is aware that many San claimants have in the past seen themselves as 'coloureds' (kleurlinge) rather than the descendants of San hunter-gatherers:

> [They are now] landowners with 40,000 hectares of farming land, and 25,000 hectares of game reserve. They'll have to train people to do the tracking and all those things to fill that space. But probably the most major challenge is trying to make the myth that we've actually created in order to win the land claim now become a reality. It is the myth that there is a community of ‡khomani San. At the moment there is no such thing. Its a group of relations who are in the Northern Cape diaspora, and Dawid Kruiper is their symbolic leader... Many of them know that he is responsible, that's why he's got his leadership position... He stepped into a gap where there was no one before, and no one is fighting for that space. He has created the

---

of cultural transmission and thereby contribute towards social cohesion and community solidarity.

[20] For a discussion on land claims and indigenous identities see Robins 2000:56–75.

[21] Chennels, personal communication.

title, the traditional leader of the Þ khomani, and no one else challenges him... SASI's job is to actually help make their lives more meaningful, and there's a need for it. We have to try and find a way of helping the ‡khomani understand what it means to be ‡khomani. Do they give jobs only to ‡khomani people? Do they have affirmative action for ‡khomani in a ‡khomani homeland? Do they call it a homeland, a cultural homeland? How will they perceive themselves, as a tribe or a people? I think SASI's role is very much about culture and development, around the cultural imperative of actually creating a community. Because there's a landowner, a legal entity, which has not yet really been filled, it's a potential entity at this moment. So that is quite a difficult thing to tell the funders, to explain that some of the people who come to the meetings and to the elections have not actually seen a San themselves. They are actually curious. They know their grandparents spoke this language or were of San, so they have this potential affinity. They're almost like members coming to a club not quite sure whether to join. They're only going to join the club if we make it meaningful for them to join, in a way that does not threaten their 'civilized' status. That I find is the real challenge.

Whereas the original claimant community comprised 350 adults, the current numbers of the ‡khomani San community are estimated to be close to 1,000 adults spread over the Mier area in the Northern Cape, Botswana and Namibia.[22] With the growing awareness of the development and income-generation possibilities of the R15 million land claim settlement, it is to be expected that the numbers could increase further. It is as yet unclear what rules of inclusion and exclusion will be used to define rights to membership and access to ‡khomani San resources. Ultimately, it will be up to the ‡khomani San leadership to come up with the criteria for membership of the CPA. In addition, the CPA will have to develop the capacity to make decisions concerning natural resource management and so on. During 1999, however, it became clear that there were tensions between the decision-making procedures stipulated in the CPA Constitution and the ad hoc decisions of the traditional leadership, for instance Dawid Kruiper's decision to shoot a few springbok on one of the farms.

---

[22] Chennels, personal communication, 1999.

Subsequent to the land-signing ceremony, tensions intensified between the 'traditionalists' under Dawid Kruiper and the so-called western 'bushmen' under the CPA leader Petrus Vaalbooi.[23] The traditionalists called for the severance of ties with their 'westernised' relatives.[24] They even went as far as calling for the division of the San land claim area into two sections: the westernised stock farmers of the Vaalbooi group could have the farms outside the Park, and the 'traditionalist' Kruiper clan would take the 25,000 hectares inside the Park.[25] The following section discusses how this divide was itself largely a product of the dual mandate of donors and NGOs that wished both to preserve San tradition and to inculcate Western ideas about 'civil society' and democratic accountability.

The Politics of Tradition and Leadership in the Kalahari

The divergent leadership styles of the key players at KGNP heightened the divide between the 'traditionalists' and the 'westerners'. Petrus Vaalbooi, the former chairperson of the ‡khomani San CPA, is an eloquent and savvy political player. He cuts an impressive figure in national and international indigenous peoples' conference circles. Vaalbooi is just as comfortable making polite conversation with President Thabo Mbeki or negotiating with the Ministers of Constitutional Development and Land Affairs, as he is occupying the centre stage at UN indigenous peoples' forums in Geneva. Vaalbooi's political style contrasts dramatically with the more low profile and parochial traditional leader, Dawid Kruiper. Moreover, whereas Vaalbooi is a comfortable and competent participant in party political manoeuvres and development and bureaucratic discourse, Kruiper is not able to engage as productively in these power plays. In addition, while Vaalbooi has commercial livestock interests, Kruiper is perceived to be only concerned with 'the bush', cultural tourism and hunting and gathering.

The responses of various San 'insiders' and 'outsiders', including donors, NGOs and academics, to these diametrically opposed leadership practices and lifestyle orientations has contributed towards exacerbating the divide. The involvement of 'Khoisan' activists in the question of traditional leadership has also reinforced these lines of division. The tension between the decision-making processes of the CPA and traditional leadership is

---

[23] Cape Times, 16 September 1999.

[24] Ibid.

[25] Ibid.

unlikely to be easily resolved. This ambiguity, I suggest, lies at the heart of NGOs' dual mandate: to promote the 'cultural survival' of indigenous peoples and to socialise them into becoming virtuous modern citizens within a global civil society.

The traditionalist leadership have drawn on dress and language as powerful signs of authenticity and belonging in the Kalahari. For instance, the Kruiper 'traditionalists' attempted to banish 'bushmen' from entering the Witdraai settlement unless they wore the traditional skins or !xai. The handful of elderly San-speakers at Witdraai have also become the embodiment of authentic San identity, and they are regularly appropriated by competing groupings in divisive power struggles and public displays of authenticity. The three San-speaking Swartkop sisters, /Abaka Rooi, Keis Brow and /Una Rooi, for example, are often appropriated by various members of the ǂkhomani community as embodied signs and custodians of San tradition. These particular processes of cultural appropriation are also made possible by SASI's concentration on San language projects.

This focus on language has led to a situation whereby Afrikaans-speaking, western dressed livestock farmers, such as Petrus Vaalbooi and his brother, have come to be seen as 'westernised bushmen', the 'impure product'. Dawid Kruiper has also become a victim of this process since he only speaks Nama and Afrikaans. Fluency in a San language, along with 'bush knowledge' and a history of employment and residence in the Park, has become a crucial marker of San identity. It has also had a powerful influence on local community politics. Whereas Kruiper's legitimacy as a traditional leader owed much to his claim that he was raised in the Park and learnt 'bush knowledge' from his late father, Regopstaan Kruiper, this narrative was challenged by some San-speaking elders who claimed that the Nama and Afrikaans-speaking Kruiper was in Botswana at the time of the forced removals. These badges of authenticity and legitimacy continue to haunt San leaders and divide the community.

For San leaders like the Afrikaans-speaking Petrus Vaalbooi, who do not have direct access to these cultural markers, alternative legitimising strategies have to be deployed. Vaalbooi's rise to prominence as the first ǂkhomani San CPA Chairperson was largely a result of his ability to engage with development and bureaucratic discourses. Vaalbooi's strength as a leader was also due to his ability as a translator and mediator of local San issues to broader national and international audiences. It is precisely these Western-style discursive competencies that are recognised and rewarded by

NGOs and donors committed to promoting the values and democratic practices of 'civil society'. At the same time, Vaalbooi's local legitimacy was built upon the fact that he is the son of the 97 year old Elsie Vaalbooi, one of a dozen known ‡khomani San-speakers in South Africa. However, Vaalbooi's Achilles' heel was his inability to speak Nama or San, as well as his refusal to wear loincloths. In other words, the Afrikaans-speaking western-dressed Vaalbooi did not conform to popular notions of cultural authenticity embodied in the image of the primordial bushman.

While NGOs and donors tended to valorise these signs of authentic San culture – language and bodily vernacular – they also valued individuals like Vaalbooi who were able to master development and governance discourses, and who appeared to be willing to embrace the virtues of 'civil society'. The ambiguities of this 'dual mandate' – of promoting San cultural survival and the values and virtues of 'civil society' such as democratic decision-making and accountability – seemed to invoke a repetition of stereotypes about 'pure' and 'detribalised' 'bushmen' that has contributed towards the re-inscription of an artificial divide between 'traditionalist' and 'western' 'bushmen'.[26]

Hybrid Discourses and Indigenous Modernities in the Kalahari

Despite considerable evidence of the hybrid character of both NGOs discourses and the everyday practices and identities of the San themselves, advocates of modernisation and traditionalism seem to share a common discomfort with the idea of 'the hybrid'. In other words, modernisers and traditionalists alike seem to believe in the necessity for pure categories and identities. However, the attempts to constitute a purified San tradition in the Kalahari created problems for 'traditionalists' who found themselves unable to . t completely their own criteria and conceptions of authentic and pure San tradition. After all, most of them are Afrikaans and Nama-speaking former farm workers or National Parks employees with extremely tenuous ties to a hunter-gatherer existence. However, the more porous and precarious these

---

[26] Similar processes of intra-community tension emerged in the violent conflicts between 'traditionalist' hostel dwellers and militant township residents (the comrades or *amaqabane*) during the apartheid era. See Robins 1998a. Elsewhere, I have written about development discourses that elide cultural hybridities in the name of modernisation and commercialisation. See Robins 1998b; and Robins 1997.

claims on authentic San identity and tradition, the more intense the struggles to eradicate the influence of 'exogenous' forces of modernity can become. Even the most fervent San traditionalists were deeply implicated in the discursive webs of modernity. This situation, it would seem, is largely a product of historical encounters with 'the West', including colonialism, Christianity, capitalist wage labour, the state, donors, NGOs, academics, journalists, white farmers, tourists and so on. These imbrications in the discursive webs of modernity are especially evident in San encounters with donors and NGOs. Here, traditionalist discourses and solidarities based on kinship ties, ethnic affiliation and narratives of cultural continuity come face to face with the 'civilising mission' of donors and NGOs whose aim is to promote liberal discourses of civil society, accountability, democracy, and Western-style individualism. Despite the efforts of outsiders, and the San themselves, to create the myth of the 'pure bushman', there is no escape from the hybrid condition that characterises the everyday social realities of the San.

It is perhaps paradoxical that the survival of San hunter and gatherer traditions has required that the 'traditionalists' expend considerable energy gaining access to 'exogenous' modern means of production, such as cultural tourism, wage labour, and government and donor grants. As Marshall Sahlins notes, the survival of indigenous peoples, such as hunter-gatherers, is often not a result of their isolation: rather, their subsistence is dependent on modern means of production, transportation and communication – rifles, snowmachines, motorised vessels and, at least in North America, CB radios and all-terrain vehicles – which they buy using money they have acquired from a variety of sources, including public transfer payments, resource loyalties, wage labour and commercial fishing (Sahlins 1999:i–xxiii; 140). Sahlins' comments suggest that these peoples need to engage with modern means of production but that this does not mean that they are simply swallowed up by the homogenising forces of modernity and globalisation. Instead, many of these groups adapt and recast their dependencies on modern means of production in order to reconstitute and reproduce their own cultural ideas and practices. Similarly, by participating in NGO and donor-driven projects, indigenous groups, such as the Kalahari San, are drawing on the modern institutions and resources of a global civil society to reconstitute themselves as a 'traditional community'. Indeed, it is precisely by invoking this dichotomy that traditionalists are able to ground an extremely unstable and hybrid San identity.

Ethnographic examples of the integration of industrial technologies in indigenous sociologies and cosmologies are what Sahlins and others refer to as indigenous modernities. However, the pervasiveness of a 'western' dichotomy of tradition and modernity continues to obscure the reality of what Sahlins also refers to as the indigenisation of modernity. Instead of recognising this hybridisation, 'western' binary thinking contributes towards the persistent reassertion of an artificial divide between tradition and modernity. As will become evident in the following section, the construction of a dichotomy between San traditionalists and 'western bushmen' in the Kalahari was, it would appear, itself partly a response to the contradictory demands of donors and NGOs for the San simultaneously to constitute themselves both as Late Stone Age survivors and modern citizens of the nation state.

Mixed Messages and Crossed Lines?
Land, 'Cultural Survival' and the 'Civilising Mission' of NGOs

Elsewhere I have written about the ways in which the land claims process has contributed to post-apartheid reclamations of Nama and San cultural identity (Robins 1997 and 2000). Land claims in the Northern Cape, as elsewhere in the country, have become a catalyst for processes of ethnogenesis[27] that reproduce apartheid-like ethnic categories and essentialist discourses. These ethnic categories and tribal discourses, however, are not simply imposed 'from above' by the state, donors or NGOs, but are also reinvented and reappropriated by land claimants themselves.[28] In the following I analyse NGOs as 'third parties', as interhierarchical brokers or mediators of state and donor discourses and agendas, as well as local community interests. Examining the ambiguous and intermediary structural and discursive location of SASI, and its involvement in the San land claim, can throw light on the complex and contradictory nature of the cultural politics of land, 'community', 'development' and identity amongst the ‡khomani San people. It can also reveal the impact at the local level of the mixed messages of donor and NGO programmes.

Given that donors and NGOs tend to view indigenous peoples as both 'First People' and modern citizens-in-the-making, it is not surprising that

---

[27] See Sharp 1996.
[28] See Robins 2000.

SASI sought to develop ways of combining charismatic and patriarchal styles of 'traditional leadership' with the establishment of the ǂkhomani San CPA, along with a Constitution and executive committee to ensure democratic procedures of accountability and decision making. However, it soon became apparent that there was tension between the followers of 'western bushmen' under the then CPA chairperson, Petrus Vaalbooi, and San traditionalists under Dawid Kruiper.

Whereas during the land claim process the San were portrayed in the media as pristine 'First People', after the settlement they increasingly came to be seen as part of a broader category of hyper-marginalised 'coloured' rural poor that needed to be drawn into the 'civilising process' through development and institutional capacity-building programmes. It was also during the post-settlement phase that rural development NGOs such as Farm Africa began to move into the Kalahari in order to assist the San to develop organisational capacity to deal with the more mundane administrative and development matters relating to land-use and livestock management. In other words, while SASI's decision to concentrate on 'First People' status may have made strategic sense during the land claims process, this emphasis was perceived to be inadequate during the post-settlement phase. The following discussion seeks to locate these developments within the context of the changing roles and influences of donors and NGOs.

In recent years, NGOs have come to be seen by policy makers, development practitioners, donors, politicians and social scientists as conduits for the dissemination of the ideas and practices of 'civil society'.[29] This identification of NGOs as custodians of the democratic virtues of civil society has, however, been brought into question by the observation that, given the limited financial resources available, NGOs are becoming more dependent on the whims and fancies of international donors, state aid agencies and corporate patrons. Nonetheless, NGOs continue to be lauded for promoting democratisation and the expansion of the core values of 'civil society'. Scholars of international relations have even examined the impact of NGO coalitions and networks on international politics and their role in the formation of a post-Cold War international civil society.[30] A key question to emerge in these debates has been the shifting relationship between globally connected NGOs and the nation state. NGOs have come to be seen as the

---

[29] See Fisher 1997.

[30] Ibid.

most effective brokers and mediators of global discourses of Western liberal democracy and modernisation in the Third World. William Fisher notes that NGOs have also been identified by advocates of neoliberalism as effective institutions for transferring training and skills that 'assist individuals and communities to compete in markets, to provide welfare services to those who are marginalized by the market, and to contribute to democratization and the growth of a robust civil society, all of which are considered critical to the success of neoliberal economic policies'.[31] It would appear from all this interest in NGOs that they are indeed 'the new panacea' for the promotion of Third World democracy, civil society and 'development'.

SASI is directly involved in mediating the development discourses of international NGOs and donor agencies, governments and human rights organisations. The San NGO participates in a complex field of regional and international indigenous peoples rights organisations, NGOs and donor bodies. Many of these agencies have invested in images of the San as pristine hunter-gatherers while at the same time actively promoting the 'civilising mission' of Western liberal civil society. SASI is often caught in the complicated webs of international funding circuits that force it to engage with these mixed messages and ambiguously defined projects. It also has to attempt to connect these trans-local ideas and practices to national and local sites and contexts.

So how do the Kalahari San make sense of these ambiguous messages and discourses produced by the state, donors, 'cultural survival' organisations, and South African and international NGOs? Recent studies of NGOs by William Fisher,[32] Elizabeth Garland (1999) and Steve Sampson (1996), as well as the emergence of a growing anthropological literature on the discourses of the 'development industry'[33], have raised important questions concerning the discursive construction of development 'problems', 'solutions' and 'target populations'.

James Ferguson's Anti-Politics Machine (Ferguson 1990), for instance, draws attention to the problematic ways in which development discourses produce homogenous target populations, such as 'less developed countries',

---

[31] Ibid.:444.

[32] Ibid.:439-464.

[33] See, for example, Escobar 1995; Esteva 1992; Cooper and Packard (eds.) 1997; Crush 1995; and Gupta 1998.

'the Third World', female-headed households, and 'traditional farmers'. The San too have been constructed as a 'target population' by a range of social actors and institutions, including the state, donors and NGOs. Whereas Geneva-based donors, the United Nations Working Group on Indigenous Populations (UNWGIP) and NGOs may conceive of the San as a uniform and homogenous 'target category' of pristine hunter gatherers, the closer one gets to the ground the more unstable, messy and differentiated this category begins to appear.

The view 'from below' can be equally confusing. For example, whereas close-up observations of the Kalahari San might seem to suggest that they are totally captured within the everyday 'Western' habitus of liberal development workers, teachers, missionaries, New Agers, and government bureaucrats, this intimate exposure to the 'civilising mission' does not necessarily mean that they seamlessly reproduce Western liberal political ideals and practices.[34] In other words, the San 'target population' is a 'moving target', unable and unwilling to live up to either 'western' fantasies of the bushmen as Late Stone Age survivors, or developmentalist visions of the San as normalised, disciplined and 'civilised' modern subjects ready to be recruited into an increasingly global civil society.

Elsewhere, I have discussed various possible explanations for the tenacity of popular perceptions of the ǂkhomani San as 'First People', as the living embodiments of Late Stone Age hunter-gatherers (Robins 2000). It is by now hardly news to note that these tenacious primordialist fantasies emanate from a variety of sources including anthropologists filmmakers, museum curators, donors, NGOs, journalists, tourists and so on. The following section investigates the specific ways in which such notions are reproduced, challenged and reconfigured in the context of the ǂkhomani San land claim. This will involve an analysis of the disjunctures, ambiguities and contradictions embedded in discourses on indigenous peoples that are disseminated by bodies such as the UNWGIP and international donors. It will also involve an analysis of how these global discourses are understood and reconfigured by the ǂkhomani San community and by SASI, given the prevailing socio-economic and political realities in San settlements adjacent to the KGNP.

---

[34] See Garland 1999.

Citizens and Bushmen: Discourses on Indigenous Identity

In South Africa there are a number of groups currently claiming 'indigenous' status in terms of the internationally recognised UNWGIP use of the term. These include the Nama (Khoi or Khoekhoe), San, Griqua and !Korrana.[35] The San, Nama and Griqua were classified as 'coloured' in terms of the 1955 race classification legislation introduced by the Nationalist Government that came to power in 1948.[36] This legislation was accompanied by vigorous state-led assimilation policies. For example, Nama children were forced to use Afrikaans in school, and an Afrikaans, Christian, coloured identity was imposed upon the Nama through the institutions of church and state. Many people with San, Nama and Griqua ancestry also opted to identify with this 'coloured' identity due to the negative connotations and racist discrimination associated with the terms *'hottentot'* and *'boesman'* under colonialism and apartheid. As a result, the San and Nama languages and culture have almost disappeared. Whereas Nama is still spoken in the Northern Cape Province in northern parts of Namaqualand such as Richtersveld, it has virtually vanished in the more missionised southern Namaqualand settlements such as Leliefontein (Robins 1997). Unlike Nama, 'coloureds' and black Africans, San people were not given their own 'Reserves' as it was assumed that they were 'extinct' or thoroughly assimilated into the 'coloured' population. This also contributed to the particularly marginalised character of San identity. This marginalisation is evident in the fact that there are only approximately a dozen identified ǂkhomani San speakers throughout South Africa.

The response of the ANC government to the dramatic reclamations of Nama, San and Griqua identity that began the early 1990s, has been one of

---

[35] Nama is the only surviving Khoe language in South Africa. There are approximately five to ten thousand Nama-speaking people in the Northern Cape, mostly concentrated in the northern Namaqualand area along the Orange River.

[36] There are some 3,600,000 South Africans who identify themselves as 'coloured' (Statistics South Africa (1998), section 2.5). The category of coloured disguises the cultural heterogeneity of people many of whom have European, African, Khoe, San, Indian, Indonesian, Malay and slave backgrounds. The majority of so-called coloureds do not identify themselves as indigenous Khoe or San. However, the gains made by a growing indigenous rights movement could encourage many of these people to reclaim and recognise African, San and Khoe ancestry, which has tended to be suppressed in favour of a stress on their European and Christian background.

caution and ambivalence. The government remains wary of an indigenous rights movement that could become a vehicle for exclusivist ethnic politics. This distrust of ethnic politics comes out of a historical legacy of apartheid and rightwing Afrikaner nationalism, as well as the bloody clashes between the Inkatha Freedom Party and ANC supporters in Kwa-Zulu Natal and Gauteng. It would also appear that the ANC, as an unambiguously modernist organisation, is concerned that an accommodation of communitarianism could end up contradicting the underlying principles of liberal democracy. From a more pragmatic position, the enormous logistical difficulties experienced in attempting to process the thousands of land claims already submitted to the Land Claim Court may have contributed towards the government's reluctance to encourage indigenous groups to agitate for aboriginal land titles along the lines of Australian and New Zealand land law.

The term 'indigenous' in South Africa has come to mean something completely different to its use by international donors, the United Nations and various indigenous peoples' forums and activist groups. There is as yet no accepted South African definition of the term, even though it appears twice in the Constitution (Articles 6 and 26). The Constitution's use of the term in fact derives from the common South African use of the word 'indigenous' to refer to the languages and legal customs of the African majority of Bantu-language speakers.[37] In South Africa, like other parts of southern Africa, the term 'indigenous' is used to distinguish the black African majority from the European settlers and Asian minorities.

Khoi and San advocates and activists are critical of the government's failure to adopt international indigenous rights legal frameworks. For instance, SASI linguist and development consultant Nigel Crawhall believes the South African government's rights-based paradigm 'ignores the inability of marginalized indigenous communities to effectively hold the state accountable for implementation of its rights' (Crawhall 1999). It is with this in mind that Crawhall continues to call for the specific recognition of 'Indigenous Africans', in line with international definitions.

The common use of the term 'indigenous' in South Africa is very different to UNWGIP's use of the term to refer to non-dominant groups of

---

[37] 76.7 per cent of South Africans are considered to be African (i.e. of Bantu-language speaking origin). Whites of European descent comprise 10.9 per cent, Coloureds 8.9 per cent and Indians 2.6 per cent. Statistics South Africa (1998).

people of aboriginal descent and with distinct territorial and cultural identities. The ANC government's apparent reluctance to take on board this UN definition is a consequence of its belief that the majority of 'black Africans' and 'coloureds' are indigenous South Africans.[38] For instance, when asked by a journalist whether the successful resolution of the ‡khomani San land claim represented the government's intention to recognise Khoi and San as 'First People', former Minister of Land Affairs, Derek Hanekom, flatly refuted this assumption. He claimed that virtually all black South Africans had suffered under colonialism and apartheid and it would not make sense to separate out and privilege the experiences of one group on the basis of claims to autochthonous, aboriginal status. As Hanekom pointed out, the land claims cut-off date is, in any case, 1913, which rules out claims to aboriginal land rights. From the ANC's perspective, redress has to address the needs of all South African citizens disadvantaged by racial legislation.

San and Khoisan activists believe, however, that the Constitution ought to recognise the very specific conditions of marginalisation of the San and Nama in South Africa. They argue that this exceptionality is evident in the observation that there are only about a dozen known ‡khomani San-speakers left in South Africa. This alone, they argue, makes the San one of the most vulnerable and marginalised groups in South Africa. The ANC, like other African governments, disagrees, and has refused to accept United Nations' declarations on indigenous peoples.

The ANC is clearly unwilling to encourage openly an indigenous peoples' discourse that would rub against the grain of the tenets and principle of liberal democracy. Since it was founded in 1913, the ANC has embraced a Western-style liberal democratic model that cannot easily accommodate communitarian political institutions and practices, such as traditional leadership. However, given the concessions granted to African traditional leaders in the recent past, including the establishment of a House of Traditional Leaders, the government is regularly reminded by Khoi and San activists that it has already set a precedent. In fact, chiefs are about to be given more powers in terms of land rights in communal areas. This perhaps explains why, despite a reluctance to ratify international conventions on

---

[38] The term 'black' is often used to refer specifically to black Africans who speak Bantu languages . It is also used more broadly to refer to Indians, Coloureds, Khoi, San and Africans, i.e. 'non-white'. The term black, like that of African and coloured, is a highly unstable and contested term.

indigenous rights, the ANC government has nonetheless taken seriously the dire predicament of the ‡khomani and !Xu/Khwe San.[39] Apart from the provision of land, the government has also initiated a process aimed at addressing the specific needs and cultural rights of San, Nama and Griqua communities, although it remains to be seen whether this will bear fruit.

Rights, Culture and NGO Priorities:
The Question of Strategic Essentialism

Rather than chasing after constitutionally enshrined rights for indigenous people, SASI's lawyer, Roger Chennels, is more concerned with the enormous challenges of creating viable local community structures and livelihood strategies. It is here, at the more mundane and immediate level of everyday life, of poverty, conflict and social fragmentation, that Chennels locates the San agenda. However, it is not only these material realities that need to be addressed. Chennels and Crawhall believe that tapping into San local knowledge and the historical narratives of elders could be a valuable source of social capital in the quest to forge a collective sense of belonging, psychological well-being and social cohesion, as well as facilitating the development of viable livelihood strategies. In other words, there need not be an artificial dichotomy between the more materialist rural development strategies of NGOs such as Farm Africa, and SASI's cultural projects aimed at stimulating social capital formation through inter-generational knowledge transfer. However, it remains to be seen to what degree these indigenous knowledge and cultural practices can be used as a basis for 'cultural survival' and economic sustainability for present and future generations of San.

Given the strong interest of international donors in the 'cultural survival' of vanishing cultures and languages, it could be argued that it still makes strategic sense for San communities, and SASI, to stress the importance of their hunter-gatherer lifestyle, indigenous knowledge and San cultural continuity. The deployment of these strategies to gain donor funding may also contribute towards reconstituting kinship and other activities that contribute towards the remaking of San conceptions of human existence. However, endorsing primordialist notions of the San as hunter-gatherers

---

[39] There are about 4,500 former Angolan Khwe and !Xu San now living near Kimberly.

could also contribute towards the devaluation and marginalisation of alternative livelihood strategies and social practices that do not conform to this stereotypical 'bushman image'. For instance, San livestock farmers are often perceived to be less authentically San by donors even though, for many ǂkhomani San, goats and sheep have been, and continue to be, the most viable livelihood strategy in the arid Kalahari region. While livestock production is in fact taking place on the newly acquired farms, it has contributed towards growing tensions between so-called 'traditionalists' who claim to prefer the hunter gatherer/cultural tourism option, and livestock farmers who are referred to as the 'western bushmen'. As was mentioned earlier, the media, academics, NGOs and donors are not entirely innocent in these processes.

Anthropologists and historians have devoted enormous time and resources towards proving or disproving 'bushman authenticity'. This obsessive pre-occupation with cultural authenticity is not, of course, limited to scholars. For example, when Donald Bain wanted to establish a Bushman Reserve in South Africa in the 1930s, he encountered strong opposition from white farmers who, fearing shortages of farm labour, claimed that the Reserve was unnecessary as there were no 'real bushmen' left. In recent years, 'bushman' tourism and the ǂkhomani San land claim have once again triggered academic and popular interest in the perennial question of 'bushmen' authenticity. More than 50 years after Bain's aborted attempt at salvaging 'bushman' culture through the establishment of a Reserve, the issue of 'bushmen' authenticity remains as loaded as ever. It would appear that the 'bushmen' have once again become the lightening rod for academic and media discourses on cultural difference and authenticity. It is as if they have come to represent the last repository of absolute alterity, as a mythic, primordial Other. Ironically, they have also become intellectual fodder for countless academic projects aimed at debunking 'bushman myths' and primordialist essentialism. Elsewhere, I have written about the political and ethnic dilemmas facing South African anthropologists and historians when called upon to provide research to support essentialist conceptions of San cultural continuity in order to buttress land claims and projects of 'ethnic revitalisation' (Robins 2000, see also Warren 1998).

The perceived uniqueness of the Kalahari San and their land claim has attracted enormous media, donor and NGO interest. It also captivated President Mbeki and the former Minister of Lands, Derek Hanekom, whose personal involvement in the claim played a particularly significant role in ensuring its success. Popular images of primordial bushmen not only fuel media and scholarly interest, but also shape government, NGO and donor perceptions and development strategies and priorities. For instance, San development projects are known to receive generous funding from international donor organisations for whom the Kalahari bushmen represent the last of the surviving Late Stone Age hunter gatherers. Similarly, it could be argued that the R15 million San land claim 'jumped the queue' precisely because the San are perceived to be such a valuable political and tourist commodity by the state, NGOs, donors and the media. President Mbeki's African Renaissance, South Africa's quest for a permanent seat on the UN Security Council, and the race for votes in the Northern Cape probably all played a significant role in the ANC government's last minute rush to address San land and language rights in the run up to the 1999 general elections. Although political opportunism alone cannot account for the whole story, it would appear that the San were indeed political pawns in the 1999 elections. This does not imply, however, that they were passive victims of the machinations of powerful political elites; after all, they managed to win back their land and continue to secure access to state resources. Neither are they passive victims of the representations, political agendas and development discourses of powerful outsiders.

The representations of 'bushmen' as 'First People' that are reproduced daily at South African museum dioramas and San tourist villages continue to ignore the devastating consequences of San genocide, land and cultural dispossession and contemporary rural poverty and social fragmentation. However, drawing attention to this devastating San past and present does not necessarily appeal to tourists who want to see the Kruiper clan dressed in loincloths and carrying bows and arrows. Neither does it necessarily appeal to donors looking for 'First People'. The Kruiper clan recognises that these 'traditional' bushman images are invaluable cultural and economic resources in their quest for a future that is more than mere 'cultural survival'. They are creative and self-conscious producers of the cultural commodities that fuel a fledgling tourist and donor-driven economy. These developments are not merely instrumental manipulations of culture and identity in order to gain access to material resources. They are also cultural practices aimed at the recuperation of social memory and identity similar to other cultural reclamations taking place throughout post-apartheid South Africa.

The problem with such strategic essentialism, as Gayatri Spivak points out, is that it can end up obscuring intra-community differences along class, age or gender lines. These 'ethnic' strategies of mobilisation also tend to ignore and degrade cultural hybridities in the name of 'pure essences' and cultural continuity, thereby encouraging the kinds of tensions between 'pure' and 'westernised' bushmen that emerged in the Kalahari. Moreover, such an approach could render the San increasingly dependent on powerful donors and create obstacles for San communities seeking to develop independent and effective local community and leadership structures. It is also likely to alienate the ǂkhomani San from their 'coloured' and Nama-speaking neighbours in Northern Cape. Growing divisions and tensions have in fact occurred between the claimant community and their communal farmer neighbours in the Mier area. This culminated in legal contestation of the San claim by Mier residents. The matter was eventually resolved through a negotiated settlement whereby Mier communal farmers also received state land and resources as compensation for land dispossession under apartheid. Nonetheless, instead of encouraging strategic ties with their neighbours, a donor focus on San exceptionalism and 'First People' status could end up isolating and alienating this claimant community from potential human resources and political allies in the neighbouring communal areas and rural towns. In other words, an 'ethnic separatist strategy' that was perceived to be strategic during the San land claim process, and which was supported by NGOs and donors, could contribute towards erecting an artificial barrier between the ǂkhomani San and neighbouring 'coloured' and 'baster' communities, even though many of the San claimants come from these neighbouring areas and have close kinship ties with people living there. In other words, a narrowly defined donor focus on 'indigenous' San could create problematic socio-spatial and political divisions and inequalities amongst these culturally hybrid and impoverished rural people of the Northern Cape Province. 'Ethnic separatist' strategies also fail to recognise the potential for San participation in broad class-based social movements and development initiatives involving 'coloured', black African and Nama communal farmers, farm workers, the unemployed and other marginalised groups in the Northern Cape region. However, given the fact that this political mobilisation is not taking place, it probably makes strategic sense for the ǂkhomani San, with the help of SASI, to continue to concentrate on taking care of their own needs and concerns. Although this approach could confine the San to an 'ethnic cage', there is nothing to prevent the San from participating in broader social movements and developmental agendas in the future. In the absence of such social movements, however, SASI is unlikely to decide to work with non-San communities as this could jeopardise its ability to tap into Northern donor circuits earmarked specifically for 'indigenous' people. It could also spread the organisation's limited resources too thinly. Restricting their work to San issues also makes sense given SASI's identification of the San as a hyper-marginalised community with very specific social and cultural needs and predicaments.

SASI could find itself in a situation where it is unable entirely to dismiss international donor desires for authentic 'First People', and yet unable to ignore the ambiguities, contradictions and messy social realities they meet in their everyday encounters in the Kalahari. This messiness is further complicated by NGO attempts to reconcile traditional leadership, values and practices, with the need to establish democratic and accountable decision-making institutions. Chennels' comments on the difficulty of explaining this complexity to funders remains a troubling one. Meanwhile, recent developments in the Kalahari suggest that donors are uncertain whether they should fund 'cultural survival' NGOs or more mainstream rural development NGOs. Some of the major donors have, in fact, recently provided significant support for rural development programmes at the Kalahari San settlement as a way of countering a perception, rightly or wrongly, that in the past the bulk of San donor resources went to cultural survival projects. This represents a significant shift towards providing donor support for more conventional rural development programmes aimed at developing livelihood strategies and natural resource management institutional capacity.

The following letter to the Sunday Independent, entitled 'Create lasting economic strategy for Nyae-Nyae', is a highly polemical attack on San 'cultural survival' projects in Namibia. The writer, who claims to have spent fifteen years at Nyae-Nyae, lambastes outsiders for promoting their own self-interested conceptions of 'bushman' culture.[40] The letter was written in response to a prior article entitled 'Alcohol makes a desert of Namibians' hopes'[41].

> The people of Nyae-Nyae have their own culture just as all other people in Namibia have their own culture. This has nothing to do with the ability to keep animals and grow vegetables. The people of Bushmanland are perfectly capable of keeping cattle and growing vegetables. It might not be 'in their

---

[40] Sunday Independent, 17 October 1999.
[41] Sunday Independent, 5 September 1999.

tradition', but neither was warfare nor alcohol. For 15 years I have witnessed NGOs, governments, trophy hunters, racketeers, conservationists, film makers, intellectuals and quasi-intellectuals and priests telling the people of Nyae-Nyae how they should preserve their 'culture' and run their lives. Culture and tradition can only survive if the people want it to. Paternalism from outsiders just won't do the trick. If anyone was really concerned about the wellbeing of the 'bushmen' of Nyae-Nyae, they would have created an economic environment diverse enough for the people to be able to feed themselves. This has not happened and never will as long as outsiders with their own agendas try to rule the roost.

The letter is an outright attack on what the author perceives to be the outside imposition of San culture survival projects that do not adequately address San poverty and so create viable livelihood options. There is a danger, however, that such blanket criticisms could be used to justify the imposition of rural development projects that fail to address adequately the specificities of the social and cultural aspects of everyday life in San communities. In other words, it could end up ignoring the valuable local knowledge and social capital that SASI development consultants such as Nigel Crawhall and Roger Chennels believe is essential for any attempt to reconstitute this highly fractured San community. It could also end up failing to recognise the ways in which representations of San tradition and culture are fashioned 'from below' by the San themselves. While the appropriation of essentialist notions of San cultural identity can contribute to the kinds of conflicts between 'traditionalist' and 'western' bushmen that occurred in the Kalahari, it can also contribute towards reconstituting the social fabric of community and revitalising local conceptions of San culture and identity. Similarly, although San cultural politics could lead to forms of 'ethnic separatism' and isolationism that undermine social and economic ties with non-San neighbours in adjacent communal areas and rural towns, this is not inevitable: San cultural politics does not have any pre-ordained script or teleology.

To break out of the ethnic mould of apartheid history, South African NGOs, and the San themselves, may have to walk a fine line between negotiating the primordialist desires and fantasies of funders, and the need to gain access to development resources to empower poverty-stricken San communities. They will also need to negotiate the ambiguous and contradictory dual mandate of donors that seek to promote San 'cultural survival' while simultaneously inculcating the values and virtues of 'civil society' and liberal individualism, development and democracy. This could be a hard road to walk.

Conclusions

This article has focused on donors, NGOs and the San claimant community in its investigation of how the apparently contradictory agendas of San 'cultural survival' and the promotion of the values and practices of 'civil society' have shaped the ‡khomani San, both during and after the land claim. It is clear that the cultural politics of San identity, community and tradition is a highly complicated and shifting discursive field, and that the San are simultaneously enmeshed in donor and NGO projects of cultural recuperation and the 'civilising mission' of liberal democracy. It would also appear that, despite considerable evidence of the hybrid character of San local knowledge and everyday practices, the dual mandate of donors and NGOs has contributed towards reproducing a 'great divide' between 'traditionalists' and 'western bushmen'. It has been argued, however, that this divide is not simply imposed 'from above' by NGOs and donors, but is also very much a product of local constructions of bushman identity and community.

San cultural revivalism is taking place within the context of a new politics of indigenous identity and cultural rights that is currently unfolding in South Africa. The stakes are being raised through tough competition over access to donor and state resources, including struggles for access to government salaries within a proposed Indigenous Council (*Inheemse Raad*), a 'KhoiSan' equivalent of the existing House of Traditional Leaders. These recent developments have exacerbated leadership struggles and social divisions amongst the Kalahari San. Such conflicts over traditional leadership and identity could also end up deflecting attention from the more mundane and material livelihood needs of these hyper-marginalised rural communities.

The ‡khomani San land claim unfolded within this complicated post-apartheid political landscape. The gains made by ‡khomani San and other 'indigenous' groups in recent years would not have been possible during the apartheid era. There are a number of reasons for this, including the fact that San, Nama and Griqua were categorised as 'coloured'. The 'authentic San' were deemed 'extinct', and the Nama (Khoe) and Griqua were seen by the

Apartheid State as part of an assimilated and hybrid 'coloured' population living in the 'Coloured Reserves' of the Northern Cape. It is only in the post-apartheid period that people with San, Nama and Griqua ancestry have been able publicly to assert themselves as indigenous peoples with specific land, cultural and language rights. Despite refraining from entrenching indigenous rights in the constitution, the ANC government has, in fact, addressed many of these claims through land restitution, by providing resources to promote Nama and San languages, and by addressing the question of traditional leadership. This political environment has enabled SASI and the San to make successful claims to land and cultural rights. While these claims have resulted in significant gains for this marginalised San community, a stress on primordial notions of San tradition and 'First People' status has also had unintended consequences in terms of generating conflict between 'traditional' and 'western' 'bushmen', as well as running against the grain of the donor and NGO 'civilising mission' and its civic culture of liberal individualism. This article has attempted to examine the ambiguities and contradictions of these donor-driven double visions and local struggles over land, tradition and identity.

References

Boonzaier, E.
1992   *Rediscovering the Nama: a Case Study of Controlled Identity Politics in the North-West Cape.* Paper presented in the Department of Social Anthropology, University of Cape Town.

Boonzaier, E. and J. S. Sharp (eds.)
1988   *South African Keywords: the Uses and Abuses of Political Concepts.* Cape Town: David Philip Press.

Boonzaier, E. and J. Sharp
1994   Ethnic Identity as Performance: Lessons from Namaqualand. *Journal of Southern African Studies,* 20 (3):405-415.

Cooper, F. and R. Packard (eds.)
1997   *International Development and the Social Sciences: Essays on the History and Politics of Knowledge.* Berkeley, Los Angeles, London: University of California Press.

Crawhall, N.

1999   *Needs Assessment Study: Indigenous Peoples in South Africa.* Report
        prepared for International Labour Organization and the South
        African San Institute. Cape Town: SASI.

Crush, J.

1996   *The Power of Development.* London: Routledge.

Escobar, A.

1995   *Encountering Development: The Making and Unmaking of the Third
        World.* Princeton: Princeton University Press.

Esteva, G.

1992   Development. In: Sachs, W. (ed.) *The Development Dictionary: A
        Guide to Knowledge and Power.* London: Zed Books.

Ferguson, J.

1990   *The Anti-Politics Machine: 'Development', Depoliticization and
        Bureaucratic State Power in Lesotho.* Cambridge: Cambridge
        University Press.

Fisher, W.

1997   Doing Good: The Politics and Antipolitics of NGO Practices. *Annual
        Review of Anthropology* 26:439-464.

Garland, E.

1999   Developing Bushmen: Building Civil(ized) Society in the Kalahari
        and Beyond. In: Comaroff, J. L. and J. Comaroff (eds.) *Civil Society
        and the Political Imagination in Africa: Critical Perspectives.*
        Chicago: University of Chicago Press.

Gordon, Robert

1992   *The Bushman Myth: the Making of a Namibian Underclass.* Boulder:
        Westview Press.

Gupta, A.

1998   *Postcolonial Developments: Agriculture in the Making of Modern
        India.* London: Durham.

Hadland, A. and J. Ratao

1999   *The Life and Times of Thabo Mbeki.* Rivonia.

Hitchcock, Robert
1982   Patterns of Sedentism Among the Basarwa of Eastern Botswana. In:
        Leacock and Lee (eds.) *Politics and History in Band Societies*.
        Cambridge: Cambridge University Press.

1987   Socioeconomic Change Among the Basarwa in Botswana: An
        Ethnohistorical Analysis, *Ethnohistory*, 34 (3):219-255.

James, D.
2000a   Hill of Thorns: Custom, Knowledge and the Reclaiming of a Lost
        Land in the New South Africa. *Development and Change* 31:629-
        649.

2000b   "After Years in the Wilderness": The Discourse of Land Claims in
        the New South Africa. *The Journal of Peasant Studies* 27 (3):142–
        161.

Lee, Richard
1979   *The Kung San: Men, Women, and Work in a Foraging Society*.
        Cambridge: Cambridge University Press.

1984   *The Dobe !Kung*. New York: Holt, Rinehart and Winston.

Mafeje, A.
1971   The Ideology of Tribalism. *Journal of Modern African Studies* 9
        (2):253-261.

Magubane, B.
1973   The Xhosa in Town Revisited: Urban Social Anthropology – A
        Failure in Method and Theory. *American Anthropologist* 75:1701-
        1714.

Povinelli, E. A.
1999   Settler Modernity and the Quest for Indigenous Tradition. *Public
        Culture* 11 (1):19-48.

2000   Consuming Geist: Popontology and the Spirit of Capital in
        Indigenous Australia. *Public Culture* 12 (2): 501-528.

Rassool, C.
1999   Cultural Performance and Fictions in Identity: the Case of the
        Khoisan of the Southern Kalahari, 1936–1937. In: Dladla, Y. (ed.)
        Voices, Values and Identities Symposium (South African National
        Parks, Pretoria).

Rassool, C. and P. Hayes
2001   Science and the Spectacle: |Khanako's South Africa 1936–37. In:
        Woodward, W., G. Minkley and P. Hayes (eds.) *Deep Histories:
        Gender and Colonialism in Southern Africa*. Amsterdam: Rodopi.

Robins, S.
1997   Transgressing the Borderlands of Tradition and Modernity:
        "Coloured" Identity, Cultural Hybridity and Land Struggles in
        Namaqualand, 1980–94. *Journal of Contemporary African Studies*
        15 (2):23-44.

1998a   Bodies out of Place: Crossroads and Landscapes of Exclusion. In:
        Hylton Juden (ed.) *Blank Interrogating Architecture After Apartheid.*
        Rotterdam, NAI:457-470.

1998b   Breaking Out of the Straitjacket of Tradition: the Politics and
        Rhetoric of "Development. In: *Zimbabwe*. World Development 26
        (9):1-18.

2000   Land Struggles and the Politics and Ethics of Representing
        "Bushman" History and Identity. Kronos: *Journal of Cape History*
        26.

Sahlins, M.
1999   What is Anthropological Enlightenment? Some Lessons of the
        Twentieth Century. *Annual Review of Anthropology* 28:i-xxiii.

Sampson, S.
1996   The Social Life of Projects: Imposing Civil Society to Albania. In:
        Hann, C. and E. Dunn (eds.). *Civil Society: Challenging Western
        Models*. London and New York: Routledge.

Sharp, J.
1984   *Rural Development Schemes and the Struggle against
        Impoverishment in the Namaqualand Reserves*. Paper presented to
        the Second Carnegie Conference on Poverty and Development in
        South Africa, University of Cape Town. Carnegie Conference
        Report No. 69.

1994   Land Claims in Namaqualand: the Komaggas Reserve. *Review of
        African Political Economy* 21 (61).403-414.

1996   Ethnogenesis and Ethnic Mobilization: A Comparative Perspective
        on a South African Dilemma. In: Wilmsen, E. N. and P. McAllister

(eds.). *The Politics of Difference: Ethnic Premises in a World of Power.* Chicago and London: University of Chicago Press.

Sharp, J. and S. Douglas
1996   Prisoners of their Reputation? The Veterans of the "Bushman" Battalions in South Africa. In: Skotnes, P. (ed.). *Miscast: Negotiating the Presence of the Bushmen.* Cape Town: University of Cape Town Press.

Wallace, Anthony
1956   Revitalization Movements. *American Anthropologist* 58:264-281.

Warren, K.
1998   *Indigenous Movements and their Critics: Pan Maya Activism in Guatemala.* Princeton: Princeton University of Press.

White, H.
1995   *In the Tradition of the Forefathers: Bushman Traditionality at Kagga Kamma.* Cape Town: University of Cape Town Press.

Wilmsen, Edwin
1989   *Land Filled with Flies: A Political Economy of the Kalahari* Chicago and London, University of Chicago Press.

Newspaper Articles:

Cape Times, 1. July 1999.
Cape Times, 16 September 1999.
Sunday Independent, 17 October 1999.
Sunday Independent, 5 September 1999.

List of contributors

Susanne Berzborn has a degree (MA) in social anthropology from the University of Cologne. She is a research fellow at the Institute of Social Anthropology in Cologne within the Special Research Unit ACACIA. After her M.A she has conducted two years of field research on household economy, social networks and land rights in the Richtersveld, South Africa which she is currently writing her PhD on.

Gertrud Boden has a degree (MA) in social anthropology from the University of Cologne. Afterwards she has worked at the Rautenstrauch-Joest-Museum for Cultural Anthropology in Cologne and the Museum for Cultural History in Duisburg where she arranged exhibitions and published catalogues on Native Americans and San respectively. Since 1998 she conducted several periods of field research in West Caprivi/Namibia. Currently she is a member of the Special Research Unit ACACIA and a research fellow at the Institute of Social Anthropology in Cologne. She is writing her PhD on "Social Change within a Setting of Severe State Intervention – A Case Study of the Khwe in West Caprivi".

Michael Bollig is Professor for Social Anthropology at the University of Cologne. He conducted research on conflict management in Northern Kenya and on risk management in Northwestern Namibia. Field research on economies, social systems and change in northern Namibia has been ongoing since 1994. His major interest has been vulnerability, risk management and socio-economic change in herding economies.

Ute Dieckmann has a degree (MA) in social anthropology from the University of Cologne. After her MA she has conducted two years of field research as a research fellow at the Institute of Social Anthropology in Cologne within the Special Research Unit ACACIA on Haiǁom identity and history in Namibia on which she is currently writing her PhD.

Thekla Hohmann has a degree (MA) in social anthropology from the University of Cologne. She has spent over a year as a research fellow at the Institute of Social Anthropology in Cologne within the Special Research Unit ACACIA working on San identity, development initiatives and resource management. Currently she is a participant at the Centre for Advanced Training in Rural Development (SLE), Humboldt University Berlin.

Ina Orth has a degree (MA) in social anthropology from the University of Cologne. She has conducted field research for her MA in 1998 in Namibia on land rights and identity among Khwe in West Caprivi.

Steven Robins PhD is Professor of Sociology at the University of Stellenbosch. He is a commentator on issues of rural development, especially in Southern Zimbabwe, Namaqualand, and the Kalahari (South Africa), and has written several articles on trauma, place, and urban identity in Cape Town.

Michael Taylor PhD currently works for the United Nations Development Programme on a project to develop models for community-driven rehabilitation of rangelands in the arid zone of Africa. His research has focused primarily on issues of environment and development in Botswana. His long-term research with San in northern Botswana on land, identity and natural resource use formed the basis of his PhD from the University of Edinburgh.

Thomas Widlok MSc, PhD (London 1994) is member of staff at the Institute of Social Anthropology in Heidelberg. He has carried out long-term field research in northern and central Namibia, as well as in northwestern Australia. His main interests are comparison and ethnography, hunter-gatherer studies, and anthropological theory. He has also done work in cognitive anthropology and in anthropological linguistics, especially with Hai‖om speakers. He is the author of "Living on Mangetti. 'Bushman' Autonomy and Namibian Independence" and of numerous articles on Namibian and Australian ethnography.

Rüdiger Köppe Verlag

Languages and Cultures (Selected Publications)

History, Cultural Traditions and Innovations in Southern Africa
edited by Michael Bollig and Wilhelm J.G. Möhlig

1. M. Bollig: *"When War came the Cattle slept...". Himba Oral Traditions*, 1997, 352 pp., 13 b/w photos   ISBN 3-89645-049-2

2. M. Fisch: *Der Caprivizipfel während der deutschen Zeit 1890–1914*, 1996, 158 pp., 32 b/w photos, 8 maps   ISBN 3-89645-050-6

3. P. Hayes: *Healing the Land. Kaulinge's History of Kwanyama*, 1997, 112 pp., 4 b/w photos   ISBN 3-89645-051-4

4. C. Mayer-Himmelheber / D. Meyer-Bauer: *Töpferei und andere Strategien der Ein- kommenssicherung. Risikominimierung im Norden Namibias*, 1997, 182 pp., 10 b/w photos, 8 maps, 13 tables, 9 graphs   ISBN 3-89645-052-2

5. P. Scheulen: *Die „Eingeborenen" Deutsch-Südwestafrikas. Ihr Bild in deutschen Kolonialzeitschriften von 1884 – 1918*, 1998, 203 pp., 1 map

       ISBN 3-89645 054 9

6. J. de Vries: *Manasse Tjiseseta, Chief of Omaruru, 1884-1898, Namibia*, 1999, 136 pp., 2 maps, 14 appendices   ISBN 3-89645-055-7

7. I. Brinkman / A. Fleisch (eds.): *Grandmother's Footsteps. Oral Tradition and south-eastern Angolan Narratives on the Colonial Encounter*, 1999, 255 pp., 3 maps, 13 b/w photos, 2 tables   ISBN 3-89645-056-5

8. J.-B. Gewald: *"We Thought we would be Free ...". Socio-Cultural Aspects of Herero History in Namibia, 1915–1940*, 2000, 273 pp., 1 map, 10 b/w photos

       ISBN 3-89645-057-3

9. W.J.G. Möhlig (ed.): *Frühe Kolonialgeschichte Namibias*, 2000, X, 207 pp., 2 maps, 2 tables, 2 figures, index   ISBN 3-89645-058-1

10. G. Menzel: *Widerstand und Gottesfurcht. Hendrik Witbooi – eine Biographie in zeitgenössischen Quellen. Mit einem Epilog von Wilhelm J. G. Möhlig*, 2000, 259 pp., 3 maps, 17 b/w photos, 2 indices, appendix   ISBN 3-89645-059-X

11. W.J.B. Chapman: *The Dorsland Trekkers. An Account of the Entry of the Trek-Boers into Angola 1879–1928*, edited by M. Bollig, 2002, 192 pp., 1 map, 10 b/w photos   ISBN 3-89645-350-5

12. D. Wagner-Robertz: *Ein Heilungsritual der Dama, Südwestafrika/Namibia*, 2000, CD-ROM: 210 pp., 2 maps, 19 coloured photos, 1 graph

       ISBN 3-89645-351-3

13. M. Bollig / J.-B. Gewald (eds.): *People, Cattle and Land. Transformations of a Pastoral Society in Southwestern Africa*, 2000, XII, 540 pp., 17 maps, 16 coloured photos, 17 b/w photos, 31 graphs, numerous tables

       ISBN 3-89645-352-1

14. A. Fleisch / W.J.G. Möhlig: *The Kavango Peoples in the Past. Local Historiographies from Northern Namibia*, 2002, 344 pp., 5 maps, 19 b/w photos, 1 folded table, 5 tables, indices of persons and localities   ISBN 3-89645-353-X

15. D. Wagner-Robertz: *Liedtexte der Dama, Südwestafrika/Namibia*, 2001, CD-ROM: 190 pp., 2 maps, 2 b/w photos   ISBN 3-89645-354-8

16. I. Brinkman (ed.): *Singing in the Bush. MPLA Songs during the War for Independence in South-East Angola (1966–1975)*, 2001, 111 pp., 5 b/w photos   ISBN 3-89645-355-6

17. J. Götz: *Ethnische Grenzen und Frontlinien in Angola*, 2002, 132 pp., 1 map   ISBN 3-89645-356-4

Namibian African Studies
edited by Wilfrid H.G. Haacke

W.H.G. Haacke / E.D. Elderkin (eds): *Namibian Languages. Reports and Papers* (Vol. 4), 1997, 451 pp., 11 maps, 104 tables, 118 lists, 1 illustration   ISBN 3-89645-080-8

C. Kilian-Hatz: *Folktales of the Kxoe in the West Caprivi* (Vol. 5), 1999, X, 338 pp., 79 illustrations   ISBN 3-89645-081-6

Research in Khoisan Studies · Quellen zur Khoisan-Forschung · QKF
edited by Rainer Vossen

H.-J. Heinz: *Social Organization of the !Ko Bushmen*, ed. by K. Keuthmann (QKF 10), 1994, 232 pp., 8 b/w photos   ISBN 3-927620-57-2

M. Szalay: *The San and the Colonization of the Cape 1770–1879* (QKF 11), 1995, 151 pp., 33 b/w photos, 1 map   ISBN 3-927620-58-0

R. Vossen: *Die Khoe-Sprachen. Ein Beitrag zur Erforschung der Sprachgeschichte Afrikas* (QKF 12), 1997, 536 pp., 5 maps, num. tables   ISBN 3-927620-59-9

E.N. Wilmsen (ed.): *The Kalahari Ethnographies (1896–1898) of Siegfried Passarge. Nineteenth Century Khoisan- and Bantu-speaking Peoples* (QKF 13), 1997, 332 pp., 1 b/w photo   ISBN 3-89645-141-3

B. Sands: *Eastern and Southern African Khoisan. Evaluating Claims of Distant Linguistic Relationships* (QKF 14), 1998, 251 pp., 1 map, 5 graphs, 56 tables, appendices   ISBN 3-89645-142-1

M. Schladt (ed.): *Language, Identity, and Conceptualization among the Khoisan* (QKF 15), 1998, 503 pp., numerous graphs and tables   ISBN 3-89645-143-X

W.H.G. Haacke: *The Tonology of Khoekhoe (Nama/Damara)* (QKF 16), 1999, XVI, 233 pp., 45 illustrations, 23 tables   ISBN 3-89645-144-8

Afrika erzählt

Vol. 5: S. Schmidt: *Sagen und Schwänke in Afrika. Erzählungen der Damara und Nama*, 1991, 245 pp.   ISBN 3 927620 69 6

Vol. 6: S. Schmidt: *Scherz und Ernst. Afrikaner berichten aus ihrem Leben*, 1998, 240 pp. ISBN 3-89645-122-7

Vol. 7: S. Schmidt: *Hänsel und Gretel in Afrika. Märchentexte aus Namibia im internationalen Vergleich*, 1999, 398 pp. ISBN 3-89645-123-5

Vol. 8: S. Schmidt: *Tricksters, Monsters and Clever Girls. African Folktales – Texts and Discussions*, 2001, 383 pp., 3 musical notations ISBN 3-89645-128-6

Grammatical Analyses of African Languages
ed. by Wilhelm J.G. Möhlig and Bernd Heine

1. Th. C. Schadeberg: *A Sketch of Umbundu*, 1990, 61 pp. ISBN 3-927620-15-7

2. Th. C. Schadeberg: *A Sketch of Swahili Morphology*, 3rd revised edition, 1992, 39 pp. ISBN 3-927620-16-5

3. J.-Cl. Naba: *Le Gulmancema : essai de systématisation*, 1994, XIV, 398 pp.
ISBN 3-927620-17-3

4. S. Brauner: *A Grammatical Sketch of Shona. Including historical notes*, 1995, 66 pp., 2 tables ISBN 3-927620-18-1

5. H. Pasch: *Kurzgrammatik des Ewe*, 1995, 93 pp., 1 map ISBN 3-927620-19-X

6. F. Ahoua: *Prosodic Aspects of Baule. With special reference to the German of Baule speakers*, 1996, 221 pp., 1 map, 65 tables, 13 diagr. ISBN 3-927620-14-9

7. G. Atindogbé: *Bankon (A40). Eléments de phonologie, morphologie et tonologie*, 1996, XXII, 273 pp., 3 maps, 2 diagrams, numerous tables ISBN 3-89645-030-1

8. F. Gbéto: *Le Maxi du Centre-Bénin et du Centre-Togo: Une approche autosegmentale et dialectologique d'un parler Gbe de la section Fon*, 1997, 220 pp., 2 maps, numerous tables and diagrams ISBN 3-89645-031-X

9. N. Cyffer: *A Sketch of Kanuri*, 1998, 80 pp., 4 graphs, 2 maps, numerous tables
ISBN 3-89645-032-8

10. J.A. Blanchon / D. Creissels (ed.): *Issues in Bantu Tonology*, 1999, VIII, 198 pp., numerous tables ISBN 3-89645-033-6

11. K.K. Lébikaza: *Grammaire kabiyè: une analyse systématique.*, 1999, 559 pp., 1 map, 23 tables, numerous graphs ISBN 3-89645-034-4

12. M. Kossmann: *Essai sur la phonologie du proto-berbère*, 1999, 316 pp., index
ISBN 3-89645-035-2

13. F. Gbéto: *Les emprunts linguistiques d'origine européenne en Fon (Nouveau Kwa, Gbe: Bénin). Une étude de leur intégration au plan phonético-phonologique*, 2000, 90 pp., numerous tables and diagrams ISBN 3-89645-036-0

14. B. Ngila: *Expérience végétale bolia (République Démocratique du Congo). Catégorisation, utilisation et dénomination des plantes*, 2000, 149 pp., 1 map, 9 tables, 6 diagrams ISBN 3-89645-037-9

15. A. Fleisch: *Lucazi Grammar. A Morphosemantic Analysis*, 2000, 363 pp., 42 tables, appendix, several indices ISBN 3-89645-038-7

16. C. Griefenow-Mewis: *A Grammatical Sketch of Written Oromo*, 2001, 117 pp., 44 tables ISBN 3-89645-039-5

17. N.M. Mutaka / S.B. Chumbow (eds.): *Research Mate in African Linguistics: Focus on Cameroon. A Fieldworker's Tool for Deciphering the Stories Cameroonian Languages Have to Tell. In Honor of Professor Larry M. Hyman,* 2001, XVI, 359 pp., 1 map, 1 b/w photo, 49 tables, 8 figures, language index
ISBN 3-89645-041-7

18. A.A. Amidu: *Argument and Predicate Relations in Kiswahili. A New Analysis of Transitiveness in Bantu,* 2001, XX, 505 pp., numerous tables
ISBN 3-89645-042-5

Wortkunst und Dokumentartexte in afrikanischen Sprachen
edited by Wilhelm J.G. Möhlig

4. K. Pfeiffer (ed.): *Mandinka Spoken Art. Folk-tales, Griot Accounts and Songs,* 1997, 310 pp. ISBN 3-927620-63-7

5. J. Heath (ed.): *Texts in Koyra Chiini (Songhay of Timbuktu, Mali),* 1998, VIII, 389 pp., 1 map ISBN 3-89645-260-6

6. J. Heath (ed.): *Texts in Koroboro Senni (Songhay of Gao, Mali),* 1998, X, 283 pp., 1 map ISBN 3-89645-261-4

7. S.G. Obeng: *Conversational Strategies in Akan. Prosodic Features and Discourse Categories,* 1999, X, 174 pp., 1 map, 7 tables, numerous figures
ISBN 3-89645-262-2

8. K. Dombrowsky-Hahn: *Nyagalen Mugan Tarawele. Une épopée bambara racontée par Bakoroba Konè. Présentation, texte, traduction,* 2001, 224 pp., 1 map, 4 tables ISBN 3-89645-263-0

9. L. Hunter / C.E. Oumarou: *Aspects of the Aesthetics of Hausa Verbal Art,* 2001, 153 pp., 10 b/w photos ISBN 3-89645-264-9

10. K. Pfeiffer: *Sprache und Musik in Mandinka Erzählungen. With an English Summary,* 2001, 379 pp., 2 maps, 11 tables, 8 charts, 11 musical notations, 13 texts from Mandinka folktales, appendix, with an audio CD ISBN 3-89645-265-7

11. R.M. Beck: *Texte auf Textilien in Ostafrika. Sprichwörtlichkeit als Eigenschaft ambiger Kommunikation,* 2001, 263 pp. ISBN 3-89645-266-5

12. W.R. Leben / F. Ahoua (eds.): *Contes et textes documentaires kwa de Côte d'Ivoire,* 2002, X, 208 pp., 1 coloured folding map, 1 map ISBN 3-89645-267-3

13. U. Reuster-Jahn: *Erzählte Kultur und Erzählkultur bei den Mwera in Südost-Tansania,* 2002, X, 573 pp., 1 map, 1 graph, 8 tables ISBN 3-89645-268-1

14. J.U. Kavari: *The Form and Meaning of Otjiherero Praises,* 2002, 329 pp., 1 map, 16 diagrams, 5 tables, appendices ISBN 3-89645-269-X

15. G. Schlee / K. Sahado: *Rendille Proverbs in their Social and Legal Context,* 2002, IV, 192 pp., 1 map, 1 figure, 1 table ISBN 3-89645-271-1

16. Chr. Kilian-Hatz: *Contes des Bakas (Sud-Est Cameroun). Le cycle de Waito,* 2002, X, 542 pp., 1 map, 2 figures, 39 drawings, 2 tables ISBN 3-89645-272-X